Through the Glass of Soviet Literature

Through the Glass of Soviet Literature

Soviet Literature

Views of Russian Society

Edited, with an Introduction by

ERNEST J. SIMMONS

Columbia University Press, New York and London

THE TRANSLITERATION SYSTEM USED IN THIS BOOK IS BASED ON
THE LIBRARY OF CONGRESS SYSTEM WITH SOME MODIFICATIONS

COPYRIGHT 1953, COLUMBIA UNIVERSITY PRESS, NEW YORK

COLUMBIA PAPERBACK EDITION 1961

MANUFACTURED IN THE UNITED STATES OF AMERICA

THE RUSSIAN INSTITUTE

OF COLUMBIA UNIVERSITY

THE RUSSIAN INSTITUTE was established by Columbia University in 1946 to serve two major objectives: the training of a limited number of well-qualified Americans for scholarly and professional careers in the field of Russian studies and the development of research in the social sciences and the humanities as they relate to Russia and the Soviet Union. The research program of the Russian Institute is conducted through the efforts of its faculty members, of scholars invited to participate as Senior Fellows in its program, and of candidates for the Certificate of the Institute and for the degree of Doctor of Philosophy. Some of the results of the research program are presented in the Studies of the Russian Institute of Columbia University. The faculty of the Institute, without necessarily agreeing with the conclusions reached in the Studies, believe that their publication advances the difficult task of promoting systematic research on Russia and the Soviet Union and public understanding of the problems involved.

The faculty of the Russian Institute are grateful to the Rockefeller Foundation for the financial assistance which it has given to the program of research and publication.

Grateful acknowledgment is made to Jewish Social Studies *for permission to reprint the part of Bernard J. Choseed's "Jews in Soviet Literature" which appeared in Volume XI, Number 3 (July, 1949) of that periodical.*

Contents

Contents

Through the Glass of Soviet Literature

Ernest J. Simmons

Introduction: Soviet Literature and Controls *

I

To ATTEMPT to use the evidence of belles-lettres, as much of this book does, to shed light on behavioristic patterns and on certain political, social, and ideological factors in the Soviet Union, may seem a dubious scholarly endeavor. The creative imagination, presumably devoted to the universal truths of life, has the primary purpose of art to serve, and such a purpose is not necessarily consistent with the revelation of scientific data. One does not expect historical fiction or drama, for example, to be entirely accurate historically, for the artist often deals in illusions of reality, and by the magic of his art he seeks to persuade his readers to accept these illusions as real. To be sure, the emergence of nineteenth-century realism and naturalism in literature placed great emphasis upon a factual representation of life. The social historian of nineteenth-century England or France could not afford to neglect the novels of Dickens, Balzac, or Zola, to mention only a few of the better-known names. And a student of Russian life of the last two decades of the nineteenth century would find that a study of the tales and plays of Chekhov would supplement historical and social material and statistical data. Yet only in a limited sense could we regard the evidence drawn from such literary sources as scientific, for they are concerned essentially with broad impressions, psychological insights, and with what might be described as the portrayal of the character of a people or a nation.

* Parts of this Introduction appeared under the title "Controls in Soviet Literature," in *The Political Quarterly* (London), XXIII, No. 1 (January–March, 1952), 15–31.

Veblen clearly recognized the evidential value of literature as the organized symbolic experience of society, and Max Weber found a fruitful field of investigation in the relation of literary institutions to power. Since then some attention has been paid to the theory of literary communications and to various problems growing out of the relation between society and literature. As yet, however, no body of material has been commonly accepted as significant to social scientists interested in literary communications and content analysis, and no very effective methodologies have been devised for the study of belles-lettres as a reflection of social norms, behavior patterns, and national characteristics.

No attempt is made here to resolve these various difficulties as a contribution to the developing sociology of literature. They have been stressed in order to indicate some of the obstacles in the way of studying Soviet belles-lettres as important evidence of Soviet life. Because access to that country is difficult if not impossible for objective foreign scholars, the vast outpouring of novels, plays, and poetry, a large part of which is available, takes on added significance as possible source material for an understanding of the Soviet Union and its people. The nature of the material, however, and many factors connected with its development only serve to complicate the problems.

The complicating factors, mentioned above, are inherent in sociological literary research. For example, in dealing with the evidence of Soviet literature, we must frankly admit that its purpose is different from that of the West, as is the Soviet conception of the artist and his function in the state. In Western esthetics, art has no ulterior purpose in the practical or moral world, and the same may be affirmed of the artist. To be sure, exception may be taken to this point of view, and the very fact that there can be varying esthetic views in the West is in itself significant in this context. According to the Marxian esthetic conception in the Soviet Union, art in a class society is a class art and must serve as an instrument in the class struggle. Since the proletariat is the revolutionary and dominant class and the Communist Party is regarded as the advance guard of the proletariat, then the point of view of the Party, *partiinost'* ("Party spirit"), must define the purpose of literature and direct all Soviet art. Further, as Stalin has pointed out, one of the principal instruments of the Party, "always and everywhere," is agitation. That is, propaganda is a basic function of *partiinost'*, and consequently "creative" effort must unfailingly fulfill a definite propaganda aim. The end sought is pointedly summed up in *New World:* "For Soviet literature there is no more important, no higher purpose or undertaking than that ordained by the Bolshevik Party" (*Novyi mir*, No. 12 [1949], p. 190). In this scheme of things the literary artist would appear to have no loftier duty than that of slavishly following the commands of the Party.

This Soviet conception of belles-lettres, of course, was not a part of Communist theory in 1917. It has developed over the more than thirty-five years of existence of the regime and in close connection with the parallel development of the power of the Communist Party. The correlation between these factors and the chronological output of literature is an essential focus for any understanding of the relation of the Soviet writer to Soviet reality. In this process the role played by Party controls over the whole period is clearly one of the most important elements in evaluating the evidence of literature as a reflection of life in the Soviet Union. To dismiss the literature as valid evidence of Soviet life because of this factor of controls is hardly warranted. Regimentation of art is not a peculiarly Soviet phenomenon. Not until the Renaissance was art emptied of its directed content, exempted from the service of religion and morals, and resolved at last into the decorative and entertainment for their own sake. Still later Catherine the Great and Napoleon attempted to compel literature to serve the state. It is true, however, that in a body of literature so largely controlled as that in the Soviet Union, it is not sufficient to examine the frequency and intensity of themes, types, and situations in order to establish what is typical or characteristic of the social structure reflected in this literature.

The fact of regimentation clearly conditions the value of the evidence. It is therefore necessary to have some precise knowledge of the chronological development, extent, implementation, and effect of controls in Soviet literature. In one way or another this element of controls is a persistent factor in the evidence studied in the discussions which follow. Hence, the present author will consider this problem solely, while being conscious of the many others awaiting investigation before there can be any comprehensive

understanding of the extent to which Soviet belles-lettres faithfully
reflect or deliberately distort the truth of Soviet reality.

II

During the early 1920s the Soviet literary scene presented a striking contrast to that of today. Freedom—one might almost say a certain degree of anarchy—inspired by the tremendous release of
energy brought about by the Revolution, prevailed among writers.
The passionate desire of radical writers to make a clean sweep of
the old was countered by a cautious policy, encouraged by the
Party, that the best of the classics of the past must be preserved and
understood and a new socialist literature built on this foundation.
Liberal convictions of the rights of authors to express themselves
freely without fear of persecution, a heritage of nineteenth-century
Russian Marxism, persisted and were shared by prominent Communists in the government. Anatolii Lunacharskii, the first Commissar of Education, declared publicly that a revolutionary government ought to preserve the right of individual creation. Though at
first publishing was nationalized, beginning with 1921 and extending through the period of the New Economic Policy, private publishers were allowed to operate, subject to rather nominal censorship controls of the newly established central government publishing house (*Gosizdat*). By 1922 there were 220 private publishers in
Moscow alone, and they had published 803 titles up to this point
with a record of rejection through censorship of only 5.3 percent.
Indeed there was much competition between private and government firms, and the Party press complained bitterly at the time that
books of private publishers were critical of Communist doctrine.

In this revolutionary atmosphere of release and comparative
freedom, numerous independent writers' organizations sprang up,
each with its manifesto declaring a variety of artistic aims and
ideological loyalties. Groups such as the Proletcult, the Serapion
Brothers, and the Formalists boldly asserted their intentions of
pursuing literature and criticism without benefit of any government controls. Leading Communists both encouraged and denounced them in print, and the brilliant Party literary critic and
editor of *Red Virgin Soil*, Alexander Voronskii, published in this
leading review in the early 1920s the works of members of various

groups—Party writers, fellow travelers, and even bourgeois authors. As an editor Voronskii made it clear that he was less interested in ideological matters than in good literature, for he felt that every work of art had an esthetic as well as a class or sociological aspect. Art, he believed, should not be devoted to agitation and propaganda, or to the service of a proletarian state or to the conscious promotion of any set of ideas or values.

Of course, the genuine democratic spirit of early Russian Marxism and the feeling of release afforded by successful revolution do not account entirely for this atmosphere of freedom. The Party in these early years was too absorbed in the fierce struggle to maintain the government and its own existence to be effectively concerned with the problems of literary controls. Yet a warning of the direction that future Party action might take occurred as early as 1920. For in that year, through the medium of the Central Committee of the Party, Lenin forced upon a Congress of the Proletcult a resolution which, in effect, ended that powerful organization's insistence that proletarian literature should be allowed to develop free of any control by the government or the Party. The Central Committee, however, felt it necessary to soften this degree of interference by publishing a letter in *Pravda* which, among other things, assured workers in the field of artistic creation that "full autonomy" would be guaranteed them.

In fact, instead of dictator, the Party played the role rather of referee in the major literary struggle of the time—that between the various left-wing proletarian groups which demanded hegemony, Party sanction, and government support for the development of proletarian literature, and the right-wing and fellow-traveler groups which insisted upon complete freedom to create as they wished. The battle raged with much acrimony in the press. Well-known Party officials publicly expressed their opinions on both sides of the issue. It is interesting to observe that Bukharin favored the position of the right wing, maintaining that the Party should scrupulously avoid issuing directives on literature since such problems were not susceptible to methods used in politics. And he urged the freest competition among writers and literary groups. Trotsky's view is summed up in his *Literature and Revolution* (New York, 1925, pp. 170, 218): "Art must make its own way and by its own means. The Marxian methods are not the same as the artistic. The Party leads the proletariat but not the historic processes of history. . . . The domain of art is not one in which the Party is called upon to command. It can and must protect and help it, but it can only lead it indirectly.''

At a meeting of the Press Section of the Central Committee in May, 1924, representatives of all factions in this controversy were invited to present their views. Nothing appears to have been lacking in democratic procedure in the discussion or in the formulation of or in the voting on the resolution that was passed. This meeting was followed by others of a special commission of the Central Committee (February, 1925) to work out a policy statement to settle the quarrel. The conclusions of the commission were embodied in the famous resolution of the Central Committee (July 1, 1925) on literature. The point of view reflected in the resolution was pretty definitely that of Bukharin, and he may even have had a hand in drafting the resolution. In substance it repudiated the extreme position of the proletarian literary groups without failing to promise future support, but it definitely encouraged the efforts of non-Party, right-wing, and fellow-traveler authors.

It is clear that up to this point the Party attitude on controls in literature was an ambivalent one. The 1925 resolution itself was a Party directive, but liberal in its intentions. Prominent leaders obviously thought that the Party should not attempt to regiment literature and should encourage the competition of various groups without favoring any. Some indication of the freedom of action that still existed is the fact that a group of proletarian writers publicly criticized the Party resolution.

The ambivalence of the Party in the matter of literary controls and the very liberalism of the 1925 resolution were no doubt connected with both the social and economic conditions of the country at this time and with the struggle for power within the Party. That is, the political struggle was reflected in the literary struggle—the right, believing that literature should be immune to the direct influence of the Party, emphasized the emotional, esthetic, and individual element in the creative process; the left demanded firm Party control and stressed the primary educational, propaganda, and utilitarian functions of literature.

It was inevitable, however, that in a totalitarian form of government the single party in power should ultimately secure full control over literature as over every other ideology. And it would be easy to offer a Marxian rationalization of this development: in a socialist state the ideological superstructure must necessarily reflect the socialist economic base. Since there is little formal treatment of literature in the works of Marx and Engels, and certain "deviations" were soon discovered in the more extensive efforts of Plekhanov in this direction, Soviet critics eventually elaborated a Marxian literary theory of their own with Lenin and later Stalin as the "authorities," which justified in terms of historical materialism the several shifts and changes in the national literature on its way to absolute Party control.

However, neither socialism nor a real totalitarian status had been achieved as yet. With the triumph of Stalin over Trotsky and his other enemies and the inauguration of the First Five-Year Plan in 1928, the Party felt able to move further in the direction of literary controls. In the summer of 1928 the Central Committee called an All-Union Conference on questions of agitation and propaganda. Among the resolutions passed was one on literature, the theater, and cinema which ordered that these media be mobilized to reach the whole population in order to fight for a new cultural outlook in keeping with the operations of the Plan. Out of this conference, in December, 1928, came a formal resolution of the Central Committee. The resolution was a primary statement of the Communist Party in literary matters for the entire period of the First Five-Year Plan. It is in the form of a directive to publishing houses, indicating the kinds of books they are to select for publication and the nature of the subjects to suggest to writers. The resolution is a frank departure from the tolerant policy of 1925 and must be regarded as the first positive effort of the Party to "take over" literature and use it as an instrument to support a national program. The move marked the end of any illusion that the Party would consider literature as the product of the free exercise of man's creative impulses.

In addition, the Party quietly dropped another of its policies— its decision not to favor any of the rival literary groups. It gave its support to the most powerful organization, the Russian Association of Proletarian Writers (RAPP), as the one best suited to organize literature as a propaganda instrument to promote the success of the Plan. With Party support and under the able leadership of Leopold Averbakh, RAPP soon succeeded in asserting its control over many of the literary journals and publishing firms, and thus could discipline recalcitrant authors who failed to heed the "social command" of the Plan by denying them an outlet for their works and even by exposing them as "enemies of the people." In many respects RAPP was able to achieve an extraordinary thematic conformity in plays, novels, and poetry which uniformly acclaimed the achievements of the Five-Year Plan.

Despite RAPP regimentation, writers within the organization and other literary groups fought back publicly, though not with much success, against these dictatorial methods. And even the leadership of RAPP, once it had obtained extensive controls, ambitiously developed its own theory of literature, a theory which had little in common with the Party's stark determination to use belles-lettres to propagandize the virtues of the Plan. Though Averbakh felt it important to help writers to be conscious of the social command, he is on record as declaring that it was impossible to dictate themes to an author. Not dictated themes, he said, but a proper view of the world was the important thing for a writer. If his view of the world is a Marxian one and is based on dialectical materialism, he will fulfill his mission to the proletariat. He even borrowed from Voronskii's theorizing, by now officially discredited, the idea that art is cognition of life, but, contrary to Voronskii, a form of cognition of reality as an instrument of the class struggle and as a means of changing social reality. Further, the leadership of RAPP advocated a literature devoted to the realistic and psychological portrayal of the "living man," and to a "tearing away of the masks" of Soviet life, revealing its evils as well as its virtues.

Such presumption on the part of a favored organization could not be tolerated, and, after several unheeded warnings, the Central Committee issued a resolution on April 23, 1932, dissolving RAPP. The resolution also suggested the formation of a single Union of Soviet Writers. The Union was actually organized in 1934, after all other literary groupings had obligingly dissolved themselves. The move was hailed as a charter of liberty in the Soviet literary world and even abroad, for it brought to an end the regimentation of RAPP. Actually the evidence appears to indicate that the Party had at last reached a point where it felt that it could safely take over control of all literary endeavor in the Soviet Union and bend it to its own purposes.

The relative success of the First Five-Year Plan had helped mightily to assure the power of the Party and Stalin's sole leadership of it. Contrary to the contention of RAPP, it was now maintained that there was no real need for a proletarian literature, for with the great progress toward socialism all literature in the Soviet Union must be socialist in essence. And with some cogency it was also argued that even non-proletarian authors, such as the fellow travelers, had been won over to the cause of socialist culture. In this spirit all authors were invited to join the new Union of Soviet Writers and adhere to the Party's own platform of socialist realism in literature.

There is good reason to believe that Stalin played a personal role in the dissolution of RAPP and fathered the idea of one big union of writers for the whole of the USSR. Dividing the opposition in order to conquer it is a familiar Party tactic, but so also is the device of combining organizational fractions into one large organization in order to control diverse activities more effectively. In a field so resistant to controls as culture, this latter device is possible only when the Party has great power. By 1932 the Party had reached that stage. Far from conferring more freedom upon writers, as was widely imagined at the time, the organization of a single union made for more sweeping controls. In place of the incomplete regimentation of the Party-favored RAPP, all literature in the Soviet Union now had thrust upon it the direct controls of the Party itself.

In what turned out to be a final exercise of the freedom of individuals and organizations to oppose in print the official decisions of the Party in literary matters, the leadership of RAPP bravely published a firm criticism of the 1932 resolution in their own journal *On Literary Guard*. In effect, it was a criticism of Stalin. The writers denounced the Party line on the publicist function of art and also those people who, knowing nothing about literary criticism, try to impose their ideas on it. In fact, this spirit of opposition to Party interference died hard among literary men. Numerous meetings of authors throughout the country and much manipulation and Party pressure over a two-year period were necessary in order to establish the proper attitude of compliance in which to launch, in 1934, the organization of a single union of writers.

From this time on to the Nazi invasion in 1941, Soviet literature developed in an atmosphere of conformity to Party dictates. The conservatism of a revolution growing old, a conservatism which had already begun to affect literature, was intensified by the enveloping domination of the Party. In general, the Party still preferred to remain behind the scenes, exercising its controlling influence largely through the medium of the Party fraction in the Union of Soviet Writers. Only occasionally did it show its claws in public, as in the case of the vitriolic denunciation of formalism in the arts in *Pravda* in 1936.

Instead of the varied and often highly individualistic schools of criticism which, before 1932, had made a brilliant and impressive contribution to Soviet literary theory, there now existed the single authority of Lenin and the official artistic credo of socialist realism. Fatuous attempts were made during this period to elevate Lenin to the position of a universal authority on literature on the basis of a few random remarks scattered through his works, several brief essays on Tolstoy, which are more social than literary criticism, and his 1905 article, "Party Organization and Party Literature." This latter piece became an unfailing touchstone for all literary critics, largely by way of justifying Party direction of literature, Communist and non-Communist, though there is reason to doubt that this was Lenin's precise intention in the article. Some measure of the success of this apotheosis of Lenin as a literary critic may be gained from a typical declaration of a later writer that "there is no important problem in the historical development of Russian literature that was not dealt with in his writings" (*Soviet Literature*, No. 1, 1951, p. 151).

Some critical battles were fought out in the press during this period, but they were concerned mostly with the problem of adorning socialist realism in the dress and loose ornament of Marxism, and such samovar tempests invariably took place within the bosom of the family, so to speak, that is, under the aegis of the all-inclusive

Union of Soviet Writers. Gone were the days when a critic such as Viktor Shklovskii could assert that the application of Marxist doctrine to literature was a matter of critical expediency rather than methodological principle, or that dialectical materialism, to paraphrase Boris Eikhenbaum, may be a fruitful concept in the field of sociology but, because of its extrinsic frame of reference, had little to offer literary scholarship. After 1932 critics were asserting in concert that only an author with the Marxist-Leninist-Stalinist world view could correctly portray life in the Soviet Union and abroad, and hence only literature written from this point of view could be considered as real art. The Marxian interpretation of socialist realism ended in the closed and vicious circle of declaring that only the reality of socialism is real and that therefore everything hostile to socialism is unreal. Such a position was the logical outcome of Party dictation, and its relation to the truth of art in literature is well summed up in a typical statement of one of the critics, M. Serebrianskii, in 1938: "Artistic truth is the ability to tell everything necessary but to tell it correctly, that is, from a definite, Bolshevik point of view" (*Literaturnye ocherki*, p. 231).

Shortly after the Second World War began and the propaganda emphasis had shifted from its focus of the directing genius of the Communist Party to that of the unity and patriotism of the multinational peoples of the Soviet Union in defending the motherland, one could detect a relaxation of Party controls on all the media of art and intellectual life. In the spirit of this unexpected freedom, writers poured forth in their works sentiments and feelings which often had little connection with the former prescribed pattern of Communist emotions. Even direct and implied criticism of Party dictation may be found in this deeply patriotic war literature. At the end of the War a public report of the tenth plenum of the Executive Committee of the Union of Soviet Writers recorded frank expressions of hope by prominent authors that interference in the arts would be discontinued.

These hopes were blasted by the resolution of the Central Committee of the Party on literature shortly after the War (August 14, 1946) and by the related speech of the late Andrei Zhdanov, member of the Politburo, in which he clearly indicated not only what literature was considered anti-Soviet, but also defined the kinds of books that ought to be written by postwar authors of belles-lettres. As is now well known, this resolution touched off a vast frontal attack by the Party on all aspects of Soviet artistic and intellectual life. In this period of "the gradual transition from socialism to communism," the shift in the ideological line must be understood as a reflection of the new postwar national and international policy of the Party. Specifically in the "purification" drive that followed there were, no doubt, several objectives, but certainly one of them was the determination that all intellectual and artistic effort must be utterly subservient to Party control and should have as one of its aims the glorification of the Soviet Union and its accomplishments over the capitalist West and America.

In fact, the most obvious feature of the interference in belles-lettres in this new period, as contrasted with the earlier ones, is the openly declared and total domination of the Party in the whole literary direction of things. In its blatant public identification with literature, the Party now demands from all writers adherence to the guiding principle of *partiinost'*—of Party spirit—which assumes an all-pervading organic connection between literature and politics. As one recent critic frankly put it, the writer can give a truthful and profound portrayal of reality in its revolutionary development only if he is guided by the policy of the Soviet state! One must conclude that anything less is not even realistic in the eyes of the Party.

Such inclusive and rigid controls in literature require an omniscient authority as an infallible point of reference for authors and critics. Naturally Stalin, who has pretty much usurped Lenin's position in this respect, has been readily, and apparently uncomplainingly, pressed into service. (It should be recalled that Lenin achieved this unearned authority as a literary critic only after his death.) However, Stalin's comments on belles-lettres, even more sparse than Lenin's, have been diligently collected and used again and again by critics, appropriately and inappropriately, to illuminate the new "line" in literature. Nevertheless, it should be added that Stalin's personal decisions behind the scenes, not recorded though occasionally hinted at, have probably played a significant part in the direction of literature, music, and the theater since 1930. Speaking of the fact, not altogether certain, that Stalin was responsible for the description of the writer as "an engineer of the human soul," a Soviet critic writes: "Indeed, how deep is the love and respect for man and the writer's labor contained in this famous definition by Stalin! Only he, the educator of the millions, the mentor of mentors, for whom there is nothing more precious on earth than man, could have defined the significance of the writer in the new society in terms so full of love and wisdom. All of Stalin's precepts on art and the artists' tasks constitute a creative development of Lenin's views on art, and primarily of Lenin's cardinal, fundamental principle of socialist esthetics—the principle of the Bolshevik Party spirit of literature" (V. Yermilov, *Soviet Literature,* No. 4 [1950], p. 126).

By now a formidable control apparatus has been developed to enable the Party to carry out its declared intention of using literature for its own purposes. Since the whole manufacturing process of the printed word (paper, presses, publishing houses, distribution) is ultimately under government control, the Party has an economic stranglehold on the output and content of literature. The propaganda line that determines the broad direction of literary content is usually initiated in the Politburo and announced in resolutions of the Central Committee which have almost the force of law. One of the main duties of the Propaganda and Agitation Department of the Central Committee is to compel active observance of the ideological line in literature and to expose through various means what it considers important deviations from it. From time to time the Department may also promulgate a new aspect or interpretation of the line or emphasize the need for special concentration on some theme by writers. This is ordinarily done through inspired articles in *Pravda, Literary Gazette,* or some other important Party organ.

Lower down in the hierarchy of controls, though capable of bringing more immediate pressure to bear on authors, is the Union of Soviet Writers, which is divided into committees corresponding to the various branches of literature. Though Communists do not predominate in the membership of the Union, they do occupy most of the key posts and control it. Authors are encouraged to read their works in progress to the relevant committee of the Union, and there the critical emphasis is on whether the writer has embodied in his work the true spirit of the Party line. A further check takes place in the editorial offices of the so-called "thick" magazines, for the best literature, even novels as serials, appears first in these publications. Their editorial boards in turn are made up largely of Communists, and one of their principal functions is to pass on the ideological correctness of manuscripts submitted to them. The same is true of the editorial boards of the huge government book publishing firms. Finally, all literary works must receive the approval of the official government censorship office (*Glavlit*).

Should a literary work pass safely through this formidable array and appear in printed form with some undiscovered ideological impurity, which occasionally happens, it is almost certain to be pounced upon by reviewers (literary magazines as well as books are reviewed). And if there is any hesitation to review the work, which is sometimes the case, or if reviewers have failed to criticize offending ideological faults, an officially inspired statement appears in the press to set matters right. This invariably elicits recantations all around—from the author, officials of the Union of Soviet Writers, the editorial head of the responsible magazine or publishing house, the incautious reviewer, and often from the editor of the publication in which the erring review appeared.

It may be observed from this brief treatment of the subject that the history of literary controls in the Soviet Union over the last thirty-five years is closely connected with the history of the Party. For the Party's interference in literature progressed from its early hesitant and ambivalent attitude, when the Party was relatively weak and divided and permitted much freedom in literary expression, to its present position of absolute control, which derives from the monolithic power of the Party today. Further, there has been a close correlation between the Party attitude toward literature as an ideology and over-all shifts in Party domestic and international policy: the 1925 resolution of the Central Committee on literature reflected the gradualist, compromise position during the NEP, as well as division within the Party; the 1928 directive to the publishing houses tied literature to the service of the "second revolution" —the First Five-Year Plan—and at the same time signified the growing unity and power of the Party under Stalin's leadership; the 1932 resolution removed the emphasis upon proletarian literature and placed it on socialist literature, reflecting the conviction that the corner to socialism had been turned, and concurrently the dissolution of all literary groups and the establishment of the single Union of Soviet Writers marked the still greater confidence of the Party in its power to control literature; the 1946 resolution on literature is an ideological reflection of the new period of the gradual transition from socialism to communism, in which the Party in various ways has publicly asserted its absolute control over all ideological matters in a national and international policy of far-reaching consequences. Early literary freedom under the Party has given way to complete subjection to the Party. If the whole of Christian art was devoted to the greater glory of God, today the whole of Soviet art is devoted to the greater glory of the Communist Party.

III

What effect has such a system of dictated Party ideology and rigorous controls on the Soviet literary artist? In conjuring up the familiar image of numerous artistic lives polluted or wrecked by the regimentation of a totalitarian regime, it is well to remember that in modern times the bulk of so-called imaginative literature is the product of skilled craftsmen rather than of indubitable literary artists. Mass production in publishing and a vast market of readers have made a commercial business of literature. Those who write literature, in the Soviet Union as elsewhere, with the sole purpose of making a livelihood out of it are primarily interested in producing what the publishers want. What Soviet publishers want is dictated not only by reader interest, but also by compliance with the latest Party line in literature. In this sense it is likely that most writers conform, without any severe wrenching of conscience, to the publishers' demands in theme and the ideological treatment of it. No doubt they often resent the gauntlet of controls they have to run and the editorial insistence upon revisions in ideological matters, and perhaps, like good craftsmen, they occasionally yearn for a wider field of thematic selection, though the field is wider than is commonly supposed and often involves subjects of no particular political significance. However, conformity becomes habitual in the process of earning a living, and the average earnings of such writers are substantial and the social privileges they enjoy as authors are not inconsiderable.

The case of the real literary artist subjected to the withering touch of such controls may be quite another matter. It has always been supposed that complete freedom was a vital condition for the proper functioning of the creative spirit. Perhaps there is some point, however, in Lenin's generalization that man cannot live in a society and be entirely free from it. Clearly the literary artist, whether his métier be realism or fantasy, cannot escape the compelling influence of the imperatives of his social environment or the idols of his own creative personality. He is never a wholly free spirit, whether he suffers from the censorship of profit and loss in the "free" market of a capitalist society or the government censorship in the controlled market of a totalitarian regime. But whatever open or hidden controls may exist for the Western artist—economic, social, legal, or personal—the fact remains that he has freedom of choice to select his subject and treat it as he desires. In a sense he enjoys a larger freedom, for the very essence of a work of art is centered in the variety of all possible relationships in exercising artistic judgment in freedom of choice. In this process the author lives his own version of freedom. Thus a wealth of human experience is at his beck and call, shaped by the powers of his imagination in the work of art, but disciplined in it by artistic principles of organization and by physical and social environment. That is, the artist is able to serve his art in any way he thinks best.

The Soviet artist today does not enjoy this complete freedom of choice. Limits are placed on the areas of human experience he can reflect in art, and his creative mind is restricted to the pattern of ideas, beliefs, and loyalties prescribed by the Party. Punishment for failure to comply usually takes the form of public denunciation. If recantation does not follow, and is not accompanied by reformed practice, the artist may be driven from literature and he may ultimately suffer a worse fate. The annals of Soviet literature contain scores of names of writers, some of great distinction, who have unaccountably disappeared from the field or whose unfortunate fate is known with reasonable certainty. Some of these may well have vanished for reasons other than literary "deviations," but in most cases the evidence indicates literary non-conformity.

The psychological effect of such enforced conformity on the individual artist and his creative process can only be guessed at, in the absence of free access to a sufficient sample of Soviet literary artists. As we have seen, in some instances this enforced conformity has resulted in rebellion, with deplorable consequences for the artist. Among those who endeavor to effect a compromise in order to continue to write and to live, the normally free-ranging mind and imagination of the true artist must stumble in constant pain and a sense of self-violation in a compulsive, suffocating atmosphere of creation. Human nature being what it is, no doubt some writers are able to sacrifice their artistic self-esteem utterly, for the sake of the large rewards and immense national prestige won by those who successfully popularize in their works the official pattern of Soviet reality and ideology.

One cannot dismiss this subject without dwelling for a moment on the speculation that profound belief in the Party and all it stands for may enable the sincere Communist writer to accept control as an article of faith in no sense inhibiting his artistic functioning. The obvious analogy is the medieval Christian artist for whom the controls of the Church were an inseparable part of his religious convictions. How passionate a faith Communism can be for its true devotees requires no substantiation. Like the Church in the Middle Ages, the Communist Party in the Soviet Union provides a hallowed pattern of life that takes its faithful hopefully from the cradle to the grave. Where faith begins reason ends; the artist believes and hence does not question the ends achieved by instruments of control, for they have become fighting convictions. Such Communists understand Party discipline not as a frame that binds from without, dictating solely their political behavior, but as an internal, ideological force directing them in all their living reality. In some strange but believable manner the Party and literature, like freedom and authority, become identical in the minds of writers with such faith. "Both the Party and artistic literature in our country," declared the prominent Soviet writer Alexander Fadeev at Paris, "have one and the same purpose. Neither the Party nor governmental power in the Soviet land interferes in the individual creation of the artist; they have never dictated and have never attempted to dictate themes and characters, to say nothing of artistic forms"

(*Literaturnaia gazeta,* March 2, 1949). Numerous similar declarations of faith on the part of Soviet Communist authors have a ring of fanatical sincerity. For example, another prominent author, Konstantin Simonov, wrote in *Pravda* (November 26, 1946): "Publicly, from the tribune of art, for all the world to hear, we say, and will keep on saying, that we are fighting for Communism, that we consider Communism to be the only path for humanity to follow in the future, that our Communist ideals have been, are, and shall be immutable, and that no one is going to change them."

Out of such faith, no doubt, can come inspired, genuine art in which ideological limitations and controls cease to be impediments to the creative process because they do not exist as such for the artist. The act of artistic creation becomes an act of faith in the system that controls it. Though the product may be stigmatized as mere propaganda, it is well to remember that propaganda can serve art by giving it a renewed purpose and meaning and a new vitality.

IV

It is against this background of the development of controls and their effect on the writer that one must appraise the value of Soviet literature as evidence of the reality of life which it describes. If good literature promotes revolution, it does not logically follow that a revolution promotes good literature. The vast volume of fiction, poetry, and drama produced in the Soviet Union over the last thirty-five years may be set down as literary reportage tendentiously conceived in the spirit of official demands. But a very appreciable part of it, judged by the usual canons of critical taste, possesses artistic qualities of high worth. Nearly all of it, however, is of evidential value to the serious student of the Soviet Union.

Soviet belles-lettres do not attempt to approximate the vitality of natural types in life by combining the highest degree of concreteness and individuality with the highest degree of universality. But if one of the principal aims of the study of literature, as Taine suggests, is to construct a moral history and move toward the psychological laws from which events spring, then the study of Soviet literature can be of aid to the social historian provided he has an awareness of the social, political, and economic development of the country. All imaginative literature tends to exalt its subject as the most adequate mirror of life; Soviet literature today exalts it as a mirror of idealized Soviet life.

On the negative side it must be admitted that literary conformity to changing ideology has been enforced in varying degrees. But of this one never need be in doubt. As has been indicated, the periodization of Soviet social, political, and economic development has been clearly reflected in literature, so much so that one may see it in operation in the textual changes made in novels that are reprinted after a lapse of years, in order to bring them "up to date" ideologically. Herein lies a type of evidence that has its own peculiar value. Yet no one could scientifically estimate from the evidence of literature the extent of real popular opposition to the regime. Many subjects are obviously forbidden to the writer. However, hostile elements are frequently treated under the familiar designation of "bourgeois survivals." A careful investigation of these manifestations would yield significant evidence of the kind and extent of the opposition in the country and at least some of the methods employed to overcome it. Finally, an official version of Soviet life, especially since 1946, dominates this literature, and one must take care to distinguish it from Soviet reality.

On the positive side there is much to be said for the value of Soviet literature over the years as a body of evidence revealing the variegated life of the people, provided the student takes the proper precautions in the interpretation of this evidence. Precautions, though of a different kind, would be essential in using the literature of any country with a similar purpose in mind, for selection is always involved in any creative effort to achieve verisimilitude in art.

Until the formation of a single writer's union in 1934, when the Party was able to exercise more effective control, literature reflected with varying degrees of faithfulness the central problem of Soviet life over those early years—the mortal struggle between the old and the new in the rapid building of a socialist society. This problem took numerous forms in poetry, plays, and novels treating successively the periods of revolution and civil war, the NEP, and the First Five-Year Plan, but the reality of its abiding tragedy was rarely sacrificed to Communist doctrine. Party motivation is nearly always there, but what is commonly forgotten in this annoying omnipresence of the Party in belles-lettres is that it is quite true to the experience of Soviet life. In fact, since it has been difficult or impossible to investigate in the Soviet Union itself the effects of Party activities in the daily lives of men and women, the literature provides in this respect substantial evidence which may now be checked against the information from numerous displaced persons from that country.

Over these early years the amount of freedom that prevailed permitted criticism of the actions of both government and Party. There were many novels, plays, poems, and short stories in which the sympathetic treatment of opposition plainly revealed the reality of opposition in Soviet life. And out of the wealth of literature emerged the changing behavior pattern of Soviet men and women as we see them portrayed in the fierce struggle of civil war and in the titanic efforts of industrial reconstruction and the merciless business of agricultural collectivization. Five-Year-Plan novelists and dramatists, who often gathered their material on the spot, bore their readers and audiences with the technical details of huge building operations, but these were details that were omnipresent in the lives of Soviet citizens at that time. Everywhere in this literature the individual is sacrificed to the drama of collective effort in an atmosphere of ceaseless struggle and incredible human privations. And Communist bureaucracy, peculation, and widespread philistinism were fearlessly satirized, especially in the literature of the NEP period. Here is more than a brief chronicle of the times. This early literature bears the authentic ring of real life, for the Party had not yet found a formula of idealized life and was in no position to enforce one.

The Party began to thrust upon writers an official version of Soviet life in the early 1930s. Although it has changed in points of emphasis and new facets have been added since then, the fundamental content of the picture has remained pretty constant. In this official version the Soviet Union has become something of a socialist utopia. Stakhanovite workers perform prodigies of labor in the factories, overfulfilling their norms amid general jubilation, and peasants on the collective farms overcome every conceivable hostile element of nature to win through to a bumper harvest. Both workers and peasants are richly honored by the state for their achievements, and all join in attributing their success to the inspiring influence of Stalin. All types portrayed seem to live lives of beauty, labor heroism, and the honest joy of accomplishment. The essential human conflict is usually between sterling Communist virtues embodied in the masses and stray "bourgeois survivals" still persistently lodged in the nature of an occasional villain. Of course, there is never any doubt of the final triumph of socialist principles. Modern realistic literature shuns the average man for the simple reason that it is difficult to make him interesting. Only an author of the stature of a Leo Tolstoy can, by the witchery of his art, transform the average man into a vital, living symbol of the conscience of ordinary humanity. Soviet literature today prides itself on portraying only average men and women, but it casts them in the official image of idealized positive heroes and heroines.

Literature did not absorb this official version of Soviet reality all at once; life, in no sense idealized, appeared in plays and novels written up to the time of the Second World War. The early concentration in literature upon the collective was replaced to a considerable extent by an emphasis upon the individual and his adjustments to the new socialist reality. Numerous types are portrayed—the factory manager, *kolkhoz* manager, engineer, country schoolteacher, scientist, oil worker, railroad worker, the brigade leader in different kinds of labor. In socialist realism, Soviet literary critics insist, the typical does not coincide with the commonplace but reflects rather a tendency to development that is implicit in real life. However much the types may be idealized, their activities in their respective milieus provide a fund of social, political, and economic data the veracity of which may be checked by elements of consistency and by other known relevant facts. A revealing study could be made, for example, of the factory manager as portrayed in Soviet plays and novels. It would yield information difficult or impossible to obtain from other sources: the factory manager's pattern of daily life, his social status, relations with his ministry, his workers, the district Party committee, the Party nucleus in the factory, the factory trade union committee, the planning system, and with many other aspects that make up the functioning and economy of a Soviet factory. About such facts, the Soviet writer is usually well informed, for in selecting a locale of this kind he would ordinarily feel obliged to learn the facts from actual experience in a factory. He might even receive a stipend from the Literary Fund to make such a study at first hand in preparation for writing a novel or play, and there would be little reason to misrepresent the factual material obtained in this manner. Belles-lettres contain a wealth of such specialized data; this is one of its chief claims on the attention of students of Soviet affairs.

Literature during the War pursued a rather free and unorthodox course and thematically is concentrated almost exclusively on the struggle with the invaders. In descriptive power it marks a return, however fugitive and unequal, to the spirit of the unvarnished realism of the great Russian classics of the nineteenth century. Pictures of stoic suffering in the rear, the amazing feats of the partisans, and the heroism at the front reveal the perennial qualities of the Russian people in time of war, now curiously emancipated from Communist direction and inspiration, although these factors appear repeatedly. This war literature is filled with abundant details of the life and character of the Red Army officer and soldier, and nearly every novel and play contains a native "enemy of the people," which serves to remind us how misled we were by reports of the early elimination of all fifth-column elements in the Soviet Union before the War.

One must make a distinction between literature written during the War and that devoted to this theme, of which there is much, after the War. Postwar literature bears the impress of the hindsights suggested by the 1946 resolution of the Central Committee on literature—in this case a marked anti-Western fervor and a glorification of Communist leadership in the fighting. As pointed out earlier, the new policy resulted in the public identification of the Party with literature and its exercise of complete control over it. The policy was quickly reflected in the thematic direction of literature: writers were to concern themselves with exalted praise of the Soviet part in the War (frequently amounting to claims that they had won the War in spite of their allies), and with themes of postwar reconstruction and the rehabilitation of returning Red Army men. Later another category was added—the hostile designs of the West, and especially of America, against the Soviet Union.

One may well wonder whether postwar literature, under the

burden of such uncompromising controls, can have any relevance at all to the reality of life in the Soviet Union. A recent interpretation of socialist realism in keeping with the new policy in literature conveys the notion of utter irrelevance. A sample passage reads: "In describing whatever contradictions he notices in life, in depicting the struggle between the new socialist principles and the vestiges of the past in the minds of people, the Soviet writer knows that to show all this correctly he must have a clear understanding of the fact that under conditions of Soviet reality the new is bound to win. . . . The writer who, in depicting the vestiges of the past in the minds of people, merely records events, without 'interfering' in their course, without taking sides as a champion of the new . . . such a writer is not a socialist realist, his position is that of an adherent of trends hostile to realism" (Anatolii Tarasenkov, *Soviet Literature,* No. 5 [1949], p. 145). This critic then goes on to condemn certain characters in recent Soviet fiction as "non-typical" and a "gross violation of the truth of life," because the cowardice of one, an army officer, leads to the destruction of a whole division, and because a soldier in another displays weakness. These attributes, declares the critic, are "slanders against reality."

In fact, the schism between the "typical" and "non-typical" in Soviet literature, as recently expounded by Malenkov in his marathon speech before the Nineteenth Party Congress (October 5, 1952), leaves one semantically baffled and esthetically bewildered: "In the Marxist-Leninist understanding, the typical by no means signifies some sort of statistical average. Typicalness corresponds to the essence of the given social-historical phenomenon; it is not simply the most widespread, frequently occurring, and ordinary phenomenon. Conscious exaggeration and accentuation of an image do not exclude typicalness, but disclose it more fully and emphasize it. The typical is the basic sphere of the manifestation of Party spirit in realistic art. The problem of typicalness is always a political problem" (*Pravda,* October 6, 1952).

In short, it would appear that in this new world of Soviet reality vice can never triumph over virtue, evil over good. The cards are stacked against the bad man; he is not even real, at least if he succeeds. It is apparently acceptable to write about "officially" bad people, but only as foils for the good. They must never win out;

they are either reformed in the end or jailed or killed off. Socialist realism in postwar literature must contribute to the forward progress of Soviet life in all its aspects or it is not realism. Thus present-day socialist realism seems to have been transformed into the unreality of the conventional fairy tale, in which the wicked stepmother always gets her just deserts in the end, and the persecuted heroine always marries the brave hero and lives happily ever after.

By and large, postwar literature supports this conception of socialist realism in its unvarying black-and-white character portrayals. However, real problems of Soviet life are dealt with, and often against carefully described backgrounds of village or town, of factory or huge construction efforts—all of which provide important social data for the investigator. And a whole new field has been recently opened up in the growing number of novels centered in the far outlying districts of the Soviet Union. These novels present fascinating material on the life and peoples of these distant regions under the impact of Soviet socialism. However, the psychological presentation of character is hopelessly stereotyped, plainly and tiresomely manufactured out of the whole cloth of official ideology. The positive hero of literature is now nearly always a Communist, cast in the father-image of Stalin. He may have certain weaknesses (often the only element of dramatic conflict in novel or play)—impulsiveness, pride, a desire to shun the collective and do everything himself, hostility to innovation, failure to educate a wife lacking in his Bolshevik qualities. In the end, however, these weaknesses are always overcome by an application of stereotyped ideological remedies.

In its postwar development Soviet literature has become the perfect propaganda instrument, for it is presenting for popular consumption a series of consistent, idealized Communist heroes who, the Party no doubt hopes, will stand in their personal lives, heroic actions, and unswerving loyalty to the regime as instructive models for the average Soviet citizen. It is in this negative sense of reality—the idealization of life which the Party foists upon the public both as a mirror of Communist aspirations and as an opiate to minister to its discontent—that Soviet literature today can best serve the purpose of the social historian.

Louise E. Luke

Marxian Woman: Soviet Variants

THE EMANCIPATION of women has been, from 1917 to the present, one of the proudest boasts of Soviet Russia in its catalogue of achievements. As test case of Marxian theory on the question of woman's place in society, Soviet treatment of this basic domestic issue has commanded much attention in the USSR and abroad, with wide divergences in interpretation, both of original revolutionary purposes and of later revisions. Although in Communist ideology departure from the precepts expounded in Marxian doctrine is now fully admissible when dictated by a new historical situation, Soviet spokesmen have tended to mask the fact that a reversal in policy has occurred or to rationalize it as one directed by the "creative faculties of the masses," which Lenin said must be left free to discover the road.[1] Non-Soviet analyses, for a variety of reasons, have also obscured the significance of the experiment.

The terms set forth in Marxian writings as constituting the emancipation of women and the early Soviet steps taken toward their fulfillment are a matter of historical record, as, in part, are later measures toward their abrogation. Less easily spelled out are the experiences of women themselves in their acceptance or rejection of the terms. Was the veering in course prompted by certain immutables in the feminine role and in durable societal structures? Or was there, as Bolshevik Marxists assert, a "new woman" with different social functions and different values emerging in socialist society? If so, what manner of woman was she? For investigation of widespread attitudes and behavior patterns engendered among Soviet women by the new social organization, Russian literature

[1] V. I. Lenin, "Report on the Land" (Oct. 26, 1917), *Selected Works* (2 vols., Moscow, 1947), II, 238.

affords the main accessible source. Belles-lettres and literary criticism up to 1936—that is, through the initial phase of Soviet policy on the "woman question"—offer voluminous documentation, particularly during the First Five-Year Plan, when the development of industry first made it possible to put the theoretical program into practice on a large scale. At this time Russian writers lavished attention on the segment of Soviet citizenry where these two issues converged: women workers in industry. Having most fully realized women's potentialities according to Soviet criteria, they must be assumed to exemplify in their lives those personal needs which evoked a modification of the Marxian doctrine in 1936 or to demonstrate that it was imposed by other considerations.[2]

Until the mid-thirties, Russian literature enjoyed relative freedom of choice either to reflect or to affect life; it was by no means the cast-iron propaganda instrument it has become now, when the demands upon it as an implement of "education" rigidly limit the exercise of its power to reflect its society. The candor and heterogeneity at first permitted in the literary representation of the Soviet scene led to the expression of a wide variety of views on the "transformation" of women then in progress. An examination of the common elements which may be abstracted from these various views, correlated with the factual data officially released, serves to clarify the impact upon women industrial workers of the original Soviet scheme of liberation and their general social orientation by 1936. At the same time this exploratory study calls into question the reliability of later Soviet reports on the status of women in the USSR. It also furnishes grounds for hypotheses concerning the effects of the later policy governing their role in society and concerning the part which literature has been called upon to play in depicting that role.

I

According to classic Marxist theory, most fully elaborated in Engels's *Origin of the Family, Private Property and the State,* the woman question cannot be isolated and solved as a separate issue.

[2] Literature dealing with the question among the peasantry and the national minorities is not discussed here. Although the theoretical principles were, of course, intended for application to these groups also, the immediate problems during the period under consideration were of a different character.

The emancipation of women, like that of any other oppressed group, is considered part of the general social question, to be realized only with the solution of the larger problem, in communism. The status of woman in society depends upon economic relations, upon her part in production; mere legal rights demanded by the traditional feminist program cannot assure equality. In the argument of Marx and Engels, under socialism, for the first time in recorded history, woman would cease to be the victim of the process of social evolution. Capitalism, with its ruthless exploitation of unskilled female labor and the deleterious effect upon the family, had resulted in the degradation of women of all classes and the demoralization of both sexes. The bourgeoisie had reduced its own family relations to a money relation, and woman to a mere instrument of production. The proletarian family had virtually ceased to exist, its children transformed into simple articles of commerce and implements of labor. In the new society all civic disabilities would be removed from woman, and absolutely equal rights conferred. Properly trained, she was to take her place in economic production along with man. The factory would become the center of political, educational, and social, as well as of economic life; the family would assume a higher form adapted to woman's new functions in the economy; and the exploitation of children by their parents would stop.[3]

The structure of the family was one of the two determinants which would shape the social organization of the future: "According to the materialist conception, the determining factor in history is, in the final instance, the production and reproduction of the immediate essentials of life." On the one side, this twofold process consists in the production of the means of existence, of food and clothing, dwellings, and of the tools needed in that production; on the other side, it consists in the production of human beings themselves, the propagation of the species. "The social organization under which the people of a particular epoch and a particular

[3] Summarized from Frederick Engels, *The Condition of the Working Class in England in 1844,* trans. Florence K. Wischnewetzky (New York, 1887), pp. 35, 95, 97–99; Karl Marx and Frederick Engels, *Manifesto of the Communist Party* (New York, 1932), pp. 11, 27; Marx, *Capital,* trans. Eden and Cedar Paul (London, 1946), I, 522, 528–29; Engels, *Origin of the Family, Private Property and the State* (New York, 1942), pp. 64–66.

country live is determined by both kinds of production: by the stage of development of labor on the one hand and of the family on the other." [4]

The *Communist Manifesto* announces that "the bourgeois family will vanish as a matter of course." [5] Engels defines the bourgeois family as the social group resulting from the current form of "monogamy" as historically evolved: the marriage of a single pair, contracted, frequently by parental arrangement, on the basis of property considerations, dominated by the male, as a rule indissoluble (at least through the wife's volition), and inevitably accompanied by adultery and prostitution. This form was to be supplanted by one founded entirely on equality and mutual inclination—true monogamy, for the man as well as the woman. Prostitution, public and private, would disappear. Individual marriage would remain, for sexual love was by its nature exclusive. Where this sole moral basis for marriage ceased to exist, however, separation would benefit both partners as well as society, without the need of wading through "the useless mire of a divorce case." Engels acknowledges that "the intense emotion of individual sex love varies . . . in duration from one individual to another." [6] Whether this means that short-term marriage might become a commonplace, Engels neglects to say.

The first practical step was to bring the entire female sex back into public industry and thus to end man's domination based on economic supremacy. This in turn demanded the abolition of the single (nuclear) family as the economic unit of society. Private housekeeping would be converted into a socialized industry, and domestic work would consume no more than an insignificant fraction of woman's time. The care and education of children were to be transferred to public institutions, with no distinction between the rights of legitimate and illegitimate children. [7]

The new order in relations between the sexes could be introduced only by a generation which had grown up possessing legal equality and which had never known mercenary considerations in the union of man and woman: "When these people are in the world, they will care precious little about what anybody thinks

4 Engels, *Origin*, "Preface to the First Edition," p. 5.
5 Marx and Engels, *Manifesto*, p. 27.   6 Engels, *Origin*, pp. 54–73, *passim*.
7 *Ibid.*, pp. 66–67, 147–48.

they ought to do; they will make their own practice and their corresponding public opinion and that will be the end of it." [8] In essence, the Marx-Engels formula is focused almost exclusively on emancipation, the removal of restraints. The principle of stern control of relations between the sexes, in the interest of the state, is a comparatively late Soviet innovation.

Lenin, declaring that the success of the revolution and the construction of communism depended on the participation and support of women,[9] at once abolished the oppressive regulations which had restricted the activities of women in tsarist Russia. Early Soviet laws conferred piecemeal what the 1936 Constitution (Article 122) sums up as "equal rights . . . in economic, state, cultural, social, and political life." In the occupational system, in addition to such fundamentals as the same pay for the same labor, special rules on working conditions for women were laid down by the Labor Code and numerous decrees, in order to offset biological differences. The "bourgeois-feminist" refusal of the preferential protection of woman by law, "under the pretext that this is supposed to destroy the equality of the sexes, was always alien to Soviet legislation." [10] Among more important provisions for women in industry were prohibition of especially heavy or injurious work; paid maternity leave to a maximum of sixteen weeks; safeguards for mothers and needy women against dismissal; establishment of nurseries, children's homes, kindergartens, maternity homes, mother-and-child health consultation centers; on-the-job training for skilled labor; measures to assure the advancement of women to administrative posts in industry and government.

The first domestic relations code (1918) [11] was designed for the transition period "before the complete realization of the social obligation for the support of those incapable of their own maintenance." [12] At the same time, the framers of the Code plainly ex-

[8] *Ibid.*, p. 73.

[9] Lenin, *Women and Society* (New York, 1938), p. 12; Clara Zetkin, *Reminiscences of Lenin* (New York, 1934), p. 54.

[10] Andrei Y. Vyshinsky, ed., *The Law of the Soviet State,* trans. Hugh W. Babb (New York, 1948), p. 592.

[11] Kodeks zakonov ob aktakh grazhdanskogo sostoianiia, brachnom, semeinom i opekunskom prave (Sobr. uzakon., 1918, No. 76–77, st. 818).

[12] Russian Soviet Government Bureau, *The Marriage Laws of Soviet Russia* (New York, 1920), "Introduction," p. 15.

pected the married woman soon to become a wage earner: it established the principle of mutual responsibility between husband and
wife for support in case of incapacity to work and for maintenance
and education of children, as well as the principle of separate property, even that acquired during marriage. Primarily to break the
monopoly previously held by the Church in matters of marriage
and divorce, civil registration constituted the only form of marriage recognized as involving these obligations between man and
woman. Toward children, however, whether born in wedlock or
not, the responsibility of a parent was the same. Actual consanguinity, not the formalization of marriage, was explicitly recognized as the basis of the family. Although Marxian theory called for
full freedom of divorce, it was made subject to court jurisdiction
unless desired by both sides. A divorced spouse was entitled to
alimony as long as in need and unable to work. Temporary protection was thus afforded to the wife as yet unemployable, but her
ultimate security was to be found in her own earnings, not in those
of the husband. The revised code of 1926,[13] equalizing factual and
registered marriage in regard to material obligations,[14] extended
to the mother the protection formerly given only to the children
of an unregistered marriage; and authorized divorce at the desire
of either member, free of judicial decision.

In recognition of the necessity of birth control in the impoverishment of the times, abortion was legalized in 1920, as an admittedly undesirable expedient.[15]

"It is a far cry from equality in law to equality in life," Lenin
told women workers, urging their participation in political activities and public administration, along with productive labor, the
basic guarantee of equality.[16] The annihilation of custom and prejudice rested on "other processes," for which the law merely opened

[13] Kodeks zakonov o brake, sem'e i opeke RSFSR (Sobr. uzakon. RSFSR, 1926,
No. 82, st. 612).

[14] Including the joint ownership of property acquired during marriage, to compensate the non-wage-earning housewife, still in the majority, for her labor in the home.
Registered marriage, facilitating establishment of paternity and responsibility for
support, as well as for statistical purposes, remained the form preferred by law.

[15] Decree of Nov. 18, 1920, quoted by N. A. Semashko, *Health Protection in the
USSR* (London, 1934), pp. 82–84. At the same time every effort was made to promote
the alternative of contraceptive measures (*ibid.*, p. 87).

[16] Lenin, *Women and Society*, pp. 18, 25.

the way.[17] The Communist Party immediately took vigorous steps to capture the allegiance of the female population through "other processes." A special apparatus of *zhenotdely* (women's sections) was formed, in Lenin's words, "to bring [women] into contact with the Party and to keep them under its influence," [18] guarding always against any separatist feminist movement. The system was designed to reach into every phase of woman's life, on the job and at home. The importance to the Party of the program among women, with its domestic and international propaganda value, is indicated by a resolution of the Thirteenth Party Congress in 1924, which admonished the *zhenotdely* to greater efforts toward keeping women in their jobs, in the face of a tendency to freeze them out whenever personnel cuts were made. "The retention of female labor in production has political significance," the resolution read.[19]

II

Women were slow to appear on the industrial scene. As it was in actuality, so in fiction: unemployment was the great problem until inception of the First Plan. For the most part, those who figure in NEP literature are Party workers or students, groping toward the future in a society ridden by moral anarchy. The ground-clearing

---

[17] Russian Soviet Government Bureau, *Marriage Laws*, p. 11.

[18] Quoted by Zetkin, pp. 53–54.

[19] "Zhenskoe kommunisticheskoe dvizhenie v SSSR," *Bol'shaia sovetskaia entsiklopediia*, XXV (1932), 244.

The main tasks of the *zhenotdel* organizers were to indoctrinate women workers in Communist principles, to enroll them in the Party and train them for government service, to assist in their advancement on the job and in the establishment of communal domestic facilities. As aides, the organizers enlisted a corps of *delegatki*, women elected by their co-workers as deputies. *Zhenotdel* representatives had a voice in selecting the factory complement of women and girls for special training. They also served on industrial arbitration committees and sponsored the election of *delegatki* to the local soviet. They sat on commissions to authorize free abortion; cooperated in campaigns to eradicate prostitution; assisted in prosecution of cases concerning establishment of paternity, alimony claims, non-support of children; worked in advisory centers maintained by *Okhrmatmlad* (Okhrana materinstva i mladenchestva [Organization for Protection of Motherhood and Infancy]), part of the People's Commissariat for Public Health. After a troubled and precarious existence within the Party, the *zhenotdely* were dissolved, with a cryptic explanation, in 1929, at the very time when women began to pour into industry in great numbers ("Zhenskoe kommunisticheskoe dvizhenie"; "Zhenotdely," *Malaia sovetskaia entsiklopediia*, 2d ed., Vol. IV [1935]; S. Smidovich, "Delegatskie sobraniia zhenshchin," *Malaia sov. entsik.*, III [1935]).

for solution of the woman question was a long process, and, in the nature of things, a destructive one. Demolition began on marriage, the family, and the morality of the past.

Within its ranks the Bolshevik "old guard" disagreed on procedure in the abolition of the single family as the basic economic and educational unit of society. Lenin anticipated its withering away and urged the establishment of all possible public facilities for taking over household functions,[20] for "the real emancipation of women . . . will begin only when . . . petty domestic economy is transformed on a mass scale into large-scale socialist economy." [21] Such expectation by no means implied that Lenin countenanced the disappearance of the family in the burst of debauchery which occurred. Quite the contrary. He inveighed against the widespread sexual license on the postrevolutionary scene, particularly among the younger generation, under the slogan of "free love" or "glass-of-water" theory.[22] Devotees of the cult declared that love was a bourgeois fable, that relations between the sexes were of a purely physiological character, in which desire demanded satisfaction as thirst demanded the drinking of a glass of water; in neither case was ethical or moral significance involved, and there was no need of continuity in the sexual alliance. If Russian men and women were less promiscuous in their relations than was noised abroad at this time, at least they were well organized for promiscuity. They had a theory. And the theory showed remarkable tenacity in spite of formidable opposition.

Whoever was the chief mischief-maker in its coinage, the "free love" slogan has become fixedly identified with the name of Alexandra Kollontai. The domestic polemics stirred by her pronouncements were all the bitterer because her position of eminence and world-wide reputation (first as Commissar of Social Welfare and later as Minister to Norway) lent a certain suggestion of Bolshevik sponsorship for the ideology expounded. In her publicist writings, Mme Kollontai proposed a new proletarian morality based on less stability in the relations of the sexes, as dictated by the fundamental tasks of the worker class.[23] In place of the "individual and

[20] Zetkin, pp. 47, 57–58.   [21] Lenin, *Women and Society*, p. 14.
[22] Zetkin, pp. 49–50.
[23] Kollontai, "Moral' kak orudie klassovogo gospodstva i klassovoi morali," *Molodaia gvardiia*, No. 6–7 (1922), pp. 128–36; *Rabochii klass i novaia moral'* (Moscow, 1919).

egotistic family," there would arise "a great universal family," in which the worker-mother would no longer differentiate between her children and other children, recognizing all as *"our* children, those of the communist state, the common possession of all the workers." [24] Kollontai's short story "Love of Three Generations" (1923) [25] depicts her new morality in practice. Zhenia, the heroine, has remained ever since the most famous exponent of the glass-of-water theory. In arranging for an abortion she voices a prevalent Komsomol view that sexual life is nothing more than a physiological pleasure, for which she changes her lovers according to her mood. Which one is the child's father she does not know nor care. Love is for those with leisure. Her own heavy duties in the Komsomol leave no time for it. Her mother, a Party organizer before the Revolution and now an important industrial executive, is herself opposed to the institution of marriage, but at the same time is revolted by the lovelessness of Zhenia's multiple and overlapping affairs and by the discovery that Andrei, her own current lover, is one of the possible fathers of Zhenia's child. To the old-guard Party woman such licentiousness is incompatible with Communism. From the triumph of the daughter, coupled with the author's pamphleteering, the conclusion was unavoidable that Kollontai championed Zhenia's credo as a relatively durable and fitting one, evolved by Soviet youth in adaptation to the new conditions, and not merely a by-product of the chaotic relations between the sexes which accompany and outlast wars anywhere.

In a savage critical attack, Kollontai was accused of ideological error in her premature formulation of a new proletarian moral code before women were converted into a skilled labor force, educated, and united in the establishment of social life on collective principles. Her intimation that, through attainment of equality in the sex relationship, woman won equal rights in general was castigated as feminist nonsense, a denial of the Marxist view that woman's economic achievement determined her social status.[26]

Lunacharskii, Commissar of Education, also objected to untimely straining toward a new moral code in order to stem or excul-

---

[24] Kollontai, *Communism and the Family* (New York, 1920), pp. 22–23.

[25] Kollontai, "Liubov' trëkh pokolenii," *Liubov' pchël trudovykh* (Moscow, 1923).

[26] P. Vinogradskaia, "Voprosy morali, pola, byta i tovarishch Kollontai," *Krasnaia nov'*, No. 6 (October–November, 1923), pp. 179–214.

pate the corruption inevitable during the transition period and arising from the very existence of the family: "What are we to do about it? Create a special militia of morals, a salvation army? . . . Nothing of the kind. Educate—that is the answer. . . . To the freedom of the unbridled human being, we oppose communist enlightenment." [27] Lunacharskii saw in state regimentation of purely private matters one of the greatest impediments to the advance toward a communist society, in which morality would consist in the absence of all precepts: "It will be the morality of the absolutely free human being." [28] Neither Lenin's authority nor Lunacharskii's "communist enlightenment" was enough to end the vogue of "free love." Until the beginning of the First Plan, the sex problem of Komsomol youth was "the most fashionable in literature." [29] Fiction writers looked upon the girl of the factory with an eye single to her erotic possibilities.

Tania, heroine of Malashkin's "Moon on the Right-Hand Side" (1926), is one of the most gratuitously dissolute in the large company. A Komsomolka who had worked for a time in a Moscow mill and then entered the university, she there became addicted to drunken orgies, narcotics and abortions, and acquired a series of "husbands," to the number of twenty-two. In her abject self-disgust, she could explain only that she was stigmatized as "petty-bourgeois" if she rebuffed the comrades.[30]

The painstaking dissection of this story in leading literary journals is indicative of the high standards of factual veracity to which critics were holding writers at the time. The critics acknowledged that the story dealt with an actual problem of serious dimensions, but found that Malashkin had failed to motivate Tania's depravity in psychological or sociological forces. Indecisive allusions to her kulak origin and to "pernicious elements" in the petty-bourgeois and left-wing intelligentsia encountered at the university did not reveal the source of contamination, but merely misrepresented the class composition of the student body. The critic Polianskii pointed out that the Party carefully sieved university candidates and that

[27] A. Lunacharskii, "Moral' i svoboda," *Krasnaia nov'*, No. 7 (December, 1923), pp. 135–36. [28] *Ibid.*, p. 133.
[29] Boris Grossman, "Knizhnoe obozrenie," *Novyi mir*, No. 3 (March, 1929), p. 265.
[30] Sergei I. Malashkin, "Luna s pravoi storony, ili neobyknovennaia liubov'," *Molodaia gvardiia*, No. 9 (September, 1926), pp. 3–54.

statistics on their class origin were available. Such falsification, he declared, was impermissible to a Soviet artist.[31] If the cause of Tania's debauchery remained indeterminate, at least the critics were certain of the cure: the factory. The healthy surroundings of the industrial proletariat would have restored her.

About Kollontai's earlier story, it was said: "Zhenia's philosophy is a disease, not a class ideal." [32] It was a classless and apolitical epidemic, which raged most fiercely in the midst of the Komsomol, despite another critic's assertion that, although rottenness crept into both the Komsomol and the Party, "these are all isolated cases which the Party liquidates without difficulty." [33] The literary output of the moment and of the next years refutes his statement. Youth was out of hand; the Party could not control it. Everywhere, young Communists floundered in a morass not of "simple self-corruption, but self-corruption with a philosophy." [34]

In Bogdanov's *First Girl* (1926), a young Komsomolka leader has been spreading disease in the performance of her obligation to the comrades; when about to be publicly denounced in retaliation, she is killed by her closest friend to spare disgrace to her and the Party youth organization. Through the girl's final protest against the brutal attitude of the Komsomol, the author frankly pleaded for more prudent and considerate behavior among youth.[35] In turn, he was cautioned in a leading literary journal to eschew didacticism, however deplorable the reality he was forced to describe: "We should prefer the absence of all moralizing. In art, only creative images are effective." [36] Again, Gladkov in the novel *Tipsy Sun* (1927) raises the question of the compatibility of current mores with Party and Komsomol membership.[37] The list of young Communists overcome by the miasma of drunkenness, sex, rape, and

---

[31] Valerian Polianskii, "O povesti S. Malashkina 'Luna s pravoi storony,' " *Pechat' i revoliutsiia*, No. 2 (March, 1927), pp. 93–103.

[32] Aaron B. Zalkind, *Polovoi vopros v usloviiakh sovetskoi obshchestvennosti* (Leningrad, 1926), p. 52.

[33] Viacheslav Polonskii, "Kriticheskie zametki. O rasskazakh Sergeia Malashkina," *Novyi mir*, No. 2 (February, 1927), p. 176.

[34] *Ibid.*, p. 172.

[35] Nikolai Bogdanov, "Pervaia devushka," *Molodaia gvardiia*, No. 2 (February, 1926), pp. 49–106; No. 3 (March, 1926), pp. 73–108.

[36] D. Tal'nikov, "Problemnaia literatura," *Krasnaia nov'*, No. 3 (March, 1929), p. 209.

[37] Fëdor V. Gladkov, *P'ianoe solntse* (Moscow, 1927).

murder, and thus frustrated in their original high purpose of "remaking the ancient worn-out principles of life," [38] might be extended indefinitely.[39] Criticism of this crop of fiction ranged from
outraged incredulity and protest against the caricature and slander
of youth, through dismayed skepticism, to final pained acceptance
of the mounting evidence as a valid reflection of reality. The fact
that much of it was given "from the inside, through the eyes of
Komsomol members," could not be gainsaid.[40]

The older Party woman, with deeper roots in the past, also joined
in the concerted onslaught against marriage, family, and the out-
moded morality, no matter how cruel the price. Gladkov's novel
Cement (1925), in which the proletarian family is sacrificed as
Dasha, the heroine, remakes her life and that of others in accordance with the principle that woman's primary function is economic
production and that wifehood and motherhood are accessory to that
function, might carry as subtitle a phrase from the book: "the too
heavy burden of woman's freedom." [41] When her husband, Gleb,
returns from the civil war, Dasha spurns his efforts to reestablish
the family on the old basis. She has been transformed from the doc-
ile homemaker, whom Gleb regarded as his private property, into
a *delegatka* (see page 33, note 19) and Party agitator. To assert her
independence and defy Gleb's jealousy, anathema to "new" men
and women, she submits almost hypnotically to the preposterous
lecher who is chairman of the local Party executive committee, and
urges Gleb not to rebuff the advances of her co-worker in the Party.
Against Gleb's will, Dasha has entrusted their small daughter
Nurka to the *zhenotdel* children's home and, under the spell of
the Communist slogan "There are no strange children for us,"

[38] S. Pakentreiger, "M. Karpov," *Pechat' i rev.*, No. 1 (January, 1928), p. 185.

[39] A number of the more widely read and discussed works on this theme are:
Lev Gumilevskii, *Sobachii pereulok* (Dog's Alley; Leningrad, 1927); Georgii K. Nikiforov, *U fonaria* (At the Light; Moscow, 1928); Nikolai N. Nikitin, "Prestuplenie
Kirika Rudenko" (The Crime of Kirik Rudenko), *Krasnaia nov'*, Nos. 9–11 (September–November, 1927); Nikolai Ognëv, *Dnevnik Kosti Riabtsëva* (Diary of Kostia
Riabtsëv; Moscow, 1928–29 [in 2 vols. under the titles *Diary of a Communist Schoolboy* and *Diary of a Communist Undergraduate*, trans. Alexander Werth, London,
1928–29]); Gleb Alekseev, "Delo o trude" (An Affair of Labor), *Inye glaza* (Moscow,
1926); M. Karpov, *Piataia liubov'* (Fifth Love; Kharkov, 1927); Boris L. Gorbatov,
Iacheika (The Cell; Moscow, 1928); I. Brazhnin, *Pryzhok* (The Leap, Moscow, 1928).

[40] A. Lezhnëv, "Molodëzh' o molodëzhi," *Novyi mir*, No. 6 (June, 1929), p. 191.

[41] Gladkov, *Tsement* (Moscow, 1927), p. 35. The novel was serialized in 1925 in
Krasnaia nov'.

denies any intenser love for Nurka than for the others there. In the terrible poverty of the time, the children are hungry and in rags. Even street waifs are afraid of being sent to the home. Yet, proposing that more houses be appropriated for nurseries, Dasha rails against the "vile kitchen" from which "free proletarian women" must be released.[42] Feverishly occupied in inciting women to abandon their homes and relinquish their children to public institutions in spite of the militant and bawdy opposition from the men and a handful of resistant housewives, Dasha even allows Nurka to die in the destitute children's home, for want of the mother's care. Dasha's unquestioning subordination of personal emotions to the cause won for her the consistent plaudits of the critics as a "new human being," "a Bolshevik." Here, as elsewhere, the breakup of the family, with its attendant communizing of daily life, was regarded complacently as a salutary phenomenon, a sign of progress toward the future.[43] In contrast, in the same novel Polia Mekhova, leader of the *zhenotdel,* irreconcilable to the NEP, protests at a Party purge against the iniquities of the new policy: the reappearance of cafés, high heels, dice and profits, the wave of drunken bestiality, in the face of starving refugees—the Revolution turned to greed. The arbiter rebukes this overzealous, romantic, rifle-carrying fighter of the civil war days as unsuited to the next phase of Soviet life: "This curly-head was born too soon. . . . We have not yet reached the stage of full communism. Little women like this should be kicked out." [44] She was expelled from the Party. Within its ranks, there was no quarter on the basis of sex.

Party philosophy and practice alone did not fix the harsh materialistic temper of the times. Stories of Alexei Tolstoy and Panteleimon Romanov show non-Communists bent on the same prosy lusts and compromises, or tasting the same bitter isolation.[45] The heroine of Romanov's "Without Cherry Blossom" (1926) and its

[42] *Ibid.,* p. 72.

[43] I. Astakhov, "O tvorchestve F. Gladkova," *Literatura i iskusstvo,* No. 12 (1931), p. 65. The creation of residence communes in N. Liashko's novel *Domennaia pech'* (Blast Furnace; Moscow, 1924) was hailed as an equal triumph to the blowing in of the furnace (Viktor Krasil'nikov, "Knizhnoe obozrenie," *Novyi mir,* No. 4 [April, 1927], p. 199). [44] Gladkov, *Tsement,* p. 281.

[45] Tolstoi, *Gadiuka* (The Viper; Moscow, 1927); Romanov, "Pravo na liubov' " (The Right to Love), *Novyi mir,* No. 7 (July, 1926), pp. 5–27; Romanov, *Voprosy pola* (Sex Problems; Moscow, 1927).

companion piece "The Big Family" (1927) capitulates out of loneliness to the unwritten credo of her environment: "For us love does
not exist; we have only sexual relations." [46] One evening she pins
a spray of cherry blossom to her dress and accompanies a fellow
student to his room. He scoffs at the flower, at her distaste for the
squalid litter of his quarters, at her hesitations. "It all ends the same
way, cherry blossom or no cherry blossom. . . . Why mince matters?" [47] The purpose accomplished, he leads her out the back way.
Throughout the story, hero and heroine are nameless. In the sequel,
"The Big Family," Sonia has finished with anonymity and humiliation. She is mother of a child, which she has chosen to bear notwithstanding her contemptuous dismissal by her peasant mother
and the availability of abortion. She has left behind the "tyranny of
the family over the individual, that obscure, dirty tyranny," and
has found "another larger family" [48] in her comrades at school, who
regard her husbandless motherhood as a triumph over bourgeois
morals and join forces to help her through her studies and into a
job. When, with the baby on an outing from the nursery, she again
encounters Alexander, now a practicing doctor, it is only the father
of the child who is discomfited. He glances furtively at her dress
and the patch on one shoe as if measuring his possible liability. On
several meetings, Sonia gives no hint of any bond between them.
Except for sidelong squints, Alexander pretends not to notice the
baby. He is obviously puzzled by Sonia's relationship to him: wife,
mother of his child, or no one? At last, lightly, piquantly, she alludes
to him as the father, but father unrelated to the baby's future.

> He sat awhile with bowed head and fidgeted nervously with the top
> of one of his boots. . . . He bit his lip. "But I have some relationship
> to him, somehow," he said, with his head still bowed.
> "A very small one," I rejoined. "In any case, no relationship that he
> will be pleased to learn about by and by." [49]

Despite Alexander's reawakened interest in her, she takes leave of
him, to go to another post, filled with "an inexplicable inner
strength . . . and freedom." [50]

[46] Romanov, "Without Cherry Blossom" (Bez cherëmukhi), *Without Cherry Blossom*, trans. L. Zarine (New York, 1932), p. 17.
[47] *Ibid.*, p. 19.
[48] Romanov, "The Big Family" (Bol'shaia sem'ia), *Without Cherry Blossom*, pp.
43–44.   [49] *Ibid.*, p. 51.   [50] *Ibid.*, p. 52.

The effect which Romanov attributes to this new estate—
motherhood without benefit of marriage, independent, sanctioned
and secured by society itself—at once raises the question: is the
characterization authentic? Is Sonia genuinely motivated to relinquish parental home and claims on the father of her child, to rely
on her own powers within "the big family," to identify herself with
the authority that has schooled her, cared for her child, and placed
her in the work for which she was trained? Or is she a concoction
calculated to embody the slogans of the day? It is a question of
Romanov's artistic practice. In the opinion of two utterly dis-
similar critics, both Russian but non-Soviet, Romanov during the
period of these stories was, in the "naturalistic" manner of reportage cultivated in the 1920s, rendering a bald, but faithful and
exact account of the actuality he observed.[51] Furthermore, he was
at this very time repeatedly turning out works which aroused ideological displeasure.[52] It seems unlikely that in these two stories
Romanov was falsifying for the sake of currying favor. There is
also indication in factual writings that life in many quarters was
being organized around the concept of "the big family," especially
in the residence communes founded by young people.[53] Whether
the concept is a viable one is another question.

In Iurii Olesha's enigmatic novel *Envy* (1927), a skeptic and
rebel fulminates against a vast mechanized food factory as symbol
of the regimentation of the new industrial order, with its inevitable
strangulation of sentiment, of romanticism, of all the poetry of living. As leader of a "conspiracy of the emotions," Babichev calls
upon women to join him in destruction of the enemy machines:

"Comrades! They are trying to rob you of your greatest possession—
your hearth and home. The horses of the Revolution are thundering up
the back stairs into your kitchen, trampling your children and your
cats, smashing your beloved little stoves. . . .

[51] Marc Slonim, "The New Spirit in Russian Literature," *Soviet Literature*, ed.
and trans. George Reavey and Marc Slonim (New York, 1934), p. 28; Gleb Struve,
Soviet Russian Literature 1917–50 (Norman, Okla., 1951), p. 146; Struve, *25 Years of
Soviet Russian Literature 1918–43* (London, 1944), pp. 63–65.

[52] Pakentreiger, "Talant ravnodushiia," *Pechat' i rev.*, No. 8 (December, 1926), pp.
86–94.

[53] A. Grigorovich, *Zhivëm* (Moscow, 1930); A. Naistat, I. Ryvkin, I. Sosnovik, *Kom-
muny molodëzhi* (Moscow, 1931); Fannina W. Halle, *Woman in Soviet Russia*, trans.
Margaret M. Green (New York, 1933), pp. 376–77; Klaus Mehnert, *Youth in Soviet
Russia*, trans. Michael Davidson (New York, 1933), pp. 162–86, 249–56.

"He mocked your pots and pans, your gentleness. . . . He is trying to turn you into wanderers in the wastes of history. Women, he spits into your soup. Mothers, it is his idea to obliterate from the faces of your little ones all resemblance to you—that sacred, beautiful family resemblance! . . . Tell him: 'Don't beckon to us, don't tempt us—what have you to offer in place of our capacity for love, for hate, hope, tears, pity, and forgiveness?' " [54]

High-tempo industrialization was imminent. The literary and philosophical organ of the Party reiterated that the development of communal facilities could no longer be postponed [55] and that the singer of "hymns to the individual kitchen" was a "loathsome egotist." [56] Polonskii, countering Babichev's tirade in *Envy*, accused him of inventing a threat where none existed: "It is about [the kitchen factory of the future] that we speak when we speak of the great proletarian revolution, of socialist construction of unprecedented scope, of the remaking of the world, and of the emancipation of man." [57] Only to the "haughty intransigents" of the old bourgeois intelligentsia, quaking in the face of Communism, the mechanization of bakeries meant also the "mechanization of procreation," "universal leveling." What reason was there to think that "the iron heel of the approaching epoch" would stamp out the heart and brain of man, that "columns of figures would replace flowers, and that the great emotions . . . would perish?" [58]

Sergei Semënov's two-volume novel *Natalia Tarpova* answers that even in the veteran Party woman "the great emotions" of the past were ineradicable and as yet intractable to the sternest self-discipline. For the heroine, secretary of the factory committee and member of the Party bureau in a Petrograd machinery plant, the central problem implicit in the Marxian design for woman—reconciliation of job with longing for home and family—is complicated by class conflict. Until her astonished realization of her love for the non-Party engineer, Gabrukh, "the word 'love' had not existed in her vocabulary." [59] The "Party formula" [60] of Communist men in

[54] Olesha, *Zavist'*, 2d ed. (Moscow, 1930), pp. 113–14.
[55] Iakov Cherniak, "Zavist'," *Pechat' i rev.*, No. 5 (July–August, 1928), p. 112.
[56] M. Bochacher, "Serdtse povelitel'," *Pechat' i rev.*, No. 4 (April, 1930), p. 20.
[57] Polonskii, "Ocherki sovremennoi literatury—preodolenie 'Zavisti,' " *Novyi mir*, No. 5 (May, 1929), p. 199.   [58] *Ibid.*, p. 203.
[59] Semënov, *Natal'ia Tarpova* (Leningrad), II (1931), 16.
[60] *Ibid.*, p. 174.

proposing a short-term life together had sufficed as prelude to a
series of free and easy alliances. Now, with Gabrukh, she felt an
indomitable urge toward a completeness and stability of relationship, banned between her, a proletarian, and a "class enemy" at
odds with the new regime. His marriage she dismissed as no barrier,
but the class difference in their blood prevented intimacy as man
and woman.

Through Gabrukh's jeers, she had perceived that ideological
acquiescence was not sufficient for the Party but that, like the medieval religious order, it must exact from its members their whole
being. As a Communist, she was committed to the task of drawing
the factory workers out of their separate family nests into an open,
socialized mode of living, in order to mobilize their total faculties
for the cause, not merely the time spent at the machines. To this
end, it was her obligation to set an example. Whereas the Party
organizer, Riabëv, had succumbed to the desire of many Communists to construct a watershed between their public life and their
everyday existence at home, by ensconcing himself in a private
apartment with a girl of the intelligentsia, collective opinion in the
factory would not permit the Party woman the same liberty with a
member of an alien class. A critic analyzing this persistent inequity
concluded that its solution must wait: Riabëv was stronger and
more experienced than Liudmila, who, "as is characteristic of the
average non-Party woman, has no firm ideology. . . . Politically,
he will subjugate her." However, Gabrukh had intellectual superiority over Tarpova, and even the force of class hegemony on her
side might not prevail.[61] Only that which harmed the Revolution
was the illicit love. The rationale of the critic stems from Lenin's
definition: "The basis of Communist morality is the struggle for
the consolidation and completion of Communism." [62]

Nevertheless, when Gabrukh's wife deserted him, Natalia instantly ceased to be a weapon in the hands of her class and joyfully
elected love. Semënov, a Party writer who allows the personal pas-
sions of his characters to override Communist conviction, typifies
the temporary lenience of the Party itself, which during the NEP

[61] G. Gorbachëv, "O romane S. Semënova 'Natal'ia Tarpova,'" *Oktiabr'*, No. 2
(February, 1929), pp. 239–40.
[62] Lenin, "The Tasks of the Youth Leagues," *Selected Works* (2 vols., Moscow,
1947), II, 670.

period refrained from resolving the struggle in the individual conscience by Party fiat. To some degree the novelist justifies Tarpova's
violation of the current taboo for the Party woman against taking
a mate outside the group by intimations that the bourgeois-
intellectual Gabrukh will gradually embrace the Communist cause.
The failure of his marriage has refuted one of Gabrukh's strongest
arguments against the new order. To the end he had attempted to
preserve his home intact, contending that marriage, the basis of the
family nucleus, "the primary unit of any society," must be maintained for life, but must also be accompanied by full extramarital
freedom for both members.[63] In socialist society, Semënov demonstrated, and a critic hastened to confirm, such a form of marriage
and family, like the others, "undergoes inevitable destruction." [64]
In the clash of antagonistic class systems resulting from the entry of
women *en masse* into the factory, the bourgeois intelligentsia lost
the life-long permanency and legal sanction it had demanded in
domestic relations; the Party proletarians were forced to concede
the validity of "the great emotions" and to abandon their practice
of casual alliances.

Not only from Tarpova's awareness of the prohibitive attitude
of the Party toward marriage with an outsider, but also from her
relations with women workers, it is clear that the women of the
Party constituted an in-group differentiated from the rank and
file, although, in the eyes of others, by no means a closed group.
Notwithstanding the heavy toll taken by the Party from its members, women of all classes in the factory aspired to admission in the
Party and followed the *zhenotdel's* lead over the stepping stones,
eagerly attending lectures on historical materialism far beyond
their grasp and putting up a dogged fight against men workers for
fabzavuch training.[65] The paucity of new recruits into the Party
which had displeased the Congress in 1924 [66] here resulted solely
from the Party's own rigid standards of eligibility, which excluded
the material so far available: cultural workers of the bourgeois in-

[63] Semënov, *Natal'ia Tarpova*, I, 45 (Leningrad, no date; author's date at end of
text: 1925–27).
[64] Gorbachëv, "O romane S. Semënova," p. 239.
[65] The *fabzavuch*, or FZU, schools (fabrichno-zavodskoe uchenichestvo [factory and
plant apprenticeship]), located at all large industrial establishments, were the chief
training centers at this time to prepare minors for skilled and semi-skilled labor
[66] "Zhenskoe kommunisticheskoe dvizhenie," col. 245.

telligentsia, still considered second-grade citizens; and proletarian nonentities left over from the old regime. The Party was only for the strong, Tarpova reflected, surprised to learn of the ambitions of one weakling. Her immediate response verges on the disdain of the member of an elite group for an inferior:

"You know, Comrade Lenin has said," whispered Raisa Pavlovna, " 'Every cook must learn to rule the state.' "
"So that's what's up," thought Tarpova in irritation. "A slogan like that shouldn't be spread around." [67]

Critics greeted with relief the resurgence of emotions from their state of anesthetization and approved Natalia, before publication of the end of the book, as a "positive Communist" who, devoted first of all to the cause, still did not stifle her feelings,[68] in contrast to the stock Party heroine whose renunciation of all thought of love only led to "the ugly excrescence of the personal." [69] Major writers such as Kataev and Kaverin also make the point that, toward the end of the NEP period, the time was ripe for an unabashed rehabilitation of love as the basis of alliance between man and woman.[70]

The negation of love, the cult of depersonalization, had drawn women into licentiousness sickening to themselves or into poignantly felt segregation. Although critics lifted their voices to deplore debauchery in youth and to censure it in Bolsheviks,[71] fiction writers, availing themselves of the indulgence of the time, did not hesitate to point out that often the example set by Party members only accelerated the trend. Gladkov refers in *Tipsy Sun* to the heavy casualties among Komsomol youth, who filled the sanatoriums and rest homes and at the age of eighteen or nineteen were burned out by overwork and libertine habits. In such matters, the Party held a slack rein during the period, relying on excesses to lose momentum of themselves.

There were two essential features of the Marxian program on

[67] Semënov, *Natal'ia Tarpova*, II, 300–301.
[68] Gorbachëv, "O romane S. Semenova," p. 235.
[69] Lezhnëv, "Molodëzh' o molodëzhi," pp. 193–94.
[70] Valentin Katayev, "Squaring the Circle" ("Kvadratura kruga," 1928), trans. Charles Malamuth, in *Six Soviet Plays*, ed. Eugene Lyons (Boston, 1934); Veniamin Kaverin, *The Larger View* (*Ispolnenie zhelanii* [Fulfillment of Desires], 1935–36), trans. E. Leda Swan (New York, 1938).
[71] Lezhnëv, "Literaturnye zametki," *Pechat' i rev.*, No. 7 (October–November, 1925), pp. 135–37.

the woman question which had, of necessity, to be realized concurrently, for any measure of success: liberation from the bonds of the old family, and employment in socially productive work. To a certain extent, the accomplishment of the first purpose lay within women's own power, and on it they fell to work with a will, more zealous than men in their attack on the family structure and in acceptance of the communal mode of life. In providing work for themselves in industry on a scale to match the breakdown of the family, however, they were helpless. The faulty synchronization left them in a quandary. *Zhenotdel* leaders, charged with the task of tugging women out of the family and into socialized labor and living, were attempting the impossible: the assignment depended upon an economic base not yet laid in the NEP period.

One achievement the *zhenotdel* could claim: the universal and detailed knowledge of the goal. The propaganda campaign was unmistakably reaching the masses of women. As yet many resisted. There was a stubborn and powerful carry-over of the prerevolutionary tradition of woman's role. Nothing could avail to break this opposition and to relieve the frustration of those ready to embrace the new program so long as industry failed to provide the conditions in which women could harmoniously combine their two basic functions, social employment and motherhood.

The remedy was obvious: jobs. And these the year 1929 provided, in abundance. Without them, the striving toward a new life was no more than an attempt to create it by incantation.

III

With the decision on high-tempo industrialization and the inauguration of the First Five-Year Plan toward the end of 1928, womanpower became a matter of life and death to the economy. Glebov's play "Inga," which had its première in March, 1929, is a blunt announcement that in the utilization of womanpower the work of the factory came first and that no interference would be brooked. Glebov, a Communist, belonged to the dominant literary faction RAPP (Russian Association of Proletarian Writers), which measured the value of a writer's work by the assistance rendered to the fulfillment of the Plan in molding attitudes and behavior to its service. The special purpose of Glebov's play is obvious, and it is one which directly contravenes the consensus of Party opinion as expressed in literature during the NEP period. The assumption had been that, upon the mass absorption of women into social employment, the family, no longer necessary or desirable to its members and to society, would swiftly vanish and emancipation proceed apace. Glebov, at the very inception of the Plan, treats this solution with misgivings and prescribes the remedy of salvaging the family as a temporary aid, not a hindrance, to immediate social goals.

In Glebov's play, Inga Rizzer, a Communist intellectual and the capable director of a clothing factory, is one of the rare women to have reached a high post by the beginning of the First Five-Year Plan. Women were winning their place in industry, but only with an ugly struggle. To her resentful old-regime subordinates, who oppose such innovations as nurseries—then an economic imperative to attract women to the factory—Inga sternly announces that everything in the plant must be linked to the interests of the workers. In the sphere of private life, she herself violates the principle by taking Dmitrii Grechaninov, chairman of the factory committee, from his wife and child. On the strength of years of self-denying service to the Party, Inga refuses to surrender her right to happiness, to sacrifice herself merely because the other woman is a mother. When Glafira, the abandoned wife, attempts suicide, gossip and angry disapproval disrupt plant operations; old Somov, voice of the Party and arbiter of all destinies at the factory, warns Inga that she cannot defy the opinion of the entire collective, that one must not love at the expense of someone else. To a Communist, constantly watched by the masses as an example, there are no personal matters. Dmitrii is condemned for dereliction of his duty to raise to his own ideological level the simple, uneducated Glafira, who had become "a rope around [his] neck," and for opportunism in turning to the more highly placed and glamorous Inga. To Somov, their action is "counterrevolution—a blow at that family which the working class is building, without which it will not be able to draw one-half of humanity into the Revolution." [72] Inga is one individual; Glafira stands for the millions. At this time of idealization of equalitarianism, Inga must wait, as long as there are millions of women still ignorantly praying to God, suffocating in

[72] Anatole Glebov, "Inga," trans. Charles Malamuth, in *Six Soviet Plays*, p. 359.

kitchen stench, and carrying bruises from their beatings. They need the family, Somov asserts. His purpose is to prevent the loss of a worker through the adverse effects of a broken marriage. Glafira's labor and that of her counterparts everywhere are needed in industrial construction.

In Glafira's remaking, the playwright demolishes his own thesis. It is only the break-up of her home which goads Glafira into putting her child into a nursery and transforming herself from a slovenly, backward housewife into a *delegatka,* working at shock-brigade tempo, fiercely shouting women's rights, and self-reliant enough to refuse alimony from Dmitrii. At the end, when Inga, embroiled with Dmitrii in quarrels and recriminations touched off by her higher economic rank and intellectual sophistication, has acceded to Somov's verdict and renounced Dmitrii, to remain free for the Party, for the good fight, Glafira takes Dmitrii back, with some reservation and saucily conscious of her new worth as heiress to the future: "If you are with me, it's all right; if you are not—well, what of it? I have my own road to travel. . . . Give us time . . . We'll not only catch up with your Ingas, but we'll outdistance them! We have more backbone . . . and more strength. And you know our blood is a bit warmer." [73] Somov's argument is further confused by the hopeless future of a peasant housewife, mother of four and victim of beatings by her drunken husband. The *zhenotdel* proves ineffectual as her protector at a factory "trial," intended to curb domestic abuses; the wife-beater refuses to relinquish his inalienable prerogative, and the woman, because of her children, submissively remains with him "to die under the flatiron." [74]

The *zhenotdel* organizer, Mera, herself seven times married and die-hard champion of the glass-of-water theory, jibes at Somov's defense of the family: "Pots? Diapers? Jealousy? . . . To hell with it!" [75] Mera, too, speaks with the voice of the Party, before the days of the monolithic front. In the play, logic lies on her side. Yet Somov, with superior authority, overrules her and arrogates to himself the role of mentor to the factory women. In him, a Communist faction previously reticent shows itself prepared to abandon the passive Party stand toward personal relations and to intervene actively on behalf of the established family, without scruple for the

[73] *Ibid.,* p. 368.   [74] *Ibid.,* p. 374.   [75] *Ibid.,* p. 359.

letter of Marxian doctrine if the exigencies of industrialization demanded compromise. There is a strong suggestion that in Glebov's eyes the Code on marriage and divorce may have been premature: in the realm of domestic relations the counterpart of premature measures in other fields—what moneyless economy was in the period of War Communism, what the *sovkhoz* was at the beginning of collectivization—an ideal unrealizable at the time, but perhaps not discarded as an ultimate goal.

At the very outset, then, the playwright clearly delineates the disequilibrium occasioned by the employment of women between the occupational system in the process of formation and the lingering family system of Soviet society. Through the medium of his dramatic figures, he presents a social tension readily translatable into the terms of contemporary Western sociologists who have described the corresponding stresses and strains in modern capitalist society. On the American scene among the urban middle class, for example, in the analysis of Talcott Parsons, the precarious balance between the family and the occupational structure is maintained at the cost of virtually excluding the married woman from highly rewarded occupation and of sacrificing the ideal of equality of opportunity for children of different social strata. In order to release the full prowess of the husband and father for effective competitive performance as breadwinner and status-seeker, he must be shielded from conflict between the essentially irreconcilable behavior patterns required in his work and in the family, from disturbing rivalry with a family member, and from ties to a particular community contracted by other individuals in his family which would hamper his geographical mobility. These hazards the segregation of the wife's role prevents. On the other hand, in order to preserve the family solidarity requisite for execution of its functions, class distinctions within it are inadmissible. Wife and children must share the place in the stratification scale won by the father. Consequent advantages and disadvantages inevitably inhere in the status thus ascribed to children on different social levels.[76] It was precisely to avoid payment of this price that Marxian theorists demanded the abolition of the unitary nuclear family. The fundamental differ-

[76] Talcott Parsons, "The Social Structure of the Family," *The Family: Its Function and Destiny*, ed. Ruth N. Anshen (New York, 1949), pp. 173–201.

ence for the Soviet woman was that the regime encouraged, or compelled, her to accept economically productive employment as a perpetual commitment and the determinant factor in her social status, rather than as a stopgap before marriage, and promised her state aid in the undertaking.

In his cross-section of Soviet women industrial workers caught at the beginning of the Plan in the collisions of the occupational system and the family, established or potential, Glebov erects the framework of the situation within which most subsequent writers represent the development of the "new Soviet woman." Other elements in the reorganization of the feminine role are treated as relatively insignificant. In advocating "an entirely new kind of family . . . *our* kind of family" [77] as interim solution of the central conflict, before the advent of abundance which would end all conflict—with its concomitant equalitarianism, the disappearance of competitive strife among workers, and public care for dependents—Glebov stands almost alone in Five-Year-Plan literature. Other solutions found by fictional characters and the degrees of sympathy with which they are related by their authors cover a wide range. With hardly a dissenting voice, however, they are agreed on the primacy of woman's role as worker.

Literature of the First Plan is a chronicle of unremitting toil. Not drudgery. Enthusiastic toil. What precisely occurred in the individual and collective consciousness to produce this mood often remains blurred. "Labor is an affair of honor, of valor," a Komsomolka, quoting Stalin, chanted for no apparent reason at a work bench in Glebov's play.[78] Yet this state of mind is the pivot upon which, theoretically, Soviet life turned, the force which built Magnitogorsk, Dneprostroi, the tractor works of Stalingrad, all the vast industrial developments of the Plan. In these times, writers of every stripe found it unnecessary to motivate for the Soviet reader the tremendous excitement and stimulation of their ideologically precharged heroes and heroines. It was being proclaimed through every channel of communication in the land that the attitude toward labor had changed with the social ownership of the means of production and the ending of exploitation; that now the workers

[77] Glebov, "Inga," p. 359.   [78] *Ibid.*, p. 355.

must build socialism in one country—industrialize at high speed, overtake and surpass the West. This was a war.

To convey the nature of the distinctive new relationship to work, the literature of a country under the dictatorship of the proletariat and in the process of becoming a socialist state of workers and peasants naturally focuses on these two classes, from which women and girls flocked into industry, most of them young, untrained, totally inexperienced in wage-earning labor. Usually they found themselves in hard, rough jobs. An endless procession of women and girls push wheelbarrows through the pages of Five-Year-Plan fiction. The Komsomolki came to industry as a matter of course, in swarms, to earn a living where they were most urgently needed, ready for any extravagant feat of labor. In the fever whipped up by socialist competition, one young Komsomolka in Valentin Kataev's *Time, Forward* (perhaps the most popular and universally admired Five-Year-Plan novel) shows a fine disregard for the provisions of the Labor Code on woman's work: "Olga caught the barrow. The palms of her hands were on fire. She strained, pushed, turned deep red to the roots of her hair, and, with a crash and a clang, rolled the heavily jumping barrow across the rails between the two uncoupled freight cars." [79] Temporarily, it was the fashion to vie with men in undertaking the heaviest tasks. In sober fact, socialist competition was the main device employed during the period to stimulate labor productivity. At Magnitogorsk, in this novel, it produces crackling excitement and herculean efforts, among men and women alike, as a local brigade challenges the champions at Kharkov for the world's record in concrete pouring. This kind of contest, stressing social incentives and competition in groups, was derided as ineffectual and ridiculous by old-regime engineers ("The construction is not a stunt," [80] one says in Kataev's book). Komsomolki took it seriously. Thirst for individual fame was frowned upon as egotistic. For their deadly earnest trial of strength, teamwork and the trustworthiness of each player in the game were so crucial that, before the shift, Olga and a comrade made a security check on the non-Party members of the brigade. Stalin's recent warning, quoted in the book, set its pace and

[79] Kataev, *Time, Forward* (*Vremia, vperëd!*), trans. Charles Malamuth (New York, 1933), p. 273.　　[80] *Ibid.*, p. 154.

its spirit: "We are fifty or a hundred years behind the advanced countries. We must make good this distance in ten years. Either we do it, or they crush us." [81]

The social incentives which affected those at the behest of the Party seldom attracted other women unless accompanied by material advantages. What brought them to industry was, axiomatically, the principle that "he who does not work shall not eat." Once there, the shock workers fared better than most. The logic of their ration card, in these days of acute material shortages, prevailed upon the peasant girl Fenia. She came to Magnitogorsk in search of the father of her child, and decided to remain. Kostia's brigadier card entitled him to good food and even some manufactured articles occasionally. Fenia, too, would work, as a carter in the mines, or as a digger. To do nothing was shameful and boring. "Then also, while one shock-brigade card was good, two were better." [82]

Ehrenburg, in *Out of Chaos,* highlights the universal thirst for knowledge and technical training as a prime motive force of raw young recruits, and the matching interest of management in converting them into skilled workers with the utmost speed. Grunia, daughter of a peasant under suspicion as a kulak, was sent away by her mother to escape the hardships at home during the collectivization drive. At Kuznetsk she was set blindly to work:

At first she shunned people. . . . Even more than people did she fear machines. She did not understand what they were for, nor how one should deal with them. Her head was reeling with questions, but she had not the courage to speak to anybody. She was rescued by the old fitter Golovin. . . .

Grunia questioned him about levers, people, words she could not understand, iron, the Communist Party.[83]

Under Golovin's fatherly tutelage, Grunia acquired skill, enrolled in the courses for advanced training, timidly found her way into the Komsomol, and became a dedicated shock-brigader who declined the special privileges of her ration book. Another girl, guard on a railway service car, barely literate but moved by a "passionate Bolshevik desire to master technique," [84] began to study a "Manual of

[81] Joseph Stalin, "The Tasks of Business Executives," *Selected Writings* (New York, 1942), p. 200.   [82] Kataev, *Time, Forward,* p. 171.
[83] Ilya Ehrenburg, *Out of Chaos* (*Den' vtoroi* [Second Day]), trans. Alexander Bakshy (New York, 1934), pp. 280–81.   [84] *Ibid.,* p. 72.

Train Dispatching" left in the train. After forty readings, she understood the mechanisms in her car. Her initiative earned the reward of *rabfak* [85] training. A young woman from Kirghizia, addressing a club meeting, explains her pleasure in Kuznetsk:

"Before we lived worse than animals. The men ate meat, and the women stood behind them and waited to be thrown a bone. Now I am in a shock brigade. Yesterday I joined the special courses." She became embarrassed and could not utter another word. She was much applauded. Sitting in the corner was an old bearded Kirghiz. He gazed around him cunningly, his eyes screwed up. He said, "Aren't they shameless?" and then began to applaud.[86]

To reveal, in his swift, staccato characterizations, precisely what the "passionate Bolshevik desire to master technique" was, Ehrenburg has not time, nor perhaps insight, for all his express curiosity.

Panfërov, a Party writer, displayed a touchy resentment of the outlander's effrontery of Ehrenburg in undertaking to meet this challenge to Soviet literature. In *Bruski*, the author sneered at a Russian writer "with a face as long as a porcupine's," who lived permanently in France but visited a vast new Soviet industrial site to plague the workers with his question: "What possesses you to work as you do?" [87] Panfërov then set out to worry the problem himself. The hero of the book, Kirill Zhdarkin, Party functionary, in the early days of the Plan watches a caravan of prospective workers tramping across the steppes to the metallurgical and tractor works and settling into barracks or mud huts; he is convinced that these newcomers, particularly the young Communists, have not come simply for the sake of piecework wages. They are moved by "something else," which it is his duty to awaken and direct: "a surge of creative faculties must be stirred up in the people, and then the desire to accumulate money would disappear, the dream of going back home would fade, and they would come to love the plant." [88] As the author describes the great tide rising among the people, much lip service is paid to the contribution of women and to the new status they attain through it. On the lower echelons, by mumbo-jumbo methods the megalomaniac hero transforms raw

---

[85] Abbreviation for *rabochie fakul'tety* (workers' faculties), attended exclusively by workers and peasants being prepared for higher educational institutions.

[86] Ehrenburg, *Out of Chaos*, p. 325.

[87] Fëdor I. Panfërov, *Bruski* (Moscow, 1947; first published in 4 vols., 1928–37), p. 697.   [88] *Ibid.*, p. 695.

peasant girls and women into incandescent workers under the leadership of the Komsomolki. One of them, Natalia Pronina, is put in charge of a section on the peatfields instantly upon her arrival. For completing its quota ahead of time, her brigade is rewarded with bonuses and with publicity over the ubiquitous loudspeakers. Natalia's picture is posted in the line-up of leading workers. To placate disaffected women living in dugouts, and sharp-tongued on the subject of the Soviet government, Zhdarkin relies on cajolery. In the case of a newly born child, he and the director of the works dispatch a warm letter of felicitation accompanied by three meters of satin. As if personal largess, he distributes to his favorites the meager new housing quarters, constructs dining rooms and a sport stadium, and promises children of the dugout colony a Pioneer's Club. As a result, girls sing as they "storm" the peatfields. Through work in the dining rooms, former household drudges blossom into real women. They pour out their gratitude and admiration in sentimental effusions, and shower Zhdarkin with presents. Nevertheless, in a coup of inconsistency, even for Panfërov, master of *non sequitur,* crowds of girl peat workers depart for their native villages, gloating over the envy they will evoke there with the kerchiefs and earrings, beads, and silk stockings bought at the cooperative store—headed home without a flicker of "creative faculties," unmoved by the lure of the Soviet factory which, in contrast to the crushing Ford plant, "gives wings to the human being, straightens out the soul." [89] Obviously, cajolery was inadequate to teach the difference to the hard-headed Russian peasant-proletarian girl. Even the thoroughly indoctrinated Fenia Panova, a gifted chemist and budding metallurgical engineer, fails to exercise woman's new prerogatives when she allows Kirill Zhdarkin to preempt her services and, as his handmaiden at the plant, cheerfully squanders her talents on petty routine details.

From such preliminaries, Panfërov leaps over the intervening years and, without the slightest substantiation to warrant the statement, as of 1935 proclaims woman's social equality to have been triumphantly realized in the Soviet Union. It was to describe the mentality of Panfërov and his ecstatic hero Zhdarkin, and on this very subject, that Lenin had said, "Scratch a Communist, and you

[89] *Ibid.,* p. 792.

find a philistine." [90] Panfërov's novel, a signal failure in interpreting the "something else" brewing among women industrial workers, is of interest as an example of the occasional tailoring of reality to fit the boast. The clumsy fit is readily detectible. Chronology can never be overlooked in reading Soviet literature. Panfërov's work was published in 1937, after the modification of policy toward woman's role in society, when achievement of equality was documented by official pronouncement, not by statistics.

A book as straightforward and stripped of pretense in its account of women in industry as Panfërov's is snarled and spurious is *People of the Stalingrad Tractor Works*.[91] In the collection of workers' autobiographies as related to a team of writers, there are three narratives by young women, all Communists, retaining the accents of their own homely, downright, slangy talk and the native didoes of their thought. Their firsthand reports bear no resemblance to the extravagant claims of Panfërov, but rather accord with the accounts of the non-Party writers Kataev and Ehrenburg in protesting much less while at the same time showing, on the part of management, serious efforts to prepare women as skilled workers and specialists through technical training, as well as a readiness to entrust to them the supervision of men operating complex machinery. The watchword of Soviet youth—"To us belongs the future"—sounds steadily in the strong proprietary attitude displayed, in the disregard of physical privation and hardships, and in the conscious solidarity with fellow workers against the challenge of the world outside the Soviet Union.

In Leonid Leonov's novel *Soviet River,* two women of mixed proletarian-peasant origin, with a bizarre indifference to the grandiose Party designs in their behalf, turn to industry as a refuge from domestic difficulties. The old woman Varvara, "of a stony breed, like her son," [92] is driven, paradoxically, into the hire of the Soviet regime out of truculent disgust for his practices as a Party official: "Burn and scorch . . . and slash your countrymen! . . . You iniquitous devils!" [93] She bundles up her feather bed and an ikon, and goes off to a job switching street car tracks. When her son

[90] Zetkin, p. 56.

[91] *Liudi stalingradskogo traktornogo,* comp. Iakov Il'in (Moscow, 1933).

[92] Leonov, *Soviet River (Sot',* 1930), trans. Ivor Montagu and Sergei Nolbandov (New York, 1932), p. 79.   [93] *Ibid.,* p. 84.

Uvadiev finds her again, she is at her post, an iron staff in her hand, towering with calm and happy face amid the traffic, reconciled to the new order. She yields to his urging and joins him in the far North, to end her days as mother of a Bolshevik. Once she has cleaned his house and mended all his clothes with fierce energy, she hankers after her iron staff and departs, rejuvenated by the mere prospect of return to independence. The new spirit infects even the passive housewife, Natalia, who, long since outdistanced by her husband, Uvadiev, "had grown used to the sorrowful role of a moon reflecting the splendor of a far-off luminary." [94] The delicately balanced mixture of the comic and the macabre with which Leonov describes the soul convulsions of the superseded Natalia, as she loses Uvadiev to a rival and is goaded by the collapse of her marriage into social utility, is a striking *tour de force* in the midst of the great stylistic wastes of Plan literature. As usual in his earlier works, however, the author delivers his laggard to the gateway of the new life, but cannot take her through.

In Suzanne, heroine of the book, the highly original, hitherto jaundiced-eyed Leonov creates one of the earliest examples of an ideal type much exalted in Five-Year-Plan literature: the Soviet-trained, Party-member "specialist," who, in the words of a critic, "sees the basic meaning of her life in the successes of the Revolution." [95] Alienated from her father because of political differences, she had left home to fight in the civil war and then to be educated as a chemical engineer. At the construction site of a paper mill in the northern backwoods to which she was assigned, a turbulent struggle, physical as well as ideological, boils up in the process of proletarianizing the area. As a Communist, she carries a double work load: her professional duties in the laboratory, and proselytizing among the recalcitrants. She faces violence with the same cool equanimity as the hard-bitten professional revolutionaries who lead the fight. To the news of her father's suicide after manhandling by an angry mob which suspected him of sabotage, Suzanne says calmly, with the "unexpected hardness" which surprised even seasoned Bolsheviks, "Yes, he felt lost in the face of the new . . . and it was too late for him to change himself." [96] Staunch

[94] *Ibid.*, p. 83.
[95] I. Nusinov, "Ot 'Untilovska' k 'Soti,'" *Krasnaia nov'*, No. 4 (April, 1931), p. 165.
[96] Leonov, *Soviet River*, p. 279.

Party women did not weep when an enemy of the Revolution was exterminated, foe or father.

The first professional women in industry had enjoyed early advantages in background. By the middle of the Plan, the new specialists began to appear in numbers, drawn from the ranks to form the workers' "own industrial and technical intelligentsia . . . capable of upholding [their] interests in production as the interests of the ruling class." [97] The career of Elena Makarova, heroine of Afinogenov's play "Fear" (1931), a former factory worker who became director of a scientific institute, illustrates how great an asset in obtaining favor and promotion it was to come of worker stock, as well as what hostility and opposition awaited the promotees especially educated by the Party and advanced into positions of authority. The scientists in "Fear" dread Elena not only as an instrument in the hands of the bureaucracy for interference in science, but also as the means of supplanting them and their class. The wrecker trials, beginning in 1928, had led to a policy of regarding "practically every expert . . . of the old school as an undetected criminal and wrecker." [98] In awe of their scientific authority, Elena proves no match for her more wily antagonists, and her class instinct falters. Her mainstay, the old factory hand Klara, berates her for cowardice: "The moment you step away from your class, you are possessed by all sorts of cosmic doubts. I suppose you think that's the result of thinking, but I tell you that it comes from lack of will, from nonpartisan scholarship." [99] Elena finally wins victory only through the weight of her class dominance. For the administrator as well as for the bench worker, individual strength and security derived from class or Party.

Party membership, for women even more than for men, was the surest road to higher levels, but not the only one. Tatiana, one of the two young women working as construction engineers at Dneprostroi in Gladkov's *Power,* had remained outside the Party as she rose to her position of trust from a harsh childhood as a homeless waif. Such detachment was a rarity, and was often questioned by her associates, without answer. More the rule was Fenia, a girl of the peasantry reared in an orphanage, who had made her way up-

---

[97] Stalin, "New Conditions, New Tasks in Economic Construction," *Selected Writings,* p. 212.   [98] *Ibid.,* p. 216.

[99] Alexander Afinogenov, "Fear," trans. Charles Malamuth, *Six Soviet Plays,* p. 424.

ward to the same profession through the ranks of the Komsomol. Both came soundly prepared for their responsibilities and able to command respect and allegiance even from the wary specialists of the old school. Mechanics, foremen, and timekeepers who streamed into Fenia's office confidently relied on her efficient distribution of the labor force. At conferences the chief engineer consulted her more often than her young male colleagues. In an emergency she worked alongside the drillers, with none of the aloof dignity of the old technical intelligentsia, or even some of the new Soviet engineers, "awkward and humiliated among simple workers and technicians . . . whom they had been accustomed to command from their unapproachable heights." [100] The chagrin at the reversed role of the sexes which Fenia's authority causes in admiring young workmen is without animus, and acts as a spur to their own ambitions. The strident antagonism with which a brigade of boys received a brigade of girls assigned, at their own insistence, to the same heavy work of concrete laying, soon disappeared as the girls demonstrated their ability to hold their own in the competition. Fenia regards the future they are all building together in terms of the current hyperbole: "She, still just a girl . . . was helping to construct this hydro-colossus as no mere dam, a kilometer in length and seventy meters wide, but was raising up the structure of a new world, which would live forever and create new generations of people, courageous, audacious, free." [101] Women specialists of the proletariat and peasantry were end-products of benefits offered to promising girls of unexceptionable class origin. Their conflicts were only external clashes with enemies of the new order. They themselves had accommodated to the necessary without inner struggle.

The process by which a young woman of the suspect intelligentsia reached the estate of full-fledged Party member is traced in Veresaev's novel *The Sisters*. Veresaev, famous long before the Revolution and even then of strong Marxist persuasion, was an oldish man in 1933, when this work, his last piece of fiction but not of letters, was published. The tone of the book is one of stark truth, and of finality, as if the author had had his say. *The Sisters* is an anomaly in the literature of the time. It is frankly concerned with the wellsprings of the individual. It is drenched in pity for its char-

100 Gladkov, *Energiia* (Moscow, 1933), p. 367.   101 *Ibid.*, p. 360.

acters—that impermissible feeling toward the new Soviet man. There is even a tinge of alarmed moralizing. Yet in this sober, documentary work, the two sisters Lël'ka and Ninka come to life with an emotional force which seldom gathers in Five-Year Plan literature. As university students, precociously mature at seventeen and nineteen, they face the dilemma of inquiring young intellectuals in the Komsomol. Reared in the revolutionary tradition, they cannot contemplate life outside the Party fold, and yet they cannot "live, act, and think 'to order.' " [102] For Lël'ka, being trained as an agitator and propagandist, the equivocation is too painful. Deliberately to stifle her individualism, to find relief from her ideological deviations in losing herself among the masses, she leaves the university and, on the eve of the First Plan, goes to work at the "Red Knight" rubber boot factory. "This is simply the instinct of self-preservation," [103] she admits. Ninka remains in engineering school, to find out everything for herself.

The main part of the book follows Lël'ka in her deepening intoxication with Party dogma and in the progressive atrophy of her "living soul." At work on a conveyor, her loneliness and isolation disappeared in the sweet feeling of inseparability from others in the common effort, while she ignored the terrible, and preventible, dangers to her fellow workers from perpetually inhaling the fumes of benzine. Tutored by more experienced comrades in the Komsomol unit, she adopted, squeamishly at first, the standard practice of informing on one's fellow workers for shirking and misdemeanors. Soon she relished reporting a woman who had poured acid on her hand in order to receive sick leave and compensation, forgetting that once, when first in the factory, she herself had purposely drawn a knife across her finger for the sake of a few days' respite from benzine poisoning. Finally rid of all "rotten compromises," she rose in a Party purge to denounce her closest friend.

Over the indifference of management and the open hostility of the rank and file, the Party and Komsomol introduced shock-brigading and socialist competition. When factory personnel responded defiantly to the idea of the Five-Year Plan and the demand for increased output, the Party began its "skillful, ingenious

---

[102] V. V. Veresaev, *The Sisters (Sëstry)*, trans. Juliet Soskice (London, 1936), p. 20.
[103] *Ibid.*, p. 62.

work." [104] The reluctant were forced into competing brigades, less by prizes of money, excursions, rest-home holidays than by means of humiliation, disgrace, and enforced overstrain. At the instigation of Komsomol timekeepers, higher production quotas were set and piecework pay was reduced accordingly. Women who failed to comply were shifted elsewhere and replaced by Komsomolki primed to set an example at any cost. Photographs of the stubborn, obtained by subterfuge, were published in the factory newspaper, with a caption accusing them of intentional failure to meet the quota. The little Pioneers were sent to the homes of absentees and to the special pay desk for defaulters, to ridicule them. In the lavatories and dining rooms, the older women complained and cursed, fell silent only at the approach of Party members. They thumped their fists on the director's desk and shouted that they would die at the conveyors. But the young girls, a few at a time, joined shock brigades. The factory raised production. Newspapers carried headlines on the "transformation of former slaves into flaming enthusiasts." "In the factory these articles were . . . laughed at. Of course, it was all true, and yet it was quite, quite different." [105] Actually, less than one tenth of the workers took part in competitions. A brigade of Komsomolki who had challenged a team of the most experienced old hands, disdainful of their foolishness, came off a bad second in the competition. A commission inspecting galoshes ready for shipment found half of them defective. Lël'ka was aware of all this, but not dismayed. It did not shake her faith. Veresaev interpolates in his own name that, through various incentives, good and bad, the Party was slowly and with difficulty teaching the workers that they must cease the old deceit and trickery once practiced against the exploiters. As in battle attack, the Communists, an organized and strictly disciplined minority, thrust themselves into the ranks of the majority, a fluid mass of average people, took ascendancy, and led the forward movement.

For her exertions in the drive and for her growing ability as agitator, Lël'ka was admitted into the disciplined minority. Party membership enabled her to win, as lover if not as comrade, a "real" proletarian, of deep class instincts, who despised her as a foreign element, a child of the intelligentsia, and let her understand that

104 *Ibid.*, p. 194.   105 *Ibid.*, p. 209.

he visited her as he would a prostitute. Children were out of the question: "With the blue blood of gentle folk in them? No, thank you!" [106] Humbled by the brand of the intelligentsia which lay upon her like a curse, she accepted Vedernikov's terms, and at the same time turned toward a meek worshiper for solace. When she became pregnant, she did not know who the father was. Seized by a terrible loneliness and longing for the child, she nevertheless procured authorization for abortion. "Ten days later [Lël'ka] returned to the factory. Her face had grown plain. It was the color of damp whitewash." [107] The last vestiges of intellectual humanitarianism obliterated, she threw herself into Party work with new intensity. In the farm collectivization drive, she was teamed with Vedernikov. As they moved to the attack upon the peasants, his iron will and hers were welded into one powerful, ruthless force. They lived together openly, and she was blissful in his acceptance of her.

In the country the sisters again met and clashed. Ninka, who believed that it was not "such a bad thing to use one's brain from time to time," [108] was pursuing, contrary to local Party instructions, a moderate course of gradual persuasion in organizing a *kolkhoz*. Lël'ka, in blind obedience to orders, was mercilessly confiscating the property of rebellious peasant families, down to the felt boots from the feet of children. Ninka escaped punitive measures by the district committee only through publication of Stalin's "Dizzy with Success" article, condemning the excesses of Party workers drunk on power: "Our policy is based upon a voluntary *kolkhoz* movement." [109] Lël'ka crumbled under the savage denunciation of a follower for the cruelties she had committed and enticed him to commit. Ninka is Veresaev's concept of the "positive" Communist woman on whom the highest authority of the Party had momentarily set the seal of approval: an engineer, strong, self-reliant, courageous, kind and quick to sympathy, humorous, unfanatic, defiant of instructions which negated the principle of Marx and Lenin: "Our teaching is not dogma, but a guide to action." [110] What process produced her, we do not witness.

A more damaging answer could scarcely have been made to the

106 *Ibid.*, p. 240.   107 *Ibid.*, p. 251.
108 *Ibid.*, p. 285.   109 *Ibid.*, p. 284.
110 Lenin, "Letter on Tactics" (April, 1917), *Selected Works*, ed. A. Fineberg (12 vols., New York, 1935–38), VI (1936), 32.

expectations of the critics that the factory and its healthy proletariat were the remedy for the NEP-time ills of Soviet women. The degradation of Lël'ka is directly due to her surrender of will to the industrial Komsomol cell, dominated by arrogant proletarians with "an entirely upper-class psychology," [111] and to her slavish acceptance of precepts handed down in a narrow interpretation of Marxist doctrine. What other writers were extolling as socialist labor, Veresaev assails as a regime of coercion which involved its ringleaders in deceit, brutality, hypocrisy, and a callous disregard of deep-rooted human emotions, ending, for Lël'ka at least, in self-destruction. Marietta Shaginian, in *Hydrocentral,* paints a similar picture, with less somber colors, as the impression of a German visiting the USSR.[112]

This interpretation seems completely at variance with that of Kataev, Ehrenburg, Panfërov, Il'in, Gladkov, and most Five-Year Plan writers, who describe rank-and-file women workers laboring "on tiptoe," with ebullient spontaneity, at Magnitogorsk, Kuznetsk, Stalinsk, Stalingrad, Dneprostroi. The discrepancy does not necessarily impugn the verisimilitude or typicality of their characterization. There is basis in fact for both views. Taking zeal for shock-brigading and socialist competition as proof of the new attitude toward labor, the larger group of writers affirm the development of the new attitude at the huge new construction sites of heavy industry, where extremely young, inexperienced newcomers, almost half of them Komsomolki, formed the vast majority of the female labor force.[113] Veresaev denies its appearance, except among a handful, in a different milieu, in light industry, where there was a much larger carry-over of women workers from the pre-Plan or even prerevolutionary period, with a smaller influx of new hands.[114] Thus, where there was a preponderance of youth, including large numbers of Komsomol instigators, the new incentives were effective. An unprecedented outburst of energy, enthusiasm, and endurance occurred, and a general mood of optimism prevailed. On the other

[111] Veresaev, *Sisters,* p. 243.

[112] Shaginian, *Gidrotsentral'* (Leningrad, 1931).

[113] G. N. Serebrennikov, *The Position of Women in the U.S.S.R.* (London, 1937), pp. 37, 39, 50–52; S. Kaplun, "Zhenskii trud v SSSR," *Bol'shaia sovetskaia entsiklopediia,* Vol. XXV (1932); S. Dmitrieva, "Woman in Industry," *VOKS Bulletin,* II, No. 2 (1931), 14–15.

[114] Kaplun, "Zhenskii trud"; Serebrennikov, *Position of Women,* pp. 37–39.

hand, the resistance of old-timers to the new methods led to the application of the punitive measures which were also inherent in the Soviet labor regime. Obviously, those who, on Party assurance, believed themselves the heirs of the future were readier to hasten the day of inheritance by Party-sponsored labor methods.

The indication of literature that women as a whole were more amenable to the new collective methods is borne out statistically: a higher percentage of women workers than of men participated in socialist competition and shock-brigading during the First Plan.[115] This was no idle, unproductive gesture. Women were acquiring skill rapidly. In the compulsory technical examinations of industrial workers' qualifications given in 1935–36, among the lower-age groups the women not only proved equal to the men but in some respects surpassed them. Even earlier, women's average labor productivity in comparable jobs, in both skilled and unskilled categories, was as high as that of men.[116] Nevertheless, for the masses of women entering industry, the heritage of illiteracy, ignorance, and lack of training was still heavy. Because of this initial handicap, the employment of women in skilled work was limited throughout the First Plan, and in 1936 still remained lower than that of men,[117] as, in consequence, did their average wages.[118] Women made up in zeal and perseverance what they lacked in skill. In these days of critically high labor turnover, while peasants, transformed into proletarians by gradual and painful degrees, found it difficult to adjust to the idea of continuity of employment, the fly-by-nights were comparatively rare among women in fiction. In general, women are depicted as more conscientious and better disciplined workers than men—a veracious reflection of actuality.[119] Their more willing compliance was due in part to the early animosity

[115] Kaplun, "Zhenskii trud"; Tsentral'noe upravlenie narodnokhoziaistvennogo uchëta SSSR, *Narodnoe khoziaistvo SSSR* (Moscow, 1932), p. 454.

[116] Serebrennikov, *Position of Women*, pp. 72–73; "Zhenskoe kommunisticheskoe dvizhenie." John D. Littlepage, an American engineer with long experience in Soviet industry during this period, goes so far as to say (in Littlepage and Demaree Bess, *In Search of Soviet Gold* [New York, 1938], p. 226), "Women average better than men in production."

[117] Serebrennikov, *Position of Women*, pp. 60–62, 195–96.

[118] 15 percent to 30 percent lower throughout the First Plan (Kaplun, "Zhenskii trud").

[119] "Zhenskoe kommunisticheskoe dvizhenie"; Serebrennikov, *Position of Women*, pp. 77–81.

of their male co-workers and to their greater dependence upon
authority for assurance. At first, in their unfamiliar surroundings,
they sheltered under the wing of the *zhenotdel* at factory meetings,
either utterly inarticulate or self-consciously aggressive in response
to the taunts of their baiters. Their huddled timidity was deplored
by Party activists, who consistently encouraged them to boldness
and self-confidence. Panfërov describes with approbation Natalia
Pronina's bearing of studied negligence and lack of obsequiousness,
"in the approved Komsomol manner," [120] and Gladkov idealizes
the bold leadership of Katiusha Bychkova in saucily overriding the
objections of foremen and engineers to assigning her brigade of
girls to heavy labor.

Until its official dissolution the *zhenotdel* continued to harp on
woman's exploitation, to fan resentment of old prejudices, and to
encourage rivalry between the sexes rather than to stress greater
labor productivity. In Gladkov's *Cement* the leader was "kicked
out" for her intransigence. In 1929, the entire organization departed by the same door. The militancy between men and women
on the industrial scene gradually wore away into easy mutual tolerance and assistance. The recalcitrants left clinging to their bias
were those held up to scorn as anti-social in other respects as well:
the confirmed wife-beaters, monastery monks, disgruntled prerevolutionary bourgeois administrators superseded by a woman
boss, and their ilk.

Generally, in fiction there is scrupulous avoidance by the Party
and management of discrimination against women. Leonov, tongue
in cheek, gives one exception in *Skutarevskii*, when the old scientist observes the effect on women janitors at his institute of Lenin's
famous and mischievous motto, "Every cook must learn to rule the
state": "Of course, we know that they're all learning to govern the
country. . . . Not that I'm against that. I'll be dead long before
they finish learning. Only what we need here just now is some
ordinary, plain, common or garden caretakers." [121]

Cooks were not learning to rule the state very fast. Literature
almost completely ignores women's role in government. Their
attention was fully occupied in the factory. On their mettle, they

[120] Panfërov, *Bruski* (1947), p. 728.
[121] Leonov, *Skutarevsky*, trans. Alec Brown (New York, 1936), p. 94.

acquitted themselves well in the job, but among the masses in fiction few had attained the proprietary class-consciousness which would form the backbone of a "new attitude toward labor" as "an affair of honor, of valor." In *People of the Stalingrad Tractor Works,* a Komsomolka to whom "class" meant a schoolroom was disabused only in the course of prolonged private instruction preliminary to her entrance into the Party. In Veresaev's *The Sisters,* the most esteemed forewoman in the plant, and an old Party hand, confessed at a Communist purge that, although she attended the Party school, she couldn't understand a word of its program. The very fact that social incentives were reinforced in 1931 by substantial material advantages, previously considered contrary to socialist principles, and that, later, the psychological deterrents to violations of labor discipline were buttressed by fixed administrative and judicial penalties, is clear recognition that human beings as then constituted had a limited understanding of their common interests in industrial production. Proletarian women were no exception.

In general, on the lower echelons during the First Plan, social origin was the telling factor in determining occupation. In literature, those of proletarian or peasant stock were at the machines or behind the wheelbarrows. Those from the bourgeoisie and intelligentsia, even if at first forced into rougher work, found their way eventually to the classrooms and libraries, the laboratories, and office desks. Dusia in Voinova's *Semi-Precious Stones,* in escaping the cruelty of her husband, a minor Trust official and secret destroyer of the new society, who has shielded her from all interests save those of the household out of his preference for a "pure, undamaged type of woman," [122] resentfully realizes that she has been disqualified for work outside the home. She has served her husband, not society, thinking she would cook all her life: "And this is what I have cooked up! . . . There has been trouble, and now I have no place to go." Under the guidance of an old Communist, who urges her to abandon family life and "come out on the open road," [123] she becomes a street-car operator. A woman of her earlier

---

[122] A. I. Voinova, *Semi-Precious Stones (Samotsvety,* 1930), trans. Valentine Snow (New York, 1931), p. 324.   [123] *Ibid.,* p. 317.

set describes the new Dusia as a peasant, quick with her curses, on the verge of blowing her nose in her sleeve, and, worst of all, proud of it, as of a great achievement. In time she learns that, however ill-equipped she is, she can be of genuine service in "cultural" work by eschewing the shopworn propaganda words, devoid of human kindness, at which the women workers merely laugh.

Without influential backing, women from the old governing classes were long debarred from such employment. In the same book, the daughter of a tsarist official, despite her identification of self with the new regime, has been expelled from a theatrical workshop and from the Komsomol. Lilia belonged to the class which felt the Terror. Stronger than her fear of detection, however, was the power of the promise of woman's equal rights. Even with her falsified documents and her desperate need of work, when she is refused a job on the basis of sex by a Trust official, she bluntly defies him: " 'I am astounded that you, a Communist, should say such things!' she exclaimed. 'You have no right to refuse me, just because I am a woman. This is the USSR we're in, not Europe!' " [124]

From their condemned gallery, unemployed women of the bourgeoisie and intelligentsia eyed the activities of their sex on the industrial stage with uneasy ambivalence. Until 1936 it was the women without jobs who were on the defensive. Sufficient numbers of the incorrigibly frivolous had drifted into industry to explain the small expectations held of them and the general attitude of wariness. An interpreter in Ehrenburg's *Out of Chaos* is drawn to the inferno of Kuznetsk by the rumor that foreigners spend their evenings with women translators and, in their special store, have access to silks, berets, and even shoes. A young sculptress in Afinogenov's "Fear" sets out to transform herself to the roots of her being in a noisy rolling mill. Her effervescent enthusiasm quickly subsides, and she scampers away. It is the intent of Nikiforov in his novel *The Woman* [125] to show the bourgeois heroine Favsta as reborn into an active builder of the epoch by renouncing her past and joining the factory proletariat. One critic complains that the author succeeds only in demonstrating how Favsta contaminated fellow workers with her waverings, doubts, and inner torments.[126]

[124] *Ibid.*, p. 10.   [125] Georgii K. Nikiforov, *Zhenshchina* (Moscow, 1929).
[126] I. Mar, " 'Zhenshchina' G. Nikiforova," *Krasnaia nov'*, No. 4 (April, 1930), pp. 202–3.

At the same time, "non-Party Bolsheviks" were emerging from the classes at first hostile to the new regime or immunized by incomprehension of its aims. Irina, heroine of *Out of Chaos,* abandons the university and an unhappy love affair with a fellow student "attached to a dying culture," to go to the Kuzbass as teacher in a factory school:

"I have no delusions about what is in store for me . . . a veritable hell. . . . It frightens me to think of the conditions under which people work. . . . You are superior to the others in intelligence . . . but you do nothing to make life better. You notice only evil, and scoff at it. . . . Is it because the socialist idea is base? Or because people are still full of the old baseness? There can be no two answers to that. . . . Do something I must, and not merely sit with my hands folded." [127]

As yet no attempt had been made to restore discipline and obedience to the classroom. In Ehrenburg's trenchant description of school conditions, Irina's triumph over the anarchy and disdain that await her becomes a feat of labor no less heroic than that of the proletarian girls at their lathes. Although she is still at an economic disadvantage in comparison with them, she feels none of the grievance expressed, for instance, by Shaginian in *Hydrocentral* over the discrimination against educational and cultural workers until the end of the First Plan. There is no time to spend what she does earn. Teachers at Kuznetsk are overburdened with their own work and with the responsibilities that parents assume in most societies:

There were thousands of children on the construction. They lived with their parents in barracks or dugouts. Fathers and mothers went to work—they were building the plant. . . .
Dasha's mother, after returning from work, groaned, cursed, and did the family washing. Pashka's father drank vodka and in his misery shouted at his son. . . . The children grew fast, and any old way.[128]

The women were doing their part, in simultaneous economic production and childbearing, but the new socialized agencies had not appeared to aid them. This is the crux of the matter.

The struggle to provide facilities needed at an industrial housing center in Iurii German's novel *Antonina* (1936) is the means of transforming the heroine from a bewildered, isolated housewife

[127] Ehrenburg, *Out of Chaos,* pp. 158–63, *passim.*
[128] *Ibid.,* pp. 231–32.

into a valuable citizen, a "non-Party Bolshevik." To free her from a deadening and unsavory second marriage to which she had consented out of chronic loneliness persisting from the solitary, skulking, back-street existence of her girlhood, a Communist couple take Antonina and her small son into their home and, with the assistance of their friends, reeducate her for social usefulness. As they tutor her and tame her audacious energy—in their eyes meaningless and without direction for lack of discipline in a workers' collective— they are all making an investment which she is to repay society as a whole.

In time, she is given the responsibility of establishing a nursery and kindergarten, with a warning that she will be discharged at once if she cannot cope with the job: "We can't afford to put this work in jeopardy. It's a job of political importance." [129] With trepidation, because she is not a member of the Party, Antonina undertakes the task. The author gives a detailed documentary account of the venture, which is laboring under stress of insufficient funds, and of the policy which guides it. As expounded in the book by an authority at *Okhrmatmlad* (the central organization in charge of mother and child care), the policy is one of developing nurseries and kindergartens to the utmost and of stamping out the unsound practice of domestic attendants, still employed by those who could afford them. The idea was to be fostered that public facilities were not a lower form of child care, but a higher—better than nursemaids, better than mothers, since it was desirable that children should spend a great deal of time with other children in order to form social habits. To take the child during the mother's working hours alone was only half the task of the Child Welfare Center. It was the duty of the director to provide twenty-four-hour service, and to persuade the mother to utilize her leisure for social and cultural activities. By the time of the publication of the book (1936), this policy was already in process of revision.

After some vacillation on the part of parents, the stampede to the Center soon necessitates tremendous expansion. Hundreds of mothers are made available for work in the local factories. Antonina is praised in the newspapers, respected and sought after throughout

[129] German, *Antonina* (*Nashi znakomye* [Our Friends], 1936), trans. Stephen Garry (London, 1937), p. 377.

the community, honored by the Party at a factory meeting. Her sense of oneness with a "big family" culminates during her preparations for examinations in the medical training which is required of her by the swift growth of the Center. Zhenia, the doctor who had first befriended Antonina, spends evenings coaching her in the dissecting rooms, declaring that it gave her pleasure to be of help, that it was useful to go over the ground again.

Antonina knew she had forgotten nothing, that she got very tired at the clinic, and that she [Zhenia] was doing all this extra work only for her sake. But she felt not at all touched by this, although she was grateful. It seemed to her that so it ought to be, that she and Zhenia and everybody else were doing common work, and that in the final reckoning it didn't matter in the least who helped whom. If the occasion arose, she in her turn would help somebody.[130]

Everywhere in fiction, women were displaying the same readiness to entrust their children to nurseries and kindergartens, and everywhere capacity remained woefully inadequate. Although there was never lack of recognition at the top that public child care could not wait if women workers were to be utilized in the drive for industrialization,[131] the chronic shortage of funds persisted. At Kuznetsk, as Ehrenburg shows in *Out of Chaos,* provision of facilities depended largely upon the individual initiative of the women themselves. At Magnitogorsk, the nurseries were overflowing. The peasant girl Fenia, the morning after her arrival and the very day of the birth of her child, joined the women who were building a nursery on their free time, in order to assure her baby a place. "Walking heavily . . . stumbling, drenched with sweat," [132] she put boards and a saw over her shoulder, and went to work. In *The Volga Falls to the Caspian Sea* (1930), Pil'niak interpolates his sardonic comment on the deficiency at Kolomstroi, where single women slept seventy-one to the barrack, surrounded by their wailing infants on the plank bunks: "Women, made equal to men in civic rights, were not rendered equal in everyday life and were certainly not made equal by biology, since children are left to the care of the mothers." [133]

130 *Ibid.,* p. 424. 131 Serebrennikov, *Position of Women,* p. 424.
132 Kataev, *Time, Forward,* p. 171.
133 Boris Pilnyak, *The Volga Falls to the Caspian Sea (Volga vpadaet v Kaspiiskoe more,* 1930), trans. C. Malamuth (New York, 1931), pp. 241–42.

After a fashion, daily living was perforce socialized in the squalid, overcrowded barracks that were the order of the day at the new industrial combines. At Magnitogorsk, whole families shared a single bunk. At Kuznetsk "people scratched themselves, embraced, and multiplied in the dark. They hung their tattered, evil smelling rags around their benches, trying to guard their nights from the eyes of strangers." [134] Those who could find accommodation in such shelter were lucky. New arrivals from the steppe and the hills, men and women, dug themselves foxholes against the Siberian winter. The administrative staff fared better. At Kolomstroi their "standardized little houses were laid out as on a chessboard, with curtains and geraniums in the windows." [135] Communal dining halls were provided for workers at the big developments. In the restaurant for the barracks women at Kolomstroi, waitresses in their spare time searched for lice in one another's hair. The food at Stalingrad is described by women bricklayers in Pogodin's play "Tempo" as "mostly sympathy and nothing else." [136] City workers continued to share multi-family apartments and to cook on individual Primus stoves in common kitchens. The sole interest of A. Dolgikh's story "Raw Stuff," [137] a paean of praise to a great factory kitchen varnished with a coat of fiction, is that it still celebrates, in 1931, the collective living stressed in theory but little advanced in practice.

Educational, recreational, and artistic activities were concentrated at the place of employment. There was a clamorous demand for reading rooms, study circles, clubs for national minorities, courses in gardening, photographic societies, theatrical performances, whether by a company from Moscow or by local talent putting on an agitational play. Programs were designed for the masses. The "cultural capital" which Natalia Tarpova in 1923 eyed enviously from a distance was coming into possession of some proletarian women. An attempt was made at the factory to discourage women's demand for consumer goods. During the lifetime of the *zhenotdel*, it fostered the notion that personal adornment, on the job or off, was a bourgeois trait. On the bulletin board at Kolomstroi, its placards ridiculed smartly dressed women. The typical

134 Ehrenburg, *Out of Chaos*, p. 8.   135 Pilnyak, *The Volga Falls*, p. 123.
136 Nikolai Pogodin, "Tempo," trans. Irving Talmadg, *Six Soviet Plays*, p. 217.
137 Dolgikh, "Raw Stuff," in *Soviet Stories of the Last Decade*, ed. and trans. Elisaveta Fen (London, 1945).

working garb was a pair of overalls. In Leonov's *Skutarevskii*, a friend of the old scientist deplored the Komsomol generation as "all plain and brutal—no more poetry, no more serenades," and Skutarevskii retorted with a Marxist explanation for their exuberant robustness: "Any young class striding forward to victory is bound to put forward girls exactly like those—sturdy and high-bosomed. It is obliged to multiply fiercely and rapidly; its children are bound to be voracious eaters and as ruddy as their mothers are powerful and fruitful." [138]

Along with the disdain for personal grooming, the *zhenotdel* left as a legacy in the minds of women the technique of the collective factory tribunal for public censure of abuses. In Pil'niak's *The Volga Falls to the Caspian Sea*, "the transformed feminine psychology, pouring out in floods of rage," [139] acts with elemental force against outrages not uncommon at construction sites. Foremen and workers have been molesting and raping women. Others have abandoned their children. Women hired by seasonal workers have been treated "not merely as cook, but also as wife" [140] for all members of the group. The barracks women protest by a near-lynching. The conditions of their lives are those of the frontier, and they turn to frontier justice. They band together in a weird combination strike and funeral procession at the burial of an engineer's wife, whose suicide has become to them the symbol of women's destiny: "In silence more terrible than abuse and shouts . . . hundreds of women smeared with earth, hardened by heavy work . . . relics of Russian antiquity, filled the ancient Kolomna streets and followed the coffin to the grave." [141] In the person of the engineer they are decrying licentiousness and their fate. The engineer is saved from interment along with the coffin only by an old Party woman, who appeals to the others to deal with him through organized action. The next day they present a notice to the director that they will boycott the engineer on the job. However preposterous their tactics in Pil'niak's inflamed symbolism, in literature it is characteristic of Russian women workers of the time that they employ the might of their new weapon, collective action, not against the subhuman

138 Leonov, *Skutarevsky*, pp. 70–71.
139 B. Aikhenval'd, "O romane B. Pil'niaka 'Volga vpadaet v Kapiiskoe more,'" *Krasnaia nov'*, No. 4 (April, 1931), p. 180.
140 Pilnyak, *The Volga Falls*, p. 169.   141 *Ibid.*, p. 75.

squalor of their barracks and dugout life, but against affront to the dignity of "women with full rights." Creature comforts could wait. Human dignity could not.

Mass employment of women was the circumstance prerequisite to a reordering of relations between the sexes. In part, the generation growing up after inauguration of the Plan was the first unconditioned by a past in which women, economically dependent, could be purchased by money or other social instruments of power. According to the theory, only such a new generation could evolve its own practice in marriage and the family.[142] As "guide to action," Engels had foreseen the marriage of the future as a union of equals based solely on love, unaffected by economic considerations, monogamous for its duration, but freely terminable whenever mutual love had ceased. Under Soviet law, this ideal was unrealizable because of one fundamental contradiction: marriage retained the form of an economic contract, imposing mutual obligations for support in case of need as long as the state was unable to assume the burden. For enforcement of these obligations, the Code of 1926, by indirection, defined marriage as constituted by official registration of a union between man and woman (Article 1) or by existence of an unregistered union under conditions of cohabitation, common household, and evidence of conjugal relations (Article 12). Delimitation of the family was more difficult. Engels's prediction of the form it would take was of a negative character, an enumeration of the historic functions it would lose, mainly economic cooperation and the rearing of children (see pages 29–31). Except for provisions to eliminate the distinction between the rights of legitimate and illegitimate children, the law and Engels were fundamentally at variance in the matter of the family—again explained as a result of the poverty of a state which could not assume full responsibility for dependents. The framers of Soviet law, after an initial fiasco in attempting to define the family in 1918, in 1926 simply declined the use of the term, establishing parent-child rights and duties, without stipulating the legal nature of the tie between the parents, which might be one of registered marriage, unregistered marriage,

[142] Engels, *Origin*, p. 73.

or transient alliance (pages 31–32). Actually, the family as an entity did not exist in law between 1918 and 1944.[143] Old customs of marriage and family, sanctioned by ecclesiastical regulation and extinct among the advance guard designated to lead the way in crystallizing new custom, had, it was assumed, been devitalized or irreparably weakened among the industrial proletariat after the NEP onslaught. Thus, the new generation would theoretically enter upon a fair field where no form of man-woman-child relationship canonized in doctrine, law, or mores hampered it in devising its own as the economic base permitted.

At the outset of the First Plan, Party women and Komsomol girls found relief from the tension between law and theory, which had created bewilderment and uncertainty of procedure in marriage and family, by the drastic measure of restricting their lives to the occupational sphere. For them, extremist emphasis on work dwarfed all human relations outside the factory. Romantic love, a bourgeois fable during the NEP days, was barely resuscitated as a respectable emotion when it was again set aside for the Plan emergency. There was no time for it. This was a non-erotic period. In Glebov's play, Inga sweeps away everything which stands in the path of industrialization: "Sentiments are mobilized, too." [144] The heroine of Platoshkin's novel *On the Road* is sharply denounced in Komsomol

[143] In law, the concept of family was a perplexed one. Marriage and family relations were entirely separated in the 1918 Code, as interpreted by its chief framer (Professor A. G. Goikhbarg, *Brachnoe, semeinoe i opekunskoe pravo sovetskoi respubliki* [Moscow, 1920], p. 104). Art. 133 reads: "Actual descent is regarded as the basis of the family." The 1926 revised Code of Marriage, Family and Guardianship shuns the word "family" in the text, and states: "The mutual rights of children and parents are based on consanguinity" (Art. 25), thus avoiding the earlier semantic and ideological boner of recognizing only the parent-child relationship as the axis of the family. To institutionalize the Soviet family in law on the basis of the economic and educational responsibilities entailed in the parent-child relationship did violence to the doctrine, which reserved for the socialist family no traditional function save that of reproduction and, consequently, necessitated primary emphasis on the man-woman relationship. Otherwise, the legally recognized father of one family might simultaneously be also the legal father of another family or families, with paternal rights and duties toward each. Such potential complexities invalidated the monogamous principle inherent in the provision that a marriage could not be registered between persons one of whom was already married, with or without registration (Art. 6). The solution was to abandon in law the attempt to define the nuclear family, while imposing economic obligations for mutual support upon an extensive kinship group (not only between parents and children, but between children and grandparents, children and stepparents, and among siblings). [144] Glebov, "Inga," p. 387.

74 *Marxian Woman: Soviet Variants*

circles for her social crime of allowing herself to be trapped in the toils of love and the swamp of domesticity.[145] Masha, a factory Komsomolka in Lidiia Seifullina's comedy *Fellow Travelers,* finds symptoms of morbid emotion, the predilection of the intelligentsia, in Nikolai, a married poet fifteen years her senior, when he attaches momentous importance to their decision to live together. She is ready to move into an available room with him on her first day off, but with none of the time-consuming silliness of registering at ZAGS[146] or of scruples about the rearing of his son. His duties as father she dismisses as a matter significant only at the time of conception.[147]

Critics, mindful of the results from anesthetization of the emotions during the NEP, were quick to scotch the implication in early Plan writings that any emotional involvement between man and woman was necessarily destructive and motherhood incompatible with woman's function in industry.[148] Pertsov decries Gladkov's conception of the young engineer Fenia in *Power,* who lives only in her work, believing that "the personal . . . paralyzes the individual as a socially useful entity, that one must reduce it to ashes, and . . . dissolve, without trace, in the thoughts of others":

Service to society is represented not as a sphere for self-discovery and self-determination of human individuality, but for its self-denial, for its annihilation. . . . This conclusion is absurd. Fenia . . . is far from that solution of the problem which socialism offers, from that unity of the personal and the social, in which the social becomes the personal and the personal the social.[149]

Other Party women, proof against the work fetishism, sought a fusion of private life and social command by recognizing ideological compatibility as the first, sometimes the only, prerequisite to a sound relationship between man and woman. For Elena of "Fear," it was good and sufficient reason for marriage that she and Nikolai had their work in common and could help each other, even in their

[145] Mikhail Platoshkin, *V doroge* (Moscow, 1929).

[146] Otdel zapisi aktov grazhdanskogo sostoianiia (Department of Registration of Vital Statistics).

[147] Seifullina, *Poputchiki* (Moscow, 1933).

[148] "Platoshkin," *Literaturnaia entsiklopediia,* Vol. VIII (1934); Nikolai Sergeev, "Kritika i bibliografiia," *Krasnaia nov',* No. 7 (July, 1929), pp. 237–38.

[149] V. Pertsov, "Lichnost' i sotsialisticheskoe delo," *Krasnaia nov',* No. 4 (April, 1933), pp. 186–87.

professional rivalry. Suzanne in *Soviet River* clung to the demand
for love to supplement shared purpose in work. She rejected
Uvadiev, director of the construction, a "cast-iron" revolutionary
who "fled tenderness worse than banality," [150] but welcomed the
love of a young Party engineer with such alacrity that, asserting her
new prerogatives as equal, she lost no time in proposing marriage—
a not uncommon initiative in those days. If love conflicted with
Soviet aims, the orthodox Communist woman automatically closed
the doors of her attention to it. The action was determined by
inner acquiescence and preparation rather than by the external
discipline needed to bring Glebov's Inga to heel. When Liubov
Poletika (in Pil'niak's *The Volga Falls to the Caspian Sea*) learned
that the irresistible satyr whom she had loved was implicated in
sabotage and involved with another woman, she cashiered him with
whimsical disdain and finality. For the strong, resilient Liubov,
there was no repining. Her capacity for love was no whit diminished, and was transferable. She retreated to the impregnable com-
pound of her ideology, and made a new choice, an up-and-coming
engineer risen from the ranks, who followed the same uncompromising code as her own. Irina of Ehrenburg's *Out of Chaos*,
the non-Party girl of the bourgeoisie, made her choice by the same
standards. "Irina had gone over to iron," [151] without reservations.
For its sake, she eliminated from her life the fastidious self-outcast
who could not believe that a blast furnace was more beautiful than
Venus, and substituted the proletarian Kolia, Party member, shock-
brigader, and builder of Kuznetsk. "Irina and Kolia felt themselves
in their proper place. They knew exactly what they had to do." [152]

With the increasing political homogeneity of Soviet society, class
and nationality distinctions frequently break down in intermar-
riage. In their identification in the common cause, Vedernikov in
The Sisters, despite his intolerance of the non-proletarian, finally
accepts Lël'ka in the role of wife. A deep gulf is bridged in German's *Antonina* when the heroine, redeemed from her futile and
law-breaking past by her contribution to the new society, com-
pletes her happiness in the love of an OGPU official. The Komsomolka Shura of *Time, Forward* knows nothing of a prejudice

[150] Leonov, *Soviet River*, p. 197.   [151] Ehrenburg, *Out of Chaos*, p. 257.
[152] *Ibid.*, pp. 336–37.

which could affect her love for the Jewish engineer Margulies.

These embryonic relationships, by implication of the authors durable relationships, arise with blithe disregard for their legal status. During a brief respite after the record-making shift at Magnitogorsk, Shura snatched a moment in the shadow of a warehouse to put the traditionally masculine question: "Will you marry me?" What she intended was not the formality of registration. Shura was barely seventeen. The marriageable age was eighteen. Margulies, who had had a wife or so, laughed affectionately at her phrase as at an amusing, but obsolete, formula. The legally unsophisticated were themselves uncertain whether they were married or not in Soviet terms. The ambiguity of the concept of marriage is indicated by the very common extension of the term "husband" and "wife" to the partners of even the most casual alliance. Fenia, in *Time, Forward,* although she and Kostia had not registered at the village soviet, considered herself married all the same, bought herself a ring, and followed him across the country, to an address she knew no more than vaguely, in order to register. At Magnitogorsk, where she arrives only in the nick of time to bear her child, the distraught little peasant girl instantly learns deference to the claims of the Plan. As Kostia drives her to the hospital, she apologizes for taking him away from his work. Another young girl in Ehrenburg's *Out of Chaos,* setting off for the wilderness in search of the father of her child, bursts into tears when asked on the train whether he is her husband: "I don't know myself. He said to me, 'Let's get married.' Then he went to Temir-Tau." [153]

To the more enlightened, registration of marriage was a matter of indifference or an absurdity. There was no correspondence between the formalizing of a marriage and its stability, little material advantage or prestige to be gained. In theory, woman's dependence upon her own efforts for social recognition, not through the intermediary of husband, precluded the enjoyment of consort status. As long as public opinion was being mobilized against the unemployed woman, on the industrial scene the wife who made no contribution of her own to society continued to live in a backwash of life from which her husband's eminence could not draw her. Irina and Kolia,

[153] Ehrenburg, *Out of Chaos,* p. 385.

applauded by the critics as "people of the future," [154] show no interest in legalizing their relationship. Like many other fictional couples with a prudent eye on permanence, they continue to live apart, because of housing difficulties regarding the arrangement as a commonplace; the Party hero of *Power* even made a virtue of such separation: "Their love will be all the stronger for it. There's nothing to oblige them to live together. . . . Love is a good thing only at a distance." [155] This is not marriage in the sight of the law. Yet Ehrenburg's Irina and Kolia find it to their taste. In contrast, the registered marriage of Irina's neighbor Varia terminates unceremoniously with her husband's transfer to Moscow. Even Panfërov, egregious propagandist for the latest Party wrinkle, in a book published as late as 1937, allows the paragon Zhdarkin and his wife Steshka to scout the formalities: "Why should they register? Every morning Steshka saw him off just as affectionately and lovingly without that." [156] Apart from doctrinaire abhorrence of any legal restraint upon love, prospective bride and groom winced in the atmosphere of a ZAGS office, where "couples sat among the posters on venereal diseases" and the Childrens' Friends Society appealed in verse to cruel parents.[157] A member of one bridal party at ZAGS comments: "In the past, people used to look on marriage from a poetic point of view . . . and this is the Soviet prose for you!" [158] Although the law preferred marriage registration, in practice it was not encouraged, much less insisted upon.

In literature, ideology dictated divorce as well as marriage, at least when the action was initiated by the wife—usually as riddance from a husband of subversive or "bewhiskered psychological makeup" [159] after her own acceptance of the new order. Men, including the staunchest Communists, availed themselves far more lightly of the easy divorce of the period, in a mass gravitation from the wife who was merely homemaker to a younger or more "advanced" independent woman. A functionary in *Semi-Precious Stones* rationalizes his abandonment of the woman who had followed him into

[154] A. Selivanovskii, "Rozhdenie novogo khudozhnika," *Krasnaia nov'*, No. 6 (June, 1934), p. 227. [155] Gladkov, *Energiia*, pp. 233–34.
[156] Panfërov, *Bruski* (1947), p. 773.
[157] Kaverin, *The Larger View*, pp. 320, 414–15.
[158] Voinova, *Semi-Precious Stones*, pp. 521–22.
[159] German, *Antonina*, p. 317.

Siberian exile: "It doesn't matter how many times a man has been married or divorced, but how much he has accomplished. . . . It's work that matters, not wives." [160] At the ZAGS office, "the gay blonde who fulfilled the part of Soviet priest" shrewdly handed divorce papers to the first wife, who had accompanied the bridal party in order that Khriapin might save time by divorcing and re-marrying on the same day. "Everybody is divorcing their old wives now," [161] she said frankly. Apart from the old wives themselves, few appeared to object. Glebov is almost alone in literature in suggesting that the disintegration of the old family produced adverse effects on the new society. By the end of the First Plan, however, the day of serial marriage was over for Communists. In *Out of Chaos:*

> The secretary of a [Party] cell, Lukianov, held a wedding celebration; he was getting married for the sixth time. In the barracks he waxed violent and smashed crockery. Zaitsev asked him sternly, "How could you, a member of the Party, become so hopelessly disintegrated?"
> Lukianov made no answer. He lay on his cot and snored. He was expelled from the Party.[162]

Five-Year Plan novelists are conspicuously chary of following the new marriages or quasi-marriages beyond their inchoate beginnings. Children were evidently as great an embarrassment to their literary creators as they were likely to be to parents in the living conditions of the time. Many unions were formed with no intention of producing children. There was seldom floor space for a new baby, from the first moment of its life. The receptionist at a Magnitogorsk hospital led Fenia to the delivery room with dismay: "Another one! . . . How do you manage it? Well, now, tell me—where will I put her?" [163] The new proletariat, drawn in good part from the peasantry, kept maternity institutions filled and overflowing. A stoker exclaims to a nurse at Kuznetsk when informed that the new baby is a boy: "What a woman! A real brick! This is my fifth—and all boys." [164] Desire for a large brood was old tradition, but a tradition in conflict with the dread of another child in the barracks or dugouts of industrial areas. Although free abortion offered relief for women in these dire circumstances, in literature it was not the women employed in industry who were causing the

160 Voinova, *Semi-Precious Stones*, pp. 133–34.   161 *Ibid.*, p. 522.
162 Ehrenburg, *Out of Chaos*, p. 103.   163 Kataev, *Time, Forward*, p. 197.
164 Ehrenburg, *Out of Chaos*, p. 368.

admittedly high abortion rate of the period,[165] except perhaps for the handful still addicted to the glass-of-water theory, such as Party worker Basia in *The Sisters*, who "changed her lovers many times and had already had five abortions." [166] Over and over again among industrial women, with or without perennial husband, there is a deep, stubborn insistence on motherhood, a decision to bear their children and risk the future on their own efforts. "Bochka," the women's organizer of Gladkov's *Power*, values her freedom too much to want a husband, but would give half her life for a child. The pregnant woman deserted by the father—a recurrent figure in literature before 1936—remained averse to abortion. In *Out of Chaos*, a worker, abandoned by her husband, who "doesn't send home a kopék," retorts indignantly to Irina's advice, "Aren't women good for anything?"

[Irina] answered that now women worked like everybody else—in short, complete equality.
She shouted . . . "I work, too, at the brick section! Talking to me about rights! I know my rights! I was a delegate at a conference. If I bear children, it means I like it. You are a teacher. You must understand yourself—it is more fun with children." [167]

However rigidly the obligation for child support was enforced when possible, the collection by a deserted mother of the famous "third" of the father's earnings usually awarded for one child was dubious. In an alimony hearing at Kuznetsk: "Stepka laughed and thrust out his broad chest. He said, 'I have ten of them—all my work. Where on earth could I make that much money? They go with a fellow—then it's their business to look after themselves.' " [168] Occasionally, however, the security of the unmarried mother "under the aegis of *Okhrmatmlad*" aroused male envy. A colleague says of a red-headed office worker in *Semi-Precious Stones* who managed to time her pregnancies to moments of staff reduction: "They get their pleasure and then a three months' leave with full salary, and no fear of being dismissed! It's a great life!" [169]

Platoshkin's *On the Road*, a novel much discussed during the early Plan period, develops the somber tragedy of a young Komsomolka, forsaken by her lover before the birth of their child, who

165 Semashko, *Health Protection*, p. 84.
166 Veresaev, *The Sisters*, p. 140.
167 Ehrenburg, *Out of Chaos*, p. 380.
168 *Ibid.*, p. 368.
169 Voinova, *Semi-Precious Stones*, p. 71.

fails in her determination to prove to doubtful comrades that the
Soviet woman can successfully play the dual role of mother and
worker. With the author's clear approval and obvious intent to
offer her as a model, Pania decides against abortion for ethical
reasons seldom voiced in earlier Soviet literature—conscience for-
bids her to commit murder. Yet even with the aid of a day nursery
and of friends, she finds the burden of work and the daily pain of
parting from the child beyond her strength. Her health injured
by overexertion, she cannot nourish the infant adequately. As
worker, she is saved for the factory only by the cruel solution of
the child's death before her own complete collapse. Society had not
yet provided the lone working mother with the necessary assistance.
At the end of the novel, a reflective Komsomol leader concedes
that the problem would be a troubling one for a long time to come,
and could be solved only with an improvement in the general
economic situation.

The decision to carry a child to birth was not always an entirely
voluntary one. In *Out of Chaos* Ehrenburg reports that in the clinics
of Kuznetsk drastic restrictions on abortion were being imposed,
four years before enactment of the 1936 law forbidding it. Varia,
left alone by her husband, was refused authorization for free abortion. Rather than resort to a licensed operator at prohibitive expense, she elected to bear the child, accepting Irina's help but not
alimony from her husband, in the widely typical preference of industrial workers for flaunting their new independence of the individual man and relying on the "big family."

After the first reckless excesses, then, women assured of employment and maternity benefits are repeatedly characterized as finding
the birth of a child in the absence of the father a less traumatic experience than abortion. If any stigma was attached to the unmarried
mother, Soviet writers consistently exclude it from the industrial
scene and confine it to the fringe groups of the superannuated. In
several works, the old slogan "There are no strange children for us"
crops up in the new variant of man's readiness to accept another
man's unborn child as his own.[170] Either cultural lag was in this

---

[170] This is the theme of Vasilii Shkvarkin's play "Father Unknown" (*Chuzhoi
rebënok* [Another's Child]; Moscow, 1933), in *Soviet Scene*, trans. and ed. Alexander
Bakshy (New Haven, 1946); the theme also appears in Libedinskii's *Birth of a Hero*
(see p. 82).

respect rather quickly overcome in a society which publicized its new laws so widely and intensively, or writers were in compact to instill a new attitude in readers by representing it as already existent.

It is at the point of a family group in the offing that most writers stop. In *Time, Forward,* Kataev permits Fenia, as representative of the woman of the masses, merely a hopeful glimpse into the future from the maternity hospital of Magnitogorsk. This is the closest approach to the creation of a new Soviet family during the First Plan. It will be a socialist family to the extent that the parents will live "in the open," with their fellow workers in the barracks of the industrial plant, and their child will be assured a nursery place, through the mother's own efforts. And with Magnitogorsk steel, Ishchenko, the baby's father, reflects optimistically, they will make everything needed for the happiness of "the little one who was not yet even in the world, but who would be. . . . Oh, how good life was, after all!" [171] It is significant that the story of such women is usually not carried further, into the actual situation in which they were able to combine job, home, husband, and motherhood into one harmonious whole, through the assistance of public institutions.

When a writer ventured to go beyond the preliminary stages, disaster generally ensued for parents and children. Gladkov, whose novel *Cement* in 1925 had, more forcefully than any other work of NEP literature, come to grips with the question of a new basis for the family, returned to it again in *Power* at the end of the First Plan, to show that no advance had been made in the solution of the problem. The Communist couple Miron and Olga Vatagin reduce their only son to a state of sullen trembling confusion by their indifference and neglect, until finally an irritated blow from the father drives the boy from home to join a band of roving waifs. Miron had known nothing of his son's life. "It never occurred to him to force himself to a gesture of affection." [172] There was neither desire nor time. Olga, too, although she found an occasional word of tenderness for the boy, always returned late from the factory, preoccupied with Party and factory affairs, too weary to cast a glance at the sleeping child. Aghast at the outcome, she says to Miron: "We think of ourselves as revolutionaries. We have a mission to

171 Kataev, *Time, Forward,* p. 139.   172 Gladkov, *Energiia,* p. 21.

build socialism. But in the family we're a thousand times worse
than the bourgeoisie. We don't know how to love our children and
bring them up." [173] After the loss of their son and their own separation because of their Party assignments, both suffer solitary,
long-festering remorse. In Gladkov's eyes, the remedy is still the
same: public facilities for child care. Miron, as secretary of the
Party committee, continues to press for the construction at Dneprostroi of "the foundations of the new life: communal dining
rooms, laundries, clubs, kindergartens, nurseries." [174] Another
Communist in the book is ashamed that his wife stays home with
their infant: "No matter what, the wife of a Bolshevik . . . has a
duty to be working outside, for society." [175] Miron and the women's
organizer "Bochka" join in insisting that the reluctant mother place
the baby in a nursery and assume her proper role. To the Communist mind in Plan literature there is no glimmering of the universal
law of human nature discovered in 1936, the necessity of the intimate and inviolable association of mother and child. Invariably
it is the Party opponent who harps on it. In *The Sisters,* the old
proletarian Buerakov, deprived of the former attentions of his wife
through her new factory activities, remains at home, resentful and
alienated, merely to rail at the break-up of the family and at her
neglect of the children, who run wild, "like hooligans." Daria,
however, goes her way resolutely, bright-eyed and vigorous in her
release from the washtubs of home.

Iurii Libedinskii in *Birth of a Hero* raises the point-blank question of fulfilling the commitment of the revolutionary state to re-
cast the family. Shorokhov, an old-guard Communist and government official, awakens with alarm to the danger in the continued
survival of the old private home only when his young motherless
sons attempt to organize a children's commune, where young citizens would live apart from their elders, in protest against their
father's domestic entanglement with a frivolous young Komsomolka
and against the general Communist neglect of children in the new
society. Stirred by his son's accusation, Shorokhov hastens to Liuba,
whom he had abandoned, to save their newborn infant from the
crippling influence of her bourgeois way of life. The ambiguity of
official policy is mirrored in the indecisive ending, as Shorokhov

[173] *Ibid.,* p. 22.   [174] *Ibid.,* p. 391.   [175] *Ibid.,* p. 131.

and the defiant Liuba confront each other over the baby's crib, each struggling for possession of the seed of Communist society.[176] Apart from Gladkov's work, literature had slighted what Trotsky called "the most important socialist function," [177] the social rearing of children. There was good reason. Little had been done toward solving this basic and delicate problem, either by extensive development of children's institutions or by open modification of Marxian theory on the subject. Libedinskii's book queried whether the socially useless mother who refused to acknowledge that the claims of the new order transcended her maternal rights should not be forced to yield and suggested that it was high time to resolve the issue.

The question was already superfluous in the case of industrial women in fiction; they were transferring the care of their children and their housekeeping to public agencies as fast as the latter could absorb them. They were, on their own initiative, pathetically attempting to supply the great deficiency. Even Dusia, the once ultra-conservative, sheltered bourgeois wife, preferred to have her son reared in a state institution—which she had earlier termed "the modern cesspool" [178]—rather than continue the old life. The resistant woman kept from the factory by fear of entrusting her child to the hands of strangers was disappearing from literature or was described, as by Gladkov in *Power,* on the verge of capitulation.

In German's novel of 1936 two women attain, or nearly attain, in work and domestic life that "unity of the personal and social" promised by Soviet society. These are exceptional women, enjoying exceptional advantages: Zhenia, doctor and Party member, and Antonina, hand-picked and hand-tended by her Party mentors. The exact coincidence of the views of the Communist and non-Communist women is pointedly stressed. With both, the strong personal ties are now always subordinate to the exigencies of the job. Zhenia, a warm-hearted, wise, gay wife and mother, without warning announces that she is going off to practice medicine for a year in the country, because doctors are needed there and "it's interesting." [179] Her astounded husband is silent. Antonina, filled with a sure, intuitively guardian, possessive tenderness for her son,

[176] Libedinskii, *Rozhdenie geroia* (Leningrad, 1930).
[177] Leon Trotsky, *The Revolution Betrayed* (New York, 1945), p. 147.
[178] Voinova, *Semi-Precious Stones,* p. 320.
[179] German, *Antonina,* p. 444.

realizes that the boy resents his small share of her time and is growing away from her while she works and studies. But she goes on
studying. She also forsakes her new husband, Altus, for the Child
Welfare Center after a few weeks with him which he has happily
assumed were prelude to a permanent life together wherever his
OGPU missions took him. Communists could only accede ruefully
to the unanticipated consequences of woman's new role. In a brief
epilogue which carries the action into 1935, Antonina and Altus,
reunited for a time, part once more as he leaves on another assignment. Antonina longs to accompany him, but she is still in medical
training. In their relationship, "this is even before the beginning,"
Altus tells her.[180] The vanguard had itself had too short a time to
crystallize its own characteristic practice. 1935 is the year. In 1936,
the unexpected new phase was introduced into the lives of Soviet
women.

Only six or seven years had then elapsed since women in considerable numbers had achieved economic independence. Even in
the highly dynamic Soviet society, little advance in the evolution
of new forms of marriage and family could have been anticipated.
Nonetheless, in the expectant watchfulness for the utterly different pattern of human relations bound to emerge in socialist society,
it had already been judged several years before that woman continued, in fact as in fiction, to show "greater zeal and decisiveness
in breaking up the old family hearth," and that in her "the potential for the creation of new forms of life reveals itself more forcefully." [181] The masses of women who had entered industry had, by
that very step, departed far from earlier practices in marriage and
family. According to the evidence of literature, they now exercised
unprecedented freedom of marriage choice in a thoroughly open
system. Love had unabashedly reasserted itself as the approved
motive after the unconscionable NEP promiscuity. With the general severance of parental ties, kinship influence on the choice of
husband or wife was reduced to insignificance, and during the
roughly equalitarian period, economic differences were too slight
to sway the decision or to lend the husband authority over an em-

180 *Ibid.*, p. 469.
181 P. Berëzov, "Protiv 'vetkhogo' cheloveka," *Krasnaia nov'*, No. 2 (February, 1933),
p. 211.

ployed wife. Domination of the male was boldly challenged where it lingered. The preferential selection of a mate within the same class, and notably within the Party, was minimized. Marriage registration rested upon individual taste, and no shadow of disapproval lay upon the prevalent unregistered union. Divorce was treated as a private affair, and recourse to it was uninhibited, even encouraged as a means of releasing women for the labor force. A succession of divorces, however, incurred censure for the Party member. Stemming from the peculiarly Soviet, and also to a certain degree peculiarly socialist, features—relatively small economic differential, optional formalization of marriage, and the complete freedom of divorce—common and distinctive attitudes toward marriage crop up in the wage-earning Soviet girl. No longer conditioned to regard her security as dependent upon the man's indulgence nor a mistake in marriage as irretrievable, she was, on the one hand, largely devoid of the compulsive courtship urge to ingratiate herself in male favor and, on the other, ready to enter upon an alliance without vacillation, trepidation, or the latent hostility against the privileged male found to work mischief in other societies.[182] Whether the new marriages would remain monogamous, whether the right to dissolve them would be exercised on a large scale in the future, remained to be seen.

In the question of the industrial family, Soviet society had reached an impasse by 1935–36. When the man-woman-children group cohered at all, the parents strained toward a common, isolated residence, where the lives of their children were at least tentatively centered and exercised still ambiguous claims—claims which the Communist-minded confidently expected soon to channel, in the main, into public agencies. Within this framework, a marked assimilation between the masculine and feminine roles was occurring, as a result of the primary orientation of both mother and father toward the job function outside the home, of the woman's assertion of equal authority in family decisions, and of the indeterminate division of responsibility in the rearing of children. Without reflection on the future emotional consequences to themselves of separation from their children, fictional women of the proletariat and peasantry display a strongly positive attitude toward mother-

[182] See Parsons, "The Social Structure of the Family," pp. 188–89.

hood whenever assured of economic security through their own efforts. Among the old intelligentsia and the newcomers in this class, the attitude toward motherhood is one of willingness rather than of demand. By the mid-thirties, the aggressive repudiation of feminine attributes which had marked the early period was becoming so rare in literature that the young engineer Fenia in Gladkov's *Power* stands out as an anachronism in her distaste for Tatiana's ripe femininity and in her own reluctance for childbearing. The one recurrent innovation in literature—the family group composed solely of mother and children—was not a premeditated creation of women out of their ingenuity in devising "new forms of life"; men initiated it by absconding, but woman, biologically bound more closely to the children, shouldered the task, the more responsible and conscientious parent, as on the job she proved the more responsible and conscientious worker of the new labor force. Some success had been achieved in the removal of distinction between legitimate and illegitimate children and in the incipient uniformity of marriage and family practices among different classes or strata. Aside from this, ultimate desiderata of the theory were precluded by the law, as long as individual parents bore the economic responsibility of children. What new relations elimination of this responsibility would develop also still remained to be seen.

Nowhere else does literature bear out Glebov's assertion that the working class was building "an entirely new, different family . . . *our* kind of family." On the contrary, "the destruction of the family was a matter of everyday occurrence," [183] wrote Leonov in *Skutarevskii,* summarizing succinctly the consensus of observation by his fellow writers on the fate of the old family among all classes. The same rupture threatened the new parent-child groups still in the rudimentary stages. Merely to stabilize them on the basis of woman's primary commitment to her own work, to prevent the mother's withdrawal from social employment, required the swift expansion of housing and of socialized domestic institutions, at temporarily indispensable private expense. Beyond the provision to the masses of these material prerequisites, there lay the further stage of removing the economic and educational core of society from the

[183] Leonov, *Skutarevsky,* p. 181.

parent-child group before any form of family consistent with the
Marx-Engels conception could be evolved.

In the early thirties, as literature has reflected Soviet society,
neither leaders nor led had any doubt that these were the next
moves. The regime of abundance on which communism was contingent demanded the increasing use of womanpower in social
production, and the price was still not grudged. In 1933, Gladkov,
most orthodox of Communist writers, observes through "Bochka,"
his highly esteemed women's organizer, "The family is dying out.
. . . Already by our very work system we are destroying it." [184]
When the feminine occupational and family roles collided, the
economic contribution was rescued at the cost of intermittent home
life. Status mobility in the job, for the woman as well as the man,
was guarded even when it involved geographical separation of the
family. The hazard of occupational rivalry between husband and
wife was freely tolerated in industry. The woman was encouraged
to consider her inferior status there a temporary contretemps and
to improve it by training. If her attainment of higher position occasionally caused the husband jealousy or resentment (both on the
professional level as in "Fear" and "Inga," and among skilled
workers as in Bakhmetev's story "Her Victory"),[185] the husband
was expected to reconcile himself without umbrage, and his protests were ridiculed. The solution was never the withdrawal of the
wife from competition, either by her volition or by administrative
debarment. No functioning family system was recognized as entitled to protection at the expense of woman's exclusion or suppression in the occupational sphere. If inequalities between husband
and wife became intolerable, either was free to abandon the marriage and try again. For the mother, generous maternity leave, at
full pay, was provided, and her job held open until her return. But
return was expected of her. It was at the factory workbench and
office desk that Five-Year Plan heroines performed their exploits.
Not a single woman of literature up to 1936 became a public hero
in the maternity ward.

Literature spares none of the ugly details in its description of

[184] Gladkov, *Energiia*, p. 249.
[185] Vladimir Bakhmetev, "Eë pobeda," *Eë pobeda* (Moscow, 1932).

the new hardships of women at work and at home. Yet it does not
hint at the slightest disposition among those in industry to resume
the old pattern of their lives. They were intent on overcoming the
obstacles to actualization of the new design. When workers in
Avdeenko's *I Love* (1933) [186] begin an exodus from Magnitogorsk
and their flooded barracks, women, to arrest it, organize plastering
brigades, in a typical attitude of forbearance and trust in the promise that their own labor in industry would eventually bring comfort and plenty. One measure of the mood of women workers is
that they manifest none of the disaffection which produced widespread sabotage on the part of men. They stand apart or vigorously
oppose conspiracy and wrecking; some denounce members of their
own family.[187] Their freedom from the Soviet "terror" is a significant factor in the psychology of industrial women. "This fear . . .
stalks behind those who wait for the return of the old order," Klara,
the old factory worker, says in Afinogenov's "Fear." [188] According
to the almost unvaried evidence of literature, among women not
one was waiting for this; among men, many.[189]

There is substantial agreement among the most diverse interpreters of the scene up to 1936 that, among all classes and on all
levels in industry, as they gave the job priority and relegated their
family functions to a secondary place, women were taking firm
root in their occupations and losing the frustrations, the personal
insecurity, and instability associated with the feminine role in
modern industrial societies. Other anxieties were being substituted, however—anxieties concerning the endurance of their
strength and the welfare of their children. The one grievance about
which they were highly vocal was the delay in providing the essentials to aid them in the performance of their double task. One interpretation outside the Soviet Union of the fact that the network
of socialized domestic facilities was never developed according to

[186] A. Avdeyenko, *I Love* (*Ia liubliu*, 1933), trans. A. Wixley (New York, 1935).

[187] As in Nikiforov, *Zhenshchina* and *Vstrechnyi veter* (Headwind; Moscow, 1931);
V. P. Il'enkov, *Driving Axle* (*Vedushchaia os'*; Moscow, 1931) trans. unnamed (New
York, 1933); Pogodin, "Tempo"; and Gladkov, *Energiia*.

[188] Afinogenov, "Fear," p. 453.

[189] It is vaguely suggested in *Belomor* (*Belomorskoi-Baltiiskii kanal imeni Stalina*
[The Stalin White Sea-Baltic Canal], ed. Maksim Gor'kii, *et al.* [Moscow, 1934]), trans.
Amabel Williams-Ellis (New York, 1935) and by Panfërov in *Bruski*, that there may
have been some exceptions to the universal loyalty of industrial women.

expectations is that the scheme failed to catch on with the population. Yet official sources admit that in the early days the state was
too poor to make the investment; [190] and fiction consistently shows
all such institutions crowded beyond capacity and without funds.
For the failure to expand them after the mid-thirties there were
reasons other than the disfavor of women.

The moral standards implicit in the new orientation of women
workers may or may not have been those which Lenin defined for
the transition period: "The basis of communist morality is the
struggle for the consolidation and completion of communism."
Acceptance of their new role was tantamount to acceptance of the
Revolution: what they elected as good and right for themselves
had, at this stage, already been declared good and right for their
society, which needed their labor. They may have been conforming
to the requirements of the regime, or they may have been sat-
isfying eternal demands latent in womankind; for the moment,
two motives coincided. The exuberance of release from the old
disabilities of their sex blinded women to the portent in the moral
code which they had ostensibly embraced. In the quotation which
follows, the heretic Pil'niak gives them due warning through the
words of a doomed outcast who discovers the significance of the
"controlling bandage" sealed on a wound by doctors in industry
to prevent self-sabotage and forestall the absence of workers from
the plant:

"I must not trust myself; I am an individual; but one cannot stop
the plant on account of cases of individual sabotage; so I am bound in
a controlling bandage for the good of the state. It is just such controlling
bandages, placed not on our fingers but on our souls, that neither of
us recognizes. . . .

"Formerly we lived by family morality; now we live by collective
morality. . . . It seems that, like boots and grain, the morals of each
of us are also property [of the state]. . . . Morality is a simple . . .
economic unit, no less necessary than coats or potatoes." [191]

It is a renegade and saboteur who speaks. Yet no one in literature
speaks more cogently of Soviet morality. Another outcast, Ehrenburg's, rounds off the prediction. "Proletarian morals," he says,
"change according to the decisions of the latest congress." [192]

190 "Zhenskoe kommunisticheskoe dvizhenie."
191 Pilnyak, *The Volga Falls*, pp. 307–8.   192 Ehrenburg, *Out of Chaos*, p. 151.

IV
> . . . bound in a controlling bandage
> for the good of the state . . .

The function of Soviet writers, in the 1932 definition attributed to Stalin, is to act as "engineers of the human soul." When a novelist interprets this dictum as literally as does Panfërov, it is easy to detect a revision in the architect's plans from which he works. The publication in 1937 of the final volume of *Bruski* signified unmistakably that construction had begun on an entirely different kind of soul in woman. In the author's literary credo, explicitly set forth in the book, all art is tendentious, and the writer devoted to the service of the people must take the reader by the scruff of the neck and lead him where he, the artist, wishes, not allowing the reader's eyes to wander.[193] Accordingly, the book opens with the tribute of the Communist organizer, Kirill Zhdarkin, to his wife Steshka: "I love the mother in woman. When I see a pregnant woman, I feel like going up to her . . . and saying, 'You're an adornment to the earth.' "[194] The book ends with Steshka posing for a painting entitled "Mother." On the canvas, she is seated, heavy with child, the exultant radiance of motherhood in her eyes, gazing at a group of women as if to say, "What are you quarreling about? Every one of you can be as I am."[195] It is the painter's intention to show that "in woman, besides everything else, higher than all else, is the mother, motherhood. Without that, she'd be a homeless bitch." Kirill thinks: "Exactly my idea."[196] Between these two points, Panfërov at every step confronts the reader with "the smile of a happy mother":[197] "A miraculous thing began to occur . . . women started to bear children as if on orders, and the secretary of the village soviet . . . could not keep the birth records up to date. . . . It was that kind of spring."[198]

For full happiness, however, Panfërov makes clear, the Soviet mother must still, from time to time, prove her mettle as a heroine of labor. During the first rapture of their life together, Steshka has been persuaded by Kirill that she will devote herself to bearing children while he will feed the family. Is she of poorer stuff than his mother, who had borne eleven, or is he not a good father? Al-

193 Panfërov, *Bruski* (1947), p. 872.   194 *Ibid.*, p. 667.
195 *Ibid.*, p. 944.   196 *Ibid.*, p. 870.   197 *Ibid.*, p. 670.
198 *Ibid.*, p. 834.

though with some misgivings to start with, Steshka, a Party woman, drops all outside activities and spends the duration of the First Plan at home, engrossed in husband, children, furniture, and kitchen, exhausted by housework but happy in Kirill's praise and relishing the envy of other women, among whom she is careful to conduct herself "as was seemly for the wife of the secretary of the town Party committee." [199] In time, Kirill comes to despise her as an idle, backward, inefficient, slovenly bore. Driven away by his "betrayal" of her with another woman, Steshka—overnight, without previous training, and as a purely sporadic effort—becomes the best tractor driver in the Union. She is acclaimed by Stalin himself as living proof that "the question of woman's equality has been solved in our country once and for all." [200] Under his wing, at a great conclave in Moscow, she mounts the speakers' platform to address herself to all women and to proclaim the new rules:

"Of course, the wife must be the mother, must be the one to make a comfortable home life. But for this, there is no need whatever to withdraw from public work. Family affairs must be combined with social affairs, with work in society on an equal footing with men. We Soviet women are given such rights, but women in other countries still only dream of them." [201]

For two decades woman had been told daily and hourly, on Lenin's authority, that it was from this very responsibility of making "a comfortable home life" that the Soviet government would liberate her, that, pending the establishment of socialized agencies, the man had equal duties in the household.[202]

Kirill, repentant, sues for pardon and for Steshka's return, enticing her with new dresses and a summer cottage, beautifully furnished, equipped with tennis courts, croquet grounds, volleyball court, hammocks in the woods, a bathhouse on the lake, and a large library of fiction, all for her. Although Steshka is, until the last minute, in love with the painter Arnol'dov, indifferent to her former husband, and resentful of the old "master psychology" persisting in him, she and Kirill are reunited. The influence of material factors, brought to bear upon a woman's decision by a man of large income and social prominence, was unthinkable to the

[199] *Ibid.*, p. 777.   [200] *Ibid.*, p. 911.   [201] *Ibid.*, p. 922.
[202] Zetkin, pp. 56–58.

earlier Marxian mentality. Despite the vaunted new prosperity, at least on Kirill's level, the same basic problem remains for the woman: the feasibility of discharging her dual obligations in the future, when in the past she has been unable to cope with the housework alone, even aided by a domestic servant. The author is discreetly silent on practical measures except for dangling the suggestion that the small son of Steshka and Kirill might be left with his *babushka,* Kirill's peasant mother, during Steshka's absence at work. This is the first hint that the *babushka,* not the nursery or kindergarten, was to become the safety pin of the Soviet economy.

Panfërov's purpose is plain: to rebalance in the mind of Soviet woman the functions assigned to her, weighting the role of wifehood and motherhood, lightening that of socially productive employment, and to confute her importunate demands with the pronouncement that her emancipation is complete. The plans and specifications to be followed by "engineers of the human soul" in directing the new construction are not so fully available as the earlier "guide to action," but the main outlines can be discerned from the open record, as annotated inadvertently by Panfërov in revisions made in successive editions of his book.

During the first writing, an intensive propaganda campaign was in progress extolling the blessings and duties of family life and pointing out the evils of abortion.[203] In 1936, the tremendous publicity and encouragement (albeit somewhat shamefaced) given the organization of the Wives of Red Army Officers, of the Wives of Engineers, Managers and Technicians, and of Wives of Stakhanovites,[204] for activities akin to those of volunteer social work elsewhere, denoted official sanction for the woman who was not a wage earner, but depended on consort status. That these organizations were not to be treated with levity, indecorum, or ideological objections is indicated by the continual textual changes made in subsequent editions of the novel *Bruski,* in order to mute the author's first sardonic description.[205]

The propaganda campaign culminated in the decree of June 27,

203 *Pravda, Izvestiia, Rabotnitsa,* and *Komsomol'skaia pravda,* June, 1935, to June, 1936.
204 *Pravda,* May 10, 1936.
205 A comparison of the following corresponding passages in different editions shows a progressive watering down of Panfërov's initial attitude of disdain, even contempt, into one closer to the benign approval given the members of these women's organiza-

1936, which prohibited abortion and established state aid in handsome amounts for mothers of more than six children. The decree provided for a great expansion of facilities for the care of mother and child as well as additional protection of the right to collect child maintenance from the father. One of the main purposes, the preamble announced, was to "combat a light-minded attitude toward the family and family obligations." Divorce was rendered more difficult; although it remained financially accessible, disfavor was emphasized in the procedure now required.[206] Shortly before the issuance of the decree, *Pravda* explained its aim as the strengthening of the Soviet family, the safeguarding of the health of millions of women, and the rearing of a numerically strong and healthy generation.[207]

The high degree of articulation between official objectives and literary reflection of life in the work of certain Soviet writers is clarified by the coincidence of this decree with the production of the final volume of Panfërov's *Bruski*. At the same time, the writer illuminates the genesis of the legislation. The preamble to the decree states: [In these provisions] "the Soviet government responds to numerous applications made by toiling women." According to Panfërov's version, apparently written not long before the decree, the initiative lay elsewhere: early in the First Plan, Stalin counseled Kirill Zhdarkin that "we must plan and build a family we may be proud of." [208] To Stalin, Panfërov also attributes the solicitude for the welfare of mothers and children expressed in the premiums for numerous progeny. In the course of the now explainable miracle of childbirths "on order," quadruplets were born to one dismayed peasant woman. Accused by her husband of trafficking with the devil, she is on the verge of starving three of her new sons to placate him, until a Party emissary arrives with money, gifts, photographers, and good wishes from Stalin:

"Do you know what he says? There must be a law, he says, so that the firstborn brings honor to the mother, the second too; and the third not only honor but . . . rubles, cash in hand. There—that's for you from

tions in the official press: *Bruski* (4 vols., Moscow, Gosizdat, 1933–37), IV (1937), 295–97; *Bruski* (Moscow, OGIZ, 1947), p. 916; *Bruski* (2 vols., Moscow, Sovetskii pisatel', 1949), II, 588–89.
[206] Postanovlenie TsIK i SNK SSSR ot 27 Iiunia 1936g. (S.Z. SSSR, 1936g., No. 34, st. 309).
[207] *Pravda*, June 4, 1936.   [208] Panfërov, *Bruski*, (1947), p. 680.

the government! And the fourth—[more] rubles for you, cash in hand. That's the kind of man he is, Stalin." [209]

If sponsorship of the project was incorrectly assigned, the Soviet censor was somewhat laxer than has been thought. It is a gauge of the reaction of women to the decree in its entirety that Stalin was dissociated from it in subsequent editions. In the rewriting of life, the filicidal impulses also disappeared.

The year 1936 signalized the fundamental reversal in policy. In contrast to the lengthy debates preceding the 1926 Code, the decree of 1936 came into force without discussion in the highest legislative body. Among apologists for the new law, a sociologist writing in the philosophical organ of the Party recanted as a "leftist error" his earlier pronouncement that "socialism leads to the extinction of the family," and asserted that, on the contrary, under socialism the family grows stronger.[210] The shift in emphasis from woman's role in social production to her role in reproducing the species has become more and more marked in subsequent years. In 1943, coeducation, a cherished Soviet principle, was abolished in secondary schools,[211] and a separate curriculum for girls was instituted, to include training in domestic science and preparation for the duties of motherhood.[212]

In 1944, without warning to the public, the July 8 decree of the Presidium of the Supreme Soviet of the USSR rescinded the two features of matrimonial law long celebrated as characteristically Soviet: recognition of factual marriage and freedom of divorce. The relief of the father from all obligations to children born outside registered marriage blasted the very foundation of "family" law, laid down on the principle of actual descent. The decree restored divorce to court jurisdiction (without specifying grounds) and put it out of financial reach of a vast segment of the population. Moreover, to invest registration of marriage with new importance and solemnity, the decree called for the introduction of a ceremonial procedure. Mothers were awarded steeply graduated money

[209] Panférov, *Bruski*, IV (1937), 220.

[210] S. Vol'fson, "Sotsializm i sem'ia," *Pod znamenem Marksizma*, No. 6 (June, 1936), p. 64, note.

[211] Postanovlenie SNK SSSR No. 789 ot 16 Iiulia, 1943g.

[212] M. M. Tsusmer, "Separate Education for Boys and Girls," *Information Bulletin of the Embassy of the U.S.S.R.*, No. 126 (Washington, D. C., Nov. 13, 1943), p. 6.

premiums from the third child on, instead of from the seventh as under 1936 legislation. In addition, various decorations were instituted in honor of mothers of large families: the "Motherhood Medal," "Order of Motherhood Glory," and "Order and Title of Heroine Mother." Taxes were imposed on bachelors and childless women and on families with fewer than three children. The most radical step was the creation of a unique estate in the position of the unmarried mother: the decree provided direct state subsidy for her, in lieu of the child support previously payable by the father, or the alternative of placing the child in an institution for rearing at state expense; she was also eligible for the premiums awarded for many children. The preamble of the decree begins: "Care for children and mothers and the strengthening of the family have always [sic!] been among the most important tasks of the Soviet state." Further, it expressly states its aim of "encouraging large families and providing increased protection for motherhood and childhood." [213]

In the face of this bald announcement of the decree itself, many other interpretations of the new family policy, Soviet and non-Soviet, have been advanced. One Soviet apologist explained that, with the attainment by parents of "a high political and cultural level," there was no necessity to transfer the care of children to public institutions for fear the home might stunt them by improper training.[214] Another spokesman for the regime gave as motive the prevention of juvenile delinquency, found to be closely correlated with weak family supervision or homelessness.[215] These arguments ignore the fact that the object in entrusting the early

[213] "Ukaz Prezidiuma Verkhovnogo Soveta SSSR ot Iiulia 1944g.," *Vedomosti VS SSSR*, No. 37 (1944), p. 32.

[214] V. Svetlov, "Sotsialisticheskoe obshchestvo i sem'ia," *Pod znamenem Marksizma*, No. 8 (August, 1936), pp. 56–57.

[215] Grigorii M. Sverdlov, *Brak i sem'ia* (Moscow, 1946), p. 6.

Among non-Soviet interpreters, Rudolf Schlesinger, in addition to the main consideration of birth rate in the 1944 legislation, suggests a number of incidental motives connected with postwar demobilization in his *Changing Attitudes in Soviet Russia: The Family in the USSR* (London, 1949), pp. 22–23, 403–4; and in his *Spirit of Post-war Russia* (London, 1947), pp. 55, 63.

An American anthropologist's view sees the new policy as a concession to old cultural patterns. It is inconceivable, however, that a propaganda campaign like the intensive one of 1935–36 was required in order to make a "concession." Nor would the flood of apologia for the 1936 decree have served any purpose if the force of public opinion had been responsible for the measure.

care and education of children to nurseries and kindergartens was
primarily to free the mother for social employment, and that for
evils such as juvenile delinquency Marxian doctrine prescribed
a remedy never applied by the Soviet state on a scale to meet the
needs: adequate institutions for child care. Nevertheless, the fundamental purpose of the new policy is obvious: an increase in the
birth rate. No less powerful motive would justify the overriding
of the grave economic and political considerations involved.[216] In
1936 a war was in sight. In 1944 there were losses to be made up.
To reconstruct and develop the vast underpopulated land while
preparing it for further tests by war, sheer numbers were required,
even at some forfeit of women workers immediately available. If it
was ever necessary to look beyond the plain words of the decree
itself for the significance of the new policy, the need was removed
by subsequent candid confirmation. Sverdlov, foremost authority
on Soviet family law, wrote in 1945, in a booklet intended for foreign consumption: "The state is interested, too, in an increase in
the population, and this can only be assured when normal conditions for family life exist." [217] Accepting the thesis, once dismissed
as thoroughly bourgeois, that legally formalized marriage was con-
ducive to greater population increase than factual marriage, Soviet
policy makers now scorned halfway measures. Sverdlov had paved
the way for drastic steps with the argument that the socialist state
repudiated the view of relations between the sexes as private matters to which society and the state were indifferent, and reserved
for itself a very considerable sphere of direct and active intervention in the relationships of marriage and family in order that it
might influence them in the direction beneficial and necessary both
to society and the individual.[218] This is a far cry from the position in
1936, when the Party had declared marriage and divorce still private

[216] In an occupational system where labor productivity is stimulated by highly
differentiated rates of pay, as in the Soviet Union since 1935, one of the most compelling incentives—expenses entailed in the upkeep of a household and in the
rearing of children—is weakened by the subsidization of large families. (See Schlesinger, *Changing Attitudes,* pp. 398, 405.)

[217] Sverdlov, *Legal Rights of the Soviet Family* (London, 1945), p. 17. For a discussion of the decline in the birth rate between 1927 and 1935, associated with an increase in the frequency of divorce and abortion, see Frank Lorimer, *The Population
of the Soviet Union* (Geneva, 1946), pp. 126, 128.

[218] Sverdlov, "O predmete i sisteme sotsialisticheskogo semeinogo prava," *Sovetskoe
gosudarstvo i pravo,* No. 1 (1941), pp. 58, 63–64, 66.

affairs, in spite of the touch of censure for divorce. The idea of non-interference in this sphere was so imbedded in the general consciousness that even Communists failed to recognize special Party control in their case. (In the first version of *Bruski*, Panfërov allowed one of his characters, in seeking Zhdarkin's advice on marital difficulties, to say, "I know the Party is not concerned with family matters." [219] Panfërov knew better in later editions; the passage vanished, along with Kirill's counsel in favor of separation).

In 1944, the conduct which disapproval had failed to effect in 1936 was made binding by law not only on Party members, but also upon the mass of Soviet citizenry. No longer was the family an amorphous institution. It rested foursquare on the base of a registered marriage, which could be dissolved only at the pleasure of the state. The publicity attendant on divorce, deplored by Lenin as the "disgusting formalities" of bourgeois court procedure,[220] in the 1944 decree was regarded as a salutary deterrent (Art. 24c). In following years Sverdlov set the stage for return of the authoritarian family, announcing categorically that parents were to inculcate in children the traits essential in every Soviet citizen: [221] "The socialist state supports the family as its own effective bulwark. In strengthening the family, it strengthens itself, increases its might, its power." [222]

Out of the urgency to accelerate population growth—a situation not provided for in Marxian doctrine [223]—the Soviet design for women was hastily revamped, and a new moral code devised. When the new code did come, it grew not out of economic relations within a socialist society, but out of relations between that society and the non-socialist outer world. The theory had been predicated on a world working toward communism, not on hostile population pressure from without. Woman's previously subsidiary function, motherhood, became the paramount one in 1936, and what has since been called "communist morality," so far as it concerns mar-

219 Panfërov, *Bruski*, IV (1937), 140.   220 Lenin, *Women and Society*, p. 13.
221 Sverdlov, *Legal Rights of the Soviet Family*, p. 17.
222 Sverdlov, *Brak i sem'ia*, p. 12.
223 Engels believed that humanity is capable of a higher rate of reproduction than bourgeois society permits (Marks i Engel's, *Pis'ma*, 4th ed. [Moscow, 1931], p. 163). Marx limited himself to attacks on the Malthusian law and to a statement that every social structure has "its own peculiar, historically valid law of population" (*Capital* [London, 1946], II, 697-98).

riage and family, has been formulated on this basis and imposed from above. A new ideal woman was created. There are ten or more children in her brood, and she carries the title "Heroine Mother," accompanied by a certificate from the Presidium of the Supreme Soviet and a sizable cash bonus. Marriage is systematically encouraged. Sverdlov, who in 1941 had ridiculed the "force majeure" measures of bourgeois societies to stimulate marriage and the birth rate by loans to newlyweds and premiums to parents,[224] in 1946, addressing a Komsomol assembly, glorified motherhood as the highest good for the individual, and mentioned that directors of industrial establishments and chairmen of *kolkhozy* were instructed by the government to furnish transportation to the registration bureau for couples being married and to assist them in obtaining furniture and household equipment.[225]

The same methods formerly mocked as the "belated, futile efforts" of a society based on private property [226] are now being tested in Soviet society, in which the state can more effectively control the performance of abortion and the availability of contraceptives. Increasingly stringent limitations have been placed upon divorce. In October, 1949, the Plenum of the Supreme Court of the USSR directed that, whether or not both parties desired it, divorce would be granted only if continuance of the marriage was "contrary to the principles of Communist morality and could not create normal conditions for life together and rearing of children." [227] The legally cemented family and the cult of fertility are here to stay, at any price, at least until the achievement of full communism or of security against aggression.[228] The successes of the program are perhaps already considerable.[229]

[224] Sverdlov, "O predmete," p. 63.   [225] Sverdlov, *Brak i sem'ia*, pp. 6, 16.
[226] Sverdlov, "O predmete," p. 63.   [227] *Pravda*, Oct. 3, 1949.

[228] In a review of a book by Sverdlov (*Brak i razvod* [Marriage and Divorce], Moscow, 1949), it was stated that there can be no thought of weakening state regulation of marriage and family relations during the period of gradual transition from socialism to communism, so long as the Soviet Union is building a communist society side by side with the capitalist camp (I. S. Gurevich, in *Sovetskoe gosudarstvo i pravo*, No. 7 [1949], pp. 78–82).

[229] Dramatic results were claimed following the 1936 decree. In 1937, the increase in the birth rate for the whole country as compared with 1936 was 18%, and in Moscow over 100% (Sverdlov, *Legal Rights of the Soviet Family*, p. 46). Between the 1944 decree and June, 1951, 33,000 mothers in the Soviet Union had won the title of "Mother Heroine" for bearing at least ten children, and over 3,000,000 had received awards of the "Order of Motherhood Glory" and "Motherhood Medal" for bearing

Along with each new measure legislating morality and happiness, inevitably came the assurance that in questions of marriage and family, "Soviet law reflects the interests, the will, the moral demands of the people." [230] Soviet literature up to 1936 replies that the law of that year contravenes the will and the moral demands of the people depicted as most valuable and favored in their society until that time. As attested in the press, numbers of women found the 1936 legislation, especially the anti-abortion clause, not to their interests: they vehemently opposed it, shrinking from an additional child in an already overcrowded room or fearing that, unable to place their babies in nurseries, they would be forced to give up their jobs.[231] In 1944, women were allowed no voice. In order to lend some semblance of plausibility to the contention that the new "communist morality" arose from the people and to justify the switch from the emancipation of women to the consolidation of the family, it has been feverishly proclaimed from 1936 on that full equality of the sexes had already been achieved. In the terms originally defined, there was little in fact to warrant the allegation at the time. There has been less since.

To recapitulate, the essential conditions formulated by Marx and Engels were: (1) complete equality of legal rights; (2) the absorption of the entire female population, on an equal footing, into public employment; (3) the centering of life around the place of employment; (4) the establishment between man and woman, as equals, of a union based solely on mutual inclination, freely entered upon and freely maintained; (5) communal organization of domestic functions; (6) transfer to the state of the care and education of children; (7) the withering away of the family as the economic and educational unit of society; (8) recognition of equal rights of all children, legitimate or not. These terms were most imperfectly realized by 1936. The bulk of the employable female population had not been brought into social production.[232] The

---

from five to nine children (Nina Popova, "Vo imia zhizni i zdorov'ia detei," *Pravda*, June 1, 1951).   [230] Sverdlov, *Brak i sem'ia*, pp. 29–30.

[231] See selections from press correspondence quoted by Schlesinger, *Changing Attitudes*, pp. 251–69; also Sir John Maynard, *Russia in Flux*, ed. S. Haden Guest (New York, 1948), pp. 483–84. Schlesinger, *Spirit of Postwar Russia*, p. 57, adds that there were numerous convictions for violation of the law against abortions.

[232] Serebrennikov, *Position of Women*, p. 50; TsUNKhU, *SSSR—strana sotsializma*, ed. I. A. Kraval', et al. (Moscow, 1936), p. 85.

greater number of those employed had by no means attained economic equality.[233] The lack of communal services was still the chief impediment to the mass entry of women into industry, and it hindered those already employed not only from further training to improve skill but also from other activities.[234]

The nursery system in 1933, near the peak of its development during the first two Plans, sufficed to accommodate less than half the crèche-age children of women industrial workers, who enjoyed priority over other groups; also, poor conditions in nurseries and kindergartens reduced their aid to the mother and thereby adversely affected her work.[235] The decree of 1936, in recognition of the shortage of child-care facilities and the further hardships to be incurred in the denial of abortion, promised a tremendous expansion of the nursery and kindergarten systems. Nursery accommodations were to be doubled before 1939, and those in kindergartens roughly tripled. From this point on, Soviet publications have been provocatively silent or evasive on the development of the "vast network," which, it was stated at the time, would thereafter provide "the most essential basis for actual equality between men and women." [236] By this criterion, the status of the average woman has been demonstrably impaired, even on the basis of the sparse figures released.

In the first place, the commitments of the 1936 decree have remained paper plans down to the present, if they were bona fide intentions at the time. The question of actual intention arises in view of the fact that by 1939, when the new facilities were to have

[233] See p. 63.

[234] Serebrennikov, *Zhenskii trud v SSSR* (Moscow, 1934), pp. 94, 107, 217–18, and *Position of Women*, pp. 142ff. Although in 1932–33, 37% of the urban population (Serebrennikov, *Position of Women*, p. 164) and almost 75% of the workers in the main industries were fed in communal restaurants (Stalin, "The Results of the First Five-Year Plan," *Selected Writings*, p. 160), the service apparently covered only one meal a day at the place of employment, with no provision for members of the family not at work or in school (Serebrennikov, *Zhenskii trud*, p. 106). In 1935, there were only 180 communal laundries in urban areas (Serebrennikov, *Position of Women*, p. 167).

[235] Serebrennikov, *Zhenskii trud*, pp. 98–101, 103–5, 217, 219. The defects of unhygienic conditions, improper food, inadequate or non-existent medical service, unsuitable premises and equipment, ill-trained staff were somewhat overcome during the Second Plan (*ibid.*), but by no means entirely, to judge from press correspondence published in 1936 (see Schlesinger, *Changing Attitudes*, pp. 256, 265).

[236] Vol'fson, "Sotsializm i sem'ia," p. 41.

been in operation, the combined capacity of the permanent nursery and kindergarten systems had dropped rather than increased, and was considerably lower than that of 1933–34. Neither in the immediate prewar nor in the postwar period has the goal of the 1936 decree been even half reached; in 1951 the network still had not regained the 1933–34 level.[237] The difficulties created for working mothers can be realized by considering these facts in connection with a rise of roughly 50 percent in the number of women employed in the national economy between 1933–34 and 1940, including a great increase in the percentage of women in the industrial labor force.[238] Furthermore, in 1935, hours of operation in nurseries and kindergartens, originally lengthy in order to afford the mother free time for public activities and self-improvement, were reduced to a period which covered only the mother's work shift and the time required to call for her children.[239] Nothing more effective could have been devised to return the woman to the home and housework.

The dearth of statistics on fulfillment of announced plans for large-scale public food purveyance and laundry service is explained unintentionally by Panfërov. In *Bruski*, Kirill Zhdarkin, after Steshka's desertion, realizes guiltily that "he had imprisoned her

[237] The 1936 decree called for a total of 5.3 million places in year-round nurseries and kindergartens before 1939 (1.8 million in nurseries, 3.5 million in kindergartens). In 1937 the combined total was 1.8 million places ("Tretii piatiletnii plan razvitiia narodnogo khoziaistva [1938–42gg.]," *Mirovoe khoziaistvo i mirovaia politika*, No. 2 [February, 1939], p. 27), and at the beginning of 1939 was still only 1.78 million (.74 in nurseries [K. Maistrakh, "Zdravookhranenie," *Bol'shaia sovetskaia entsiklopediia*, supplementary volume entitled "SSSR" (1947), col. 1173] and 1.04 in kindergartens [E. Volkova, *et al.*, "Narodnoe obrazovanie," *Bol'. sov. entsik.*, Vol. "SSSR," col. 1218]), as against 2.09 million in 1933–34 (.77 million in nurseries [Serebrennikov, *Zhenskii trud*, p. 219] and 1.32 in kindergartens [TsUNKhU, *Kul'turnoe stroitel'stvo SSSR v tsifrakh (1930–34)*, Moscow, 1935, p. 26]). Just before the Second World War, combined facilities provided 1.98 million accommodations (B. Markus, "Trud," *Bol'. sov. entsik.*, Vol. "SSSR," col. 1143); and in 1951, fewer than 2 million ("Schast'e sovetskoi materi," *Izvestiia*, June 27, 1951).

[238] In these years, the number of women in the national economy rose from 7.1 million to over 11 million, and the percentage in the industrial labor force from 33 to 41 (Serebrennikov, *Zhenskii trud*, p. 228; Markus, "Trud," col. 1125).

[239] Postanovlenie SNK SSSR ot 6 Iiulia 1935 (S. Z. SSSR 1935g., No. 35, st. 309). Despite the great demand, the 24-hour type of institution, formerly considered to contribute most to women's advancement and by the mid-thirties comprising a majority of the nursery accommodations in many industrial centers, was written off as no longer "expedient" except in cases where women on night shift had no other members of the family to care for children (Serebrennikov, *Zhenskii trud*, pp. 100–102, and *Position of Women*, p. 149; E. N. Medynskii, *Narodnoe obrazovanie v SSSR* [Moscow, 1947], p. 33).

in housework, chained her to the kitchen, [where] she had begun to suffocate." [240] In later editions of this novel, there was a neat, clean hole where this passage had first appeared. In short, Panfërov and the censor had expurgated Lenin, who had put the matter more pungently: "Woman continues to be a domestic slave because petty housework crushes, strangles, stultifies and degrades her, chains her to the kitchen and the nursery, and wastes her labor on barbarously unproductive, petty, nerve-racking . . . and crushing drudgery." [241] After 1937, it was impolitic to refer to housework as an unseemly occupation for the Soviet woman, at least if the housework was done after a day's labor at the factory.[242]

As corollary to the new emphasis on woman as wife and mother, the logically inevitable inroads have now been made on her previous rights to education and vocational training. Significant retrenchment has occurred in the preparation of skilled and unskilled female labor, beginning long before the abolition of coeducation in 1943.[243] The reduction in training of women technicians and minor specialists for industry must be judged mainly from the fact that publication of statistics previously given on numbers and percentage of women in *rabfak* schools was discontinued after 1936, and in *technicums* after 1938. As yet no serious curtailment is apparent at the university level. There, the percentage of women rose steadily until, at the outbreak of the Second World War, they

---

[240] Panfërov, *Bruski*, IV (1937), 315.   [241] Lenin, *Women and Society*, p. 14.

[242] Similar changes are made in Gladkov's *Tsement* (Cement) between the editions of 1927 and 1947.

[243] In 1931, girls made up 37–38% of the trainees in industrial FZU schools (Serebrennikov, *Zhenskii trud*, p. 137); and, by official order in that year, they were thereafter to constitute 50% of all factory school pupils (Serebrennikov, *Position of Women*, pp. 69–70). Nevertheless, they accounted for only 27–29% of admissions and graduations from FZU and type schools from the fall of 1935 to 1938 (TsUNKhU, *Kul'turnoe stroitel'stvo SSSR 1935* [Moscow, 1936], p. 136; TsUNKhU, *Kul'turnoe stroitel'stvo SSSR* [Moscow, 1940], p. 136). When Labor Reserve training schools for skilled and semi-skilled labor were organized in 1940 to replace the FZU system, girls were at first excluded from the program (Ukaz Prezidiuma Verkhovnogo Soveta SSSR, "O gosudarstvennykh trudovykh rezervakh," *Pravda*, Oct. 3, 1940). On their later admission, recruits were taken only from former FZU trainees (Philip R. Lever, "State Labor Reserves System of the Soviet Union" [unpublished Columbia M.A. thesis, 1948], p. 40). Shortly after the end of the Second World War, girls constituted only 15 percent of the total number in the factory training courses, the larger of the two divisions of the Labor Reserves, and about one third of those in trade and railroad schools (Sergei Kournakoff, "Building the Builders," *Soviet Russia Today*, XV, No. 9 [January, 1947], p. 20).

exceeded male students in numbers [244] as a temporary result of mobilization. From the sparse data released since the War, it cannot be determined whether the prewar ratio of women students will be maintained in the higher educational institutions.[245] Nevertheless, the proportion of women to the total number educated for the top professional levels has considerably exceeded the proportion trained in the lower specialized courses from the mid-thirties to the present.

There is no other conclusion than that a relatively small intellectual elite of women has been maintained high on the industrial ladder, but that after 1935 mass industrial training at state expense was not a sound investment in the case of girls whom it was desired to direct into large-scale motherhood and home life. Refusal of employment would, of course, be unthinkable in view of the chronic need of labor; but the drudge jobs, which offer low reward and small prospects of advancement and which may be abandoned at any time without severe loss to the enterprise, would suffice for those whose main contribution to society is preferred elsewhere.[246] On this score, again the novelist Panfërov reveals more than does Gosplan. In the tell-tale *Bruski*, Stalin is described joining in the singing of popular songs: "Especially that one about the girl getting on a tractor. He sang it, and then said: 'So she got on the tractor. Just try to take her off—and she'll start a revolt.' " [247] Perish the

[244] The proportion of women was then 57% (Sverdlov, *Legal Rights of the Soviet Family*, p. 25).

[245] In the mid-thirties, the percentage of women students in higher educational institutions ranged from 37 to 41 (TsUNKhU, *Kul'turnoe stroitel'stvo SSSR* [1940], p. 113); after the War they constituted about 40% of the number in industrial, transport, building, and agricultural colleges (Popova, *Women in the Land of Socialism* [Moscow, 1949], p. 81). The latter figure may still reflect the extremely high enrollment of women during wartime mobilization.

[246] After the early thirties, graduates of higher educational institutions, *technicums*, and labor-training schools were compelled to work for a period of three to five years on administrative order; later, certain categories of specialist personnel were made subject to transfer to any locality at any time; and ultimately labor in general was deprived of freedom of movement from job to job (see Alexander Baykov, *The Development of the Soviet Economic System* [New York, 1947], pp. 213ff., 350ff.; Markus, "Trud," col. 1129). The increasing rigidity of the occupational structure indicated by such measures inevitably meant some exclusion of women from the labor force, once the family became a paramount consideration. On the one hand, female labor could be less profitably utilized if exemptions from these liabilities were necessitated; on the other, refusal of exemption would separate the family.

[247] Panfërov, *Bruski*, IV (1937), 295.

thought! Out went the passage in later editions. If, at the very moment when women were convincingly demonstrating their marked aptitude and the economic profitability of their employment as skilled labor in industry, plans for their future there were being scuttled, it ill behooved an engineer of Soviet souls to suggest rebellion as the inevitable reaction.

The same danger of dissatisfaction and protest among the upper intelligentsia may have been averted by pursuance of an entirely different policy toward them in preserving their equality of opportunity, at no punishing cost to the paramount population objectives. These women in any case would not be the large-scale child-bearers, accustomed as they are in their milieu to birth control and, surmisably, untempted by the medals of "Motherhood Glory" and "Mother Heroine," or by premiums for large families. In view of the always compelling need of expert professional personnel, the services of those already trained are unlikely to be wasted, and the continued higher education of young women of the upper strata, yielding an increment to the professional pool with little or no loss to the population pool, is a good risk, particularly since, after the introduction of tuition fees in 1940, it need not be at government expense.

It is now this relatively small group of women alone which can be exhibited as token of the emancipation of women. Indeed, in the postwar showcase they are prominently displayed, above the legend reading, "Almost half of the country's specialists with completed higher education are women." [248] The crucial qualification in the phrase "with completed higher education" is frequently slurred. Although this achievement at the top is in itself impressive, it is by no means, in the words of a propagandist, "proof enough that in the USSR the position of women is equal to that of men not only in law but in fact." [249] The concept of "specialists" or intelligentsia in the Soviet Union is a very broad one, embracing not only the professions as the term is used here, but also such occupations as those of factory technicians and foremen, cooperative store managers, bookkeepers, medical assistants, teachers, *ad in-*

[248] Among specialists *with completed higher education,* the percentage of women rose from 42.3 in 1947 (Markus, "Trud," col. 1126) to approximately 50 in 1950 (E. Furtseva, "Zhenshchiny strany sotsializma," *Pravda,* March 8, 1950).
[249] Popova, *Women in the Land of Socialism,* p. 77.

finitum. The size of the female contingent in these wider ranks, the placards never reveal. Presumably, for the small elite, as Soviet publicists reiterate, "in the Soviet Union there is no contradiction between motherhood and participation in industrial work and social activity." [250] To perform the household duties once slated for transfer to social agencies, these women are in a position to hire domestic workers. As yet there is no evidence that, on this plane, young women who are inclined to make the effort are excluded from competition with men on the job.

The less privileged woman worker, however, must now often bear children willy-nilly [251] and at the same time maintain herself in industry without the assistance which the socialist system by its nature promises her. Her income and job are assured during maternity leave (now greatly reduced in length from the original term),[252] but the reservation of job means little unless the mother has means of caring for the child while she works; lacking such help, she is today frequently forced out of employment, and sacrifices the economic independence which is the Marxian key to social equality.[253]

Both for the married woman thus constrained to work only sporadically as a wage-earner and for the unmarried mother, a basic disadvantage has been introduced in the establishment of motherhood as the prime social function and in the simultaneous failure to compensate this function on a scale comparable with the earnings of even unskilled workers.[254] The mother's material position

[250] Serebrennikov, *Position of Women,* p. 252.

[251] On the financial level of the average worker, contraceptive resources are relatively restricted; according to Schlesinger (*Changing Attitudes,* p. 18), no serious effort has ever been made to overcome the shortage of contraceptives on the market.

[252] From 16 to 11 weeks. See decrees of June 27, 1936, Art. 8 (p.93, note 206), and of July 8, 1944, Art. 6 (p. 95, note 213).

[253] Many such complaints have appeared in the press: for instance, "Po-Stalinski zabotit'sia," *Izvestiia,* July 7, 1946, and "Gosudarstvennaia zabota o sem'e," *ibid.,* July 8, 1947; O. Kozlova, "Nekotorye voprosy povysheniia proizvoditel'nosti truda zhenshchin-rabotnits," *Pravda,* Jan. 24, 1949; V. Safonov, "Za materei-rabotnits," *Izvestiia,* June 15, 1949, "Zabota o zhenshchine-materi i detiakh," *ibid.,* June 30, 1949, and "Pis'ma materei," *ibid.,* Aug. 11, 27, 1949.

[254] State financial assistance in child rearing was never sufficient to support the married woman and her children until they became so numerous as to bar any other activity for the mother, who would then, upon cessation of the short-term payments (4 to 5 years), face later life with no security (see decrees of June 27, 1936, Art. 10, and of July 8, 1944, Arts. 2, 3; also Schlesinger, *Changing Attitudes,* pp. 396–97). For the unmarried mother, the likelihood of keeping her children with her and giving

deteriorated still further with the halving of state subsidies for child support in November, 1947, on the grounds of a rise in the value of the ruble,[255] although wages were not then reduced. The explicit reestablishment of the legal family as the economic and educational unit of society,[256] in which the husband is perforce the chief provider, according to Marxist lights returns the wife to a subordinate position in the family, dominated by the husband because of his economic superiority. No matter how assiduously Sverdlov asserts that decision on marriage in the Soviet Union is not tainted by material considerations,[257] no matter how categorically the law states that "all steps in regard to children are taken by both parents jointly," [258] it is implausible that, in a society, which, since 1935, has utilized high differential of income and prestige as the main incentive to work, the influence of these factors can be ruled out in other spheres of life or that the wife restored to mere consort status wields equal authority in family matters. Panfërov would lead the reader to think that material considerations are not negligible, as would actual reproof in the Soviet press to girls seeking rich husbands.[259]

For a time after 1944, to some observers the new estate of the unmarried mother, independent of the individual father and directly subsidized by government, forecast a possible solution for the

---

them an equal start in life with the children of legal families was relatively small, since state payments instituted in 1944 were lower than the average amount awarded earlier from the father's earnings, and continued only until the child reached the age of twelve, whereas the father is obliged to support his legal children until they reach majority.

[255] Ukaz Prezidiuma Verkhovnogo Soveta SSSR, "O razmere gosudarstvennogo posobiia mnogodetnym i odinokim materiam," *Pravda*, Nov. 26, 1947. The significance to the mother of state payments as the basic means of livelihood may be judged by comparing them with government expenditures for children in orphanages. Beginning in 1948, upon the birth of the seventh child, the mother, married or unmarried, received, in addition to a single lump-sum payment of 1,250 rubles, a monthly allowance of 100 rubles for each child over a period of four years from its second birthday. The unmarried mother received 50 rubles a month for each of the first two children, and 150 rubles for three or more. In contrast, government expenditure for an orphanage child averaged 600 rubles monthly in 1949 (I. Kairov, "Zabota Sovetskogo gosudarstva o podrastaiushchem pokolenii," *Izvestiia*, June 1, 1950).

[256] Sverdlov, *Sovetskii sud v bor'be za ukreplenie sem'i* (Moscow, 1949), p. 5.

[257] Sverdlov, "O predmete," p. 63.

[258] Kodeks zakonov o brake, sem'e i opeke RSFSR (Sobr. uzakon. RSFSR, 1926, No. 82, st. 612).

[259] An article in *Komsomol'skaia pravda*, quoted by Joseph Newman, "Soviet Girls Chided for Seeking Rich Husbands," New York *Herald Tribune*, Nov. 14, 1948.

predicament of the married woman as well, by which the bearing and rearing of children might be established as an indispensable service to society as a whole, commanding a livelihood from the entire community.[260] A turn in this direction now appears out of the question. The flimsy material foundation provided in 1944 for the autonomous institution of the unmarried mother was largely cut away in 1947. Furthermore, a tolerable position in society was guaranteed her only through scrupulous official efforts to prevent prejudice and discrimination which would affect her earning capacity. Despite demands upon the birth rate and assertion that "no social stigma is attached to the unmarried mother or her child," [261] numerous intimations from Sverdlov of moral censure for the woman "entering into irregular relations with a man" [262] and of state interest in the birth of children in registered marriage exclusively,[263] as well as the ceaseless preaching of prudish sex morals in all quarters, suggest that discrimination against the unmarried mother is far from a remote possibility. From this, it is only one step to full legal prejudice against "illegitimate" children, a prejudice which is now only partial.[264] With such reversal, the one principle of Marxian doctrine still applying to the masses of women would be the formal assurance of their equal legal rights as set forth in the Constitution.

The experiment in emancipation of women according to Marxist terms during the First Plan and part of the Second was an inconclusive test, proving nothing about the feasibility of the scheme at a later stage of Soviet development. The plea of men and women in fiction, "Let us get enough time for it, and we shall learn how to live," [265] failed. It has been tacitly admitted that the classic Marxian program for realization of women's potentialities in society is unworkable under present international conditions (and perhaps at any time), if the population law which Marx saw inherent in any social structure necessitates permanent interference and

[260] See Schlesinger, *Changing Attitudes,* pp. 401–5.

[261] Sverdlov, *Sovetskoe zakonodatel'stvo o brake i sem'e* (Moscow, 1949), p. 51.

[262] Sverdlov, "Soviet Laws on Family and Marriage," *Moscow News,* March 28, 1945.

[263] Sverdlov, "O predmete," p. 63.

[264] In addition to the lessened chances of education because of the father's release from responsibility (see p. 94), the child born outside marriage is now also deprived of the right to inherit from the father or to bear his name.

[265] Ehrenburg, *Out of Chaos,* p. 77.

control. Unless the present Soviet deadlock represents a temporary, localized contradiction between the Marxian doctrine of
emancipation and the need to gather forces in readiness for future
international struggle, then a new basis must be sought for social
equality of men and women, or the ideal abandoned. The myth of
its achievement on Marxian terms in the Soviet Union cannot be
endlessly perpetuated.

Straws in the postwar wind show that an interim solution was
being threshed out at a high policy level, under the goad of pressure from below. The press has voiced lively criticism of the dis-
continuance of coeducation in 1943,[266] of the failure to restore and
expand the network of institutions for child care and other household aids, of the handicaps created for women, and of the loss to
the economy of this potential labor power.[267] Significantly, Lenin's
diatribe against housework as the great oppressor was taken out of
mothballs. Whatever the next tack to be taken, there is a manifest
reluctance to repudiate openly the much publicized early Soviet
platform. Its grip on the popular mind has been too powerful, and
its international propaganda value too great. Most important, the
possibility of its future resurrection must be considered.[268]

The record of literature testifies that the original Marxian doctrine had gained the staunch adherence of Soviet women in industry. The reversal on principles risked the alienation of this large
and powerful segment of support for the regime. The ideological
conditioning of all the years up to 1935 was certainly not undone
overnight. The same success of the later objectives is conceivable
only if women had been so remade by "socialist" life that they have
knowingly acceded to their disadvantageous position for the sake
of survival on any terms, that is, for the sake of survival of the
state, still acquiescing in Lenin's definition of morality as rooted
in the struggle for the consolidation and completion of communism. But, to themselves at least, many women must have questioned whether the role allotted them after 1936 was a step toward

[266] See "The Discussion on Coeducation," *Soviet Studies,* II, No. 2 (October, 1950),
180–92; II, No. 3 (January, 1951), 322–24.   [267] See p. 105, note 253.

[268] In 1949, Sverdlov served notice that only wives physically incapable of work
have the right to expect support from their husbands (*Sovetskoe zakonodatel'stvo,*
p. 44). The abrupt reduction in 1947 of state payments for child support had warned
the mother that she could not expect to live by fecundity alone.

communism, and how compatible it was with the concept of "socialism in one country." Could the millions who "got on the tractor" or took to the lathe during the first two Plans be disposed of as cavalierly as those who balked at the first adaptation required of them in Soviet society? Can women disestablished after their strong early indoctrination have the same loyalty to the regime and inculcate it in their children within the family which that regime has forced them to patch up, under duress? What of the unified parental authority of which the publicists speak? Or is the authoritarian family being revived in which the mother perforce subordinates herself; and the children, taught discipline and submission to parental rule, will make it their nature to submit to government in general? How long are the memories of Soviet women, and what tension is generated in them and in the social organism as they balance their double load? Have they justified the Party conviction that people can be remade at will?

The circumspect official record will give no answers. We must turn to the brave men of belles-lettres. These questions are the very stuff of their practice. They cannot help but answer, in one guise or another.

What Soviet literature since 1936, and particularly since 1944, tells us on this score also tells us a great deal about later Soviet literature itself, about the task assigned it, about the role adopted by writers (whether by choice or by constraint), and about the extent to which fiction and drama have been free to mirror Soviet reality. As preliminary to an exploration of the answers, the present paper has been merely an attempt to define the point of departure for Soviet writers as they depict this one specific social situation, in a literature under stern restraints.

Bernard J. Choseed

Jews in Soviet Literature

I

ANY REPRESENTATIVE LIST of Soviet belles-lettres will inevitably include a considerable number of Jewish characters, as well as authors of Jewish origin. Of course, no literature reflects with complete faithfulness all aspects of a given society. This is not the role of creative literature whether in the USSR or elsewhere. Nevertheless, the special nature of Soviet literature, with its tendentiousness and "social commanding," suggests its usefulness for the study of social patterns and trends growing out of the complex and often paradoxical Soviet policy on national minorities. By using Russian literature as the primary source, as well as Yiddish and, to a lesser extent, Ukrainian literature as corroborative evidence, we shall try to see: how Jews have been presented in literature; what social patterns have been pictured; the relation between Jews and non-Jews; and, concomitantly, the attitudes and patterns of thinking, with relation to Jews, that have been imparted to the Soviet reading public.

Jews, of course, had appeared in Russian literature before the Revolution, invariably as stereotyped, often grotesque, and sometimes vitriolic caricatures. Even the "good" Jews, like Gogol's Zhid Iankel in *Taras Bul'ba* and Isai Fomich Bumshtein in Dostoyevsky's *House of the Dead*, combined the qualities of the clown and the vulture. At the end of the classic period, new stereotypes appeared —portrayals that betrayed the pangs of the Russian conscience rather than depicting the real, living Jew—in the sympathetic characterizations of Gorky, Andreev, and others.[1] Yiddish literature, too, by virtue of its continued emphasis on the little, pathetic,

[1] See Joshua Kunitz, *Russian Literature and the Jew* (New York, 1929).

comical characters (for example, in the works of Mendele Moikher Sforim and Sholem Aleikhem) pointed toward an equally typed national self-image, though one that lacked the unreality or malice implicit in the Russian picture. Both the Russian and Yiddish versions saw the Jew as a separate being, set apart from society as a whole, and both regarded his attempts to transcend national stigmata and enter into the more open arena of modern life as a tragic problem or as a matter for ridicule and contempt.

The Revolution, with its sweeping social and economic upheavals, lifted the bars of what had for so long been known as the "Prison of Nations." The initial abolishment of all religious and national distinctions was soon implemented by an official policy of guaranteeing the right to self-determination and "the free development of the national minorities and the ethnographic groups living within the confines of Russia." [2] These points were incorporated into the 1936 Constitution, Article 123 of which states:

Equal rights for citizens of the USSR, regardless of their nationality or race, in all spheres of economic, state, cultural, social, political life shall be an irrevocable law. Any direct or indirect limitations of these rights or, conversely, any establishment of direct or indirect privileges for citizens on account of their race or nationality, as well as any propagation of racial or national exclusiveness or hatred and contempt, shall be punishable by law.[3]

Other articles contain additional guarantees as to language, education, and legal proceedings; and specific provisions were also written into the criminal codes of the various republics.

These principles and decrees profoundly affected the ghetto character of Jewish life. Freed from the shackles of the Pale of Settlement and from the restrictions of the *numerus clausus* operative in all fields, Jews rushed forward into the turmoil of the new society. By 1939, almost 40 percent of the Jewish population lived outside the area of the former Pale; [4] and, although they represented only 1.78 percent of the total population of the USSR, approximately 10 percent of the entire intelligentsia, 17 percent of all doctors, and 10 percent of students in higher education were Jews.[5]

[2] V. I. Lenin, *On the Jewish Question* (New York, 1936), p. 21.
[3] *Konstitutsiia SSSR* (Moscow, 1938), p. 88.
[4] L. Zinger, *Dos banaite folk* (Moscow, 1941), p. 37.
[5] Harry Schwartz, "Has Russia Solved the Jewish Problem?" *Commentary*, II (February, 1948), 129.

Literature, too, shows the relatively high degree of prominence which Jews were able to attain in the general life of the country. Among the leading figures in Russian prose have been writers like Fink, Babel, Ehrenburg, Il'f, Grossman, Kaverin, Libedinskii; in poetry, Utkin, Bagritskii, Aliger, Svetlov, Marshak, Inber; in criticism, Lifshits, Gurshtein, Viner, Shklovskii, Bialik. Jews entered some of the other national literatures of the Soviet Union as well: in Ukrainian, Pervomaiskii, Rybak, Tikhii, Holovanivskii; and in Belorussian, Biadule, Kagan, and Zamerfeld.

II

With emancipation also came a drastic, if temporary, increase in Jewish misfortunes. During the period of civil war and intervention, the fiercest fighting somehow always took place in the areas most densely populated by Jews—and with the fighting came pogroms. Nikolai Ostrovskii's novel *The Making of a Hero* (1937) pictures one of these pogroms in the Jewish quarter of a Ukrainian town:

Many were never to forget those two horrible nights and three days. Innumerable lives were mutilated and ruined, innumerable young heads turned grey during those bloodstained hours. . . . It is even doubtful if those who remained among the living were happier, with their spirit laid waste from the ineffaceable shame and mockery they had suffered . . . with that ache of the heart for the near ones lost.[6]

The Jewish towns were devastated, and for those who survived the future seemed very dismal indeed. "My people will die with a kiss on the fields of the Revolution," [7] mourned the Yiddish poet S. Halkin, and for well over a decade after the Revolution, Soviet Yiddish poetry was filled primarily with this lament for what the Jews had gone through during the years of battle. Later literary critics aptly termed this period in poetry the "Wailing Period."

In much the same way, some of the Jewish characters who first appeared in Soviet Russian literature were in many instances too overwhelmed by events to be cognizant of the changes that were taking place. In many cases the tie with the old stereotype was very close. This was true in the works of Isaak Babel, who during his

[6] Ostrovsky, *The Making of a Hero (Kak zakalialas' stal'* [How the Steel Was Tempered]), trans. A. Brown (New York, 1937), p. 93.

[7] S. Dimanshtein, ed., *Yidn in FSSR* (Moscow, 1935), p. 145.

chief creative period presented a series of romantic "little" Jews of the Wailing Period. In his popular collection of tales, *Red Cavalry* (1926), about the Polish campaign of 1920–21, he described several of the Jewish towns and people he encountered. Of one small town, he wrote: "A violent smell of rotten herrings emanates from all its inhabitants. The little town reeks on awaiting a new era; and instead of human beings there go about mere shadows of frontier misfortunes." [8] Babel's Jews are still caricatures, although true to life; they are helpless and confused, much as their counterparts in real life, who were horrified by the pogroms and then puzzled when their "saviors," the Bolsheviks, called many of them class enemies. Old Ghedali, a poor little trader, sits in front of his crumbling house in Zhitomir and tries to reason with a Red soldier:

"Then how is Ghedali to tell which is the Revolution and which is the counter-revolution? . . . The Poles are bad tempered dogs. They take the Jew and tear at his beard, the curs! . . . And then those who beat the Poles say to me: 'Give up your gramophone for a possible requisition, Ghedali.' " [9]

This was the tragedy of the poor, middle-class Jew, of Tevye and Menakhem Mendl, who clung tenaciously to the little property and trade that remained to them. And as they appear in Babel's tales, the unmistakable stamp of the ghetto is still with them. The one exception, a rabbi's son who joins the Communists, is still a frail, oversensitive "little" Jew, even though a Bolshevik.

The Soviet literary critics, while praising Babel and putting him on a level with Flaubert, found much to complain of in these romantic, bewildered characters. Of course, since Babel himself came from the milieu he described, none of the critics found fault with the so-called "Jewish traits" of his characters. One critic, however, felt that the sketches of Ghedali and the rabbi's son showed Babel's own sympathies torn between the old and the new. In the journal *New World,* Polonskii wrote: "In *Red Cavalry,* the rugged iron of Lenin's skull and the faded silken portraits of Maimonedes live side by side. But they cannot go on living in peace. . . . Maimonedes is incompatible with Lenin." [10] Later Babel came under increasing attack for failing to go further than his pathetic wail-

[8] Babel, *Red Cavalry* (*Konarmiia* [Cavalry], 1926), trans. N. Helstein (New York, 1929), p. 122. [9] *Ibid.,* p. 31.
[10] V. Polonskii, "Kriticheskie zametki o Babele," *Novyi mir,* No. 1 (1927), p. 286.

ing Jews and his picturesque Odessa jargon. In 1933, the critic
Plotkin declared that Babel showed only the ideology of the petty-
bourgeois intelligentsia, who, while accepting the Revolution, "frequently exaggerated the element of violence inherent in every
social change, and painfully sought justification in the negative
aspects of the Revolution." [11]

This lack of perspective on the part of many Jews may have been
annoying, but it was real; the persistence of the hopeless "little"
Jew down through Five-Year Plan literature is ample proof. Even
more annoying were those Jews who engaged in active opposition
to the Revolution because of political convictions,[12] or because
they had been successful bourgeoisie under the old regime. In his
novel *A Week* (1922), Iurii Libedinskii presented an interesting
member of this latter group in the person of Rafael Antonovich
Senator, a dispossessed former druggist in a revolution-wracked
town in the Urals. Senator mourns his vanished glory and writhes
whenever he passes his old shop with the new sign, "Communal
Drug Store No. 1." Out of his almost pathological hatred for the
Communists, Senator offers his home as a secret meeting place for
a group of Whites, despite the fact that they refer to him as *zhid*.[13]
When the White revolt breaks out, Senator gleefully faces a captured Communist leader and says: "They will shoot you all, like
mad dogs, and tomorrow I shall take down the placard from my
shop. Do you hear? From *my* shop. Yes, I am rich. You hear, I am
a bourgeois. . . . I was a bourgeois, and always will be one." [14]

The Senators, however, were exceptions. Sooner or later, the mass
of Jewish population sided with the Bolsheviks, perhaps not so
much for political reasons as for the fact that everywhere counterrevolution and antisemitism marched hand in hand. But there were
also many Jews who had been associated with left-wing movements
before the Revolution and became active participants in it when the

[11] L. Plotkin, "Tvorchestvo Babelia," *Oktiabr'*, No. 3 (1933), p. 180.

[12] The major Jewish political parties, ranging from the socialist Bund to the
conservative Ahduth, all opposed the Bolsheviks. See Jacob Lestchinsky, "Jews in the
USSR" (reprinted from *Contemporary Jewish Record*, September–October, November–
December, 1940), p. 5.

[13] *Zhid* in Russian is a derogatory term denoting "Jew"; it has been eliminated from
public usage since the Revolution. See D. N. Ushakov, ed., *Tolkovyi slovar' russkogo
iazyka*, Moscow, 1935.

[14] Libedinsky, *A Week* (*Nedelia*, 1922), trans. A. Ransome (New York, 1932), pp.
180–81.

upheaval began. It was from these people that Soviet literature drew its first Jewish hero types and set the pattern for almost all the later Jewish "positive heroes."

Another novel by Libedinskii, *Commissars* (1926), features a Jewish commissar, Iosif Mindlov, in a leading role. Although the scene is laid at the close of the Civil War, all the characters in the novel have only recently returned from the battlefields. Mindlov's nationality is not stressed, but the physiognomy of the "total Bolshevik" is true to the stereotype: curly black hair, a hooked nose, a weak body, and a habit of hissing "the disdainful, eternally Jewish *psst*." [15] He has a weakness for introspection: "Here I am, an intellectual and even the son of a big bourgeois—so what? A Marxist must thoroughly acknowledge his class being to himself, and he must understand that being a Communist means he must adopt the point of view of the proletariat." [16] Although seriously ill with tuberculosis, Mindlov almost sacrifices his life to organize a school for practically illiterate commissars. So ardent is his devotion to the Party that even his superiors marvel at his perseverance. Mindlov is a model of virtue and always makes the right decisions with almost monotonous regularity. In the generally favorable reviews and articles on *Commissars,* Mindlov received his share of attention, but his Jewish origin practically none whatsoever. Only one writer found Mindlov's nationality worthy of mention. I. Kleinman, in 1929, wrote that the innately "Jewish" in Mindlov lay in that his physical description is "as characteristic for him as are his external exaltation and combustion." [17] The main body of critics examined Mindlov as a Soviet-hero type and not as a member of any particular national group.

It is especially interesting to note that from these early heroes [18] has come one of the most important of all the heroes in Soviet literature, Alexander Fadeev's Levinson, in *The Nineteen,* written in 1926. The central character in the novel is Osip Abramovich Levinson, who valiantly guides a partisan detachment through the fighting in Siberia during the Japanese intervention. He is por-

[15] Libedinskii, *Kommissary* (Leningrad, 1926), p. 76.

[16] *Ibid.,* p. 83.

[17] Kleinman, "Evrei v noveishei russkoi literature," in *Evreiskii vestnik,* ed. S. Ginzburg (Leningrad, 1928), p. 163.

[18] Among them, mention should also be made of Iosif Kogan, the commissar hero in Bagritskii's famous poem "The Elegy on Opanas" (*Duma pro Opanasa,* 1926).

116 *Jews in Soviet Literature*

trayed as a fearless, disciplined Communist with a red beard, a frail body, but with the "indomitable will of past generations," and a "patience and an obstinacy which were alike rare." [19] He displays the decisiveness and almost machinelike will power that have become the trademarks of the positive heroes of literature. Like Mindlov, Levinson is physically weak, and occasionally he accuses himself of spiritual weakness as well. He remembers that his father was a second-hand furniture dealer who "all his life had dreamed of becoming rich, but was afraid of mice and played the violin very badly." [20] But Levinson is far removed from his father and the old way of life; he is with the new and he knows why:

He had crushed in himself everything that he had inherited from past generations brought up on the lying tales of pretty little birds! . . . To see everything as it is, in order to change everything that is, to control everything that is . . . Levinson achieved this wisdom, the simplest and the most difficult a man can achieve.[21]

Throughout the novel, Levinson appears as a new, positive man who has broken with his past and has not only joined, but is actually leading, the revolutionary forces.

The majority of the critics hailed *The Nineteen* as a great event in Russian literature, and its prestige has remained undiminished with the years. There were, however, very definite objections to Fadeev's psychological approach, one that overlooked external features as well as significant background data. One critic asked: "But surely Levinson must have lived a personal life. Surely, he must have had sex, nationality . . . personal associations?" [22] and concluded that Levinson was too geometric. But a later critic pointed out that Levinson seemingly ignores family and personal life not because they are incompatible with him, but "because he cannot busy himself with creating his own personal life at this moment. For Levinson, the revolutionary struggle is his personal business as well." [23] None of the critics who were favorable touched on Levinson's national origin. Lezhnëv, however, who was not par-

[19] Fadeyev, *The Nineteen* (*Razgrom* [Rout]), trans. R. Charques (New York, 1929), p. 31.   [20] *Ibid.*, p. 65.
[21] *Ibid.*, p. 207.
[22] V. Pravdukhin, "Molodoe vino," *Krasnaia nov'*, No. 5 (1927), p. 240.
[23] M. Serebrianskii, " 'Razgrom' Fadeeva," *Literaturnyi kritik*, No. 10–11 (1937), p. 181.

ticularly impressed, exhibited an interesting sensitivity. He argued that the anecdotal tone set by Levinson's red beard, his father's violin, and the "lying tales of pretty little birds" indicated that Fadeev did not know much about the milieu from which Levinson had come: "There is nothing indispensable in Levinson's physical weakness, in his red-beardedness, or even in his Jewishness. These are all accidental traits—Levinson might just as well not be a Jew at all. There is nothing specifically Jewish in him." [24] But the same writer who had found Mindlov so "Jewish" also answered Lezhnëv's questions about Levinson. In his critical microscope he discovered that Fadeev had deliberately not given Levinson "either Russian impetuousness or Russian boldness. So, in his own way, without using emphasis or characteristically Jewish expressions, Fadeev has given us an interesting, living portrait of a fighter-Jew." [25] The question of "Jewishness," whether much or little, played no role in the official praise that followed Levinson through the years, until he became a part of Soviet literary catechism. An editorial in 1941, honoring Soviet soldiers in the Finnish War, said: "Not a few have learned their bravery and courage from the heroes of these books— from Chapaev, from Levinson, from Pavel Korchagin." [26] By 1947, *The Nineteen* was the most popular, after Sholokhov's, of all works of fiction written during the Soviet period, and had been published in 75 editions, in 16,250,000 copies.[27] And to the Soviet high-school student of 1950, Levinson was presented as a "particularly significant" hero because "basically, what is shown in him is the Party during the Revolution." [28]

The author even more popular than Fadeev, Mikhail Sholokhov, in his epic novel *And Quiet Flows the Don,* also pictures a Jew of this early group, although in a less important role. Anna Pogudko, a memorable figure in the episodes of the Civil War in the Rostov region, emerges more nationally defined and less open to question

[24] A. Lezhnëv, "O 'Razgrom' Fadeeva," *Novyi mir,* No. 8 (1927), pp. 173–74.
[25] Kleinman, "Evrei v noveishei russkoi literature," p. 163.
[26] "Dolg sovetskoi literatury," *Molodaia gvardiia,* No. 2 (1941), p. 6. Chapaev is the hero of D. Furmanov's *Chapaev;* Pavel Korchagin, of Ostrovskii's previously cited *The Making of a Hero.*
[27] N. Matusev, "Ob izdanii khudozhestvennoi literatury v SSSR za tridtsat' let," *Znamia,* No. 11 (1947), p. 187.
[28] L. I. Timofeev, *Russkaia sovetskaia literatura* (Moscow, 1950), p. 327; this was a textbook for the 10th class.

than Levinson. When the nineteen-year-old girl joins a machine-gun detachment, the commander, Bunchuk, asks her:

"Are you Ukrainian?"
She hesitated for a moment, then firmly replied, "No."
"A Jewess?"
"Yes, but how did you know? Do I talk like one? . . ."
"Your ear—the shape of your ears, and your eyes. . . . It's good that you're with us."
"Why?" . . .
"Well, the Jews have a certain reputation. And I know that many workers believe it to be true—you see I am a worker, too—that the Jews only do all the ordering and never go under fire themselves. That is not true, and you will prove splendidly that it isn't true." [29]

While Anna's mother speaks Yiddish and is obviously of the old pattern, there is little in the novel to indicate how Anna made the transition to the new. But Anna is not a mechanical Communist. Her devotion to the cause is humanized by her love for Bunchuk and her hatred for death. Yet, when the test comes, Anna is as exalted as Mindlov and, giving up her personal life, courageously meets death in an attack on the Whites.

Thus, from these first Jewish heroes, it can be seen that not all Jews were in mourning during the early period. The Revolution had opened the gates for Jewish heroes in literature as well as in real life.[30] That a Levinson could be created by a Russian author and could achieve such high acclaim is a significant sign of the fundamental changes that had taken place. Not only was a Jewish Communist hero something very new in the pages of Russian literature, but also he was a new Jewish type. His plane of action was not confined to his own national horizon, but was extended to society as a whole. Even at this early date, he had stopped using Yiddish as his language of daily communication, and he was not preoccupied with the "Jewish Problem." The very term "Jew," therefore, while still denoting a specific group origin and a common upbringing, now had to be broken down into the Yiddish speaking people, living in nationally homogeneous groups and

[29] Sholokhov, *And Quiet Flows the Don* (*Tikhii Don* [The Quiet Don], 1928–40), trans. S. Garry (New York, 1945), p. 426.
[30] Jewish figures at the top level of the new regime included Communist leaders like Trotsky, Sverdlov, Kamenev, and Zinov'ev.

cherishing the national traditions and mores, and people no longer using Yiddish who had moved into heterogeneous situations. This was not a completely new phenomenon in Jewish history, but the social conditions engendered by the Revolution greatly facilitated the transition from the first group into the second.

III

The introduction of the New Economic Policy in 1922 seemed to offer new hope to the less idealistic Jews. With trading once more free, a large number returned to the only profession they had ever known; some prospered and entered the pages of literature as the notorious "NEP Jews." At the same time, some of the Communist Jews carried the "social abstractness" of the era to extremes that created types as ludicrous and fixed as the anti-Soviet Nepmen.

Sergei Malashkin's story *The Moon on the Right Side* became a literary *cause célèbre* when it appeared in 1926. Attempting to satirize what he felt was the degeneracy of the younger generation, Malashkin pictured a group of Komsomols in drunken and dope-filled orgies called "Athenian Nights." One of the leaders of the group is Izaik Chuzhachok,[31] whom Malashkin pictures as "of slight stature; his face and body were shriveled, his pinched face looked like a canoe, and had only three points of interest—a big red nose, yellow, protruding, rapacious teeth, and two beadlike coffee-colored eyes." [32] Izaik is a fop, and is fond of expounding his ideas on free love to every girl he meets. His friends openly poke fun at the trace of a Jewish accent that he diligently tries to hide, but Izaik considers himself above his origin. "I am an internationalist," he says, and brags that back home in the Ukraine he was known as a "little Trotsky." [33] Despite this crude caricature, the critics remained oblivious to any of the implications. One, in fact, wrote of Izaik: "His external and internal aspects . . . give a clear and correct type of 'fop' met among the Komsomols at some of our large centers of higher education." [34] The story was roundly attacked for

---

[31] The name in Russian means "little alien."

[32] Trans. in Kunitz, *Russian Literature and The Jew*, p. 179.

[33] Malashkin, *Luna s pravoi storony* (Moscow, 1926), p. 92.

[34] V. Klechkovskii, "Luna s pravoi storony," *Na literaturnom postu*, No. 8 (1927), p. 47.

portraying Communist youth in a pornographic light, and was
officially denounced as "sex degeneracy" in 1932 in the *Literary
Encyclopedia*.[35]

From 1927 to 1929 there appeared a series of novels about the
NEP with Jewish speculators in the leading roles. One of these,
Minus Six, by Matvei Roizman, has the typical pattern of cunning,
avaricious NEP Jews. Aaron Solomonovich Fishbein, whose shady
past includes robbing his own father, stalks through a series of
NEP intrigues until he is apprehended and exiled from Moscow.
Fishbein does not quite grasp the tremendous changes that have
taken place; when Sverdlov dies, he grumbles, "I don't understand
what this excitement is all about. Such a parade? There's only a
Jew lying there—like any other Jew!" [36] But he knows enough to
try to thwart everything Soviet. When the NEP is first proclaimed,
he maliciously says, "To us it means: New Exploitation of the Proletariat!" [37] In the course of events, Fishbein eagerly courts the
good graces of violently antisemitic Russian Nepmen. The presence of a Russian Nepman of course suggests impartiality, but
most of Roizman's interest is centered on the Jews. By means of a
steady flow of religious references, half-Yiddish sentences, and
smutty anecdotes, Roizman leaves no doubt as to the "Jewishness"
of his characters. The fact that Roizman himself was of Jewish
origin did not save him from hostile attacks by all the critics. The
nature of the charges against him were in the vein of Rozental's:
"As Roizman presents it, all trade, with rare exceptions, is in the
hands of Jews. Subjectively, the author wants to whitewash the
Soviet regime—since it *is* for the Jews. But objectively, the novel
can play into the hands of the antisemites." [38]

A Jewish Nepman quite different from Fishbein appeared in
Rable's Factory, a novel by Mikhail Chumandrin. Mark Iakovlevich
Rable, the owner of a chocolate plant, is almost an active supporter
of the Soviet order. He argues that even his desire to make money
is not so selfish as it sounds. "The principle of profit is not important
to me," he says. "The setting up of a goal and its attainment, this is
what fascinates me." [39] Although he has his bad sides, including a

[35] "Malashkin," *Literaturnaia entsiklopediia*, VI (1932), 735.
[36] Roizman, *Minus shest'* (Moscow, 1930), p. 61.   [37] *Ibid.*, p. 99.
[38] S. Rozental', "Minus shest'," *Krasnaia nov'*, No. 8 (1928), p. 285.
[39] Chumandrin, *Fabrika Rabl'* (Leningrad, 1929), p. 6.

mistress and a fondness for sweets, he is pictured as a skillful, careful, and calculating businessman, with none of the "Jewish" traits
that were attributed to Fishbein. The critics were largely inclined
to dwell on the ideological aspects of *Rable's Factory,* and found
little to quarrel about in Rable himself. On the surface everything
appeared in order: the novel seemed to meet the "social command,"
and was moreover written by a leading member of the Association
of Proletarian Writers. But in 1930, an analyst of antisemitism,
L. Radishchev, had this to say: "Chumandrin never uses the word
'Jew,' he says nothing about the Jewish origin of Rable. . . . He
needs a Nepman for his novel and he knows that the Nepman must
be a Jew." [40] Radishchev saw something very ominous in the continued appearance of literature in which Jews played such a large
role on the counterrevolutionary side, and he pointed out that "in
the era of socialist realism, the 'principle of pairs,' 'parallels,' and
'proportionality' have become necessary so that the spectator, the
listener, and the reader should not draw socially dangerous conclusions." [41]

Radishchev's attack was not accidental. During the late twenties,
many readers had been drawing "socially dangerous conclusions,"
not only from certain literary works, but from other sources as well,
and antisemitism once more showed itself in public.

A Yiddish play by Perets Markish, "The Fifth Level" (1933),
touches on antisemitic manifestations at the beginning of the First
Five-Year Plan. Two Jewish workers come from the Ukraine to
work in a Donbass coal mine. The miners, hesitant to use new
machinery, are even more reluctant to work together with Jews.
A committee, headed by a Central Asian, Gulai Beda, goes to see
the head technician Prokopenko. Beda complains: "Work with a
Jew? A miner can never work with a Jew or with an old lady. . . .
Since they've come to the mines, we've had nothing but wrecks and
troubles." [42]

A similar situation occurs in a Yiddish novel about small-town
Jewish youths who have come to help in the construction of a blast
furnace. At first, they encounter opposition from some of the Rus-

[40] Radishchev, *Iad—ob antisemitizme nashikh dnei* (Leningrad, 1930), pp. 118–19.
[41] *Ibid.,* p. 106.
[42] Markish, "Der finfter horizont," *P'esn* (Moscow, 1933), p. 100.

sian and Tatar workers. One night, each of the Jewish group finds a note on his bed which reads:

> Can Jews do anything?
> If they try to weld, their eyes smart!
> If they start drilling, their ears hurt! [43]

The Jewish boys and girls accept the challenge and propose to meet the situation by doing even more work in the factory.

In literature, antisemitism is shown as halted by non-Jewish Communists. The Jews involved have faith in the official utterances on their behalf and fight antisemitism by proving their worth as active participants in socialist construction. Those who instigate antisemitism are clearly portrayed as counterrevolutionary elements, as kulaks in the village, as saboteurs in the mine, or as wreckers in the factory.

The campaign to stamp out these renewed manifestations was vigorously pushed in all fields. The press carried reports of trials against antisemites; [44] *agitprop* (agitation and propaganda) literature was turned out in considerable quantity with titles like *Who Slanders the Jews and Why, Hatred of Jews,* and *The Truth about the Jews.*

Russian literature, too, saw several works directed against antisemitism,[45] among them Mikhail Kozakov's "The Man Who Kisses the Ground" (1928),[46] which is particularly interesting in view of the critical reactions it aroused. In the brief space of his work, Kozakov manages to squeeze in all aspects of antisemitism: from the passive variety exhibited by a commissar who feels that an eligible Jew should not be given a leading factory post for fear that this will arouse antisemitism, to the violent type shown by a group of workers who mutilate a Jewish beggar. Basically, the Jews presented by Kozakov are still the "little" Jews of Babel and prerevolutionary literature, and it was just this that one critic singled out for attack:

[43] H. Orland, *Aglomerat* (Kiev, 1935), p. 31.

[44] For one such trial see reports on the Barshai trial, *Izvestiia,* Jan. 6, 16, 18–20, 1929.

[45] Including Dmitrii Stonov, *Sem'ia raskinikh* (The Raskin Family [a novel]; Moscow, 1929); Roizman, *Eti gospoda* (*These Gentlemen* [a novel]; Moscow, 1932); and M. Mal'tsev, *Sud nad antisemitizmom* (The Case against Antisemitism [a play]; Leningrad, 1928).

[46] Kozakov, "Chelovek padaiushchii nits," *Zvezda,* No. 4 (1928), pp. 5–45.

For Kozakov, the persecuted Jew is largely the personification of the little man in general, a man who must be *pitied* because he is unhappy and forgotten. Therefore, Kozakov's tales, despite their thematic reality and dynamic quality, hardly arouse the conscience and the psyche of the reader against antisemitism.[47]

As a rule, the critics showed no hesitancy in criticizing "The Man Who Kisses the Ground" and other works directed against anti-semitism. They were consistent in demanding accurateness and careful analysis rather than good intentions coupled with journalistic reportage.

Political leaders and critics took pains to interpret the pattern of antisemitism as a continuation of the old alliance of the Whites with racial and national hatred. There remained, however, the chagrin caused by the appearance of antisemitism even among supposedly class-conscious elements. Radishchev in his examination of the problem concluded:

The October Revolution has solved the National Question. . . . But national impatience has not been wiped out. . . . The political essence of antisemitism is hidden from many workers, even from those who are conscious Communists. . . . Antisemitism is a flag, a screen behind which hides the counterrevolution.[48]

IV

For the many Jews still living in the small towns, the NEP period was not always the sensational event that the series of speculators and antisemitic disturbances might seem to indicate. Although by 1926, the number of traders had fallen to 11.5 percent, some 32.3 percent of all Jews were still classed as "unproductive." [49]

"The Outcome," a Yiddish story by S. Persov, describes a typical Jewish small town of this period. Faivl Shub, a cranky disadvantaged Jew, together with his equally cranky wife and son, operates a tumble-down pub in the marketplace. He talks disparagingly of the Soviet government that wants him to give up his business, and is panic-stricken when his house is mortgaged for arrears. A Jewish tax collector comes to the house, sees the misery, and asks Shub: "What will be the outcome?" Faivl retorts, "That's what I say!

---

[47] A. Tarasenkov, " 'Chelovek padaiushchii nits,' " *Mol. gvardiia*, No. 9 (1929), p. 105.
[48] Radishchev, *Iad—ob antisemitizme*, p. 49.
[49] Zinger, *Yidn proletarier in FSSR* (Moscow, 1933), p. 6.

What will come of one Jew slaughtering another without a knife?"
The tax agent, a somewhat overconscientious Party member, who
has taken on himself the entire burden of his disenfranchised
brethren, replies: "I am speaking about what will come of your
just sitting here? Of business like this? And what will become of
that youngster?" [50] Faivl is finally convinced that the only way out
of his dilemma is to sign up as a settler in the Crimea.

It was for solving the problem of these small-town Jews that the
Soviet government had set up various Jewish administrative and
organizational bodies. The Jewish Commissariat, the *Evsektsii*,[51]
and the OZET,[52] together and in turn, concentrated on helping the
unproductive Jews to enter new occupations and industry, particularly to settle on the land. Large tracts were set aside for Jewish
colonists in the Ukraine and in the Crimea, and some of these grew
into Jewish National Districts. By 1939, in addition to Jewish farm
areas in the Ukraine and Belorussia, there were five Jewish National Districts: Kalinindorf, Nai Zlotopol, and Stalindorf in the
Ukraine; Fraidorf and Larindorf in the Crimea. An article in a
literary journal in 1938 painted a glowing picture of Stalindorf:

The endless collective fields, the pastures, the truck-gardens, the or-
chards, the vineyards, and of course, the tractors, the combines, the
threshing machines, the machine-tractor stations on the steppe . . .
the socialist competition. The sunburned faces—in a word: life at work,
like everywhere else in the Soviet Union.[53]

The end of the NEP also saw further steps in the utilization of
national feelings to help bring about social and economic changes.
The fervor that political Zionism had once aroused for a single
Jewish national homeland was now channeled into realizing such
a state within the confines of the USSR [54] and coupled with the
specific needs of the Five-Year Plan. The project to develop a
Jewish state in the 15,000-square-mile area of Birobidzhan in the
Far East was initiated on March 28, 1928, and the call for settlers
was sent throughout foreign as well as Soviet Jewish communities.

[50] S. Persov, "Takhles," *Tog un nakht* (Moscow, 1933), p. 179.

[51] Evreiskie kommunisticheskie sektsii (Jewish Sections of the Communist Party).

[52] Obshchestvo zemleustroistva evreev trudiashchikhsia (Society for the Settlement
on Land of Toiling Jews).

[53] Viktor Fink, "Evreiskii vopros," *Krasnaia nov'*, No. 12 (1938), p. 210.

[54] Thus in 1928, an Odessa Yiddish newspaper (*Di gezerd shtim*, April 1, 1928)
carried the headlines, "Far vos epis Biro-bidzhan un nit Palestine?" (Why Birobidzhan
and not Palestine?).

But while the appeals abroad stressed the national aspects of the undertaking, internally specific emphasis was placed on changing the character of the people who went there. In a Yiddish novel about Birobidzhan, a young settler on his way to the area turns to a friend and asks: " '*Nu,* Comrade Motl Shklover, what was it you said this would be called? What is it that we're going to build here?' His friend answers: 'It is really very simple. Is it really so hard to remember? We are going to build—Socialism.' " [55]

The project was carefully kept from becoming a "ghetto" venture: no Jews were arbitrarily "shipped" to Birobidzhan and nothing in the setup of the new area prevented non-Jews from participating; but in the early years the Soviets gave generous aid and support in an organized fashion primarily to Jewish settlers. Birobidzhan saw considerable development in agriculture and in industry, and on May 7, 1934, amid much heraldry, achieved the status of the Jewish Autonomous Region in the Russian Soviet Federated Socialist Republic, and was duly listed as such in Article 22 of the 1936 Constitution. Despite the comparatively small number of Jews in the Region,[56] Soviet leaders pointed out that the existence of a large political area with Yiddish as the state language and with Yiddish cultural institutions would insure the continuity of the Jews as a nationality.[57] The Region was used as a rallying point for Jewish culture and sentiment. Yiddish writers visited it frequently and came back with works that received wide circulation in both Yiddish and Russian. One of the leading Yiddish poets, Itsik Fefer, wrote:

> With all other peoples, hand in hand,
> We have here our home, a Stalinite land.[58]

However, Birobidzhan in no sense superseded Jewish projects in other parts of the Union,[59] and legally had no authority over

[55] David Bergelson, *Birobidzhaner* (Moscow, 1934), p. 47.

[56] Of the 108,400 total population of Birobidzhan in 1939, "over 20,000" were Jews (M. Chekalin, "Vozrozhdenie narodnostei i konsolidatsiia natsii v SSSR," *Pod znamenem marksizma,* No. 10 [1939], p. 25). The 1939 census listed 3,020,171 Jews in the Soviet Union as a whole (Zinger, *Dos banaite folk,* p. 126).

[57] See Kalinin's speech in 1934, quoted by Dimanshtein, *Yidn in FSSR,* p. 32.

[58] Fefer, "Birobijan March," in *The Golden Peacock,* ed. and trans. J. Leftwich (London, 1939), p. 221.

[59] Agitation, for example, to settle Jews on land in the Crimea continued all through the thirties. The Moscow *Emes,* Feb. 15, 1938, complained that the 1937 quota of planned settlers had not been met in full.

Jews outside the Region itself. Pride was taken in the fact that
Birobidzhan had contributed the marble for one of the Moscow
Metro stations, and at the All-Union Agricultural Exposition in
Moscow in 1938–39 the JAR had its own pavilion. But in view of
the largely non-Jewish ethnic make-up of the Region, it is not
surprising that from the end of the thirties less and less mention
was being made of Birobidzhan as a "national center" of Soviet
Jewish life. While the number of Jewish migrants kept falling, the
area continued to grow, on the basis of echelons composed of other
nationalities. The latter were welcomed with the same hospitality
and help as were the earlier settlers.[60] A new spurt of government-
aided Jewish migration took place during 1946–48;[61] and by the
end of 1946 the circulation of the Region's Yiddish newspaper was
double that of 1939.[62] This, however, did not perceptibly alter the
former trends. Success was measured in terms of the number of
schools and doctors, not in terms of the number of Yiddish schools
and Jewish doctors. The national aspects that were still being
stressed occasionally abroad, or even in the Moscow Yiddish press,
played no role in the Yiddish publications of the Region itself. Russians, Ukrainians, Koreans, and Jews were all regarded as valid
members of the JAR, and all were pictured as proud of being "Birobidzhaners." As the external significance of the JAR decreased, internally it expanded and developed as an efficient part of the Soviet
Far East, and in 1950 its capital city, Birobidzhan, was described as
"one of the new industrial cities" of the Khabarovsk Krai.[63] Although the JAR eventually lost its exclusiveness as "the only Jewish state in the world," during the thirties and forties it acquired
importance as a symbol of Jewish nationality, particularly as a symbol of the Soviet nationalities policy—as opposed to the solution
offered by the Germans. In a Birobidzhan Yiddish play about the
Second World War, "He Is from Birobidzhan," a Russian officer

[60] See reports on Russian and Ukrainian settlers from Kursk, in *Birobidzhan shtern*,
Dec. 28, 1940, and Jan. 1, 1941.

[61] The Moscow *Einikait* carried an editorial on Feb. 28, 1946, under the banner
"Tsum veiterdikn ufbli fun der yidisher avtonomer gegnt" (To the further development of the Jewish Autonomous Region); it carried reports on decrees, echelons, and
so on, through 1948.

[62] In 1939 the *Birobidzhan shtern* had a circulation of 1,500 (*Ezhegodnik periodicheskikh izdanii SSSR* [Moscow, 1940], I, 31; in 1946, 3,000 (*Letopis' periodicheskikh
izdanii SSSR 1946* [Moscow, 1947], p. 197).

[63] "Birobidzhan," *Bol'shaia sovetskaia entsiklopediia*, 2d ed., V (1950), 250.

at the front says of the Jewish hero: "Looking at this young lieutenant who has come here from Birobidzhan, I kept thinking: the ravines with slaughtered Jews—that is his accomplishment, Hitler's. But this commander of a sapper platoon, and the place he comes from—this is our achievement, the Soviet achievement." [64]

Stalin had defined a nation as "an historically evolved, stable community of language, territory, economic life, and psychological make-up." [65] When he made this statement in 1913, the Jews in Russia lacked the qualification of territory, and their economic life was certainly not that which Stalin must have had in mind. But in language, at the time of the Revolution, the Jews did qualify; [66] and the right to speak, learn, and create in Yiddish was not only guaranteed, but a large network of Yiddish schools and cultural institutions was set up with state support wherever Jews lived. Within the general framework of Soviet society, and under the specific demands of the "dictatorship of the proletariat," the Yiddish-speaking Jews in a relatively short time succeeded in creating a Soviet Yiddish culture of real quality and quantity. At the high point in 1933, the four leading Yiddish publishing houses put out an aggregate of 391 titles in 1,351,000 copies. [67]

Yiddish literature, taking as its own the heritage of the prerevolutionary Yiddish classics, produced writers and poets who achieved significance throughout the Soviet Union, as well as among Jews. Prose writers like Bergelson and Daniel and poets like Kvitko, Fefer, Hofshtein, and Markish received their due share of official awards and honors. Their works were accepted as part of the culture of the Soviet Union as a whole: between 1922 and 1939, Perets Markish's works appeared in 1,193,000 copies, in three languages; and the works of Leib Kvitko, 1928–39, appeared in 6,429,000 copies, in 22 languages. [68]

Like all the other literatures of the USSR, Yiddish literature was conditioned by Stalin's definition of national culture in Soviet society, as "a culture socialist in its content and national in its form,

[64] Buzi Miler, "Er iz fun Birobidzhan," *Birobidzhan*, No. 3 (1947), pp. 37–38.
[65] Joseph Stalin, *Marxism and the National and Colonial Question* (New York, 1935), p. 6.
[66] In 1897, 97 percent of the Jews used Yiddish (Zinger, *Evreiskoe naselenie v SSSR* [Moscow, 1932], p. 27).
[67] Dimanshtein, *Yidn in FSSR*, p. 169.
[68] *Tsifry o pechati SSSR* (Moscow, 1940), pp. 57, 60.

having as its object to educate the masses in the spirit of internationalism and consolidate the dictatorship of the proletariat." [69]
Unlike the various Jewish organizations and projects, Yiddish literature, in the process of fulfilling the social command, retained many
distinct national features for a longer period. Whereas Russian
literature had the task of guiding workers and peasants into socialism, Yiddish literature first had to make Jews into workers and
peasants and then guide them into socialism. This "double transformation" left very distinctive impressions on the pages of Yiddish letters. And while Russian literature agitated against all forms
of national hatred, Yiddish in its turn agitated against any emphasis
on the differences between Jews and non-Jews. The poet Fefer once
said: "We are against national exclusiveness. . . . Our Soviet Yiddish literature, our culture, is growing and developing thanks to
the fight against nationalism." [70]

The end of the thirties witnessed the transformation of the Soviet
Union into an industrialized and collectivized state, and the transformation of the Jews as a whole into a "productive" group. The
1939 census showed the following social grouping of all Jews in the
USSR by percentage: [71]

Workers and employees	71.2
Collective farmers	5.8
Cooperative artisans	16.1
Independent artisans	4.0
Others	2.9

Thus, in Soviet eyes, Jewry was changed from a separate, petty-
bourgeois milieu into one that was a contributing part of the society
in which it lived, no longer the "alien" and "corruptive" element
that the Slavophiles had called it in the nineteenth century.

It is not indicated in the data just cited what percentage of the
"workers and employees" consisted of industrial proletarians and
what percentage of Jews in managerial positions, in office work, in
administrative positions, in the arts and the professions. In Russian
literature the number of Jewish factory workers is much smaller
than the number in supervisory and higher posts. In the case of
agriculture, the occurrence of Jews in Russian collective farm litera-

[69] Stalin, *Marxism and the National and Colonial Question*, p. 401.
[70] Fefer, "A natsionalistisher paskvil," *Einikait*, March 2, 1948.
[71] Zinger, *Dos banaite folk*, p. 46.

ture is rare (excluding works devoted to specifically Jewish collective farms). Yiddish literature on the other hand, did focus largely on manual laborers and peasants. Once the bars were lifted, no propaganda was needed to make Jews enter the offices and the professions: the old reverence for education and for the security and prestige of the professions found scope in reality.

V

This process of transformation involved a dramatic struggle, not necessarily a political one, between anti-Soviet and pro-Soviet elements; more often than not it was a deep emotional conflict between the older people who, while accepting the Soviet regime, still tried to retain the old patterns and mores of the Pale, and the younger generation that impatiently wanted to create a completely new way of life. In literature, it was the older people who often benefited from better artistic treatment and emerged as the more plausible and interesting characters.

In Ilya Ehrenburg's novel *Out of Chaos,* old Rabbi Schwartzberg is subjected to the feverish tempo of construction in the Kuznetsk Basin. After trying to explain to his little son why Jewish holidays do not call for red flags and parades, he finally gives up: "He cursed his wife, his son, and himself. He cursed Minsk and Tomsk. He cursed the Revolution and life." [72]

In literature, these older people wonder what is expected of them; they mean well, but everything they try turns out wrong. In a Yiddish novel about industrialization, *Aglomerat,* the author works hard to transform old Wolf Landishever into a worker, and externally he succeeds. Wolf comes to the factory because his pride would not let him sit by and watch his son become an honored Communist, while he himself is classified as a nonessential citizen. Wolf does become a worker, but he is unable to accept the change as a total one. In one scene, he says: "I crush stones for a living, and I like it. But you won't convince me. They should never have taken Jews away from trading." [73] A similar air of confusion surrounds Alexander Mironovich, an old Jew who appears in Vasilii Shkvarkin's Russian comedy "Father Unknown" (1933). When his Com-

[72] Ehrenburg, *Out of Chaos (Den' vtoroi* [Second Day], 1933), trans. A. Bakshy (New York, 1934), p. 63.   [73] Orland, *Aglomerat,* p. 40.

munist daughter Raya, pregnant after an ill-fated love affair, decides to marry a Mohammedan student who is willing to raise the child as his own, Alexander Mironovich is shocked: "What a country this is! You'd think they had turned enough things upside down! Now tell me, is it really so hard to get married first and have the rest of it afterwards?" When he sees that he cannot dissuade Raya, he shrugs his shoulders, grumbles: "What is the world coming to! And still we go on living." [74]

In contrast to these as yet "unorganized" people, who are treated with a certain amount of tolerance mixed with derision, stand the Jewish heroes of Five-Year Plan literature, people who follow as firm a course of action as any of their predecessors in the Revolution and Civil War. Elke Rudner, the heroine of Lurie's *The Steppe Calls*, was considered by one Yiddish critic to be the perfect example of a positive Jewish hero,[75] and the reasons are apparent. Everything about her meets the requirements: her lowly origin, her training as a Komsomolka, her personal courage and bravery, her wise leadership, and her loyalty to higher Party echelons. As the young organizer sent to a Jewish agricultural area in the Ukraine, she dramatically exhorts the Jewish peasants to join in a collective, comparing their lot with that of farmers on a neighboring collective farm:

"With their wheat they will build a school for their children, raise a flock of sheep. . . . They are even thinking of installing electricity already. And you—what will you have? Soon, you will run short of wheat. You will be eating bread made from oats and cornmeal. So think, farmers, maybe we too can begin to live!" [76]

Elke's romantic transports on balmy spring days breathe of something quite different from love: "She had visions of how they would turn up the furrows and begin to build a new socialist village . . . and she suddenly felt a wave of joy sweeping through her—from the breaking down of the old, and the building up of the new." [77]

Another Yiddish portrayal places the hero in Birobidzhan. In Bergelson's *Birobidzhaners*, Prisker, the organizer in charge of the

[74] Shkvarkin, "Father Unknown" (*Chuzhoi rebënok* [Another's Child]; Moscow, 1933), in *Soviet Scene*, ed. and trans. A. Bakshy (New Haven, 1946), pp. 199–201, *passim*.

[75] I. Dobrushin, *In iberboi* (Moscow, 1932), pp. 173–96.

[76] Note Lurie, *Der step ruft* (Moscow, 1935), pp. 43–44.   [77] *Ibid.*, p. 107.

new settlers, is as determined and high-principled as Elke. He is a
model of tireless energy and constantly sets an example for the
other settlers. Although Bergelson tries to give him some human
failings, Prisker nevertheless emerges as a cold, pure hero. He
speaks Yiddish, his work is with Jews, and his thoughts are typical
Soviet thoughts. He has no doubts about his mission and his ideals.
At the October celebration he declares: "And from what do you
think I drew the strength to do all this? From the Soviets. I am a
member of the Communist Party. I am responsible to the Party,
and that means responsibility to the whole world. This is no small
thing." [78]

There is essentially no great difference between these Yiddish
portrayals and that of the hero who is generally considered the outstanding Five-Year Plan figure in Soviet Russian literature—David
Margulies, in Valentin Kataev's novel *Time, Forward,* written in
1932. Throughout the saga of socialist competition in the construction of Magnitogorsk, Margulies, the conscientious engineer of
the Sixth Sector, emerges as a Soviet ideal type. Like the typical
heroes, he is "precise, neat, and well organized," the most selfless
man on the construction project, and has thoroughly subordinated
his personal life to the social goal. There is nothing about Margulies
that separates him as a Jew from his fellow workers. The only clues
to his origin are his name and one allusion to his past: "In 1905,
there was a pogrom, father was killed, and for some reason we fled
to Nikolaevsk." [79] As far as the workers in the novel are concerned,
Margulies is regarded and honored as a fellow worker and a Communist. Nor did the critics make any attempt to extract Margulies
as a Jew. A few found fault with Kataev's purely external approach,
but the majority seemed to feel that Margulies was the personification of the "New Soviet Man" awaited in literature. A review of the
novel began with the dramatic words: "The new man has become
an actual fact." [80]

Thus, both Yiddish and Russian literature of the Five-Year Plan,
with its aim to create the new Soviet man, converged on essentially
the same type. Elke and Prisker both speak Yiddish and work with

[78] Bergelson, *Birobidzhaner,* p. 270.
[79] Kataev, *Time, Forward (Vremia, vperëd!),* trans. C. Malamuth (New York, 1933),
p. 320.
[80] M. Rozental', "O vremeni i ego geroiakh," *Literaturnyi kritik,* No. 2 (1933), p. 135.

Jews on Jewish undertakings; but Yiddish literature pictured
many other hero Jews in heterogeneous situations. A good example
is the ardent miner hero Shapiro in Markish's play "The Fifth
Level." When asked whether he fears an outbreak of antisemitism
in the coal mine, Shapiro says: "Let them recognize me! Now in
the light I am also a miner. Let the lamps be lit in all the levels and
I will show my face to everyone. This is it—and that's all: the face
of a miner and a shockbrigader." [81] Neither Russian nor Yiddish
literature paid attention to the fervor with which these heroes
spoke or did not speak Yiddish, and did not regard their national
origin as a crucial factor. Whether in Magnitogorsk or in Birobidzhan, they worked for the same goals and won the same titles
of "socialist hero." However, literature did show their parents, the
older generation, the confused "little" Jews, as retaining varying
degrees of ethnic separateness. The consciously anti-Soviet Jews of
the early period disappeared from the literary scene, and there
remained these two distinct groups: the apathetic "little" Jews
and the zealous hero Jews. The decidedly more "Jewish" characters of the first group, while no longer pictured as objects of
hatred, as were the kulaks and Nepmen, were shown in a somewhat
negative light. But the persistence of these "Jewish Jews" meant
that somewhere along the line compromises were being made.

VI

Toward the end of the thirties, with the adoption of the slogan
"Life has become better," there were definite indications in literature that Lenin and Maimonedes were getting along a little better
than had been expected. The fact that Maimonedes was now much
older and less hostile, and Lenin a bit more secure, may have aided
in the rapprochement.

Yiddish art began to search a little more deeply into Jewish past
history than hitherto. The hit play of the 1938 Yiddish theater
season was S. Halkin's *Bar Kokhba,* about the Jewish slave revolt
in ancient Rome. In the campaign against the growing German
menace, a certain stress on Jews as such played a large role, particularly in the series of Soviet anti-Nazi films, including those based
on Feuchtwanger's *The Opperman Family* and Wolf's *Professor*

81 Markish, "Der finfter horizont," p. 172.

Mamlock, which focused on the antisemitic policy of the Nazis. The climax came in the spring of 1939 with the All-Union celebration of the eightieth anniversary of the birth of Sholem Aleikhem. Just as the nationalities policy has never been dictated by abstract humane and moral absolutes, so this festival of "the Friendship of Peoples" served several immediate and practical purposes at once. At the celebrations in Minsk, a Russian writer said:

Today, when the Fascist barbarians are organizing bloody Jewish pogroms, passing new laws directed against Jews, physically destroying the best representatives of progressive, creative intelligentsia . . . the jubilee celebration of a great Jewish writer in our country takes on special significance.[82]

The dialectical nature of the Soviet nationalities policy found special expression in the Yiddish appeal for using the event "to destroy what may be called the national exclusiveness of this jubilee and to emphasize its international importance and scope." [83]

The German-Soviet Pact, while arbitrarily dismissing from the scene all references to the Nazi atrocities against the Jews and other peoples in Europe,[84] did not change the increasing interest in the more nationally colored Jewish theme. The Yiddish theaters added another historical play, *Solomon Maimon,* by M. Daniel; in Odessa, the Ukrainian theater staged Sholem Aleikhem's *Tevye* in Ukrainian; and the Maly Theater's 1940 revival of *Uriel Akosta* was called "the best theatrical event of the season." [85]

The "little" Jews were presented in a more and more positive light. A Russian play by the Tur brothers and Sheinin, "Unequal Marriage," in 1940, showed signs of this trend.[86] A young American, Michael Shpiegelglass, falls heir to his father's millions on the condition that he return to the Ukraine and marry a "home-town" Jewish girl. But when Michael reaches the old habitat, he finds in its place the Sholem Aleikhem Collective Farm and strangely new people. The Jewish girls scoff at the prospect of exchanging their Soviet life for foreign luxuries. Shpiegelglass is rejected by the girl

82 I. Serebrianyi, "K 80-letiiu so dnia rozhdeniia Sholom-Alekhema," *Lit. kritik,* No. 2 (1939), p. 151.
83 Fefer, "A balibter shraiber fun di sovetishe felker," *Shtern* (Kiev), Sept. 12, 1938.
84 This was true in Yiddish publications, as well as in Russian.
85 I. Al'tman, "Uriel' Akosta," *Teatr,* No. 7 (1940), p. 114.
86 "Neravnyi brak," by the Tur brothers (L. Tubel'skii, P. Ryzhii) and L. Sheinin.

he chooses, and even her elderly father, Samuil Godes, a collective farmer, proves no more agreeable to the offer. Godes and his friends are all very nationally colored, so much so that the critic Kara detected a trace of "anecdotal quality," but this did not prevent him from praising the play for showing "the marks of the great upheavals that have taken place in the soul and surroundings of the Soviet man, and in particular in the man from the old Jewish town." [87]

In Nikolai Pogodin's play "Chimes of the Kremlin," written in 1941, attention is once again focused on the early Soviet period, and here there appears a little Jewish watchmaker who is as typed as anything found in earlier literature. Like his predecessors, he is cast in a humorous vein, and just as Fishbein shrugged his shoulders at Sverdlov's funeral, the watchmaker is not overawed by Lenin's importance. But this "little" Jew, who is commissioned by Lenin to make the Kremlin chimes play the *Internationale*, while not a Communist, regards the Party with respect. He accepts his assignment with a touch of traditional humor and complacency, and then takes pride in his responsibility. When Lenin offers payment, he refuses, declaring: "There can be no terms. I'm the first watchmaker in the world who's going to tune the chimes of the Kremlin to play the *Internationale*." And when he succeeds, he reluctantly admits: "Damned if I don't feel like a real hero!" [88]

The incorporation of some two million Jews from the old Jewish centers in Poland and the Baltic states gave further impetus to the national coloring of the little heroes, and coincided with the increasing national "self-consciousness" on the part of Soviet Yiddish literature and culture. For, although rich and flourishing, Yiddish culture had reached the stage where it was no longer the culture of the Soviet Jews, but rather of an increasingly older and smaller *section* of Soviet Jews. The decreasing number of Yiddish readers was particularly evident in the steady decline in the output of the Yiddish press and publishing, even in the National Districts. [89]

[87] S. Kara, "Oblik vremeni," *Iskusstvo i zhizn'*, No. 8 (1940), p. 19.

[88] Pogodin, "Chimes of the Kremlin" (*Kremlëvskie kuranty*), in *Soviet Scene*, p. 150.

[89] In 1935 there were over 39 Yiddish newspapers in the USSR; in 1939, there were 10. The *Kolvirt Emes* in Kalinindorf in 1935 had a circulation of 2,500, in 1939, 1,000; the *Birobidzhan shtern* in 1935 had a circulation of 1,600, in 1939, 1,500 (see *Letopis' periodicheskikh izdanii SSSR* [Moscow, 1935], p. 760; *Kul'turnoe stroitel'stvo*

Moreover, one of the prime prerequisites for the perpetuation of a culture—new generations of young speakers, readers, and writers—was in this instance rapidly disappearing. The Ukraine proper (exclusive of the new areas), which at the beginning of the Second Five-Year Plan had a network of 467 Yiddish schools and 5 Yiddish pedagogical institutes,[90] by 1941 had 19 Yiddish schools in all.[91] It is not surprising, therefore, that Soviet Yiddish culture, in the process of fulfilling the social command—that is, sovietizing the new areas—began to concentrate on its new audience of Yiddish speaking and reading Jews. A considerable number of the latter in turn joined the ranks of Soviet Yiddish literature as writers and poets. Despite their protestations of faith and allegiance, there now emerged on the scene the paradox of a Soviet culture drawing life-blood and nourishment from essentially non-Soviet sources.

While this process was occurring, the former synthesis of the traditional Jew with positive values was still growing in proportions. The welcoming of the new Jewish people found literature adding religion as part of the make-up of the specifically Jewish type. In a Russian one-act play by Grigorii Romm, "The Watchmaker and the Doctor," put on in 1940, the scene is western Belorussia, three days after its annexation. Zalman Abramovich, another little watchmaker, is a pious Polish Jew, with a certain resemblance to the confused Russian Jews right after the Revolution. Zalman, however, is not regarded as a negative character. A Soviet woman doctor, whom he knew as a child, convinces him of the benefits of the Soviet way of life. Zalman wavers between joy and confusion. The next day is Yom Kippur, and he says: "Akh, how the Jews weep on this day! But tomorrow we will laugh. No, we will weep, as well, but our tears will be tears of joy." [92]

SSR [Moscow, 1940], p. 221; *Ezhegodnik periodicheskikh izdanii SSSR* [Moscow, 1940], I, 31, 209; *Tsifry o pechati*, p. 35). The fact that the *Birobidzhan shtern* doubled its 1939 circulation by 1946, as noted on p. 126, does not indicate a larger number of Yiddish readers in the Soviet Union as a whole. This one increase did not make up for the losses of the Ukrainian, Belorussian, and Crimean Yiddish press, none of which survived the War.

[90] Dimanshtein, "Tsvantsik yor groise sotsialistishe revoliutsie," *Forpost*, No. 3–5 (1937), p. 26.

[91] "Ukrainskaia SSR," *Bol'shaia sovetskaia entsiklopediia*, supplement entitled "SSSR" (1947), col. 1821.

[92] Romm, "The Watchmaker and the Doctor," in *Soviet One-Act Plays*, ed. and trans. H. Marshall (London, 1944), p. 64.

VII

Friend Zalman was soon weeping tears of another sort. The German invasion in June, 1941, brought with it the special horror that the Nazis reserved for Soviet Jews, who paid the penalty for the double crime of being Soviet citizens as well as Jews.

In his case against the Germans, Academician Trainin wrote: "The Jewish people during the thousands of years of its existence has more than once been subjected to persecution; but the Hitlerite villainies against the Jews far exceed in their inhumanity everything that is known to history." [93] And the Russian poet Alexei Surkov described the "ravaged nests" in the areas overrun by the German armies:

> Once more for miles to east and west
> Has murdered Jews' blood stained the ground.[94]

Although a large number of Jews succeeded in evacuating in time (in Zhitomir, for example, the Nazi newspaper reported that 88 percent of the city's Jews had left before the Germans arrived),[95] hundreds of thousands were caught by the rapid advance. The bloody carnivals that had been staged all over Europe were now performed on Soviet soil, and left equally bloody pages in literature.

A Russian novel by Tatiana Velednitskaia, *The Sun Is from the East* (1946), traces in graphic detail the events in a ghetto in the Western Ukraine, where the Germans decide to slaughter all the Orthodox Jews. Dressed in their prayer shawls, the old men are driven to an open square:

The orchestra began to play a "Freilakhs." A German officer, trying to keep from laughing, asked the rabbi to dance. . . . The old violin kept squeaking. The rabbi, dressed in his white woolen shawl and his fur hat, surprised even the Germans with the grandeur and ancient severity of his movements. Then, with a wild shout, one of the younger Gestapo men took to beating the rabbi over the head.

93 A. N. Trainin, *Hitlerite Responsibility under Criminal Law*, ed. A. Vyshinsky, trans. A. Rothstein (London, 1945), p. 58.

94 Surkov, "Like Birds above Their Ravaged Nest," in *The Road to the West*, ed. and trans. A. Williams (London, 1945), p. 73.

95 Joseph Shechtman, "Jews in German-Occupied Soviet Territory" (reprinted from *Hitler's Ten-Year War on the Jews* [New York, 1943]), p. 5.

The music acted as a stimulant—and all the Germans began to wield their clubs in rhythm. . . .

The music finally stopped toward evening. Surrounded by corpses, lay the rabbi—stretched out over the torn pages of the Torah.[96]

People who had lived without percentage norms and "special permits" for so many years were now subjected to indignities that even their grandfathers had never known. The enormity of this paradox is emphasized in Fëdor Panfërov's Russian story "The Green Gate." A guerrilla translator, parachuted into the Stalindorf region during the occupation, recalls a visit he had made to this same area at the end of the thirties. He remembers the prosperous Jewish farmers who no longer had "those typical mannerisms—the hands stretched upward, as if to defend themselves from something"; and then he remembers how he had asked them:

"And aren't you afraid of pogroms?"

The grown-ups were silent for a few moments, as if trying to recall something very distant, and then one of the children asked: "What is 'pogroms'?" [97]

What "pogroms" meant was soon learned, in the grimly familiar pattern: the herding of Jews into ghettos, the gas vans, the mass shootings, and the total humiliation and extermination. Episodes in Boris Gorbatov's prize-winning war novel *Taras' Family* picture the suffering of dignified old Dr. Fishman who meets his death along with the other Jews of the small Ukrainian town in a ravine.[98] The Belorussian poet Ianka Kupala in his unfinished ballad "The Nine" told of nine Jews who are commanded by the Nazis: "Jews, dig graves here!" and are then buried alive.[99] The Ukrainian novelist Iurii Smolich, in his war novel *They Did Not Pass* (1945–46), described the scenes in Kharkov when the Germans entered:

Entire families were going through the streets—old and young, with bundles, with suitcases and with pillows. They walked in silence, even the babies in their mothers' arms uttered no sound. These were the Jews who were walking. They had left their homes and were heading for the ghetto as the commandant had ordered.[100]

[96] Velednitskaia, "Solntse s vostoka," *Oktiabr'*, No. 1–2 (1946), pp. 46–47.

[97] Panfërov, "Zelënaia Brama," *Oktiabr'*, No. 12 (1946), p. 55.

[98] Gorbatov, *Taras' Family* (*Nepokorënnye* [The Unvanquished], 1943), trans. E. Donnelly (London, 1944).

[99] Kupala, "Deviat kilkiv osikovikh," 1942 (cited from the Ukrainian translation by Pavlo Tichina, in *Vibrani tvori*, Kiev, III [1947], 42).

[100] Smolich, "Voni ne proishli!" *Ukrainska literatura*, No. 10–11 (1945), p. 73.

Shortly afterwards, the Jews are evicted from the ghetto supposedly for deportation, and word reaches the terrified inhabitants of Kharkov: "All the Jews expelled from the ghetto have been shot by the Germans. Tens of thousands!" Ida, one of the novel's leading characters, adds, "I am probably the only Jew left in our city." [101]

Although there are no figures on the total number of Soviet Jews who perished in this manner, the many references to single instances offer a sufficiently stark account. At Babi Yar in Kiev, over 52,000 were shot in a group; [102] in Dnepropetrovsk, 26,000; in Pavlograd, 4,000; in Kharkov, 13,000.[103] The writer Vasilii Grossman wrote: "Over a hundred thousand Jews were killed in Minsk in the course of two years." [104] And Alexei Tolstoy in one of his burning essays reported: "But I saw something still sadder. In the North Caucasus, the Germans killed the entire Jewish population, the majority of whom had been evacuated during the War from Leningrad, Odessa, the Ukraine, and the Crimea." [105] A tale from the West Ukraine, "The Sokorin Family" by Panas Kochura, gives further evidence of the priority the Jews received at the hands of the Germans. A bedraggled refugee from an occupied town reports, with full details, that over 10,000 Jews were killed there.[106]

Once again, it was Yiddish literature that concentrated on picturing the experiences that were peculiar for Jews, and there was more than enough material. The Yiddish writers looking at the tragedy strove to draw from it hope and inspiration. In a scene of Bergelson's play *I Will Live* (1942), an elderly Jewish agricultural specialist is tortured by the Nazis for information. When he refuses, they drag in his daughter Frida and show him the alternative. The Nazi officer says: "Come on, open your old Bible eyes and look at her. Give her your blessing on her high station in life—from today on, she's going to satisfy the lust of our brave lads at the front. . . . Bless her, you old Maccabean, bless her holy prostitution!" And Avram Ber, raising his hands over his daughter's head, offers up a

[101] *Ibid.*, p. 97.

[102] "Evrei," *Kratkaia sovetskaia entsiklopediia* (Moscow, 1943), p. 461.

[103] Ehrenburg, *We Will Not Forget*, Supplement of *USSR Information Bulletin*, (Washington, 1944), p. 18.

[104] Grossman, "Good Is Stronger Than Evil," *The Years of War*, trans. E. Donnelly (Moscow, 1946), p. 413.

[105] Tolstoi, *Izbrannye proizvedeniia* (Moscow, 1945), p. 487.

[106] Kochura, "Rodina Sokorin," *Ukrainska literatura*, No. 12 (1945), pp. 13–85.

blessing: "Safeguard your purity, my child. Pay for it with your life if necessary, but stay pure. I give you my blessing on this—with the blood that is dripping from my hands on to your head." [107]

The call was for hope and for revenge. Itsik Fefer mourned the "poor Jews, the Kings of the Ghetto," who heroically died in the revolt of the Warsaw Ghetto, but found inspiration in their deed:

> Let these holy ones teach us to die
> Let these shadows lead us to life.[108]

In a similar vein, the poet Osherovich, describing the agony of Jews burned alive in their synagogue, heard their deathless call: "Jews! Quiet our pain with revenge!" [109]

In the midst of the suffering, literature also noted instances of "national impatience" among Soviet citizens in the occupied areas. The Nazi divide-and-rule policy was even more vigorously pushed on Soviet territory. Soviet *agit-prop* organs repeatedly warned of the method in the German madness. Thus, in 1942, the mass propaganda organ *Agitator's Handbook* showed how Hitler set the Belgians against the French, Russians against Ukrainians, and "incites everybody to hatred of the Jews, to antisemitism." [110] A similar organ, *Propagandist,* carried a very specific command:

The slightest attempt of the Fascists to sow national hatred in any form, and especially in the form of antisemitism, must at once be repulsed by our agitators and propagandists. Do not forget that the Fascists . . . like to set rumors in motion in the hope that there will be found credulous and hasty people who will spread them further. . . . Not a single such machination of the enemy must be allowed to remain unexposed.[111]

In addition to data citing Jewish participation in the war, further material was given the agitators in the form of the standard Soviet definition of antisemitism as stated by Stalin in 1931:

Antisemitism as the most extreme form of racial chauvinism is the most dangerous hangover of cannibalism. . . . Antisemitism is dangerous for the toilers as a false sidetrack . . . leading them into the jungle. Therefore, Communists as consistent internationalists cannot but be uncompromising and mortal enemies of antisemitism. In the USSR,

---

[107] Bergelson, "Kh'vel lebn," *Einikait,* Dec. 27, 1942.
[108] Fefer, "Wonder of the Ghetto," *Jewish Life,* II, No. 6 (1948), 10.
[109] H. Osherovich, "Yidn," *Fun klem arois* (Moscow, 1947), p. 60.
[110] "Dvadtsat' piat' let druzhby narodov," *Sputnik agitatora,* No. 19 (1942), p. 7.
[111] I. Petrov, "Krakh gitlerovskikh raschëtov," *Propagandist,* No. 15–16 (1943), p. 19.

antisemitism is most severely prosecuted as a manifestation deeply hostile to the Soviet order.[112]

Just as in earlier periods antisemitism was shown as linked with counterrevolution, so this time literature connected it with traitors and renegades. Vasilii Grossman's highly praised Russian story "The Old Teacher" (1942) centers on the dilemma of Jews in a small town in the Ukraine. With emphatic bitterness, Grossman pictures the elements who join the Germans. The day the Germans arrive, "the turbid dregs rose from the bottoms of rivers and lakes; toads swam to the surface." [113] Several deserters from the Red Army come out into the open, and their first move is against the Jews: "Where have all our Jews got to?" one asks. "All day long there hasn't been a brat or an old man in sight, not a soul, just as if they didn't exist at all." [114] Ehrenburg refers to similar people in Kiev, in the novel *The Storm:* "The former stagehand hunts for Jews, and after receiving his reward from the Germans sings 'Marfusha Wants to Get Married.' " [115] In a Soviet Latvian novel, *Toward the New Shore* by Vilis Latsis, the Germans find eager helpers among the people of a town near Riga. The Nazi commander thanks his Latvian henchmen: "Gentlemen, I'm pleased with your work. . . . In a few days we shall be able to post the sign of honor, 'Judenfrei,' in our city. And for this, we are chiefly indebted to you." Then, in a jovial mood, he asks one of his Latvian favorites to repeat the tale of "how in one day he had killed all the Jews in a small town." [116]

Yiddish literature, too, referred to similar episodes, as well as to instances where the struggle for sheer existence in the occupied zone led people to grasp at any straw; Jews as well as non-Jews served the Nazi purpose. I. Falikman's moving novel about the life and death of a Polish ghetto, *The Light Comes from the East,*

112 V. P. Volgin, "Chem obiasnit', chto Sosnkovskii i ego stavlenniki rasprostraniaiut antisemitizm sredi podchinënnykh im voinskykh chastei?" *Sputnik agitatora,* No. 15–16 (1944), p. 29. The same definition appears in Soviet reference works, and in *Slovar' sovremennogo russkogo literaturnogo iazyka,* eds. Chernyshev, *et al.* (Moscow, 1950), I, 152.

113 Grossman, "The Old Teacher," *The Years of War,* p. 160.

114 *Ibid.,* p. 162.

115 Ehrenburg, *The Storm (Buria),* trans. J. Fineberg (Moscow, 1948), p. 288.

116 Latsis, "K novomu beregu" (Russian translation by Ia. Shuman), *Zvezda,* No. 9 (1951), pp. 11–12.

includes graphic descriptions of members of the *judenrat* [117] and of the Jewish police who, to save their own lives and families, acted as agents for the Germans and even helped drive Jews to the extermination camps.[118]

In Hirsh Dobin's Yiddish story "Sugar," a Belorussian peasant, desperate to find food for his starving wife and child, is finally attracted by a solution: "If you catch a Jew for them [the Germans] they'll give you half a pood of sugar, so they say. It's even posted somewhere." [119] It is significant, however, that the peasant in the end actually feeds the old Jewish woman he had set out to "catch" and does not turn her in. Kochura's "Sorokin Family" also emphasized a Ukrainian peasant family who risk their lives to save an old Jewish neighbor, despite her reluctance to endanger them. Compassion was carried a step further in a Russian short story by Alexander Bezymenskii. Here, a Russian woman, married to a Jew, chooses to share the fate of her husband's people. When the Germans round up all the Jews, she goes along with her half-Jewish little son. To the bewildered people around her, her presence becomes a source of hope and fortitude:

She remembered an evening when she and her husband had read Lenin's article "On the National Pride of the Great Russians." Now she understood it all in a new light, and much better. She—Tamara—is a Russian. And the Russian people is the defender of all oppressed peoples, an older brother to the toilers of all nationalities. These words, once so abstract, now became as dear and meaningful as the ground she walked on, as the air she breathed. . . . It was not only love for her child that had kept her from leaving, but also pride—yes, the pride of which Lenin had spoken.[120]

When the Jews are finally led to the slaughtering ground, Tamara proudly leads the procession, with a placard on her breast: "My husband is a Jew!" and perishes with the group.

In Grossman's story, too, major stress was laid on the Ukrainians who helped Jews, and not on those who either directly hurt them or were merely indifferent to them. It is possible to assume that Radishchev's criterion of "proportionality" and "perspective"

---

117 Jewish councils set up by the Nazis in the ghettos.
118 Falikman, *Di shain kumt fun mizrekh* (Moscow, 1948).
119 Dobin, "Tsuker," *Af der vaisrusisher erd* (Moscow, 1947), p. 235.
120 Bezymenskii, "Tamara Savitskaia" (Yiddish translation by B. Kotik), *Tsum zig* (Moscow, 1944), p. 65.

142 *Jews in Soviet Literature*

needed for the portrayal of Jews in literature (see page 121), was in this and other cases applicable to non-Jews. The social command —"friendship of peoples"—ordained that the reality of Ukrainians standing by while Jews were slaughtered had to be coupled with, and overshadowed by, the reality of Ukrainians helping Jews. The outlines of this "controlled reality" stood out in sharp relief when the poet Holovanivskii in his Ukrainian poem "Avraam" pictured a scene in Kiev where Russian and Ukrainian spectators calmly watch a Jew being killed by the Germans. For this, Holovanivskii was later castigated by the head of the Ukrainian Writers' Union: "This is a terrible slander on the Soviet people, who in hard bloody battle, at the cost of great sacrifice and pain, defended the freedom and independence of Soviet people of all nationalities. But Holovanivskii throws a lump of mud into the face of the Soviet people." [121] Ehrenburg in his novel *The Storm* gave an almost identical scene in Kiev, but since in other parts of the novel he paid much more attention to Jews being aided by their neighbors, it is evident that he obeyed the "social command."

That the "command" did not mean that the Jewish tragedy could not be presented is evident from the continued treatment of this theme in Soviet literature since the polemics of late 1948 and early 1949. The prize-winning novel by the young writer Vladimir Popov, *Steel and Slag* (1949), describes the struggle against the German invaders in an industrial city in the Donbass. One chapter is devoted to the Jewish suffering in the city. Details are given of the fate of Faina Solomonovna Zamberg and her older daughter, first in the ghetto and then as they march away to the inevitable slaughter. But the novel also describes how Faina's youngest daughter is heroically saved by Russian friends, as well as the attempts of the Germans to play on Zionist memories among some of the older people.[122] Boris Polevoi's novel *Gold*, which appeared at the end of 1949, has another Jewish doctor, Abram Isaakovich Goldshstein, who is captured and tortured by the Nazis.[123] In May, 1950, a Kiev literary journal featured a series of "Lvov Sketches" by the Ukrainian writer Iaroslav Galan. In a section "People of the Lvov Ghetto,"

[121] L. Dmiterko, "Sostoianie i zadachi teatral'noi i literaturnoi kritiki na Ukraine," *Lit. gaz.*, March 9, 1949.
[122] Popov, *Steel and Slag* (*Stal' i shlak*) trans. H. Altschuler (Moscow, 1951).
[123] Boris Polevoi, *Zoloto* (Moscow, 1949).

Galan described the tragic end of the Yiddish writers Katsaizn, Perle, Veber, and Kenigsberg, as well as the heroic deeds of the Yiddish poet Shedrikh, who "died with glory" as a fighter in the underground. "The tortures of the Jewish population in occupied Lvov defy description," writes Galan. And among the ghetto horrors he pictures is the following incident:

There, where hangs the balcony railing twisted by fire, once lived a mother of two small children. . . . When the importunate demands of the SS men failed to achieve results, they devised a means of revenge: they threw their victim on a bed and disemboweled her with a kitchen knife. Even the shrieking of the terror-crazed children did not distract them.[124]

Galan, however, does not isolate the Jewish tragedy from the tragedy that enveloped all of Lvov, and he sorrows for the earth of Lvov that was drenched with "Ukrainian blood and Jewish blood and Polish blood." [125] Again, Latsis, a leading Soviet Latvian writer, in his novel of 1951 (see page 140), by labeling his villains as Latvian "bourgeois-nationalists," implies that antisemitism is an intrinsic part of the nature of traitorous and anti-Soviet elements; and the collaborationist Ludis, who had excelled at killing Jews, is captured and executed by pro-Soviet Latvian partisans.

Thus, the "social command" did not remove the tragedy from literature, but required that various aspects of the tragedy be conditioned by immediate social needs and situations. That it may not have been easy for Yiddish interpreters of the tragedy to see this and other realities in all their ramifications was natural enough, and this became particularly clear in the lengthy debates among Soviet Yiddish literary circles during and after the War. In 1946 a Yiddish newspaper editorial charged that wartime Yiddish literature had run into several major pitfalls, the most important being that "the German-Fascist crimes against the Jewish population are shown as isolated, and are not tied in with the Hitlerite murders of the Soviet people in general." [126]

[124] Galan, "Lvivski narisi," *Vitchizna*, No. 5 (1950), p. 121.
[125] *Ibid.*, p. 122.
[126] "Dekn dem khoiv farn land un folk!" *Einikait*, Dec. 14, 1946.

VIII

In *The Storm,* old Khana Alper's daughter-in-law asks her if she really believes in God, and Khana answers: "I don't know, when all is going well I don't think of it. But when anything happens . . . Don't be angry, Rayechka. You have your books, you go to the theater. But I have only this—I remember how I used to pray and I feel better." [127] As has been noted, even before the War, the positive portrayal of the "little" Jew saw an increasing identification of his "Jewishness" with religion. This trend was greatly accelerated during the War, in the Russian as well as in the Yiddish presentations. A play by the Tur brothers and Sheinin, "For Whom Time Bows," [128] put on in 1946 and still current in Soviet theater repertoire,[129] introduced yet another little Jewish watchmaker, Rubinshtein, this time in a drama of ghetto and partisan intrigue. Rubinshtein, who outwits the Nazi *Gauleiter,* is imbued with the faith and will of the positive man; he also makes frequent allusions to the Jewish past and celebrates Passover.[130]

In Yiddish literature the trend was even more marked. The older generation, which in some respects suffered most from the Nazi holocaust, like Khana Alper turned in time of supreme trial to the specifically "Jewish"—in Soviet terminology, "national self-consciousness"—which to many meant religion. Of course, it must be realized that even before the war the great majority of Yiddish writers and their readers belonged to this older generation.

In S. Gordon's vivid story about the evacuation of one of the Jewish National Districts in the Ukraine, the young organizer El'e Yehudin passes a wagon in which are several old Jews dressed in holiday clothes:

> In their hands, each one of them carefully held a long container.
> "What are you carrying?" he asked them.
> "The Holy Books," the Jews answered. "Should we have left them for the Hamans *imakh shmom* [may his name disappear]?"
> "El'e Yehudin, do you know the meaning of *lekh-lekho meartsekho*

127 Ehrenburg, *The Storm,* p. 173.
128 *Komu podchiniaetsia vremia* (Moscow, 1945).
129 See listing for the Vakhtangov Theater in Moscow in *Pravda,* Oct. 15, 1951.
130 See I. Liubomirskii, "Ver is balebos iber der tsait," *Einikait,* April 18, 1946.

umimoiladtekho [Go away from your country and from your birth-place]?"

"I know, Shmuel-Khaim, I know."

"That's what it is." [131]

The appearance of "Holy Books" in one of the Jewish National Districts, while somewhat surprising, is not too improbable: there was never any prohibition of the right to practice Judaism. It is more surprising that El'e understands biblical quotations in He-brew (italicized above), especially since Soviet Yiddish culture had from the very start cleansed its schools of all things religious and He-brew. Still, there was nothing to stop El'e from learning these things at home. In addition to indicating an increased identification of some Jews with religion, this story, by virtue of its very form, betrays a complex paradox that had arisen in Soviet Yiddish literature in its address to the readers for whom it was theoretically functioning. The Hebrew quotations cited were still printed in Yiddish trans-literation and for the most part, though not in every case, trans-lated into Yiddish in footnotes. The tendency shown here developed into a trend toward more and more frequent use of religious refer-ences and Hebrew words printed in the original; this reached its climax in 1948 with the first appearance of publications in the pre-revolutionary Yiddish orthography.[132] As one Yiddish critic astutely pointed out: "It is simply not readable for the young Soviet gen-eration of Yiddish readers who were raised in the Soviet Yiddish schools." [133] Thus, the culture that had lost its self-perpetuating traits by the end of the thirties now showed evidence of losing even those cadres that it had raised up to that time. The dynamic quality of this process can also be seen in the cases of leading Yiddish figures who had begun to shift into other spheres before and during the War. The foremost Yiddish poet of Birobidzhan through 1941, Emmanuil Kazakevich, by 1946 was one of the most promising young writers in Russian literature. His first novel *The Star* (1946) received a Stalin Prize in 1947, and another novel, *Spring on the Oder* (1949), a similar award in 1950.[134] A leading actress at the

---

131 Gordon, "El'e Yehudin," *Tsum zig* (Moscow, 1944), pp. 143–44.

132 The book chosen for this innovation was *Joseph Stalin, a Short Biography*.

133 M. Shapiro, "Khaver I. V. Stalins kurtse biografie in yidish," *Einikait*, May 13, 1948.

134 Although still active in Yiddish literary circles after the War, Kazakevich was no longer creating in that language.

Odessa State Yiddish Theater at the end of the thirties, Lie Bu-
gova, went on the Russian stage in the early forties, and in 1950,
as an Honored Artist of the Ukrainian SSR, was a featured player
at the Ivanov Theater of Russian Drama in Odessa.[135] Still others
had taken a bicultural path: the critics Nusinov and Viner played
an important role in Russian as well as Yiddish letters, and the poets
Motl Talalaevskii and Khana Levina had achieved prominence in
Ukrainian as well as Yiddish verse.

Therefore, in a sense Gordon's tale merely acknowledged the
dichotomy already in existence; and in writing for his dwindling
audience, the Yiddish author was identifying himself with one
group and depicting their mores and patterns, rather than those
of Soviet Jews as a whole. The Yiddish critic Loitsker in 1948
complained that "while Jewish life has become more and more
worldly, the literature [Yiddish] has crawled more and more into
a corner." [136]

We have already seen that the *raison d'être* of a national culture
within Soviet society was based not on altruism, but on the practical need "to educate the masses in the spirit of internationalism
and consolidate the dictatorship of the proletariat." [137] Soviet Yiddish literature had in a sense fulfilled its purpose so well that it
had educated its readers away from itself. Coupled to this development was the phenomenon of a diminishing base, characteristic
also for Yiddish culture in other areas outside the Soviet Union. At
any rate, a combination of factors—the inherent nature of the culture, the Soviet nationalities policy, the war, and the very natural
desire of leaders of culture to perpetuate their culture—led to signs
that the "national" was being placed on a *par* with the "socialist,"
rather than *after* it. In one of his war stories, Itsik Kipnis, a prominent Yiddish writer in the Ukraine, wrote: "I would like to see all
the Jews, as they march boldly through the streets of Berlin, wear
on their breasts, alongside the decorations and medals, a small,
pretty Star of David." [138] As a result of this and other works, Kipnis
was expelled by the Yiddish Section of the Ukrainian Writers'

135 L. Zhukova, I. Osipov, "V teatrakh Odessy," *Sovetskoe iskusstvo*, Nov. 25, 1950.
136 Khaim Loitsker, "Far ideisher reinkait fun undzer literatur," *Shtern*, No. 2
(1948), p. 106.   137 See pp. 127–28.
138 Quoted in H. Polianker and Talalaevskii, "Pro odne shkidlive opovidannia,"
Literaturna hazeta (Kiev), Sept. 18, 1947.

Union in 1947.[139] Yiddish critics now turned to other writers and poets, and through 1948 increased the bitterness and frequency of their attacks on instances in Yiddish literature of "national exclusiveness, nationalistic egocentrism, and bourgeois nationalism." [140]

The question whether the Kipnis affair and similar incidents contributed to the enforcement of arbitrary controls over several organized Jewish activities at the end of 1948 is a matter of speculation.[141] No official notice was ever given publicly as to when, how, or why the Jewish Anti-Fascist Committee, its organ *Einikait,* and the publishing house *Der Emes* were closed in Moscow sometime in November, 1948. Public mention was made only of the cessation of the Kiev journal *Der Shtern* in September of the same year because of "bourgeois nationalism" and "control-lessness" of its staff.[142] That this may have been a typically arbitrary Soviet reaction to an immediate crisis situation and not a planned or coordinated step against Jewish culture per se is suggested by the continued functioning of a number of Yiddish activities and personalities in other parts of the USSR *after* November, 1948. The Jewish theaters in Moscow, in Chernovits, and in Birobidzhan were all listed as operating in the fall of 1949.[143] Of these, only the Kaganovich Theater in Birobidzhan was listed in operation in 1950.[144] Although none of the best known Yiddish writers, all in the Moscow Section of the Writers' Union, was mentioned after 1948, important Yiddish writers in other areas continued their work after that

139 *Ibid.* The expulsion was of short duration since in 1948 Kipnis was being published again by the Kiev Yiddish journal. See *Der Shtern,* No. 3 (1948), p. 69.

140 Loitsker, "Far ideisher reinkait," p. 111.

141 For a detailed interpretation of this and other critical Soviet Jewish developments, see Solomon M. Schwarz, *The Jews in the Soviet Union* (Syracuse, N.Y., 1951).

142 "Printsip bilshovitskoi partinosti—virishalna umova rozvitku radianskoi literaturi," *Radianska Ukraina,* Jan. 21, 1949.

143 The last mention of the Moscow and Chernovits theaters appeared in *Izvestiia,* Nov. 16, 1949, and in *Pravda Ukrainy,* Sept. 11, 1949, respectively. The Birobidzhan theater was listed in *Teatr,* No. 8 (1949), p. 105. In January of 1949, the Baku Yiddish Drama Ensemble was also still operating (*Bakinskii rabochii,* Jan. 15, 1949).

144 "Birobidzhan," col. 250. The director of the Minsk State Jewish Theater (not listed in operation after 1948), Peoples' Artist V. Golovchiner, in 1951, as chief director of the Irkutsk Regional Russian Theater, was playing a prominent role in Soviet theatrical discussions (see Golovchiner, "Iskusstvo otobrazhat' zhizn'," *Sovetskoe iskusstvo,* March 3, 1951). The veteran director of the Chernovits Jewish theater (until 1946 the Kiev Jewish Theater), Honored Artist M. Goldblatt, in 1951 was producing plays at the Theater of Ukrainian Drama in Chernovits (Ia. Gan, "Iskusstvo ne terpit ukrashatel'stva!" *Sovetskoe iskusstvo,* Oct. 3, 1951).

date. Sporadic evidence hints that some continued to create in
Yiddish. Thus, in 1950, the Moscow Children's Publishing House
issued in Russian a new volume of poetry by the Yiddish poet
Iosif Kotliar, listing it as "translated from Yiddish." [145] In the
case of other writers, no language was listed, but their literary work
was mentioned. The Yiddish novelist Note Lurie and the critic
Irma Druker, in 1950, were both completing new works in their
usual habitat, Odessa.[146] Several previously cited as "bicultural"
continued as prominent figures in Ukrainian literature: the poetess
Khana Levina was counted among the leading Ukrainian children's
writers in 1950,[147] and Motl Talalaevskii, the former head of the
Yiddish Section of the Writers' Union in Kiev, remained active on
Ukrainian periodicals and in dramaturgy.[148]

After 1948, no reference to any of the chief Yiddish writers in
Moscow was made in any of the central publications. There was no
criticism directed at them publicly, and no polemics appeared
against Soviet Yiddish culture as such or as a cultural entity.
Whereas formerly it had been possible to gather a general and
sometimes detailed picture of Soviet Jewish affairs from the Moscow Russian periodicals and press, the same publications after 1948
paid almost no attention whatsoever to such affairs. However, it is
open to question whether major central publications available
abroad by themselves furnish grounds which in turn can be safely
used to generalize on the situations in every part of the Soviet
Union. The tightening of controls after the War was accompanied
by an increasingly rigid limitation on the number of regional and
local newspapers and periodicals sent abroad. But it is just these
publications, occasionally available in isolated issues, that point to
interesting possibilities. Thus, while no criticism of the major Yiddish writers appeared in the central literary journals after November, 1948, a Kiev journal in 1949 made a single allusion to one of
Bergelson's postwar stories as a typically "nationalistic" work.[149]
Since there is no amplification of this allusion, it is possible that
other issues of the journal or other publications did carry some

[145] *Uchitel'skaia gazeta*, April 5, 1950.
[146] Iu. Dold-Mikhailik, "Literaturna Odesa," *Radianska Ukraina*, April 20, 1950.
[147] A. Korneichuk, "Ob Ukrainskoi detskoi literature," *Lit. gaz.*, Feb. 7, 1950.
[148] *Vitchizna*, No. 7 (1949), p. 178; *Teatr*, No. 11 (1950), p. 119.
[149] "Visoko nesti prapor radianskogo patriotizma," *Vitchizna*, No. 3 (1949), p. 16.

discussion leading up to such a verdict. In the same manner, although the central press made no reference in 1949 to the ninetieth anniversary of the birth of Sholem Aleikhem, the republic Russian newspaper in Stalinabad, *Kommunist Tadzhikistana,* on March 2, 1949, featured an article by L. Bard, "Sholem-Aleikhem (On the Ninetieth Year since His Birth)." [150] Again this suggests that items on Jewish affairs and activities may have appeared in other regional publications after 1948.

Nevertheless, the central press and periodicals serve the All-Union reading public and set the official tenor for Soviet culture as a whole.[151] In this case their relative silence since 1949 meant that for the general Soviet reader Yiddish culture was no longer considered a component part of multinational Soviet culture. The varied lists of nationalities included in frequent discussions on "The Friendship of Peoples" in the arts almost never cited the Jews as a separate entity.[152] Yiddish activities that may have continued to serve the cultural needs of the older Jews in various localities were no longer inflated to symbolize the creative achievements of "the Soviet Jews," most of whom were busy creating and working in other cultures.[153]

[150] Item 9445, *Letopis' gazetnykh statei,* No. 15 (1949) p. 56.

[151] See Alex Inkeles, *Public Opinion in Soviet Russia* (Cambridge, Mass., 1950).

[152] A similar situation can be found in the two versions of a textbook on Soviet literature for the tenth class, put out by Professor L. I. Timofeev. In 1946, a section devoted to the Ukrainian poet Pavlo Tichina carried the following sentence: "With great mastery he translates Pushkin, the Georgian poet Vazha Pshavela, the Armenian Akop Akopian, the Yiddish Osher Shvartsman, the Bashkir Saifi Kudash, and others" (Timofeev, *Sovremennaia literatura* [Moscow, 1946], p. 410). In 1950, the same textbook, under a new title and with additions and revisions, still contained the identical passage on Tichina, with one addition and one deletion: "With great mastery he translates Pushkin, the Belorussian poet Ianka Kupala, the Georgian Vazha Pshavela, the Armenian Akop Akopian, the Bashkir Saifi Kudash, and others" (Timofeev, *Russkaia sovetskaia literatura* [Moscow, 1950], p. 381). This, too, however, is inconclusive since in 1951 a long newspaper article devoted to Tichina once again praised his "translations of Russian, Belorussian, Armenian, Georgian, Osetian, Bashkir, Lithuanian, and Yiddish poets, writers, and dramatists" (Lev Ozerov, "Blagorodnoe delo poeta," *Lit. gaz.,* June 14, 1951).

[153] The virulent charges of "cosmopolitanism" leveled against many writers of all nationalities in all parts of the Soviet Union during the first half of 1949 saw the eclipse of a considerable number of Jewish writers (non-Yiddish) as well. However, the large majority of Jews working in Soviet literature were not touched by the polemics, and of those attacked a significant number have since reappeared. The continued prominence of Jewish figures in all branches of Soviet belles-lettres is indicated in the following partial listing taken from a larger survey of the period June, 1949, to October, 1951. The writers whose names are italicized were among the "cosmopoli-

IX

In the furor over the Kipnis affair in 1947, the leaders of the
Yiddish Section of the Ukrainian Writers' Union charged: "He
does not want to acknowledge that Soviet Jewish soldiers did not
fight for David of the Old Testament nor for his ideals, but for
their Soviet way of life, for their Soviet State, for their Soviet
Fatherland." [154] These "Jewish soldiers" who were being argued
about in the halls of Moscow and Kiev were far removed from the
disputes and little affected by their outcome. And for the most
part, in literature, these were not the people who were gassed in
the German motor vans or shot in the ravines. In *The Storm*,
Khana Alper on her way to the final agony at Babi Yar, looks at
the people marching with her and asks herself, " 'Where are the
young people?' And she at once remembered: 'The young people
are fighting.' " [155]

During the War, Jews were fifth among nationality groups in the
number of battle awards conferred, with 63,373 receiving decorations, and 6,134 the title of "Hero of the Soviet Union." [156] In the

---

tans," and a sample reference to their active status is indicated in each case. Jews in
Russian prose include: M. Egart, I. Ehrenburg, V. Fink, R. Fraerman, V. Grossman,
L. Kassil', *V. Kaverin* (*Lit. gaz.*, April 5, 1950), M. Kozakov, Iu. Libedinskii, V. Lidin,
L. Ostrover, M. Slonimskii; in poetry; M. Aliger, *P. Antokol'skii* (*Bol'shaia sov. entsik.*,
2d ed., II [1950], 524), A. Bezymenskii, S. Kirsanov, S. Marshak, A. Oislender, I. Sel'-
vinskii; in drama: A. Brushtein, L. Kompaneits, I. Rubinshtein, L. Sheinin, V. Shkvarkin, E. Shvarts, Tur Brothers; in literary scholarship and criticism: I. Aizenshtok, M.
Aronshtam, S. Bernshtein, *B. Bialik* (*Literatura v shkole*, No. 5 [1951], p. 71), *M. Blei-
man* (*Sovetskoe iskusstvo*, Dec. 12, 1950), S. Breitburg, A. Daich, L. Eidlin, B. Eikhenbaum, *A. Gurvich* (*Novyi mir*, No. 9 [1950]), *E. Kholodov* (*Teatr*, No. 4 [1950]),
E. Kriger, *A. Leites* (*Lit. gaz.*, Oct. 6, 1951), *G. Lenobl'* (*Znamia*, No. 1 [1950]), A. Mar-
golina, B. Meilakh, M. Mendel'son, F. Rappaport, G. Rozental', V. Rubin, *V. Shklovskii* (*Lit. gaz.*, July 27, 1950), M. Shneerson, *S. Tregub* (*Oktiabr'*, No. 7 [1949]), *A.
Tseitlin* (*Novyi mir*, No. 12 [1950]), *V. Vsevelodskii-Gerngross* (*Teatr*, No. 3 [1950]),
M. Zilbershtein.

In the Ukraine, Jewish figures in prose, poetry, and drama (writing in Russian,
Ukrainian, or both) include: S. Akhmatov, V. Bil'-Belotserkovskii, Io. Fel'dman, L.
Gal'kin, Ia. Gorodskoi, *S. Holovanivskii* (*Vitchizna*, No. 2 [1950]), *A. Katsnel'son* (*Vitchizna*, No. 9 [1950]), *L. Pervomaiskii* (*Lit. gaz.*, June 14, 1951), G. Plotkin, E. Raitsin,
N. Rybak, N. Tikhii, M. Zisman; and as critics and littérateurs: M. Bernshtein, O. Brod-
skii, *Ia. Burlachenko* (*Sovetskoe iskusstvo*, July 22, 1950), L. Feigel'man, *Ia. Gan* (*Radianska Ukraina*, April 2, 1950), *A. Gozenpud* (*Sovetskaia muzyka*, No. 6 [1950]), *L.
Iukhvid* (*Kul'tura i zhizn'*, Nov. 20, 1949), G. Levin, V. Liberman, *Iu. Martich* (*Sovetskoe iskusstvo*, July 10, 1951), B. Shnaider, F. Sholom.

[154] Polianker and Talalaevskii, "Pro odne shkidlive opovidannia."
[155] Ehrenburg, *The Storm*, p. 214.   [156] *Einikait*, Feb. 24, 1945.

military services, Jews participated at all levels and appeared in prominent positions; among them, Major General Kremer, Lieutenant General Krivoshein, Major General Vainrub,[157] "Hero" Senior Guards Lieutenant Polina Gelman, and "Twice Hero" Guards Colonel David Dragunskii.[158] It is among these people that we meet Khana Alper's son, Major Osip Naumovich Alper, one of the leading figures in Ehrenburg's prize-winning novel.

Major Alper is not too different from the hero Jews of earlier works in literature, although at times he is probably the least emotional of the group. Before the War, together with his wife and little daughter, he lived in Kiev with his mother, and worked as an important engineer. When the war comes, he soon manages to get to the front, where he becomes a daring and skillful soldier. In battle, as well as in civilian life, Osip is portrayed as an exemplary character:

He fought as he had worked before the war—coolly and in dead earnest—to him it was like being in the factory, he was only grieved at having to destroy. . . . He dreamed of the day when the war would end and it would be possible to work, to build, to organize.[159]

Since Ehrenburg, sparing no details, follows Major Alper's mother and daughter to the ravine in Kiev, and his Parisian brother Leo to the gas chamber in Auschwitz, Osip's very direct relation to specifically Jewish problems is obvious from the start. Yet he does not appear to be any more "national" than were Levinson and the others. His suffering is deep and overwhelming, but, unlike his mother, he does not seek solace in the national idiom. To his wife, he writes: "A terrible thing has happened, but you and I will live, we will forget nothing." [160] And Raia, his wife, an army nurse at first, when she hears about Kiev, immediately applies to her commander for a transfer to the snipers. The latter asks:

"You want to go where it's livelier, eh?"
"No, my little daughter remained in Kiev, and my husband's mother."
"But you are doing useful work here, too."
"I know, but I can't stand it any longer, I must kill." [161]

When Raia, too, is killed and the War ends, Osip does not return with any sense of being part of a "lost people." In his eyes, all the

---

[157] *Ibid.*, May 9, 1946.
[158] *Ibid.*, Feb. 1, 1947.
[159] Ehrenburg, *The Storm*, p. 410.
[160] *Ibid.*, p. 538.
[161] *Ibid.*, p. 339.

people around him are "his people," and the fate of his family is
their tragedy as well as his. He is mournful, but he knows he must
start life anew: "There's work for me everywhere. In Kiev. On the
Pechora. And I have a home everywhere—I have fought for it." [162]

Among the several Jewish soldiers in Viktor Nekrasov's prize-
winning Russian novel, *In the Trenches of Stalingrad,* a leading
role is played by young Captain Farber. Although offered jobs in
the rear, the former mathematics student, "obviously from the intelligentsia," [163] joined a rifle company on the fourth day of the
War, and eventually finds his way to the historic fighting at Stalingrad. He is so obsessed with the fighting that he finds little time for
his comrades. One of them says: "He gave the impression that nothing in the world interested him. . . . Sickly pale like most red-
headed people, he hardly ever talked with anybody." [164] But in one
of the battle lulls, Farber lets down his reserve to confess that his
attitude is partly the result of a lack of self-confidence: "I'm not
bad at solving problems in higher mathematics. . . . But an elementary problem like how to expose a sergeant-major who steals
supplies from his soldiers—this has me completely baffled." [165] The
critics greeted Nekrasov's first novel as an important contribution
to war literature. He was often compared to Tolstoy, and Farber
was praised along with the other characters in the novel. One critic
even felt that the chief figure in the novel, the narrator, was too
weakly portrayed, while the picture of Farber, his growth, his ma-
turing in battle, "is a true biography of a Soviet man . . . and the
reader believes in him unconditionally." [166]

Jews on the home front also played a role in literature.[167] Vasilii
Azhaev's complicated and drawn-out novel *Far From Moscow* was

[162] *Ibid.,* p. 719.
[163] Nekrasov, *V okopakh Stalingrada* (Moscow, 1947), p. 100.
[164] *Ibid.,* p. 134.   [165] *Ibid.,* pp. 214–15.
[166] P. Gromov, "Geroi i vremia," *Zvezda,* No. 4 (1947), p. 170.
[167] Other portrayals of Soviet Jewish participation in the Second World War include
Commissar Mirovich in Libedinskii's novel *The Guardsmen* (*Gvardeitsy,* 1942); war
correspondent-photographer Vainshtein in Konstantin Simonov's play *Wait For Me*
(*Zhdi menia,* 1943); the real-life war hero Leizer Papernik in Natan Rybak's Ukrainian
novel *The Weapons Are with Us* (*Zbroia z nami,* 1942). Jewish partisans appear in Ivan
Kozlov's prize-winning memoirs *In the Crimean Underground* (*V krymskom podpol'e,*
1947); in P. Vershigora's prize-winning memoirs (Ukrainian) *People with a Clear Conscience* (*Liudi z chistoiu sovistiu,* 1946); and in G. Lin'kov's Belorussian memoirs *War
Behind the Enemy* (*Voina v tylu vraga* [Russian translation of Belorussian original],
1947).

met with unusual superlatives when it first appeared in 1948 and has since become one of the most talked-about novels of the postwar period. Although it deals with the laying of a vital pipe-line in the north during the war years, by obvious implication it is meant to spur on the postwar Five-Year Plan; its presentation of Jewish characters thus serves as a bridge from the war to the present. In a minor role, the fat and clownish chief of supplies, Vasilii Maksimovich Liberman, consistently doing things wrong, is everywhere the object of ridicule. "I see nothing of socialism in Liberman," [168] says one engineer, and the chief of the project calls him "You humorist, you unsuccessful descendant of Mark Twain." [169] Liberman antagonizes all around him, until he reveals his actions as a form of escape: "My relatives remained in Mariupol and Berdiansk. My wife and daughter got stuck in Leningrad." [170] But his family manages to survive, and by the end of the novel, Liberman's transformation into a positive character is included as part of the success of the entire project: "Even the 'difficult customer' had now become a more or less reliable assistant." [171]

In contrast to Liberman, who is in a class with the "little" Jews, stands one of the purest of the "positive" types, Zalkind, who plays the all-important role of the Party organizer on the project. An old Bolshevik from the days of the civil war in Siberia, with a gold tooth, black hair, a "sunburned face and a clean smile," [172] Zalkind provides the necessary ideological direction to the work at hand. He quotes Lenin and Stalin at the appropriate moments, and is obviously of their mold: "The Partorg spoke simply, confidently, with that special strength of logical conviction which is always characteristic of experienced Bolshevik political leaders." [173] Unlike some of the other pure heroes, Zalkind is shown as a well-rounded man: he has wide intellectual interests and a good family life with several grown children. Zalkind's specific nationality receives exactly the same amount of emphasis as Liberman's, in both cases almost negligible. Like Osip Alper, Zalkind is part and parcel of the society in which he lives, and with Zalkind this identification extends to the past as well as the present: "We are not only descend-

---

[168] Azhaev, *Daleko ot Moskvy* (Moscow, 1948), p. 47.
[169] *Ibid.*, p. 76.   [170] *Ibid.*, p. 105.   [171] *Ibid.*, p. 524.
[172] *Ibid.*, p. 24.   [173] *Ibid.*, p. 146.

ants of Yermak, we are followers of Lenin, Soviet people; we have given this region a new life!" [174]

In the critical cheers for *Far from Moscow* no national criteria were applied to either Zalkind or Liberman. One critic found Liberman "part of the petty vanity of bourgeois individualism," [175] but in general Liberman was paid the attention proportionate to his role in the novel. Zalkind, on the other hand, was held up as a new model for the Soviet reader. In the eyes of a Leningrad critic, Zalkind "wonderfully reveals how great is the role of the Party," [176] and as a Siberian critic saw him: "The typical traits of a Bolshevik-leader are embodied in the character of Zalkind. He is the soul of the collective, a real leader of the masses." [177]

X

The arbitrary classification of these "hero" Jews as a group is almost uncannily justified by literature itself. In *Far from Moscow,* after one of Zalkind's inspiring speeches, the chief engineer of the project remarks: "Listening to Zalkind, I was sort of transported to the days of Fadeev's *The Nineteen,* and I almost fancied it was Levinson standing before me." [178] He could, of course, have chosen Osip Alper or Margulies or even Elke Rudner for his analogy, for, while their individual natures may differ, they all exhibit a similar social pattern.

As a group, they appear to have a greatly lessened "national consciousness" when compared with the older Jews or with the Jews pictured in prerevolutionary literature. The degree of their assimilation into the culture patterns of the society in which they live is shown as being extremely high. Soviet literature does not treat assimilation as a "problem," and in fact rarely treats it at all—directly. Nor does literature show any sign of a policy or drive *for* assimilation, but it does reveal a concerted effort to remove all the obstacles in the way of assimilation, and to minimize the tensions incurred on the part of the parent group, the assimilating group,

[174] *Ibid.,* p. 31.

[175] M. Kuznetsov, "Slava cheloveku stalinskoi epokhi," *Molodoi bol'shevik,* No. 1 (1949), p. 68.

[176] T. Trifonova, "Liudi idushchie k kommunizmu," *Zvezda,* No. 12 (1948), p. 180.

[177] I. Sotnikov, "O samom tsennom i prekrasnom," *Sibirskie ogni,* No. 1 (1950), p.
138.   [178] Azhaev, *Daleko ot Moskvy,* p. 560.

and the receiving group. The "hero" Jews show few signs of belonging to an "in-group" at home and to an "out-group" in the street. Zalkind and Liberman show as much and as little feeling of "belonging" to each other as they do to the other people on the scene. At the same time, literature shows few traces of an "assimilated" versus a "non-assimilated" group among the Jews as a whole. Osip Alper is not ashamed to live with his typically "Jewish" mother, and she in turn is very proud of her "assimilated" son. In her eyes the fact that he is fighting at the front makes him a loyal son of his people. And so in her hour of trial she, too, is not "lost." In the midst of the horror at Babi Yar, she defiantly shrieks: "Osya will come! The Red Army will come! You will answer for everything." [179]

While the hero types are not ashamed of their parents, as individuals they are set against having their day-to-day life in any way conditioned by or even identified with the fact that they are Jews. In Markish's 1933 Yiddish play, the miner Shapiro, when asked whether he feared being discovered by the antisemites among the miners, answered: "I will show my face to everyone . . . the face of a miner and a shock-brigader" (see page 121). Almost a decade later, in a Russian work, when the city of Kerch is being evacuated as the Germans approach, a Jewish Komsomolka, Polia Govardovskaia, insists that she be allowed to stay behind to serve with the partisans. The reluctant partisan leader explains the obvious added risks in store for Jews operating in German territory. Polia is indignant: "I was born and raised under the Soviet regime and have never felt any difference between Jews and Russians. And now, when it is necessary to defend the motherland, you remind me of this? How insulting!" To the organizer's repeated warning that "toward the Jews the Germans behave with special cruelty," Polia answers promptly, "But in my opinion, the Germans behave the same toward all Soviet people." [180]

The pattern of this assimilation is attentuated and further complicated by the hostility Soviet literature shows toward any shame or denial of national origin. Here, too, there is a consistent attitude in both early and later Soviet works. In Kozakov's 1928 story di-

[179] Ehrenburg, *The Storm*, p. 217.
[180] Ivan Kozlov, *V krymskom podpol'e* (In the Crimean Underground; Moscow, 1947), pp. 23–24.

rected against antisemitism (see page 122), a young Jewish factory official preached that only the complete disappearance of the Jews would remove their "shameful" racial stigma; and, quite logically, he acquired as a close friend an outspoken Russian antisemite. His Russian wife, however, revealed him in his true light: "God! You reminded me of a converted Jew who has hidden his origin. This shows a lack of respect for yourself, for your work—and for the work of hundreds of thousands of your people." [181] This attitude becomes even more pointed in Smolich's Ukrainian novel of 1945 about Kharkov under the Germans (see page 137). Ida Slobodianik, "the only Jew left in our city," can be saved only by having three "Aryans" vouch that she is not Jewish. Both Ida and her three Ukrainian girl friends are humiliated. One of the latter sees the efficacy of the solution, but, before agreeing, argues with her own conscience:

What a terrible thing! To claim that you are not a Jew! Is it something shameful—to be the son of your own people? . . . Olga had never thought that such a thing could happen, that she would be covering up for someone who denied his nationality. To renounce the blood of one's fathers! To maintain that you are not you at all!! And as for vouching that someone is not a Jew, this is just the same as sanctioning antisemitism.[182]

The fact that some of the heroes in Yiddish literature chose to operate in national situations does not materially alter the pattern of lessened "national consciousness." Although the agitation for the land projects and for Birobidzhan was often framed in terms of developing a new Soviet "national" Jew, in effect this did not take place. The Soviet "national" Jews as they came into literature were merely the older, more nationally tinged people who had gone through a process of adjustment and accommodation. Had sufficient numbers of Jews followed the pioneers to the Jewish Autonomous Region and reversed the traditional minority dispersion within a defined political area, then conceivably the tendency of their cultural institutions to lose functional value in a state of relative freedom might also have been reversed. Literature shows no such development and after the early years uses Birobidzhan as a symbol, but no longer speaks of it as the "homeland" for Soviet

181 Kozakov, "Chelovek padaiushchii nits," p. 41.
182 Smolich, "Voni ne proishli," p. 72.

Jews. To the Soviet reader Birobidzhan was eventually presented as a successful *socialist* venture in the Far East initially inspired by Jewish settlers.

The linguistic phase of the assimilation of the "hero" group gives additional light on aspects of control and planning within the Soviet nationalities policy. Stalin's several formulations of this policy indicate that both increased emphasis on the national at one point and arbitrary restriction at another were equally provided for and rationalized many years in advance. While explicitly defending the right of Jews to "free development," Stalin just as strongly opposed any program the goal of which was

the maintenance of everything Jewish, the preservation of all the national peculiarities of the Jews, even those that are patently noxious to the proletariat, the isolation of the Jews from everything non-Jewish, even the establishment of special hospitals.[183]

There was no compulsion to make Russian the language of the Jews. The right to speak Yiddish was secured and enforced with tangible material aid in the form of schools, publishing facilities, and the like. At the same time, the slightest manifestation of any drive to work for the Yiddish rather than the social goal, that is, the intimation that Yiddish *should* be spoken, was quickly eliminated. When the writer Kipnis wrote a story in which he speaks of meeting several Soviet Jews, and then adds whimsically that he wished "they would speak to me in Yiddish," [184] the immediate rebuttal from Yiddish higher quarters was: "And suppose they do speak Russian? Are they no longer *kosher,* no more Jews? And when the Ukrainian or Belorussian speaks Russian, does he become a non-Ukrainian or a non-Belorussian?" [185] Thus, the matter of national language is surrounded with the same air of paradox as is the much vaunted right of secession from the USSR. On this subject, Ida, the tragic survivor in Kharkov, replies to a Ukrainian friend who asked the meaning of her expression *"Ikh bin a Yid"*:

In Yiddish this means: "I am a Jew!" . . . This is the only expression I know in Yiddish. My parents were assimilated, I was raised in Russian culture, and I went to a Ukrainian school. But now our Jewish traditions often come back to me, and these Yiddish words which my mother

183 Stalin, *Marxism and the National and Colonial Question,* p. 47.
184 Quoted in "Natsionalizm untern shleier fun felker fraintshaft," *Einikait,* July 3, 1947.   185 *Ibid.*

taught me keep running through my mind. And I shall marry, I shall have children, and I shall tell them these words.[186]

On the whole, the question of how "Jewish" or how "un-Jewish" these heroes in literature may be depends on the frame of reference applied. Literature makes it clear that these people *are* Jews, either by name or by family and background data, but it does not specify them as Jews by the sum of their *differences* from non-Jews around them.[187] Nor are they characterized as Jews by their not being Gentile. In the situation depicted by Soviet literature, the Gentile and non-Gentile categories no longer operate as significant social factors. Thus, the presentation of these Jews in literature further affirms "the historical *fait accompli* that the Jew, however defined, seems to be." [188]

These at any rate are Jews as presented in Soviet belles-lettres and by Soviet literary critics to the Soviet reading public. Their heroic qualities are the heroic qualities assigned to Soviet heroes of all nationalities. They are not represented as heroes because they are Jews or despite the fact that they are Jews. Moreover, since other Jews appear in literature in a less heroic light, there is no sign that the word "Jew" and the word "hero" have become synonymous.

The Levinsons and the Zalkinds appear in various situations and at various levels, and are as natural to the specific situation as are any of the other participants. Their entry into a novel does not envelop the action with "the Jewish problem." They are judged by their words and their deeds. In literature they are shown as having the same access to all social situations as do all other members of the society in which they live, and, conversely, they are subject to the same limitations and controls. And they are endowed with just as much responsibility for making the society what it is as that society is for making them what they are. The laconic statement that appeared during Soviet polemics over the State of Israel may well apply to the presentation of Jews in literature: "The Soviet Union has no pro-Jewish position and no pro-Arab position. The Soviet State has a Leninist-Stalinist position." [189]

---

[186] Smolich, "Voni ne proishli!" *Vitchizna*, No. 5 (1946), p. 106.

[187] See Elliot E. Cohen, "Jewish Culture in America," *Commentary*, No. 5 (1947), p. 414.

[188] Melville J. Herskovits, "Who Are the Jews?" *The Jews*, ed. L. Finkelstein (New York, 1949), II, 1168.

[189] Fefer, "Arum Gromikos rede vegn Palestine," *Einikait*, June 19, 1947.

Gene Sosin

The Children's Theater and Drama in Soviet Education

We must educate through the theater not observers, but fighters and builders—Natalia Satz

I

THE SOVIET CHILDREN'S THEATER is officially defined as "a powerful educational and pedagogical medium for molding the personality of the young citizen." [1] The purpose of this study is to demonstrate how the theater functions in Communist education by examining the social content and ideological direction of its repertoire. Almost all of the plays discussed here are cited repeatedly in Soviet sources as outstanding examples of their genre and of the period in which they were written.

A distinctive characteristic of the Soviet educational apparatus is the deliberate cooperation between the school and the arts in striving toward a common goal: "The aim of the education of children in Soviet society is the preparation of well-integrated fighters for and builders of Communism." [2] Faith in the victory of Communism, loyalty to the socialist motherland, and subordination of one's personal interests to those of the "collective" are constantly reiterated touchstones of the educated Soviet citizen. In order to prepare people who are devoted to the cause of Communism, the Soviet government and the Party consider essential a planned, systematic inculcation in children of views and behavior compatible with the stated purpose of education, through the

[1] B. Rostotskii, "Teatry detskie," *Bol'shaia sovetskaia entsiklopediia,* LIII (1946), 732.
[2] A. K. Bushlia, *Vospitanie kommunisticheskoi morali u detei* (Moscow, 1948), p. 14.

school, the Pioneer and Komsomol youth organizations, the family, and the so-called "extra-school institutions." [3] These institutions compose a vast organization of leisure-time activities created especially for children: Pioneer Youth palaces, technical, agricultural and naturalist stations, clubs, libraries, excursion and tourist stations, sport societies, parks, art education centers, radio and television programs, and a network of professional theaters.

The whole system of extra-classroom and extra-school work which has been developed is directed at solving the same problems as the activity of the school—the Communist education of a cheerful, well-integrated generation of adolescents capable of taking an active, creative, conscious part in the building of Communist society and struggling actively and unselfishly with its enemies. [4]

In this complex machinery of Soviet education the children's theater is regarded as one of the vital cogs:

Special theaters for children and youth belong to the most important victories of Soviet culture. For our country, which is boldly paving the way toward mankind's future, believing in its bright Communist tomorrow, this is a characteristically solicitous, attentive and loving attitude toward the education of the growing generation, toward developing in it lofty feelings and noble traits of character. We cannot underestimate the means which aid in forming the consciousness of the man of Communist society, and among these means one of the most important places belongs to the theater. Attending the theater leaves an indelible impression on the consciousness of a child and deeply engraves itself upon his memory. [5]

The children's theater consists of a network extending throughout the principal cities of the USSR. [6] Each theater has its own per-

---

[3] *Ibid.* The organization of Young Pioneers enrolls children between the ages of nine and fourteen. Every school has a Pioneer detachment, and in the summer there are Pioneer camps in the country. The organization is guided by the Komsomol, or Young Communist League, which is made up of boys and girls in the senior grades. Both organizations assist the school in fulfilling the tasks of Communist education. See Y. N. Medinsky, *Public Education in the USSR* (Moscow, 1950), pp. 56–57.

[4] E. Volkova, *et al.*, "Narodnoe obrazovanie," *Bol'shaia sovetskaia entsiklopediia*, Supplement entitled "SSSR" (1947), cols. 1223–24.

[5] S. Mikhalkov, "O teatre dlia detei," *Kul'tura i zhizn'*, June 11, 1949. Similar statements emphasizing the importance of the children's theater can be found in various Soviet sources during the past 25 years.

[6] In 1937 there were 112 children's theaters, with 72 in the RSFSR alone. In that year over 30,000 performances were given in Russian and 20 national languages to more than 10,000,000 spectators (I. Beletskii, "Teatr iunogo zritelia," *Teatr*, No. 10–11 [October–November, 1938], p. 210). The number of theaters dropped sharply during the War, when many were forced to close or evacuate to the East. There seems to be

manent "collective" of adult professional artists who devote their careers to producing plays for young spectators. Most children's theaters bear the name of "theater of the young spectator," abbreviated as *tiuz*.[7] The audience is composed, in the main, of children and adolescents between the ages of seven and seventeen. They are students in the primary school (ages seven to eleven), junior secondary school (eleven to fourteen), and senior secondary school (fourteen to seventeen). Most of the school children under fifteen belong to the Pioneer organization, which boasted a membership exceeding thirteen million in 1949. Senior graders are eligible to join the Komsomol. The repertoire is divided into two categories of plays, one for children under twelve, and the other for those in their teens.

The professional children's theater, or *tiuz*, should be distinguished from puppet theaters[8] and amateur dramatic circles in schools and Pioneer palaces. Plays from the repertoire of the children's theater are frequently published for use by these amateur groups, which are known as "self-activity theaters." Each script contains detailed instructions by the *régisseur* regarding the interpretation of the play and its characters. Thus, dramas performed before thousands of young theatergoers reach thousands more outside the auditorium, including children who live far from the large cities. Furthermore, radio dramatizations of scripts for the children's theater provide an additional medium for reaching the juvenile audience, as do film versions of successful plays.

The educational ministries of the various republics control the activity of these theaters, as well as all the extra-school institutions mentioned above. Additional supervision is carried out by the

---

a discrepancy in postwar figures: Rostotskii, "Teatry detskie," col. 733, gave the number 51 as of 1945. But as late as 1951, fewer than 40 were said to be operating (V. Sperantova, "Children's Theaters," *Soviet Union*, No. 11 [21] [November, 1951], p. 34).

[7] From *teatr iunogo zritelia*. It is often prefaced by the name of the city in which the theater is located: *Kievskii tiuz, Tbiliskii tiuz*, etc.

[8] In 1941, there were 111 puppet theaters out of a total of 926 Soviet theaters (adult as well as children's) (*Teatral'nyi al'manakh*, Book 2, Moscow, 1946, p. 186). Such puppet masters as Sergei Obraztsov of the State Central Puppet Theater in Moscow and Evgenii Demmeni of the Leningrad State Puppet Theater have become famous throughout the world for their skill in this age-old art. The puppet theater is designed mainly for the amusement and instruction of the preschool child, although children of all ages attend. Indeed, there are puppet theaters for adults, so great is their popularity in the Soviet Union. See "Kukol'nyi teatr," *Bol'. sov. entsik.*, XXXV (1937), 435–36.

Committee on the Arts of the Council of Ministers. Through its organ, *Theater,* the Committee criticizes the work of theaters for children along with that of adult theaters. Every theater has a staff of permanent workers—actors, directors, playwrights,[9] musicians, scene designers, and technicians. Many theaters have a *technicum* for training young performers, since acting for the children's theater is a difficult vocation. Great skill is required of an adult to act the part of a child to the satisfaction of stern young critics. Those who master the art have gained the affection of their audience and official accolades.[10]

Along with the artistic section of the theater, there is a "pedagogical" section. A constant interchange of information takes place among staff members, pupil-delegates, teachers, and parents concerning present and future repertoire. Frequent discussions are held, letters and drawings are encouraged, the children are observed during and after the performance. Schools may ask for a special play based on a subject in the syllabus. More often, the theater makes its own production plans for the season, but always in close cooperation with its audience. This is exemplified by the remarks of one young girl about the Moscow Theater of the Young Spectator:

> When I say to my schoolmates, "Today I am going to our theater," nobody laughs at me because there are thousands of other schoolchildren like myself who consider the Young Spectator's Theater to be their very own.
>
> I was only six the first time I went to the theater. Now I am sixteen. In these ten years, I have seen every play in the repertoire, many indeed several times.
>
> This year I came to know our theater even better. Actors and pedagogues from the theater came to our school, asked us how we liked the plays they put on and what we would like to see. . . . Soon after this visit we started a MTIuZ club in our school. . . . Thirty-five Moscow schools have similar theater clubs, with a total of 350 boys and girls as members from the senior classes. Club members attend rehearsals and

9 The Union of Soviet Writers has a special section for *tiuz* playwrights, who had reached over 80 in number by 1940. Among the best known are A. Brushtein, V. Liubimova, S. Mikhalkov, S. Marshak, N. Shestakov, E. Shvarts. Well-known playwrights from the adult theater who have written for children include A. Afinogenov, A. Tolstoy, K. Trenëv, A. Kron, P. Pavlenko, V. Kataev.

10 Konstantin Stanislavskii of the Moscow Art Theater once said, "The way to act for children is the same as for adults, only better" (Rostotskii, "Teatry detskie").

discussions of repertoire plans. We are also invited to listen to readings of new plays and are encouraged to pass on our opinions.[11]

Tiuz actors serve as sponsors and coaches to such clubs. A former artist in the Leningrad Theater of Young Spectators, describing his contacts with school children while in charge of three dramatic clubs in Leningrad schools from 1934 to 1936, stated that twice a week he advised the club members on repertoire and helped them to produce their own plays. If, for example, Pushkin's *Dubrovskii* was currently being studied in class, the school principal would ask the actor to suggest that the children stage a play on that subject. According to him, there was not a single school of the more than three hundred in Leningrad at that time which did not have a dramatic club under the guidance of a *tiuz* actor.[12]

The theater interacts with Soviet society in still another way: All-Union surveys of its activity are held periodically. Play festivals in local areas determine the best productions for a tour in Moscow, with prizes awarded to the finalists. One survey, conducted by the Committee on the Arts, took place in 1939–40. As the final tour began in November, 1940, the head of the Leningrad Theater called it the greatest event in the life of the "Soviet pedagogical theater." In a book devoted to this survey, the author comments:

The Soviet children's theater is at present [1940] one of the strongest factors in the ideological-political, and esthetic education of the growing Soviet generation, one of the most original elements in the general system of Soviet theater culture. However, the Soviet theater for children did not become that way overnight: for twenty years of its existence it went along a trying ideological-creative path, full of strenuous searches, defeats, victories.[13]

The "trying path" traveled by the children's theater in its search for a repertoire began soon after the 1917 Revolution, but its direction did not become clear for several years.

[11] A. Sonova, "Teen Ages Look Ahead," *Moscow Daily News*, Jan. 1, 1947. This enthusiasm for the theater is a typical reaction of school children, according to former spectators of the children's theater among Russian Displaced Persons in Germany with whom I talked during 1950–51. In addition to these informal talks, interviews were conducted in Munich, Paris, and New York with persons who were active in the children's theater as playwrights, actors, directors, and artists. Some of their testimony appears in these pages.

[12] From an interview with Boris N., Munich, Germany, Feb. 10, 1951.

[13] S. Aronov, *Teatr iunogo zritelia v SSSR* (Moscow and Leningrad, 1940), p. 3.

II

The children's theater is an original phenomenon of the Soviet regime. It is frequently called "a child of October." In prerevolutionary Russia, the only satisfaction of youth's natural hunger for theatrical spectacles lay in family or school dramatics, both of which had a wide repertoire of fantasies. But there was no professional theater especially designed for children. Sons and daughters of the aristocracy might be treated occasionally to special matinees in major adult theaters, particularly during Christmas and Easter time, but the ordinary worker's child had to be content with a singing blind man, a wandering puppet show, or a trained bear in the streets.

Soon after the Soviets came to power, all theaters were put under government control. On November 22, 1917, a decree of the Council of People's Commissars placed them under the State Committee on Education (later the People's Commissariat of Education, and today the Ministry of Education). Attention was quickly turned to establishing special theaters for children. On July 15, 1918, the first one was opened in Petrograd (Leningrad), presenting two dramatized fairy tales by Andersen and fables of Krylov.

Meanwhile, in Moscow, a girl of fifteen was chosen to head the children's sub-section of the theater-music section on the Board of Education. She was Natalia Satz, daughter of composer Il'ia Satz. For almost two decades this talented and energetic young woman was a leading figure in the theater movement, as a producer, director, playwright, and theorist. Satz is known chiefly for her work in the Moscow Theater for Children, which she founded in 1921.[14]

[14] During the season of 1937–38, Satz was arrested and removed from her theater in Moscow. While it is true that her productions had been criticized for their "formalism," there were undoubtedly political reasons rather than mere esthetic causes leading to her arrest. Several hypotheses have been advanced by Russians and Americans in the West: that a mine was discovered in her theater intended for use against Soviet leaders; that she was the friend of a Polish singer accused of spying; that her father was arrested the day before; that she was the wife of Tukhachevskii, the famous marshal shot in the purges. There have been rumors that she was shot; others said she was exiled. After years of silence concerning her whereabouts, the Soviet magazine *Theater*, in 1949, twice carried the name of Natalia Satz in its chronicle of productions throughout the USSR. She was listed as the producer of two plays for the children's theater of Alma-Ata, capital of the Kazakh Republic. ("Khronika teatral'noi zhizni," *Teatr*, No. 4 [April, 1949], p. 112; No. 5 [May, 1949], p. 112).

But as early as 1918 she had opened a puppet theater in Moscow, which was converted into a dramatic theater in 1920 and called the First State Theater. At that time it was placed under the leadership of Henriette M. Pascar, a gifted director whose approach to theater for children was destined to clash head-on with the forces of Communist pedagogy.

Mme Pascar believed that the child should not be exposed to reality inside the theater:

Did we need a realistic repertoire, a painting of daily life in cruel and brutal colors, or rather plays where fantasy dominated? . . . The goal of this theater was precisely to lead the child away from this reality which injured him to a better world where he might taste a little joy. They often told us it was a mistake to feed him the unreal, instead of preparing him to live and struggle. But that is the role of the family and school, not our role.[15]

By refracting life through the prism of the fairy tale, Pascar hoped to enable the young spectator to escape from the outside world during those turbulent days. In the early period of her work, she had received the support and encouragement of A. V. Lunacharskii, Commissar of Education. But there were increasing protests against her insistence on divorcing the theater from pedagogy. In 1924, when she was rehearsing *Treasure Island,* Mme Pascar was summoned before an extraordinary commission of official pedagogues for failing to consult with them on repertoire. There she expressed her astonishment and explained that her motives were to work for children. As for Communist pedagogy: "In my opinion it has no relation to the theater, none whatsoever!" [16] Within a short time, Pascar was removed from the State Theater,[17] which was taken over by the Moscow Board of Education and soon produced a play on Soviet life, S. Auslender's *Kol'ka Stupin,* about a homeless waif.

A totally different rationale of theater for children was held by Professor A. A. Briantsev, who founded the Leningrad State Theater of Young Spectators in 1921. Briantsev believed in bringing

---

[15] H. M. Pascar, *Mon Théâtre à Moscou* (Paris, 1930), pp. 13–14.

[16] *Ibid.,* p. 95.

[17] In an interview with Mme Pascar in May, 1951, in Paris, where she has made her home since her departure from the Soviet Union soon after losing her theater, I learned that she considers Natalia Satz chiefly responsible for her removal. Satz was described as "an ambitious little girl" and *"l'enfant russe"* who "did little things to please the government."

together "artists capable of thinking like pedagogues with pedagogues capable of feeling like artists." [18] His theater has been regarded as the most influential children's theater.[19] The first performance of the Leningrad *Tiuz* was held on February 23, 1922.
The play was *The Hunchback Horse*,[20] adapted from Ershov's
classic Russian tale. For the next two years there was little to distinguish the repertoire of this theater from others relying heavily
on fairy tales. However, the Leningrad collective was searching for
an original approach: "While propagating the fairy tale, the theater could by no means let up in its search for a content which was
contemporary and, on the level of the child's comprehension, socially significant." [21]

The first play written especially for the Leningrad Theater had
its première in January, 1924. It was *Abductor of Fire*, by P. Gor-
lov, which dealt with primitive man's victory over the forces of
nature.[22] Despite the remoteness of the epoch, the play was considered as closely related to the contemporary scene because it depicted man's earlier struggle for survival. November, 1924, saw the
first attempt to portray tsarist Russia with B. Zhitkov's *The Traitor*,
which dramatized an episode from the Revolution of 1905.[23] The
audience was unexpectedly transported from 1905 into the present
by the singing of the *Internationale* at the end of the play, an attempt to draw the spectators into a political demonstration. In
December, 1925, the Leningrad Theater presented a play about
the Civil War in Russia: *Timoshka's Mine* by L. Makar'ev (see
pages 168–69). This was the first play to treat a Soviet theme and,
as such, it occupies an important historical place in the repertoire
of the children's theater. From these beginnings, plays by Soviet
writers on prerevolutionary and contemporary subjects appeared
with increasing frequency during the next twenty-five years.

Natalia Satz's Moscow Theater for Children opened on June 13,

[18] A. I. Piotrovskii, ed., *Teatr iunykh zritelei 1922–1927* (Leningrad, 1927), p. 7.

[19] Rostotskii, "Teatry detskie"; Aronov, *Teatr iunogo zritelia*, p. 44.

[20] *Konëk-gorbunok*. See Piotrovskii, *Teatr iunykh zritelei*, pp. 33–37. Pushkin has
been credited with providing Ershov with the famous opening lines: "*Za gorami, za
lesami. . . .*"

[21] Piotrovskii, *Teatr iunykh zritelei*, p. 30.

[22] *Pokhititel' ognia*. See Piotrovskii, *Teatr iunykh zritelei*, pp. 50–53.

[23] *Predatel'*. See Piotrovskii, *Teatr iunykh zritelei*, pp. 59–60.

1921, with a play called *The Pearl of Adal'mina.*[24] Adapted from a
tale by Topelius, the Finnish writer, it showed the "indissoluble tie
between tsar and executioner, the stupid ignorance of many of
those who decided the 'fate of the people.' " [25] Although Satz was
pleased with the "political direction" of the subject, she was anx-
ious to find new plays. Recalling some of those which came into
her hands at that time, Satz remarked that she would never forget
a play in verse, *Donkey Skin,* which began with the words:

> I am a little donkey, ho-ho-ho,
> I gallop on my little feet, hee-ho-ho,
> Though my skin is gray and my body small,
> Though I am an ass, I'm not dumb at all.

Not much improvement was an opus by a doctor in which the cast
of characters included a sandwich. "The first act took place in the
mouth, the second in the stomach, and the third in the large intes-
tine." [26]

As a result of such suggestions, Satz decided to commission someone to adapt the *Thousand and One Nights* for her theater in order
that "its social attraction might activate children from eight to
twelve in the necessary direction." [27] But whom should she choose?
A dramatist from the adult theater did not know the peculiarities
of the child spectator, while a teacher was unfamiliar with the
theater. Satz decided to order a play from each. The adaptation
chosen for production was the one written by the teacher, N. Ognëv,
later to become famous as the author of the *Diary of a Communist
Schoolboy.* In 1923, Satz again called on him to write a play, this
time based on *Hiawatha.* Ognëv responded with *Hiawatha—Chief
of the Iroquois.* This was the first play produced by the Moscow
Theater for Children in which there were no fairy tale themes.
Satz regarded the "struggle for the primitive commune" as a subject both interesting and educational for her audience, since it was
filled with heroism "close to our Soviet reality." [28]

In the autumn of 1924, S. Rozanov, head of the theater's pedagogical section, wrote *Be Ready,* a play about Soviet Pioneer youth

[24] *Zhemchuzhina Adal'miny.* See Satz, *Nash put'* (Moscow, 1932), p. 9.
[25] Satz, *Nash put',* p. 9.   [26] *Ibid.,* p. 10.
[27] *Ibid.,* p. 12.   [28] *Ibid.,* pp. 12–13.

who fight oppression abroad (see pages 170–71). According to
Natalia Satz: "In this play for the first time red neckties on stage
matched the red neckties in the audience. This was 1924, when the
Pioneer organization was celebrating only the second anniversary
of its existence." [29]

By 1925, the theaters of Moscow and Leningrad were respond-
ing to the appeal contained in the resolution of the Twelfth Party
Conference of 1923 devoted to problems of propaganda and agitation:

It is necessary to pose in practical form the problem of using the theater
for the systematic mass propagation of ideas in the struggle for Communism. To these ends it is necessary to attract forces both central and
local to strengthen work in creating and selecting appropriate revolutionary repertoire, using above all heroic moments in the struggle of
the working class.[30]

From 1925 until the outbreak of war in 1941, the number of
children's theaters swelled to more than one hundred, stretching
from Archangel to Tbilisi, from Orël to Tashkent, Irkutsk, and
as far east as Sakhalin. The spread of the network was accompanied
by the growth in repertoire, with the central theaters taking the
lead. Plays produced in the several theaters of Moscow and Leningrad soon appeared on stages throughout the USSR. Many were
translated into the local languages.[31] Although the theaters continued to produce fairy tales and classics, the path of repertoire was
unmistakably headed in the direction of plays about contemporary
events at home and abroad. But regardless of its genre, every play
was expected to reflect life in the mirror of Marxian dialectics.

III

Timoshka's Mine (1925), the first children's drama to portray
life under the Soviets, dealt with a subject close to the experience
of its spectators—the Civil War. Timoshka is a thirteen-year-old
Donbass peasant boy whose Communist father has been murdered

[29] *Ibid.*, p. 15.
[30] Rostotskii, "Osnovnye etapy razvitiia sovetskogo teatra," in *Sovetskii teatr,* ed.
M. S. Grigor'ev (Moscow, 1947), p. 47.
[31] Sometimes a play originally written for a local theater was accepted for production in Moscow or Leningrad. A further source of repertoire was the adult theater,
which contributed several plays including L. Rakhmanov's *Restless Old Age* (the film
version of which was known as *Deputy of the Baltic*). See Rostotskii, "Teatry detskie."

by bandits. He overhears the brigands and a counter-revolutionary, Denisov, plotting to blow up the near-by Balakinskii mine. Denisov arrives at the mine posing as an American citizen, supposedly a journalist on an inspection tour of Soviet mines. Inside the mine the workers discuss the new arrival as they wait for the cage:

First Miner: That one came alone.
Second Miner: Who?
First Miner: The American.
Third Miner: They say he writes for the newspapers.
First Miner: All of them are traveling around in droves, in deputations. They're interested in how our work is going.
Third Miner: But they lie in the newspapers, fellows. He comes here to us, gathers up what he wants, but I'm afraid they won't print it. Besides, it's a bourgeoisie there.[32]

Timoshka, after considerable difficulty, convinces his friends, the young miners, that Denisov is really a spy. As they run for help, Timoshka descends the shaft of the old mine to extinguish the fuse. In the last scene, the miners and a Red Army detachment wait anxiously near the entrance to the shaft, fearing an explosion at any second. After a suspenseful pause, Timoshka crawls out, exhausted, and announces: "I put it out. My hands are all burnt." [33] Everyone shouts for joy, the would-be saboteurs are arrested, and the mine is promptly renamed in honor of Timoshka. The play was one of the most frequently performed in the early repertoire and was still being performed as late as 1936. It provided the young spectators with an exciting drama of Reds *versus* Whites as well as a hero with whom to identify themselves. The stage was transformed into a mine at the height of its activity, with cages moving up and down, machines clattering, and workers busy filling norms. *Timoshka's Mine* brought to three-dimensional life a "heroic moment in the struggle of the working class."

The machinations of kulaks in the countryside were exposed and condemned in the children's theater even before the collectivization program began in earnest. *Black Ravine,* dramatized in 1927 by A. N. Afinogenov from a children's book by Gumilevskii, is often cited as one of the outstanding plays of the early repertoire. Elections to the rural soviet are scheduled to take place in a village.

[32] L. Makar'ev, *Timoshkin rudnik* (Moscow, 1926), p. 30.
[33] *Ibid.,* p. 44.

170 Soviet Children's Theater

The authorized government agent is delayed in a near-by town.
Kulaks take advantage of this by attempting to force the election
to be held immediately, thereby assuring the seating of their own
candidate. They arrest a young peasant, Sofron, who has been
agitating against them, and try to drown a shepherd boy, Egorka,
who has overheard their plans. But Egorka swims to safety and
rescues Sofron, the agent arrives, and the kulaks are punished.[34]
Timoshka and Egorka were "among the first portrayals of contemporaries of the *tiuz* spectator, of those Timoshkas and Egorkas who
sat in the auditorium." [35]

The theme of internationalism and sympathy for the oppressed
workers abroad found expression in such plays as *Be Ready* by S.
Rozanov, which ran in the Moscow Theater for Children from 1924
to 1926. Like many plays of this period, especially those for the
younger age groups, it sought to draw the audience into the action.
The young spectators were called upon during the play to answer
the command "Be ready" by shouting the motto of the Pioneers:
"Always ready." As the play opens, a group of Pioneers decide to
build an airplane and fly abroad to help their brother-proletarians.
Fascists dressed like black beetles attack the plane with powerful
rays and force the Pioneers to land on another planet. Here a socialist state has already been established, and the children are
assisted in their war against the Fascists with the latest scientific
equipment of the Martian-like, advanced civilization. The Fascist
leader tries to persuade the "planetary engineer":

What? You want to get rid of us and leave these Bolsheviks on your
planet? Why, they'll cause a revolution among you. Why, they'll annihilate the capitalists, who give work to everyone.

Engineer: Listen, you dummy, all the machines are ours in common;
we have no capitalists, this was done by us workers, our own revolution.[36]

The Fascist soldiers are impressed. They admit that "we, too, are
workers, our cause is a common one." They beg forgiveness, claim-
ing that their leader, who talks of Mussolini, has deceived them:
"We were assured that Communists were wild people with bushy
hair, knives in their teeth, trying to annihilate everything." [37] The

[34] *Chërnyi iar.* See *Repertuarnyi biulleten'*, No. 5–6 (May–June, 1928), p. 39.
[35] A. Brushtein, "Sovetskii teatr dlia detei," in *Sovetskii teatr,* ed. Grigor'ev, p. 580.
[36] Rozanov, *Bud' gotov* (Moscow, 1925), p. 38.   [37] *Ibid.*, p. 39.

Fascist leader is thrown off the planet, and the Pioneers prepare to return to the earth: "Here there are no oppressed. There is nothing for us to do. Remember our chief aim—to help the oppressed. Let us carry the example of their planet to the earth." [38] Through a giant loudspeaker, the Pioneers hear voices from earth calling, "Lenni, far-off Lenni." The Pioneer captain says it sounds like someone calling for Lenin. The source is identified as India, and the Pioneers take off on their mission of mercy.

The scene shifts to India, where a British *sahib* is shown mistreating the natives. One beggar tells his fellow sufferers of a prophet named "Lenni," who "rose up against the power of the rich" in a "far-off cold country," and "freed his people." As the *sahib* beats his servant, Sami,[39] the boy cries out: "Lenni, far-off Lenni—if you are really so powerful, if you are really more powerful than Brahma or Vishnu—come. Come from your cold country. You are needed more here. Lenni, far-off Lenni." [40] Whereupon the Pioneers appear and dissuade the *sepoys* from attacking: "Listen, say that we are Russian Pioneers, who have attacked you, conquered you, and released you unharmed so you can tell them that the liberation of the oppressed people of India is taking place." [41] As the natives prepare to leave with the Pioneers, they ask whether they will see Lenin. One Pioneer sadly explains that Lenin is dead, but the captain adds: "The deeds of the leader cannot die. Here are his descendants." [42] With this cue, the audience begins to sing Pioneer and Komsomol songs. A screen is lowered, and a film strip flashes on, showing Lenin delivering a speech. All join in singing the *Internationale*.

An example of a play for older children on the international theme is *Fritz Bauer,* written by Natalia Satz and V. Selikhova. The Moscow Theater for Children first presented it on February 7, 1928, and it continued to be performed until 1935.[43] Fritz is the son of a Bavarian Communist who is sought by the police for his part in provoking strikes. Despite the boy's loyalty to his father, Karl Bauer is caught by the police when Fritz is tricked into going to the house of a policeman. News is circulated that the boy has met

[38] *Ibid.,* p. 40.
[39] The name of a poem by N. Tikhonov, on which this episode in India is based.
[40] Rozanov, *Bud' gotov,* p. 52.
[41] *Ibid.,* p. 55.   [42] *Ibid.,* p. 56.
[43] The play was shown to 45,000 spectators during the season of 1928–29 alone.

with an accident, and Karl is thereby lured home. In prison, a fellow inmate consoles Karl Bauer:

You're not the first and you're not the last. The "righteous" court is in their hands. The "just" newspapers are under their dictation. Communist Max Hoelz sits in jail for setting fire to a house he never saw. The "criminal offenders" Sacco and Vanzetti, after seven years in prison, are sent to the electric chair.[44]

At the end, after the boy and his mother have managed to get to the USSR through the help of the MOPR,[45] Fritz appears before the curtain dressed in the uniform of a Pioneer, and tells the audience:

Mother and I are living in Moscow. Yesterday I got a letter. My father is coming to us. Comrades, we have it good, very good, in the land of the Soviets. But I will never forget how workers and their children live in other countries. I know well what the expression "Be ready" means. And I am ready, always ready. Comrades, are you ready for the workers' struggle?[46]

And the audience shouts back: "Always ready."

Discussing this play, Natalia Satz described how her young spectators would sob during the performance:

Children who in real life have not experienced the class struggle in all its implacable cruelty should experience it in the theater. Tears, if they are weakening, are harmful. Tears of protest, which are ammunition for the struggle, which strengthen preparedness to aid the oppressed of all the world in their struggle, are useful.[47]

Even after the victory of the theory of "socialism in one country" in the late twenties, the theme of assistance to revolutionary movements abroad continued to appear in children's plays (see page 177). The theater lagged behind official policy until the middle thirties, when Pioneers were no longer shown taking part in world revolution. However, international brotherhood and compassion for the oppressed remained fundamental precepts of Soviet education which found expression in drama for children.

In addition to the nascent repertoire based upon Soviet life and the class struggle abroad, the children's theater continued to pro-

44 V. Selikhova and Satz, *Frits Bauer* (Leningrad, 1929), pp. 68–69.

45 *Mezhdunarodnaia organizatsiia pomoshchi bortsam revoliutsii* (International Aid Organization for Revolutionary Fighters).

46 Selikhova and Satz, *Frits Bauer*, pp. 69–70.

47 Satz, *Nash put'*, p. 17.

duce fairy tales and classics from Russian and Western literature.[48] Beginning with 1923, when Ostrovskii's *Poverty Is No Crime* was produced in Briantsev's Leningrad Theater, classical drama came to occupy a prominent place. Ostrovskii and Pushkin were the most frequently performed Russians,[49] while from Western dramaturgy works by Shakespeare,[50] Molière, Goldoni, Schiller, and Calderón appeared and reappeared in the *tiuz*. Stage versions of American and Western European novels were especially common in the twenties, when there were still few original Soviet plays: *Tom Sawyer*, *The Prince and the Pauper*, *Uncle Tom's Cabin*,[51] and novels by Dickens were adapted. Natalia Satz said that her production of *Robin Hood* was aimed at making "an excursion into other times, into the life of other people, but from the point of view of our present Soviet times." [52]

In this remark lies the *raison d'être* of classics in the repertoire: Soviet education requires that the young citizen be familiar with the great literature of the past; however, in order that he may clearly understand through artistic images the Marxian view of history, the classics are usually reworked to point up the "class contradictions" of feudal and capitalistic societies with the aim of helping the Soviet child to acquire a broad "world-outlook," a proper perspective of his own socialist society and its place in history.

[48] At the time of the first All-Union survey of the children's theater in 1939–40, there were at least 200 plays in the repertoire. Of these, 25 percent were fairy tales, 40 percent were classics, and 35 percent were original Soviet plays on realistic subjects (Aronov, *Teatr iunogo zritelia*, pp. 17–28). The trend toward realistic and contemporary themes is marked. In 1951, out of 177 plays in the repertoire, 84 were based on contemporary subjects, 33 on literary classics of the Soviet republics, 17 on foreign works; and 43 were adaptations of fairy tales (Sperantova, "Children's Theaters," p. 35).

[49] As many as 16 of Ostrovskii's plays have been produced. Pushkin is represented by his tales, little tragedies, *Boris Godunov* and *Dubrovskii*. Fonvizin, Gogol, and Griboedov are also popular.

[50] *Twelfth Night, Romeo and Juliet*, and *A Midsummer Night's Dream* are the most popular.

[51] Mrs. Stowe's classic first appeared in 1927 and was still popular in 1939, when it was played 201 times in 5 different theaters. In 1949, a new version appeared in Moscow, with a prologue showing a young Negro girl injured at a political rally in New York. As she awaits medical aid, her mother tells her the story of Uncle Tom, and the play itself unfolds. Harrison Salisbury, reporting his visit to one performance (New York *Times*, April 18, 1949), described the audience's cries of protest at the injustices they witnessed on stage, including the hanging of Tom.

[52] Satz, *Nash put'*, p. 15.

IV

The advent of the First Five-Year Plan brought new demands on the children's theater, as it did on all Soviet art. Between 1929 and 1932 there was increasing insistence on contemporary plays portraying the efforts of children in socialist construction. The search for appropriate themes led directly away from fantasy:

The fairy tale was soon put under suspicion, and a little while later, through the painstaking solicitude of many ultra-left ideologists, was completely exiled as a harmful remnant of the capitalistic past; as if, in the struggle for realism in the Soviet theater for children, it were necessary to drive out fantasy, fable, and poetry.[53]

Never-Never Land was off-limits for Soviet children. Blame for this extremism has since been placed on a group of child psychologists who protested, "How can you show children a fairy tale when in a fairy tale miracles occur capable of destroying the concrete, materialist understanding of reality?"[54] Also censured in subsequent years was the RAPP (Russian Association of Proletarian Writers), which demanded works dealing with the immediate problems of the day. Fantasy had no place in literature for these extremists, and it was to remain in disfavor for some time (see pages 187–88).

Thus, the period of the First Five-Year Plan saw the production of agitational plays such as *Four Million Authors* (1930) by Alexandra Brushtein and Boris Zon. The four million authors are all the Soviet Pioneers who help to build socialism. As the curtain rises, an actor in the role of Misha, a Pioneer leader, discusses with the spectators what kind of play they prefer to see. Various subjects are suggested, until Misha says: "Comrades, in view of the fact that the votes are scattered, I propose this solution: Let our play, which we are going to compose, be about foreigners, Pioneers, the countryside and all the rest."[55] But, adds Misha, the audience cannot simply sit and watch, for they are Soviet people and must, therefore, work. He divides the auditorium into four groups, each having a task. One group "mows," another "hammers," a third "builds," and a

---

[53] Aronov, *Teatr iunogo zritelia*, p. 28.
[54] S. Tsimbal, "Vozvrashchenie skazki," *Rabochii i teatr*, No. 7 (July, 1937), p. 20.
[55] Brushtein and Zon, *Chetyre milliona avtorov* (Moscow and Leningrad, 1931), p. 7.

fourth "writes." At a sign from Misha, the children all stand and "work" as they shout what they are doing, ending with: "We are building socialism." [56] Foreign capitalists appear on the stage periodically to interfere with the construction program. First, they promise the Soviets machines if socialism is not built. The spectators are asked whether they will agree. They shout their protest and resolve to show the foreigners that they can succeed without outside help. The decision is made to complete the Five-Year Plan in four years. Scrap is collected, and a factory built. The foreigners are called in to witness that "we don't need your machines, we don't need your bosses. We are our own bosses—we are building socialism!"

Next appear bars with prisoners behind them. Misha tells the audience that "our best friends, the workers, sit in prisons abroad." [57] A letter with money for the prisoners is sent by the spectators. A policeman tries to intercept it, but the children pass it from row to row until it finally reaches the prisoners on stage. Misha urges the audience to sign up as friends of the International Aid Organization during the intermission: "By the end of the show there must not be anyone who is not a friend of the MOPR." [58]

In the next act, the Pioneers on stage and in the audience continue to build socialism by eliminating everything which impedes it. To conquer illiteracy, Misha enlists the children:

According to the socialist contract with Moscow and the Ukraine, the Leningrad Pioneers have promised to teach five thousand people this year. So you will teach them, too. Any objections?
Audience: No, no! [59]

Drunkenness is defeated as a huge bottle of vodka is knocked over by two boxers. Next, absenteeism from work is fought, followed by an attack on religion. Small figures of a priest, rabbi, mullah, and God are placed on the stage. Misha asks the children: "What does a Pioneer do with religion?" "He fights it!" retort the spectators as the actors overturn the figures.[60] Misha cautions the spectators:

Only remember, comrades, that here it is a game. We knock over a bottle like a roly-poly and a priest like a block. But in life we must not

[56] *Ibid.,* p. 4.   [57] *Ibid.,* p. 21.   [58] *Ibid.,* p. 22.
[59] *Ibid.,* p. 27. It is maintained that Soviet children actually played a significant part in the fight against illiteracy.   [60] *Ibid.,* p. 31.

fight that way against religion and drunkenness. We must unfrock them and force them out of our life so that they will vanish and not prevent us from living! [61]

The Pioneers fight uncleanliness by exterminating bugs, which enter singing a clever song by Marshak. Misha asks the audience whether they have enemies in the countryside, too. "Yes, yes—the kulaks!" [62] An old kulak woman is kept from poisoning some pigs by the shouts of the spectators: "To jail with her, to jail!" [63] With kulakism defeated, only one more enemy remains: the foreigners, who declare war against the Soviets. But actors and audience rise to the occasion fearlessly. The stage Pioneers march about to the accompaniment of a vigorous poem by Mayakovsky, while those in the audience shoot at targets of enemy ships and soldiers. When victory is won, Misha tells the children that the construction program can now continue and signals the four sections of the audience to perform their respective tasks as they shout, "We are building socialism."

In the published text of *Four Million Authors,* an introduction by Zon emphasized the "fighting political content" and "agitational" character of the play, which, through the active participation of the audience, helped children under ten to understand the reality about them in forms they could grasp.[64] Critics praised the Leningrad *Tiuz* for its production of a "real Soviet play, permeated with up-to-date political content." However, the theater was accused of "the simplification of political problems [which] leads to a perversion of the actual state of things." [65] Objections were made, for example, to depicting all foreign workers behind bars and powerless in the class struggle. Moreover, it was charged, the play contained too many ideas for the children to digest. Perhaps some of the didactic passages of the play were lost on the young spectators in the excitement engendered by the kaleidoscope of theatrical tricks. Nevertheless, it was felt that the play prepared children for real life through the medium of this "game-montage." The youngsters dutifully joined the MOPR during the intermission and left their addresses in order to be called upon as volunteers in the cam-

[61] *Ibid.,* p. 32.   [62] *Ibid.,* p. 40.   [63] *Ibid.,* p. 45.
[64] *Ibid.,* p. 4.
[65] S. Mokul'skii, "4,000,000 avtorov," *Rabochii i teatr,* No. 1 (Jan. 11, 1931), p. 12.

paign to eliminate illiteracy.[66] A number of former spectators of
the *tiuz* who are now Displaced Persons stated to the writer that, as
children, they took seriously what they were shown on the stage
and believed what the actors told them.

A persistent theme of plays about the Five-Year Plan period appears in *Cracking* (1932) by N. Shestakov. The action takes place in
an oil-cracking plant, but the title has a symbolic meaning as well:
"The author and actors show the intricate process whereby the
individual, too, is remade in the course of socialist construction as
a result of the Soviet environment as a whole." [67] Plays about industrialization and collectivization appeared with increasing frequency during this period. Children's theaters toured factories
and farms and presented these plays before workers and peasants as part of the drive to enlist their support in socialist construction.

In addition to such timely themes, the repertoire continued to
promote long-range desiderata of Communist education. *This Is
the Way It Was,* also by Brushtein and Zon, focused upon antisemitism and the class struggle in tsarist Russia.[68] Even in the hectic
days of the early thirties, the theater did not neglect its task of
teaching its audience international brotherhood. *The Far Road*
(1930) by N. Shestakov showed Pioneers traveling with a Russian
actor to rescue his son from a Chinese prison. The children succeed
and return home with new friends—French and Chinese boys.[69]
Hsiang-Feng, written by R. Landis and produced in 1931, described
revolutionary events in China and the role of its youth in the
"war of liberation of the Chinese Red Army against the imperialists
and their hireling, the Kuomintang." [70] The same year saw *More
Hindrance Than Help,* by V. Kurdiumov, about Pioneers fighting
Fascists in Italy.[71] In *We Are Strength,* co-authored by Natalia Satz

[66] V. Petushkov, "4,000,000 avtorov na stsene tiuza," *Rabochii i teatr,* No. 1 (Jan.
11, 1931), p. 19.
[67] L. N. Cherniavski, ed. and trans., *The Moscow Theater for Children* (Moscow,
1934), p. 74.
[68] Brushtein and Zon, *Tak bylo* (Moscow and Leningrad, 1930).
[69] *Put' dalëkii.* It was the second most frequently performed play of the Moscow
Tiuz between 1930 and 1932. See F. Muskatblit, ed., *Piat' let Moskovskogo teatra
iunogo zritelia* (Moscow, 1933), p. 6.
[70] N. Verkhovskii, ed., *Teatr iunykh zritelei* (Leningrad, 1932), p. 53.
[71] *Medvezh'ia usluga.* See Muskatblit, *Piat' let,* p. 16.

in 1931, Soviet Pioneers build a ship and sail to Africa to free the natives from their colonial oppressors.[72]

Dramatists also attempted to tell children about the national minorities of the USSR. In 1929, the Moscow Theater for Children sent playwright Shestakov to Ashkhabad, capital of the Turkmen SSR, where he studied the new life of the young Republic and gathered material for his play, *The Village of Gidzhe,* about "the struggle of the old Turkmen life with the new Soviet culture, which freed Turkmen women from age-old bondage":

The spectator is an indignant witness to the public display of the enslaved wife of Muhamed Jemal Kizi and to the sale of a ten-year-old girl as the wife of an old cripple. The spectator is stirred by the fate of the Turkmen teacher . . . whom the dark forces of the old existence are ready to destroy.[73]

Another aspect of Soviet life portrayed in the theater was the problem of juvenile delinquency. The civil war and its aftermath had left a legacy of vagrant children: so-called *besprizornye,* homeless waifs whose crimes became a serious threat to law and order. During the NEP period (in the twenties), a program was initiated to reclaim these vagabonds for useful citizenship by placing them in workshops and factories to learn a trade.[74] The children's theater contributed its services as a place to which the waifs could come regularly, assured of sympathetic treatment, and where, at the same time, they could see plays with educational value. An amusing anecdote told by Natalia Satz illustrates one of the successes of the theater:

I recall one of our audience of vagrants, nicknamed "Guitar," who attended the theater regularly. He particularly enjoyed *Mr. Bubble and Cherviak* [by S. Zaiaitskii in 1927] in which there was also a vagrant, Vas'ka Cherviak. This Vas'ka stole some money, but later returned it.

[72] *My—sila.* See Cherniavski, *The Moscow Theater,* pp. 39–41. These fantastic missions of mercy by Pioneers were increasingly condemned as superficial and "pseudo-ideological." After Satz fell from grace in 1937, historians of the theater held up these plays as examples of her "notorious influence." See Brushtein, "Sovetskii teatr dlia detei," pp. 557–59.

[73] *Aul Gidzhe.* See V. Liubimova, "N. Ia. Shestakov," *Teatr i dramaturgiia,* No. 7 (July, 1934), p. 16.

[74] A. S. Makarenko (1888–1939), considered as the foremost Soviet pedagogue, was especially successful in the rehabilitation of young criminals in the "Maxim Gorky" colony which he directed from 1920 to 1928. See his *Road to Life,* trans. Stephen Garry (London, 1936).

But that part "Guitar" couldn't stand to see. As soon as Vas'ka Cherviak got ready in the second scene to return the stolen money, "Guitar" would invariably go out to the lobby with the words, "Oh, the fool." But this play had a strange attraction for him. And immediately after seeing it for the seventh time he triumphantly returned a pair of scissors he had stolen from the pedagogical section of the theater at the first show.[75]

The Squealer, by L. Vepritskaia in 1929, showed a group of vagrants put to work in a shoe repair shop. One of them continues his thieving ways, presenting the others with a dilemma: should they adhere to the rigid ethics of their gang, which forbade tattling, or should they subordinate their own code to a higher principle? One boy reports the thief and thus gives evidence of his progress toward rehabilitation in acting for the good of society as a whole.[76]

Rifle No. 492,116 by Alexander Kron was produced in 1930 and became a great favorite. The play is laid in a Red Army camp, where four boys are sent for correction. The commander has been ordered to discipline the quartet, to "educate them in the Bolshevik way and create a healthy, comradely environment for them." [77] The boys are put in the hands of a young officer, Eino, who soon learns what he is faced with when his soldiers complain of thefts in the barracks. But Eino believes that "you must not consider people thieves all their lives because they spent their childhood in the streets." [78] The audience is provided with some understanding of one boy's past life when young Ivanov tells how his father was caught by the Whites and tortured to death. Left an orphan, he fell in with a band of thieves. Ultimately, the discipline of army life and Eino's patience help reform the boys, and they earn the right to have their own rifles.

The *Rifle* not only showed the transformation of delinquents, but is important as the first children's play on the Red Army. In the most significant speech of the play, Tonia, a political worker in her twenties, tells the soldiers:

Comrade Mozharov asked last time why everyone is not taken into the Red Army. . . . Because the Red Army is a class army, my friends.

[75] Satz, *Nash put'*, pp. 42–43.
[76] *Liagavyi.* See Cherniavski, *The Moscow Theater*, p. 44.
[77] Kron, *Vintovka No. 492,116* (Moscow and Leningrad, 1931), p. 8.
[78] *Ibid.*, p. 23.

The Red Army is not trying to conquer foreign lands, but to safeguard our country's borders from the bourgeoisie, who are preparing to attack us. And when war comes, workers and toiling peasantry will rise to the defense of the USSR in order to prevent landowners and capitalists from taking what is ours and again sitting on our necks. But the kulak and merchant are enemies of our work, and if we give them a rifle we will be arming our enemy. And such an enemy is more dangerous to us than the foreign soldier whom the bourgeoisie will send against us in its power and deceit. Sooner or later he will be on our side because, comrades, the real boundaries exist not between nations, but between classes.[79]

The class character of the struggle for socialism expressed here by Tonia was underlined in most plays written during the First Plan and the early part of the Second. Once that victory was won, the children's theater turned its attention from the epic of proletarian construction and the sharply delineated lines of the struggle between classes. As one critic put it: "The dialectic of life brings forth new problems to take the place of those solved." [80]

V

With industrialization and collectivization well advanced under the First and Second Five-Year Plans, the Soviet Union entered a new period in its history, one of vigorous efforts to stabilize the new institutions of socialist society. For the greater security of family life, legislation discouraging divorce was enacted in 1936. Strengthening of the family was declared essential to prevent juvenile delinquency. Abortion was prohibited. In the educational system, great authority was restored to the teacher, and discipline to the schoolroom.[81] The theater was called upon to do its part in producing the desired change in attitudes.

[79] *Ibid.*, pp. 57–58.

[80] S. Lunacharskaia, *Teatr dlia detei kak orudie kommunisticheskogo vospitaniia* (Moscow and Leningrad, 1931), p. 30.

[81] In the early days of Soviet pedagogy, when the regime experimented with new techniques, modified forms of American progressive education such as the Dalton Plan and Project Method were popular. Teachers had little or no authority, and the emphasis was on group activity rather than individual learning. In 1932, a Party decree abolished these methods and stressed the importance of individual studies as well as the role of the teacher. A further step in strengthening the teacher's authority came in 1936, when another decree liquidated pedology, a branch of educational psychology which relied heavily on intelligence tests. The teacher was now left free

The importance of the school and its teachers became the theme of several new plays in the repertoire. *Serëzha Strel'tsov* by V. Liubimova, produced in 1936, merits attention as one of the first of this genre and easily the most controversial. Serëzha is a fifteen-year-old in the seventh grade. The son of a kindly old science professor, he is of better than average intelligence, but suffers from fits of depression and is incapable of getting along with his classmates. His teacher, Natalia Petrovna, makes an effort to understand the motives behind his behavior. She suggests a visit to Serëzha's mother, but the boy begs her not to come, saying that his mother is sick. The boy's family background gives a clue to the cause of his maladjustment: his mother has deserted the family. Serëzha keeps her photograph under his pillow, staring at it half in anger, half in love. Unjustly accused of complicity in a theft of school property, Serëzha attempts suicide. When Natalia Petrovna learns that he needs a blood transfusion, she volunteers although she is anemic: "I have no children of my own and all my students are my children." [82] Freed from his former feelings of self-pity and loneliness after his recuperation, and realizing the heroic self-sacrifice of his teacher, Serëzha asks how he can repay her. Natalia Petrovna replies: "If you really want to make me happy, then be worthy of your country. I want to be proud of my students. That will be the best reward for me." [83] The playwright evoked respect and affection not only for Natalia Petrovna, but also for teachers in general. The spectator was shown the daily life of a Soviet school which probably resembled his own. When the children mischievously play a prank on one old professor of biology—they put a top hat and scarf on the classroom skeleton—Natalia Petrovna lectures them:

Is that respect for a teacher? Is that respect for your studies, your knowledge, for the whole school?. . . You wear red neckties [that is, are Pioneers]. This obligates you to a great deal, but I don't see the difference between you and the old *gymnasium* students who thought it smart to make fun of their teachers. I'm very glad when you enjoy

---

to evaluate pupils from personal contact and knowledge of family conditions, rather than on the basis of tests. See Beatrice King, *Russia Goes to School* (London, 1948), pp. 9–12.

[82] Liubimova, *Serëzha Strel'tsov* (Moscow and Leningrad, 1937), p. 74.

[83] *Ibid.*, p. 94.

yourselves, but there is a big difference between merriment and such
wicked thoughtlessness. Anton Antonovich could have retired on a
pension long ago, but he wants to transmit his knowledge to you . . .
because he loves you a great deal.[84]

For a time in 1936–37 *Serëzha Strel'tsov* was accepted as driving
home many valuable precepts to the Soviet schoolchild. During
that period, the play was produced by forty children's theaters and
by hundreds of "self-activity" theaters. At first, critics reviewed the
play favorably:

The central conflict is far from convincing in all respects. But all the
defects of the play are involuntarily forgotten since the play is timely
and fired with the author's real concern for her heroes. Education,
school and the family, questions of comradeship, friendship, love, relations with teachers—all this stirs schoolchildren today, and in it lies
the secret of *Serëzha Strel'tsov,* with all of its dramatic imperfections.
The dramatist, V. Liubimova, obviously is familiar with school material; her heroes are living Soviet children with all their good and
bad qualities. In the play there are no "bad" children, only children who
are mistaken. The greatest mistake is made by Serëzha Strel'tsov—he
strayed too far from his comrades. But aren't his comrades really to
blame for that? And the schoolchildren aren't the only ones mistaken,
for their teachers are, too. And so is Serëzha's father, for failing to detect the loss of spiritual equilibrium in his son caused by the mother's
departure.[85]

However, in October, 1937, the play was ordered off the stages
of the children's theater by the Central Committee of the Komsomol. A long article in *Soviet Art,* entitled "The Lie About Soviet
Children," charged that the play "shows school life in a crooked
mirror":

What is the role of the school, of teachers, of the Pioneer collective in
the education of Serëzha? Do they give true direction to the passionate,
romantic urges of children of a transitional age, when everything is perceived with extreme sharpness? The play gives incorrect answers to
these questions. By showing Serëzha's comrades and teachers as dull,
slow-witted, plain people, the play slanders our school.

After citing other examples of unsuitable plays, the critic concluded:

[84] *Ibid.,* p. 50.
[85] L. Maliugin, *"Serëzha Strel'tsov v oblastnom tiuze," Rabochii i teatr,* No. 7 (April,
1936), p. 14.

All these plays are testimony that dramatists still have a poor knowledge of the life of children, of the schools and their good and bad points. And it is not accidental that authors in search of interesting subjects and sharp situations exaggerate the role of an isolated phenomenon and pervert our reality.[86]

The marked change in attitude toward *Serëzha Strel'tsov* which took place between 1936 and 1937 provokes speculation. Did the play indeed pervert reality, or was it condemned because, as a former student-*régisseur* told this writer, "several touching scenes were too close to Soviet reality"?[87] Perhaps, in addition to the description of school life, the portrait of a boy deserted by his mother also influenced the decision to remove the play from the boards. At a time when the Soviet regime was doing its utmost to bring stability to the school and the family, it would hardly approve of showing children a hero who was a misfit in school and the product of a broken home.

By the end of 1937, it was clear that drama for children would henceforth be monitored vigilantly in order to serve the aims of Soviet education more efficiently. In following years more and more plays on school, family, and Pioneer life repeatedly stressed the positive qualities which every Soviet child should possess: love of one's motherland, devotion to studies, affection and respect for parents and teachers, cooperation in work and play with one's classmates, joy in the heroism of everyday tasks, and subordination of one's own selfish interests to the interests of the group.[88]

At the same time, the young spectator also saw in the theater many aspects of non-Soviet life calculated to make him count his blessings. For example, tsarist schools were recreated in such popular plays as *The Gymnasium Students* by K. Trenëv and *Blue and Pink* by Brushtein. *Blue and Pink* takes place in a school for girls in 1904. Scenes showing the ritual of prayer in front of the tsar's portrait and the detention of one girl in the empty auditorium for an entire night communicated to the spectator a Soviet version of the stifling atmosphere and repression of schools in his parents'

[86] Beletskii, "Lozh' o sovetskikh detiakh," *Sovetskoe iskusstvo*, Oct. 5, 1937.
[87] From an interview with Igor K., Munich, Germany, Feb. 17, 1951.
[88] Before the War such plays included *Skates*, on the power of the Pioneers to reform one of their erring members (Mikhalkov, "Kon'ki," *Oktiabr'*, No. 3 [March, 1939], pp. 83–105), and *Brother of a Hero*, on hero-worship of children for a Soviet flier (L. Kassil', *Brat geroia* [Moscow, 1940]).

childhood. The drama of the imminent Revolution of 1905 is reflected through the eyes of the girls. Zhenia, the heroine, reads a leaflet brought in from the street:

We're tired of working for bosses. We're tired of going hungry. We can't stand watching our children growing up without bread, without sunlight, without a school, without a childhood. . . . Two days ago we went out on the street. The bloody tsar's servants met us with whips and bullets. . . . Today we are burying our comrades. All who are with us, come out to the street! Drop your work, leave your vehicles, put out your furnaces—everyone to the streets, comrades! [89]

The Gymnasium Students chronicles the activity of pro-socialist students during the same period. They hold secret meetings, read Marx's *Capital* and Lenin's *The Spark,* publish clandestine magazines, and challenge the authority of their panicky parents and spying teachers.[90] *Lone White Sail,* adapted by V. Kataev from his popular novel, showed the people of Odessa stirred by the revolutionary speeches of a sailor from the battleship Potëmkin.[91]

The youth of famous Bolsheviks is another favorite theme in the prerevolutionary gallery. *Sergei Kostrikov* by A. Golubeva is the story of Sergei M. Kirov's youth and underground work, of the struggle between school authorities and revolutionary students.[92]

The young Stalin figures prominently in a play by two Georgians, *Lado Ketskhoveli,* which first appeared in the Tbilisi Theater of the Young Spectator in the Georgian language, but was soon translated into Russian and presented in Moscow in 1939. The character of Lado, the hero, is modeled after a fiery young revolutionary who operated a clandestine printing press in Baku in 1900. Lado's chief is twenty-year-old Soso (a Georgian diminutive of Joseph) Dzhugashvili, who later took the name of "Stalin." Before Soso's entrance, Lado and other revolutionaries argue about tactics, about publishing their own illegal newspaper. Soso takes over the meeting immediately upon arrival, and tells his assembled comrades of his plan to set up an illegal press in Baku under Lado's

[89] Brushtein, *Goluboe i rozovoe* (Moscow and Leningrad, 1940), pp. 101–2. First produced in 1936, it was still among the most popular plays in 1939.

[90] Trenëv, "Gimnazisty," *Teatr i dramaturgiia,* No. 6 (June, 1936), pp. 364–81.

[91] Kataev, "Beleet parus odinokii," in *Shkol'nyi teatr,* ed. S. Sadomskaia (Moscow and Leningrad, 1947), pp. 7–33.

[92] Golubeva, *Sergei Kostrikov* (Moscow and Leningrad, 1939). The play was adapted from her novel *The Boy from Urzhuma.*

command, while he remains in Tbilisi: "We will form close contact with the workers of Baku. We must unite the workers' movement all over the Trans-Caucasus." [93] The others agree with his proposal. Although he appears only in this brief scene, Stalin is portrayed to the audience as a bold leader who commands the respect of his comrades with a mixture of quiet humor and acknowledged authority. His guiding hand is shown throughout the subsequent action of the play.[94]

Other plays about Bolshevik heroes included such figures as Sverdlov, Budënny, Bauman and Gorky. Also drawn from Russian history were plays about Lomonosov, Pugachëv and the anthropologist Miklukha-Maklai.

The children's theater of the thirties took its audience back into the past of Western Europe, as well as of Russia. Galileo, Columbus, and Gutenberg made history before their eyes. James Hargreaves invented his "spinning jenny," and the spectators saw its effect on England's industrial revolution. Plays depicting contemporary conditions outside the Soviet Union concentrated on the struggle against the forces of reaction and oppression.

In 1934, N. Shestakov wrote an anti-Nazi play called *Mik,* in which the hero is the little son of a German Communist. Mik explains that his name is an abbreviation for the words "We shall destroy capitalism" (*My istrebim kapitalizm*). He helps a scientist, Doctor Strauss, to smuggle an invention out of Germany to the USSR: a miraculous powder which makes things grow to tremendous proportions. Strauss appears before the audience to demonstrate its powers. When he pours a few grains on a plant, it shoots up to the ceiling. Strauss explains that the powder could be used to grow food in great quantities, but that he fears its use for evil purposes:

Unfortunately, comrades Soviet children, the country where I live has a Fascist government. Would it be good if I gave my discovery to the Fascists? What do you think?

[93] G. Nakhutsreshvili and B. Gamrekeli, *Lado Ketskhoveli* (Moscow and Leningrad, 1940), p. 30.
[94] In 1930, school texts which included a biography of Stalin gave him no credit for setting up a clandestine press. But by the late thirties, as is indicated in this play, he was being glorified as the leading force in the Trans-Caucasus. Although there are many portrayals of Stalin in Soviet drama and fiction, this is one of the rare occasions when his youth is depicted. It is appropriate, of course, that the youth of their leader should be dramatized for children.

Audience: No, no good!

Strauss: I think so, too. . . . But what to do, then? Perhaps the best thing would be to send it to you, in the Soviet Union. Only there can my powder be used in the interests of workers of all the world. Isn't that so?

Audience: Yes. Right! [95]

Strauss is opposed in his efforts by the German Minister Crooks, who wants the powder as a Nazi weapon: "We can feed it to the whole nation. Casting aside the impure element—Jews, Negroes, Communists—we can make our citizens twice as tall. And who will rule the world then? What nation? Our nation!" [96] With Mik's aid, Strauss finally gets the powder out of the clutches of the Nazis— but not before the playwright has used this clever device many times over to point up the ideological opposition of Nazism to Communism.

Germany on the eve of Hitler's rise to power is the subject of Brushtein's *To Be Continued* (1934).[97] The printed program distributed by the Leningrad *Tiuz* at its performances exemplifies the theater's attempt to broaden the spectator's knowledge of the subject beyond the compass of the play itself: along with the cast of characters, the playbill contained numerous suggestions on background reading, such as the reports and resolutions of the Seventh Congress of the Comintern and various books on Germany.[98]

An American coal-mining town is the scene of *Son of a Scab,* by L. Vepritskaia in 1934. The hero is teen-age Cliff House, who is shocked to learn that his father, a veteran miner, is a strike breaker. Actually, Ed House is merely playing the role of "scab" in order to persuade the real strike breakers to join the miners on strike. But before Cliff finds this out, he has organized his classmates in a demonstration against his father. He learns the truth from House's victory speech at the mine after converting the "scabs" and from his arrest by the police. As Cliff struggles in vain to reach his father, the boy cries out:

[95] Shestakov, "Mik," in *Teatr detei,* ed. Satz (Moscow, 1935), p. 20.

[96] *Ibid.,* p. 41.

[97] See Zon, "Prodolzhenie sleduet," *Rabochii i teatr,* No. 17 (June, 1934), p. 15.

[98] This playbill, along with several others, is in the Soviet theater collection of the late H. W. L. Dana in Cambridge, Mass.

Papa, you were right and I—
   House: You, too, were right. Don't take it to heart. The fight isn't
an easy one, Comrade Cliff.
   Cliff (in despair): Papa!
   House (turning, cheerfully): Now you buck up! Keep your chin up,
like a real fellow from the Northern Mines.[99]

As the fear of war grew in the late thirties, Soviet children were
educated to the need for defending the homeland against potential
enemies. The children's theater cooperated with such plays as *At
the Cove,* by D. Del in 1938, which told how spies and "diversion-
ists" penetrated into a border town before they were captured by
a Soviet patrol.[100] *Our Weapon* by A. Kron, first produced in 1937,
was still one of the most frequently performed plays of 1939. It
is a sequel to *Rifle No. 492,116,* the first play about the Red Army
(see pages 179–80). The erstwhile vagrant boys are here shown
eight years later in a border town in Siberia, where they help the
Red Army round up a group of spies. One of their former officers
praises them and offers advice: "I will tell you the most important
thing I have learned in my thirty-three years and my eight years
in the Party: Keep growing, fellows, keep reaching higher. Get
knowledge and Bolshevik hardening. That is our weapon." [101] The
play ends with a joyful celebration, at which the final toast sums up
the sentiments of all present: "Let us drink, dear comrades, to our
motherland—may she grow and strengthen! To the Soviet people
and good people all over the world, and especially to Comrade
Stalin! That is the whole story." [102]

   In the repertoire before the Second World War the fairy tale
had returned to a place of honor after its temporary banishment
during the First Five-Year Plan. The principle of "socialist realism," established for Soviet literature in the early thirties, recognized the contribution of fantasy in stirring the imagination. At
the first All-Union Congress of Soviet Writers, in 1934, Gorky
opened the discussion of Soviet literature. The "co-report" supple-
menting his speech was made by Samuil Marshak, well-known

[99] Vepritskaia, *Syn skeba* (Moscow and Leningrad, 1934), p. 27.
[100] *U lukomor'ia* (these are the opening words of Pushkin's *Ruslan and Liudmila*).
See L. Levin, "Dramaturgiia Delia," *Iskusstvo i zhizn',* No. 8 (August, 1938), p. 17.
[101] Kron, *Nashe oruzhie* (Moscow and Leningrad, 1938), p. 131.
[102] *Ibid.,* p. 132.

writer for children. Marshak dealt with the state of children's literature, which was considered to be one of the most urgent problems
facing the Congress. Analyzing the role of fantasy, Marshak declared:

We do not intend to regenerate the old fairy tale in the Soviet land.
. . . In our country and in our day there can emerge not a *Wunderbuch,*
but a true fairy tale, because here people have entered a race with time,
breaking paths where man never before set foot. . . . Well then, do
we have a children's fairy tale, that is, a poetic, fantastic story which
asserts new ideas and facts? We must say bluntly that we do not yet
have such a fairy tale.[103]

Within a few years, however, the "Soviet fairy tale" was born and
has thrived ever since in children's literature. It consists of an inter-
weaving of fantasy with elements of realism from everyday Soviet
life.

In the theater, the best loved and most frequently cited example
of this genre is Mikhail Svetlov's *A Tale* (1939). The play begins in
a geological institute, where a group of students are gathered at
dinner. They persuade Vania, the school poet, to tell them a tale
which includes three themes: gold, friendship, and courage. One
of the girls pleads, "No magicians, I can't stand magicians." [104]
Vania thinks for a while, then says, "Attention! The tale is beginning. Come in, Ivan Anisimovich!" [105] The head of the institute
enters and informs his students that they are all to accompany him
on an expedition into the *taiga,* the Siberian forest. There they will
prospect for gold, not as fortune seekers, but for the good of the
government: the gold will be used to finance collective farms. The
location of the deposits is the Golden Valley, a place of "fearful
legends" which can be reached only by crossing "ten canyons, a
hundred peaks, a thousand obstacles." [106] Svetlov makes excellent
use of poetry, songs and phrases from folklore to infuse a romantic
quality into Vania's story of a scientific expedition. The essential
point of the play is not the search for gold or its discovery, but
rather the heroism of the young geologists and their joint efforts in

---

103 "Sodoklad S. Ia. Marshaka," *Pervyi vsesoiuznyi s"ezd sovetskikh pisatelei 1934*
(Moscow, 1934), pp. 27–28. Gorky was himself deeply concerned with the question
of children's literature; see his *O literature* (Moscow, 1935).
104 Svetlov, *Skazka* (Moscow, 1939), p. 12.
105 *Ibid.,* p. 28.   106 *Ibid.,* p. 56.

attaining the goal, a process through which "the collective is forged, grows and becomes strong." [107] When Vania finishes his tale, it would seem that the play is over. But at that moment Ivan Anisimovich enters and is informed by telephone that he and his students are to organize an expedition for gold. With this device Svetlov relates the tale to real life, for perhaps everything which Vania invented, and which was acted out before the audience's eyes, will now come true.

In their notes on *A Tale,* the producers drew a striking contrast between fantasy before the Revolution and under the Soviets:

While the dreams of the three sisters in Chekhov to go "to Moscow, to Moscow" were . . . ephemeral and unattainable, one of the heroes of *A Tale* merely makes a wish to go "to the *taiga*" and, as if by the stroke of a magic wand . . . the fabulous *taiga* becomes a reality, and in this reality is the fairy tale of our day.[108]

Folklore from old Russia and the West has also enriched the repertoire.[109] In adapting the Western tales, Soviet dramatists often introduce new characters to give the story a Soviet atmosphere. Thus, in *Laughter and Tears,* which Mikhalkov adapted from Gozzi's *Fable of the Love for Three Oranges,* the hero is Andriusha, an "ordinary Soviet boy." In bed with a cold one day, he amuses himself with some playing cards and falls asleep. The cards come to life and lead Andriusha to their kingdom, where he experiences a series of exciting adventures with Gozzi's creations. In his conversations with them, he always makes it known that he is "a most ordinary Soviet boy, a student of the 4-B class of boy's school 117," and he proudly asserts: "I am a Soviet citizen." [110] When he is summoned before the throne, Andriusha shouts: "I do not bow down to kings!" [111] He reveals himself as resourceful, clever, self-sufficient,

[107] *Ibid.,* p. 189.
[108] *Ibid.,* p. 191. Adult theaters also produced *A Tale*—a rare distinction for a children's play.
[109] These include Pushkin's tales, Marshak's *Twelve Months* (the first play of the children's theater to receive a Stalin prize), Ostrovskii's *Snow Maiden,* and old favorites from Russian folklore such as *Baba Yaga, Vasilisa the Beautiful, Il'ia Muromets, Finist the Bright Falcon.* National folk heroes appear in their respective theaters. From the West, tales of Andersen, the Grimm brothers, Perrault, and others have been dramatized.
[110] Mikhalkov, "Smekh i slëzy," in *Teatr iunogo zritelia,* ed. N. Stepanov (Moscow and Leningrad, 1946), p. 79.   [111] *Ibid.,* p. 81.

loyal to his parents, friends and country, and capable of surmount-
ing all obstacles—in short, the very model of a modern Soviet
schoolboy.

Although often the object of criticism, the fairy tale is firmly entrenched in the theater since it is considered to be a "powerful
supplementary means for educating the spectator." [112]

VI

The War forced the children's theaters of Moscow and Leningrad to evacuate eastward, but by the end of 1943 they were returning home. Their popularity and influence had spread so widely
during their sojourn in the East that the Committee on the Arts
recommended in July, 1943, that new theaters be established in
many cities where none existed before the evacuated companies
came. Brigades of *tiuz* actors also toured the fighting fronts and
military hospitals. [113]

During the War and long after, plays depicted the struggle for
the homeland against the German invaders. In 1942, Arkadii
Gaidar's novel *Timur and His Team* was adapted for the stage. [114]
Timur is a bold young leader of a band of children who help families of Red Army men at the front. Both book and play stimulated
the "Timur movement" throughout the Soviet Union, in which
thousands of "Timurites" behind the lines collected scrap, set up
workshops, assisted in hospitals, and performed countless chores. [115]
It was inevitable that A. Fadeev's famous *Young Guard* appear on
the stages of the children's theater. There Oleg Koshevoi and
his brave young comrades of Krasnodon faced the German firing
squad with fervent prayers for their motherland and contempt for
their executioners. [116] In 1945, a contest was held by the Committee
on the Arts for the best children's plays, with special emphasis on
contemporary themes. One of the winners was *The Girls* by Vera
Panova, noted Soviet novelist. It is a poignant drama of two mother-

[112] Aronov, *Teatr iunogo zritelia,* p. 28.

[113] See Brushtein, "Sovetskii teatr dlia detei," p. 583.

[114] A. Grossman and A. Gol'dberg, "Timur i ego komanda," in *Shkol'nyi teatr,* ed.
S. Sadomskaia, pp. 157–200.

[115] See Brushtein, "Sovetskii teatr dlia detei," p. 583.

[116] See G. Grakov, "Molodaia gvardiia," in *Shkol'nyi teatr,* ed. Sadomskaia, pp. 255–
311.

less sisters whose father is at the front, and of their heroism during the three long years before he returns.[117]

Perhaps the most moving war play was *Tale of Truth* by the poet Margarita Aliger, who in 1946 won a second Stalin prize for this work, in addition to the one awarded in 1942 for her poem *Zoia*. The play deals with the same subject—the martyrdom of a young Komsomol girl, Zoia Kosmodem'ianskaia, who was tortured and killed by the Germans in the 1941 attack on Moscow. Several passages from the poem are delivered as monologues by the heroine, infusing the play with rich lyricism. In the final scene, as she lies dying, Zoia imagines she sees Stalin before her, telling her that Moscow has held firm: "Thank you, Joseph Vissarionovich, for coming to tell me this. Now I am no longer afraid of anything." Now she can die peacefully and, turning to face the audience, she says: "Why are you silent, comrades? It's all right. It's all right. Live proudly, boldly, beautifully! Do not fear for me. It is a joy to die for one's people!" [118]

Even the fairy tale was recruited for war work and served well as allegorical representation of the Soviet-German struggle. Russian folk heroes fought such nefarious enemies as Duke Iron-Heart, King Spider, and Koshchei the Deathless. But the disguises were thin: they were all quite like Hitler. Plays extolling wartime heroism continued to appear long after victory, for in the postwar years patriotism has been stressed above all as a most vital aspect of Soviet education.

VII

The path of postwar repertoire for children was in large measure determined by the now famous resolutions and pronouncements of 1946 on literature and drama. The Party resolution of August 26, "on the repertoire of dramatic theaters and measures for its improvement," declared: "The chief defect of the present . . . repertoire of dramatic theaters is that plays by Soviet authors on contemporary themes are virtually excluded." [119] Playwright Alexandra Brushtein interpreted its meaning for children's drama:

[117] See Panova, "Devochki," in *Teatr iunogo zritelia,* ed. Stepanov, pp. 173–223.
[118] Aliger, "Skazka o Pravde," in *Shkol'nyi teatr,* ed. Sadomskaia, p. 250.
[119] *Teatral'nyi al'manakh,* Book 3 (5), p. 3.

Like the whole country, the children's theaters are looking ahead to tomorrow. If, in all the prewar period of their history, the *tiuzy* remembered that they were called on to educate children, tomorrow's warriors and fighters, then in our day they have again heard the battle cry of the Party, government, and whole country. . . . The theme of education of youth runs through [the resolutions] like a red thread. This call to the education of a new Communist generation through the medium of art is also directed at the children's theater.

Do we have plays which would educate this future youth in the way our Party wants? Of course, we have, but they are still few in number.[120]

In the most frequently performed and highly praised dramas since 1946 contemporary problems have been given precedence to a degree unparalleled in the history of the repertoire. Moreover, certain themes are so often repeated as to indicate a conscious attempt to keep them uppermost in the child's mind.

Red Necktie by Mikhalkov was first produced in 1947. The chief characters are two thirteen-year-old boys: Valerii Vishniakov, son of a factory director, and Shura Badeikin, a war orphan. Valerii is a talented boy, but listless, inconsiderate of others, and uncooperative. He refuses to carry out an assignment in his Pioneer detachment, angrily takes off his red necktie (part of the uniform), and throws it on the table in front of his superiors. For this, Valerii is expelled from the Pioneers. When his father hears the news he is deeply troubled:

If they said to me, "You will assume responsibility for setting up a lathe"—and a lathe is a complicated thing, it's no easy job to do—what if I went to the district committee, took out my Party card, laid it on the table, and said, "It's too hard. I don't want to set up a lathe." I dare say I would be expelled, too. They would kick me right out. Who needs someone like me?

Valerii (timidly): But a Party card isn't a red necktie.

Vishniakov: A person who cannot value his red necktie when he is a child will not pay any attention to his Party card.[121]

Valerii's father reminds him of his favored position as the son of a factory director:

Think of those children who are not so well off as you. They don't take off their Pioneer neckties. Because they are young Leninists, they respect what their fathers fought for, and they are also fighting for it.

120 Brushtein, "Sovetskii teatr dlia detei," pp. 583–84.
121 Mikhalkov, "Krasnyi galstuk," in *Shkol'nyi teatr*, ed. Sadomskaia, p. 485.

If you cannot be a real Pioneer, you will hardly make a real Communist.[122]

The scene stresses for the audience the significance of the Pioneer
organization in building the future Communist. In the end, the
collective triumphs over the egotist: Valerii realizes that he must
do his share, confesses his error and wins his way back into the
Pioneers. The fact that the "spoiled" child is the son not of a rank-
and-file worker, but of a factory director and Party member, raises
the question whether Valerii's behavior pattern is a not uncommon
one among children of privileged parents in Soviet society, whether
social distinctions in this "class-conflict-less" society may not be
strong enough to produce the phenomenon. One critic deemed
Valerii's actions "a reflection of survivals of capitalism in the young
consciousness." [123] That conduct unbecoming a socialist persists
among certain Soviet youngsters is indicated not only by *Red Necktie,* but also by other plays in the repertoire. In every case, such
willful egocentrism is held up to scorn, and Soviet youth is urged
to emulate quite another type.

The "positive hero" of *Red Necktie* is Shura, the orphan. Un-
daunted by the war years, optimistic and fearless, he is the quintes-
sence of the ideal postwar Pioneer. Shura's faith in the limitless
opportunities for youth in the Soviet Union is seen in his thoughts
on his happy life as compared with life elsewhere: "How can you
be happy if, say, you are a Negro and live in America? They don't
even consider you a person there. Suppose you were born there
today. You are already nobody if you were born black instead of
white." [124] And again: "I have a dream of becoming a doctor, like
Pirogov! So fewer Soviet people will die. Who is preventing me?
No one! But if I didn't live in the Soviet land, I would see all my
dreams only in my sleep, unless I had gold in the bank. . . . (He
stands.) Enough philosophizing, let's go skating!" [125] *Red Necktie*
is typical of the emphasis in postwar plays on the power of the
collective, the joy of Soviet life, and the misery of non-Soviet life.

In *Matriculation Certificate* (1949) by A. Geraskina, seventeen-
year-old Valentin Listovskii, capable and intelligent, has begun to

[122] *Ibid.,* p. 486.
[123] E. Mindlin, "O chuvstve novogo v detskom teatre," *Teatr,* No. 10 (Oct., 1947),
p. 29.
[124] Mikhalkov, "Krasnyi galstuk," p. 480.　　　　　　　　[125] *Ibid.,* p. 481.

neglect his obligations (such as writing an article for the Komsomol paper). He teases his teacher in class, treats his friends superciliously. His teacher tells him: "To act the way you do is shameful for a Soviet schoolboy, and all the more for a Komsomol member." [126] A Komsomol meeting is held after class to thresh out charges against Valentin. His chief accuser, Lenia, rehearses the lad's offenses. Valentin hotly defends himself, citing his contributions, but his position is untenable. "What kind of example do you set for the Pioneers?" shouts Lenia.[127] Listovskii is voted out of the Komsomol and is told by the district secretary:

You have worked poorly. You have torn yourself away from the collective. May today's meeting serve as a bitter lesson to you. You yourself have seen where you get by disliking your work, failing to make a habit of work, by arrogance and conceitedness. "Only in toil," said Vladimir Il'ich [Lenin], speaking to the Komsomols, "only in toil with workers and peasants can you become real Communists." (Applause. Curtains close.) [128]

After he has had time to digest the full meaning of his actions, Valentin comes to the district secretary and says, "It is hard for me, Boris Ivanovich, I am alone." He is told: "You will have to speak about your errors honestly. And without false egotism. Honestly. In the Bolshevik way. Understand?" [129] A scene of general rejoicing follows when the Komsomols learn that Valentin has acknowledged his guilt. The play comes to a close with the school director raising his glass in a toast: "Boys! To your friendship, to your happiness, to our motherland, my sons!" [130] Although the social status of Valentin's family is never made clear, his home is described as "well appointed," and contains a piano, on which the lonely boy plays a symbolic bourgeois survival—Chopin's *Funeral March* (Beethoven's *Moonlight Sonata* in the version of the Moscow *Tiuz*). Critics charged that the character of Listovskii was "not typical of a Soviet tenth-grader," [131] and reproved the playwright for evoking too much sympathy for her hero, instead of focusing attention on the work of the collective in reforming him.

The action of *Precious Grain*, by A. Musatov in 1949, takes place

126 Geraskina, "Attestat zrelosti," in *Detskii teatr v klube*, ed. L. Shilovtseva (Moscow, 1950), p. 64.   127 *Ibid.*, p. 81.   128 *Ibid.*, pp. 82–83.
129 *Ibid.*, p. 96.   130 *Ibid.*, p. 100.
131 Liubimova, "Dramaturgiia dlia detei," *Teatr*, No. 12 (December, 1949), p. 73.

on a collective farm and shows Sania Konshakov, thirteen, orphan son of a famous agronomist, contemptuous of Pioneer and school-work, preferring to become a *kolkhoznik* (collective farmer). Sania quits school, remains aloof from the Pioneers, and follows the familiar anti-social pattern of egotist *versus* collective. Like the others, Sania ultimately repents his past errors, returns to his studies, and asks to be accepted into the Pioneers. Cooperative work with his comrades in cultivating grain results in a fine crop which wins praise from the adult workers on the farm and the allocation to the Pioneers of two hectares of the best land to farm on their own.[132]

In these and similar plays the leitmotif is repeated: the individual is nothing without the collective; serious study in school is the greatest contribution to be made to one's people and country. Discussions of specific careers by children seem to indicate the theater's attempt to stimulate interest in certain directions. Shura in *Red Necktie* wants to be a doctor. But a girl in *Matriculation Certificate* objects to her mother's wish that she become a doctor, and instead hopes to be a "Michurin horticulturist." [133] Inasmuch as medicine was heretofore considered as woman's province, this shift of emphasis from girls to boys is striking. A bid to interest the spectators in agriculture is manifest in Sania's promise to become a distinguished agronomist (*Precious Grain*). *Stern Comrades* is devoted to life in a Suvorov military academy, where future Red Army officers are produced.[134]

While postwar drama has concentrated on the importance of the school and the Pioneer organization in the upbringing of the Soviet child, the repertoire has not neglected life beyond Russia's borders. Present-day America is the background of *Snowball* by V. Liubimova. First produced in 1948, the play became one of the most popular in the repertoire, and was translated into several national languages of Soviet republics and serialized on the radio. Most of the action takes place in a high school in a Northern state. "Snow-

[132] Musatov, "Dragotsennoe zerno," in *Pionerskaia estrada,* ed. N. Mervol'f (Moscow and Leningrad, 1949), pp. 118–41.

[133] Geraskina, "Attestat zrelosti," p. 91.

[134] I. Motorin and E. Ryss, "Strogie tovarishchi," *Zateinik,* No. 3 (March, 1951), pp. 8–26. Since the abolition of coeducation in 1943 this is the first play to stress military training, which was one of the objectives in adopting the new program. To my knowledge, however, there has been no play answering the call to prepare girls for domesticity and motherhood.

ball" is the nickname of Dick Dempsey, a Negro boy. He gets along well with all his classmates except for a bully, "Butch," and a Southern girl, Angela Biddle, just arrived from Georgia. Angela complains to her father, a fat, cigar-smoking factory owner: "If only those black-faces wouldn't sit so close. Right next to you! . . . In the South, they sit separately, in the back, but here . . . That Mr. Thompson is too nice to them." [135] Thompson is the principal of the school. He encourages Dick to study hard and to ignore the prejudiced people who would have him believe that Negroes are inferior: "Your people are talented, intelligent and have made great scientists, musicians, and artists." [136] Biddle puts pressure on Thompson to seat the Negro in the rear of the classroom, but is refused. In his position as a member of the Board of Trustees, Biddle urges that Thompson be removed. Although he succeeds, Thompson's spirit is unbroken. Gathering his youngsters together, he faces Biddle defiantly: "You are celebrating victory prematurely, Mr. Biddle. We are going to fight for our children, for the future America. We will have them grow up for the world, for real freedom, for friendship! We won't back down! You can't frighten us! We'll fight!" [137]

The playwright portrays America as a land of extremes: Biddle is anti-Negro, a millionaire, and is working on atomic production for the government.[138] Thompson, the leader of the progressive forces, is shown as pro-Russian. In one scene, he invites a group of his students to his home, where they listen in awe as a passage from Fadeev's *Young Guard* is read to them. In the history classroom, where Roosevelt's picture hangs on the wall, the students ask ill-tempered Miss Feller to tell them about Russia. She replies abruptly: "The history of Russia offers nothing interesting or heroic." [139] When she is asked what Russia is like at present, she says: "Now it is chaos . . . disorder! The Russians fully intend to conquer the whole world and put it under their power. We must always be on our guard and remember the danger." [140]

[135] Liubimova, "Snezhok," *Detskii teatr v klube*, ed. Shilovtseva, p. 259.

[136] *Ibid.*, p. 267.   [137] *Ibid.*, p. 287.

[138] Atomic research has been made the subject of a play called *The Secret of Eternal Night*, in which Russian scientists compete with foreign attempts to harness an underwater volcano in the Pacific (I. Lukovskii, "Taina vechnoi nochi," *Komsomol'skaia pravda*, May 7, 1949).

[139] Liubimova, "Snezhok," p. 272.   [140] *Ibid.*, p. 273.

One observer in Moscow reported that when he saw *Snowball* in the Central Children's Theater, the children reacted to these words by jumping up and shouting, "It's a lie! Why don't you go there yourself and see." He was informed that this happened at performance after performance.[141]

Snowball was awarded a Stalin prize, as was another play about conditions abroad: *I Want to Go Home* by Mikhalkov, produced in 1949 and made into a film in 1950. The play takes the audience into an orphanage in the British zone of Germany, where displaced Russian children are mistreated and prevented from being repatriated despite the efforts of a Soviet major, who tells the British authorities:

I cannot help but express my surprise and the surprise of my people that the children of fathers who saved Europe from Fascism, Soviet children, are for some reason detained in Germany by English occupation authorities. Why are they not sent home to the parents who await them? Why is the truth concealed from them? Why are they told that they are orphans when many of them have mothers and fathers alive? [142]

The spectators learn why the children are kept there when one English officer privately tells a Red Cross woman: "So that your son won't have to work in the South African mines. So that your son won't have to parachute behind enemy lines." [143] One of the boys, Sasha, escapes to the Soviet zone, and finally is brought back home to the USSR. In an epilogue in front of the curtain, Sasha appears in Pioneer uniform as another Pioneer declaims:

We cannot control indignation; in wrath and aware of the truth,
We ask for their repatriation. Give back our Soviet youth! [144]

Both *I Want to Go Home* and *Snowball* have been praised as "fighting, politically sharp plays, which evoke in the hearts of children hatred and scorn for American fascism." [145] In such plays as these the children's theater has joined with adult drama in presenting the same general picture of the non-Soviet world, in accordance with the demands of the new postwar ideology.

[141] S. Kournakoff, "Soviet Kids and a White Supremacist," *The Worker Magazine*, Feb. 13, 1949, p. 4.
[142] Mikhalkov, "Ia khochu domoi," *Detskii teatr v klube*, p. 223.
[143] *Ibid.*, p. 225.   [144] *Ibid.*, p. 243.
[145] "Doklad K. Simonova," *Literaturnaia gazeta*, Jan. 28, 1950.

At the Thirteenth Plenum of the Executive Committee of the
Union of Soviet Writers in 1950, Vice-Secretary Konstantin Simonov devoted a long speech to the problem of children's literature.
Citing Gorky's dictum, Simonov explained its meaning for writers
with a juvenile audience:

It means to educate a person from his youngest years to think and to
act in a revolutionary way. And to act as a revolutionary means to build
Communist society, build it assiduously and constantly, fulfilling any
task assigned to you. . . . Thus, the first task confronting our literature, our children's literature in particular, is the task of educating an
active builder of Communism, not a benevolent onlooker, but a person
building Communism, with his sleeves rolled up, contributing to this
cause all his efforts and all his passion.

Simonov went on to say that since "our country is not building
Communism in a vacuum, because of the presence abroad of
enemies armed with an ideology hostile to us and materially armed
for war with us," literature was faced with a second task: "to educate a fighter, a person thinking politically, battling furiously with
all manifestations of ideology hostile to us, with all the machinations of the old world in the sphere of politics, ethics, mores, education, and upbringing." [146]

Dramatic literature for children between 1925 and 1952 discloses
the intensification of the theater's activity in educating "builders"
and "fighters." A striking trend is discernible in the number and
character of plays which aimed to mobilize children and guide them
along prescribed channels. The evolution in repertoire was in no
way spontaneous, but consciously directed from above and conditioned by changes in the social situation.

The twenties saw a period of tolerated experimentation, against
the background of a growing demand for plays with a "Marxist-
Leninist" viewpoint. On the eve of the First Five-Year Plan, the
future role of the theater was unmistakably defined: it was to serve
not as a temple of art for art's sake, but as a "weapon of Communist
education," an ally of the school and the youth organizations. Before 1929, plays dealing with the class struggle at home and abroad

[146] *Ibid.*

were in the vanguard of the new repertoire. With the Stalinist revolution came the demand for drama capturing the tempo of industrialization and collectivization. For a time fantasy fell a victim to the excessive emphasis on the contemporary. While the theory of socialist realism was hammered out in the thirties, the call sounded for more contemporary plays, but the repertoire was broadened to include the fairy tale as a fillip to the child's imagination. For reinforcement of the new regime in the school system, plays began to appear which sought to foster disciplined behavior, respect for teachers, application to schoolwork, affection for classmates. The *cause célèbre* of *Serëzha Strel'tsov* demonstrated the determination of the authorities that the children's theater should avoid "negative" aspects of the new society, and bend every effort to cultivate in young citizens the newly redefined ethics of socialism: love of the motherland and its leaders, devotion to family, love of work and pride in the efforts of fellow citizens, suppression of selfish instincts for the good of the group, intransigence toward enemies of Communist ideology. The war years saw the full flowering of these themes in plays glorifying the good fight and the victory.

Since 1946, under the vigilance of the Party, the children's theater has conformed even more closely to the standards set by Soviet pedagogical and literary theory. While it is true that a gap has always existed between the demands of official criticism and the fulfillment of those demands by the theater, the general tone of approbation during recent years indicates that the gap is closing. The chairman of the Committee on the Arts, the head of the school administration of the RSFSR, the vice-secretary of the Writer's Union, and others have praised the theater's progress and spreading influence.[147] The award of Stalin prizes is further evidence of official approval.

However, according to recent criticism, the theme of the young individualist who is torn from the "collective" has been unduly labored in the repertoire, to the exclusion of subjects equally important as educational material: young workers in factories and

[147] The influence of the Soviet children's theater has extended into East Germany, Poland, and Czechoslovakia. Not only have Russian companies toured there, but theaters modeled after the *tiuz* have been established and are producing well-known plays of the Soviet repertoire in Berlin, Leipzig, Prague, Warsaw, and other cities.

farms as builders of Communism, positive adult heroes whom children can emulate.

Simonov concluded his speech to the Union of Soviet Writers:

Our children's literature is growing and strengthening. It is fundamentally a healthy literature, growing in the right direction. The question now is only to give active and firm support to what is ideologically progressive, valuable, and important for the education of young Leninists, the people of a new society.[148]

The "young Leninist" of today was born after socialism was officially declared to have been established in the Soviet Union. He has seen his country emerge victorious in war and enter a period of peacetime reconstruction. Every day he is exposed to a battery of communications media repeating the slogans of Communist education in his school, his Pioneer detachment, his newspaper, his books, his films, and his plays. The theater operates, above all, on the emotions of its audience. When children enter the auditorium, they project themselves on to the stage and live every moment of the drama. They see transmuted into dramatic form the ideas and ideals which are inculcated in them outside the theater. Here those concepts breathe life and leave a profound and lasting impression.

Marshak once said that the theater is the child's favorite artistic medium. Former spectators and artists of the *tiuz* have repeatedly stressed the unquestioning belief of children in what they saw and heard in the theater. Such a reaction to the drama is, of course, characteristic of children throughout the world. How much more effective, then, must be an extensive theatrical system for children, long practiced in combining in its repertoire artistic entertainment and official educational ideology. In harnessing the great potential, which is drama, to Soviet education, the USSR delivers incalculable power to the machinery geared to produce generations of loyal young citizens.

[148] "Doklad K. Simonova."

Rebecca A. Domar

The Tragedy of a Soviet Satirist:
The Case of Zoshchenko*

I

ON AUGUST 14, 1946, the Central Committee of the Soviet Communist Party, in a public statement, severely reprimanded the editorial boards of the literary journals *Star (Zvezda)* and *Leningrad* for publishing certain works of Zoshchenko and Akhmatova, ordered the *Star* to print no more of Zoshchenko's works, appointed A. M. Egolin as chief editor of the *Star* while retaining him as assistant director of the Board of Propaganda of the Central Committee, and abolished *Leningrad* on the ground that at that time there did not seem to be enough artistic literary works to fill the pages of two journals in the city of Leningrad.[1]

Later that month, in his report at meetings of the active Party members and of writers of Leningrad, A. A. Zhdanov, Secretary of the Central Committee of the Communist Party, enlarged upon the Resolution.[2]

At its meeting on September 4, the Presidium of the Board of the Union of Soviet Writers resolved, among other things, to expel Zoshchenko and Akhmatova from the Union, on the ground that only those writers can belong to the Union who "stand on the platform of Soviet power and participate in socialist construction."[3]

* The author gratefully acknowledges the extensive editorial assistance of Miss Louise E. Luke in the preparation of this article.

[1] "O zhurnalakh 'Zvezda' i 'Leningrad.' Iz postanovleniia TsK VKP(b) ot 14 avgusta 1946g.," *Zvezda*, No. 7–8 (1946), pp. 3–6.

[2] "Doklad t. Zhdanova o zhurnalakh 'Zvezda' i 'Leningrad,'" *ibid.*, pp. 7–22.

[3] "Rezoliutsiia Prezidiuma pravleniia Soiuza sovetskikh pisatelei ot 4 sentiabria 1946g.," *Oktiabr'*, No. 9 (1946), pp. 182–87.

In regard to Zoshchenko, the publication of his story "Adventures of a Monkey" (*Prikliucheniia obez'iany*) by the *Star* in its May–June issue of 1946 was given as the immediate reason for these drastic decisions of the Central Committee and of the Union of Soviet Writers. At the same time it was made clear that Zoshchenko's previous writings and his past in general were not without blemish. Particular attention was drawn to his autobiographical story *Before Sunrise,* which had been published three years earlier.[4] Finally, Zoshchenko was accused of having done nothing during the war to help his country and his people.

In the resolution of the Central Committee and in Zhdanov's report Zoshchenko's works and ideas were described as "shallow, insipid, and cheap," "encouraging a putrid ideological neutrality, crassness, and an apolitical attitude, intended to disorient our youth and poison its mind," "sinking to the lowest moral and political depths"—"a crude lampoon on Soviet life," "filth and obscenity." Zoshchenko himself was referred to as "a philistine," "a vulgarian," "a vile mind," "an unprincipled literary hooligan," "the dregs of literature."

These epithets and accusations were hurled at a writer who for the last quarter of a century had been extremely popular among Soviet readers, who had been regarded as an outstanding, if not the leading, Soviet satirist and humorist, who had often been elected by his fellow writers to positions of responsibility, who in 1939 had received the medal of the Red Labor Banner "for outstanding progress and achievements in the development of Soviet belles-lettres," [5] and who as late as April, 1946, had been awarded a medal for his "valiant work during the Great Patriotic War of 1941–45." [6] Zhdanov himself testified to Zoshchenko's popularity and high position in the Soviet literary world when he said in his report that the journals *Star* and *Leningrad* had been very willing to publish his works, that theaters had been "readily and gladly" placed at his disposal for the reading of his works, and that the story "Adventures of a Monkey" had been read in a great number of them in Leningrad.

[4] See p. 236.   [5] *Literaturnaia gazeta,* Feb. 5, 1939.
[6] *Ibid.,* April 27, 1946.

Moreover, he was permitted to take a leading part in the Leningrad branch of the Union of Writers and to play an active role in the literary affairs of Leningrad. . . . Zoshchenko almost became a coryphaeus of literature in Leningrad. . . . He is extolled on the Leningrad Parnassus.

In its resolution on Zoshchenko, the Union of Soviet Writers pointed out with great indignation that in 1946 a collection of Zoshchenko's stories, including "Adventures of a Monkey," had been published by both the Leningrad branch of the State Publishing House and a Moscow organization ("Biblioteka Ogonëk"), in a large number of copies. The very magnitude of the storm indicates Zoshchenko's importance in the Soviet literary world and his popularity among the people.

It is difficult to reconcile the vilification of Zoshchenko as "the dregs of literature" with the familiar assertion that the tremendous progress of the Soviet people in the realm of culture has made them far superior to the peoples of the Western world, that their highly developed literary tastes clamor for the very best which Soviet and world literatures can offer them. How, then, could "the dregs of literature" have been so popular among such people? Why have they been so badly mistaken during a quarter of a century as to be unable, without the aid of the central organ of the ruling Party, to perceive the real nature of the writer? This contradiction is merely sharpened by investigation of the immediate complaints against Zoshchenko by the Central Committee and Zhdanov.

"Adventures of a Monkey," published by the *Star* in its section "New Stories for Children," was evidently intended as a tale for children, in a humorous, jocular tone. The following is a summary of the story:

In a southern city of the USSR during the War, a little monkey, a marmoset, escapes from its cage when a bomb explodes in the zoo. Not seeing any use in remaining in a town under bombardment, the monkey runs off into the countryside, climbs a tree, and falls asleep. A passing military man sees the monkey. Fearing that it will starve to death in these parts, he takes pity on it and carries it off to a town where he has friends who will take care of the little animal. On the way to his friends, he stops off on some business. The unguarded monkey escapes and walks along the streets of the town until it becomes hungry. Now, where can a monkey get food in a town? It cannot go to a restaurant. It cannot buy anything in a store because it has neither money nor a ration card. While passing by a cooperative food store, the monkey sees fresh vegetables on the counter. There are people standing in line, and the saleswoman is selling them food. But what does a monkey know about waiting in line, buying, selling, paying? The animal is hungry and sees food: there is no reason why it should go on being hungry while there is food. So the monkey runs over the heads of the customers to the counter, grabs a bunch of carrots, and dashes out of the store.

One can easily imagine what happens next. A whole crowd, preceded by a dog, joins the chase: first, the street boys, then a great number of adults, and after them a militiaman with his whistle. While trying to escape from this crowd, the little monkey says to itself that it should never have left the zoo: after all, it could breathe more freely in a cage than here in the street. Finally, the monkey climbs a fence, jumps into a backyard, and there is found by a boy who takes it home and feeds it. While they are having tea, the boy's grandmother puts her piece of candy on her saucer, and the monkey snatches the candy. Of course, a monkey is not like a human being: the latter would not take anybody's candy when that person could see him doing it. But the grandmother grows very angry and says that she does not want to share her house with a monkey. One of them will have to go to the zoo. The boy assures his grandmother that he will train the monkey and that she will have nothing to worry about.

Next day, when the boy is at school, the monkey gets out of the house through an open window. In the street, the animal is caught by an old man who is on his way to the bathhouse. It occurs to the old man that he can sell the monkey in the market and buy himself a few drinks for the money. But since he does not feel like returning home, he takes the monkey along to the bathhouse and starts to wash the animal there, saying to himself that he can get more money for a clean monkey than for a dirty one. At first the monkey likes the warm water and the heat in the room, but when soap gets into its eyes, it bites the old man's finger and rushes out of the bathhouse.

And, of course, there is another chase in the street. But it so happens that the boy who had kept the monkey in his home is returning from school and sees the chase. The military man who brought the monkey to the town is also passing by, as the old man comes running from the bathhouse with his boots in his hands. The boy takes the monkey in his arms and says that it is his. But the old man also claims it, and, as proof that the monkey belongs to him, shows his bitten finger. But the military man declares that he was the first master of the monkey and that he wants to give it to the boy because the boy is kind to it. The boy takes the monkey home and cares for it. He trains the little animal in such a way that the monkey learns very good manners. Children and many adults can learn their manners from the monkey.

Analysis of this story led the Central Committee of the Communist Party to the following conclusion in its decree:

"Adventures of a Monkey" . . . is a vulgar lampoon on Soviet life and on Soviet people. Zoshchenko disfigures and caricatures Soviet customs and Soviet people, slanderously portraying Soviet people as primitive, uncultured, stupid, with philistine tastes and customs. Zoshchenko's malicious, hooligan-like depiction of our way of life is accompanied by anti-Soviet attacks.

Zhdanov added in his report:

The meaning of this "work" by Zoshchenko is that he portrays Soviet people as idlers and monsters, stupid and primitive. . . .
If you read the story "Adventures of a Monkey" very carefully and think about it, you will see that Zoshchenko bestows on the monkey the role of a supreme judge of our social customs and makes it teach the Soviet people a moral lesson. The monkey is presented as an intelligent being with the right to appraise the conduct of people. Of necessity, Zoshchenko had to give a monstrous, caricatured, and vulgar portrayal of the life of the Soviet people in order to make the monkey utter the foul, poisonous, anti-Soviet quip that it is better to live in the zoo than outside it, that one can breathe more freely in a cage than among Soviet people.
Is it possible to sink any lower morally and politically? And how can the people of Leningrad tolerate such filth and obscenity on the pages of their journals?

The story is a humorous portrayal not of the Soviet people, but of mankind in general—a type of writing hardly consistent with the official conception of socialist realism. There are no specifically Soviet elements in it. The Soviet Union has no monopoly on zoological gardens, cooperative food stores, and public bathhouses: such establishments exist in many other countries as well. During the War there was rationing in many countries, and people often had to stand in line. Stupidity and alcoholism are universal evils, and not peculiarly Soviet traits. There is not one country on our planet where the manners of children and of many adults could not be improved. The only Russian element in the story consists in the proper names. The action could take place in any country of the "capitalist" world, including prerevolutionary Russia. Of all the

characters in the story, only the old man is drawn as a complete
fool. The grandmother, the salesgirl in the store, and the cashier
in the bathhouse are treated with good-natured humor, as is the
crowd which chased the monkey down the street. The boy who
took care of the monkey and the military man who saved it are
portrayed as kind, intelligent, and sympathetic. The only custom
mentioned in the story is that of going to the public bathhouse, the
sole personal "taste" or habit that of having a piece of candy with
one's tea; and Zoshchenko does not make fun of them. The monkey
regretted leaving the zoo, where it could breathe more freely in its
cage, only while being pursued down the street by a dog and a crowd
of people. The charge that Zoshchenko's story is a lampoon slander-
ing Soviet life is an absurdity. It conveys the idea that life in the so-
called "civilized" world has become rather complicated and that
there are people, both children and adults, who are not perfect.
There is nothing new or outrageous in this idea except that it is
not treated by the one method prescribed for Soviet literature:
socialist realism.

As unfounded as the criticism of "Adventures of a Monkey" is
that given by the Central Committee, in the same vituperative
terms, to Zoshchenko's story *Before Sunrise* (1943), although, it is
true, some objections on the grounds of taste may be raised in this
case.

The Party branded Zoshchenko as unpatriotic by its charge that,
safe in his refuge at Alma-Ata, he had done nothing during the
War to help the Soviet people in their struggle against the Germans. In sober fact, Zoshchenko, at the age of forty-six, suffering
from a bad heart and shattered nervous system ever since he was
wounded and gassed in the First World War, would have been a
liability in besieged Leningrad or at the front. He was one of a
considerable number of writers who found refuge in Central Asia,
where the state of his health would not handicap his work. After
about a year and a half there, he returned to the West.[7] Occasional
mention of Zoshchenko in the *Literary Gazette* and *Literature and
Art* indicates that he was quite active during the war period, that
his work was praised several times, and that in April, 1946, four

[7] In May, 1943, if not earlier, he was in Moscow (*Literatura i iskusstvo*, May 8,
1943), and on Nov. 4, 1944, made a public appearance in Leningrad (*Lit. gaz.*, Nov. 11,
1944).

months before the "storm," he received the medal for his work in the War.

Zoshchenko's expulsion from Soviet literature cannot be explained on the basis of the reasons given in the Resolution of the Central Committee and in Zhdanov's report. The real motives must be sought in the nature of his work in general and in the relations between him and the Communist Party, or what may be considered its official literary critics, from the very beginning of his career up to 1946.

II

Mikhail Zoshchenko was born in Petersburg in 1895. His father was Ukrainian, a painter, and his mother a Russian actress. The family belonged to the gentry. After graduating from a *gymnasium* (secondary school) in 1913, Zoshchenko entered the faculty of law of Petersburg University. Two years later he volunteered for military service and was sent to the front as an officer. From 1917 to 1921, after the combat injuries which left him in poor health for the remainder of his life, he tried a number of occupations, including voluntary service in the Red Army. In 1921 he began to write.

Zoshchenko made his appearance on the literary scene in that year as a member of the Serapion Brothers. The well-known manifesto of this early Soviet literary organization, written by Lev Lunts, was accompanied by short autobiographies of most of the "Brothers." Zoshchenko's, entitled "About Myself, about Ideology, and about One or Two Other Things," [8] was particularly frank and irreverent. Twenty-five years later this piece was quoted by Zhdanov as a proof of Zoshchenko's "hooliganism" and "complete lack of moral principles." In spite of the frivolous and joking tone, this early autobiographical note reveals a political and ideological position in regard to Communism and the Bolsheviks which appears to have changed very little over the years. Zoshchenko wrote that he did not attach much importance to political ideology and that his own consisted in the lack of hatred for anyone. He could not

[8] Zoshchenko, "O sebe, ob ideologii i eshchë koe o chëm," *Literaturnye zapiski,* No. 3 (1922), pp. 28–29.

have any "exact ideology," as demanded by the critics, because no political party satisfied him entirely. Still, he stood closer to the Bolsheviks than to any other party, and he was willing to go along with them. But he himself was not a Communist or a Marxist, and he doubted that he would ever be.

The manifesto and Zoshchenko's "confession" aroused strong criticism. On the whole, the critics recognized the talents of the Serapion Brothers, and some commended them for not running away from the Revolution. But the critics objected to what they considered the "incorrect" approach of the Brothers to the Revolution: they wrote in a detached manner not about this great event itself, but about petty occurrences of everyday life. One critic predicted a short life for this literary movement, while another declared the movement already dead.[9]

Zoshchenko very soon became a favorite of Soviet readers. If the popularity of a writer can be measured by the size of the editions of his books, then during 1917–27 Zoshchenko shared second place with Gorky and Neverov (about one million copies each), after Dem'ian Bednyi (over two million copies).[10] If, like the others, Zoshchenko had been publishing throughout the entire period, instead of during the second half only, he might well have reached the top of the list.

The works which made Zoshchenko so popular at the beginning of his literary career were, first of all, his numerous satirical short stories. In them he describes everyday incidents which take place in an overcrowded community apartment, in the street, public garden, or park, restaurant, cinema, theater, store, tavern, street car, office, village—wherever there are people. The characters are ordinary human beings drawn from all walks of life. They see the Revolution

---

[9] Il'ia Sadof'ev, "Mucheniki mody," *Krasnaia gazeta*, Aug. 12, 1922, and "Oktiabr' i literatura," *ibid.*, Nov. 4, 1922. V. Polianskii, "Serapionovy brat'ia," *Moskovskii ponedel'nik*, Aug. 28, 1922. P. S. Kogan, "O manifeste Serapionovykh brat'ev," *Krasnaia gazeta*, Sept. 23, 1922; I. Oksenov, "Puti sovremennoi literatury," *ibid.*, Dec. 9, 1922; A. Mechislavtsev, "Tiukha," *ibid.*, Dec. 16, 1922; M. Alatyrtsev, "Literatura sinteza," *ibid.*, Dec. 30, 1922.

A detailed description of the first appearance of the Serapion Brothers on the literary scene is given by William Edgerton, "The Serapion Brothers: An Early Soviet Controversy," *The American Slavic and East European Review*, VIII, No. 1 (February, 1949), 47–64.

[10] I. V. Vladislavlev (Gul'binskii), *Literatura velikogo desiatiletiia (1917–1927)* (Moscow and Leningrad, 1928), p. 25.

not as a great event which marked the beginning of a new and better life for Soviet citizens, but simply as a change of conditions necessitating readjustment on the part of the individual. One has to fight in order to keep or to regain one's place in life, especially one's material well-being, and, whenever possible, one may even use the new conditions to gain new advantages. Some of Zoshchenko's characters have managed to find a comfortable and warm place under the new regime, while others have difficulty in adapting themselves.

Human foibles of all kinds are the object of Zoshchenko's satire: ignorance, stupidity, cruelty, pettiness, greed, bad manners, rudeness, selfishness, narrow interests, lack of culture—in short, everything which now comes under the convenient and all-embracing titles of philistinism (*meshchanstvo*) and crassness (*poshlost'*). Zoshchenko sometimes ridicules certain defects of Soviet life, such as the housing shortage, poverty and dirt in the community apartments, the penchant for changing names and titles, incessant meetings and conferences, and what he considers the excessive concern of literature with such problems as the "liquidation" of illiteracy and the fight against alcoholism. Almost all of these early stories are told by a narrator, who speaks the language of people with little education and culture. It is full of peculiar expressions, slang, bookish and scholarly words used out of place, high-sounding slogans applied to petty occurrences of everyday life. This inimitable style —remarkable for its cleverness, wit, pointed phrases, for all shades of irony from the utterly frank to the most subtle, and sometimes very skillfully blended with lyricism—was probably one of the main reasons for Zoshchenko's great popularity; he had numerous imitators, but no successful rival.[11]

In the few longer tales written during this period, again as satirist and humorist, Zoshchenko is content to treat only the "negative" sides of human nature and life, here mainly in members of the intelligentsia. He does not think highly of human beings in general: in his ironical prefaces, digressions, and asides, he often complains about their imperfections, both physical and mental, of

[11] A. G. Barmin, "Puti Zoshchenki," *Mikhail Zoshchenko* (Leningrad, 1928), p. 41; Evgeniia Zhurbina, "Mikhail Zoshchenko" (Foreword), in Zoshchenko, *Sobranie sochinenii*, 2d ed. (Moscow and Leningrad, 1931), p. 11.

their insignificance, of the mercenary motives hidden behind even their most ordinary civilities. He asserts that he does not exaggerate, that he lives in the midst of the people whom he portrays and sees them in their true colors.[12] In his depiction, human foibles (or, let us say, "philistinism" and "crassness") are not confined to any one social class of Soviet society. From former aristocrat to poor peasant, Zoshchenko finds these traits in almost every human being, regardless of social class. And he believes that there will be enough of these topics to last him for the rest of his life. The idea that life in the future will be good and that people will live well and happily he views with frank irony.[13] For him, "philistinism" and "crassness" are everywhere, and, what is more, they are here to stay.

By implication, then, if not by outright declaration, Zoshchenko was convinced at the beginning of his literary activity that human nature could not be changed by a revolution and a different form of government and that, consequently, the efforts and the promises of the Communist Party to reeducate the people and to create superior men and women were doomed to failure. To prove his point, of the ubiquitousness and persistence of the unregenerate homunculus, Zoshchenko drew from the life around him and from the newspapers (which often supplied him with topics for his stories) enough material for the several hundred satirical short stories and *feuilletons* which he wrote during the 1920s. Their tremendous popularity can hardly be explained by the excellence of his style alone: the wry realism of his stories must also have appealed strongly to Soviet readers, who found in them a reflection of the life they lived and saw around themselves, without the usual tiresome emphasis on official ideology and strident propaganda motives.

For this very reason, critics were placed in a peculiarly difficult dilemma in dealing with Zoshchenko, and tended to shy away from discussion of this nonconformist author whom the Soviet public read with conspicuous delight. Throughout the twenties the amount of critical attention given to a writer with such a large and

---

[12] Zoshchenko, "Siren' tsvetët," *Izbrannye povesti* (Leningrad, 1937), p. 175 (from *Sentimental'nye povesti*, first published in 1927).

[13] Zoshchenko, *Vospominaniia o Mishele Siniagine* (Berlin, 1930), pp. 9-10.

enthusiastic following was disproportionately small. This neglect could be partly justified by the fact that most of his writing fell into the category which he himself ironically called "the disrespected small form," the form of the very short story, or sketch, and of the *feuilleton*, which the critics considered unworthy of their notice. They were inclined to regard him, according to Zoshchenko himself, as a mere newspaper reporter.[14]

His longer stories, however, received more attention. (In this respect, Zoshchenko's experience paralleled that of Chekhov, between whose early work and that of Zoshchenko there is a certain similarity.) Some acclaim greeted Zoshchenko's first published pieces, the *Stories of Sinebriukhov* (1922), a series of tales told by a hapless braggart who, intent on easy pickings and the saving of his own skin, survived the horrors and absurdities of war and civil war only to find that the incomprehensible new society had no place for him.[15] In the several long stories collected under the title *Sentimental Tales* (1927), there is a steady undercurrent of tragedy in the comic and farcical lives of the misfits and derelicts from the intelligentsia who are the heroes.[16] At this time, before the entrenchment of the dogma that pity toward the new Soviet man was misplaced and unnecessary, critics pointed out as a virtue the sadness, sympathy, gentleness, and lyricism in Zoshchenko's narration of these stories.[17] Other critics voiced various degrees of indignation at his "incorrect" approach to the Revolution and to Soviet life. They objected to the fact that Zoshchenko wrote not of the Revolution itself, but only of its "backyard": the trifling little incidents, the anecdotes, the man-in-the-street to whom the Revolution meant nothing but a change of government. One decrier hinted that Zoshchenko himself was no better than the heroes of his stories. And the writer was warned that, without that "complete and lofty"

[14] Zoshchenko, "O sebe, o kritikakh i o svoei rabote," *Mikhail Zoshchenko*, pp. 8, 10.
[15] Zoshchenko, *Rasskazy Nazara Il'icha, gospodina Sinebriukhova*, Berlin, 1922. For criticism, see Il'ia Gruzdev, "Vechera Serapionovykh brat'ev," *Kniga i revoliutsiia*, No. 3 (1922), pp. 110–11; Iu. T-v, "Serapionovy brat'ia," *ibid.*, No. 6, pp. 62–64; V. R., "Mikhail Zoshchenko, Rasskazy Sinebriukhova," *ibid.*, No. 8, p. 41; and A. Voronskii, "M. Zoshchenko, Rasskazy Sinebriukhova," *Krasnaia nov'*, No. 6 (1922), pp. 343–44; N. Aseev, "Rasskazy Sinebriukhova," *Pechat' i revoliutsiia*, No. 7 (1922), p. 316.
[16] Zoshchenko, *Sentimental'nye povesti* (Moscow, 1927).
[17] A. R. Palei, "Mikhail Zoshchenko: O chëm pel solovei, Sentimental'nye povesti," *Novyi mir*, No. 6 (1927), p. 205; A. Lezhnëv, "Mikhail Zoshchenko: O chëm pel solovei, Sentimental'nye povesti," *Pechat' i rev.*, No. 6 (1927), pp. 220–21.

ideology which he had mentioned slightingly in his works, he would soon lose his place in Soviet literature.[18]

Slyly and adroitly, Zoshchenko parried the criticism directed at him, through the fictitious narrator whom he employs in most of his work during the late twenties—a half-educated, ostensibly naive observer who, passively accepting the new order while betraying his nostalgia for the less strenuous days of the past, describes the current scene in the slang and political catchwords of the hour. In "Hidden Treasure," he ridicules the new literary imperative that every piece of writing, no matter how short and insignificant, must have an ideological basis. In another story Zoshchenko's habitual mouthpiece regards with considerable irony the very idea of his writing, as the Communist critics recommended, on the subjects of the Revolution, the civil war, the changes in human life, the heroism of the people or of individuals, and the other "great" issues. He refers in the same tone of banter to the argument that belles-lettres should aid in solving problems of the day, such as a shortage of packing material, the building of silos, or the organization of collective farms. He himself did not refuse to write about such topics, but he intimated that their only proper place was in the newspaper *feuilleton* or the satirical sketch.[19] In the long story "What the Nightingale Sang About" (1927), his narrator protests against the "materialistic" view of love he sees as prevalent among Party members, who are generally inclined to disparage this emotion. Zoshchenko's "author" cannot possibly agree with their opinion. He is loath to reveal intimate facts of his past life to unkind critics, but he remembers from his youthful days a young girl with a pathetic, silly little white face, before whom, transported by joy and all sorts of noble emotions, he would fall to his knees and kiss the ground "like a fool."

Now, when fifteen years have passed and the author's hair is turning a little gray from various ailments and the shocks and worries of life, when the author simply does not wish to tell lies and has no reason to

18 Voronskii, "M. Zoshchenko"; Georgii Gorbachëv, *Ocherki sovremennoi russkoi literatury* (Leningrad, 1924), pp. 76–88, and *Sovremennaia russkaia literatura*, 3d ed. (Moscow-Leningrad, 1931), pp. 82–116; Iakov Braun, "Desiat' strannikov i osiazaemoe nechto," *Sibirskie ogni*, No. 1 (1924), pp. 201–40; V. Veshnev, "Razgovor po dusham," *Na literaturnom postu*, No. 11–12 (June, 1927), pp. 55–58, and "Komicheskie bliznetsy," *Kniga kharakteristik* (Moscow and Leningrad, 1928), pp. 85–96.

19 Zoshchenko, *Vospominaniia o Mishele Siniagine*, pp. 11–12.

tell them, when, finally, the author desires to perceive life as it is without any falsehood or embellishment, he still maintains, without fear
of appearing a ridiculous creature out of the past century, that scholars
and politicians are very much mistaken about this matter [of love].[20]

He deplores the concept of a human being as "out of tune" with
the times and therefore to be denied a place on earth, and pleads:
"Let me talk, comrades! Let a man express his idea at least as a part
of the discussion!" [21] In response to the critical imperative that
the works of Soviet writers should be optimistic and cheerful, Zoshchenko describes in "A Gay Adventure" the most "cheerful" occurrence he can recall, an episode reminiscent of Dostoyevsky's
Crime and Punishment and intended as a parody on the forced
optimism ground out at Party behest. He does not spare Party members his direct satire. In the play *Esteemed Comrade* (1929), the
Communist hero is a boor and a bully who takes advantage of his
Party card to keep his fellow tenants in a community apartment
cringing before him. In a dexterous coup at the end, Zoshchenko
deflects censure from himself by having this "negative" character
expelled from the Party.

In general, Zoshchenko's extremely subtle irony, his trick of not
meaning what he says and not saying what he means created many
pitfalls for the unwary critic. Several made fools of themselves by
treating a satirical piece seriously. The most vociferous of Zoshchenko's critics fulminated from the tribunal of the official newspaper of the Soviet government. While recognizing Zoshchenko's
talent and popularity, this critic charged him with having no love
for mankind and no faith in its future, with being himself "a low,
crude man-in-the-street, who with a kind of malicious joy rum-
mages around in human refuse." The success of Zoshchenko's
works ("vile anecdotes and utter slander against man") was explained by the fact that his portrayal of the contemptible little
human being created by tsarist Russia and, in the author's eyes,
unchanged by the Revolution, provided for some readers "a blissful
escape from the loud slogans of the Revolution." [22]

That Zoshchenko was able to publish his work in spite of the
castigation by such a spokesman exemplifies the comparative free-

[20] Zoshchenko, "O chëm pel solovei," *Izbrannye povesti* (Leningrad, 1937), pp. 129–
30.   [21] *Ibid.*, p. 131.
[22] M. Ol'shevets, "Obyvatel'skii nabat," *Izvestiia*, Aug. 14, 1927.

dom which Soviet writers then enjoyed. Obviously, there was much that invited satire in the tenacious residue of the old order left in the minds of the people, and in the incongruities created by the New Economic Policy in a country striving toward socialism. Throughout the twenties such material was recognized as fair game for the satirists. A license could always be revoked, however, as offenders were warned who grew careless in the vicinity of a Party preserve. In 1928, despite the warning of the preceding year, it was still possible to publish a ninety-page book devoted exclusively to critical analyses of Zoshchenko's work from the point of view of literary form, and not of political ideology. The several contributors to the volume, including the famous Shklovskii and Vinogradov, attributed Zoshchenko's distinction not to the superficial comic element and other "disrespected" features usually singled out by critics, but to his literary merits: good construction, the device of telling a story on two planes (that of the narrator and of the hero), his deft and ingenious language, deceptively simple in appearance, but actually exceedingly complex.[23]

Again, in a foreword to the book, Zoshchenko seizes the opportunity to retort to his critics: "In literature there is a so-called 'social command.' As I see it, this command is at present erroneously formulated." What is called for is not a red Leo Tolstoy, as is demanded by the injudicious, but something like his own "disrespected" small form, associated in the past at least with the very worst literary traditions. This is the social command he obeys.

I'm not trying to sneak into "high" literature. There are already enough writers in "high" literature as it is. . . .

The thing is, I am a proletarian writer. Rather, I am parodying that imaginary, but genuine, proletarian writer who might exist in the present conditions of life and in the present milieu. Of course, such a writer cannot exist, for the time at least.

I am only parodying. Temporarily I am pinch-hitting for the proletarian writer. For this reason the themes of my stories are shot through with the naive philosophy which is cut to measure for my readers.[24]

In his longer pieces he is also parodying; in this case he is "pinch-hitting" for the writer from among the intelligentsia who perhaps

23 Barmin, *et al.*, *Mikhail Zoshchenko.*
24 Zoshchenko, "O sebe," *ibid.*, pp. 8, 10, 11.

does not exist at the moment, but who would have to exist if he were to fulfill the social command actually given by public opinion.

A few years later one of Zoshchenko's most sympathetic critics found the "positive" value of his work to lie in these longer pieces, where "the outlook of the intelligentsia [understood here as the former privileged classes in general] is exposed with exceeding fullness and clarity, almost with declarative statement." In this respect the novelettes are the key to his work:

Zoshchenko takes to pieces fiber by fiber the psychology of the person of the old world: . . . the combination of crassness, mercenary calculation, profit-motive, all this pillar of bourgeois society, based on private property, with an elaborate system of "elevated" ethical and esthetic standards.

The man of the bourgeois world, caught in the vicious circle of its inconsistencies, cannot accede to the Revolution, which strips away all masks and exposes all contradictions. He is doomed to complete disorientation . . . and to moral destruction.[25]

At the end of this first period of Zoshchenko's career, the writer himself answers point-blank the importunate question put to him by the critics from the beginning, the question of his work as a social factor in socialist reconstruction:

In our time, is the role of an exposer and satirist like Zoshchenko adequate if the writer wishes to be in reality a writer of his epoch?

[It has been shown] what forces the work of Zoshchenko disposes of and destroys. What forces, then, does he . . . affirm in his work? What is contrasted to that twisted metaphysical system of the philistine outlook which he has exposed? . . .

This question was put to Zoshchenko in one of his talks with beginning writers. "You boldly satirize our social deficiencies. Why do you not unite these deficiencies with achievements? Will you be able to work in this way?" To this question Zoshchenko answered: "The thing is that my genre, that is the genre of the humorist, is incompatible with description of achievements. That is the concern of writers of another genre. To each his own way: the tragic actor plays in *Hamlet;* the comic actor plays in *Revizor.* It seems to me that each one must proceed according to his own bent." [26]

III

Zoshchenko's insistence in 1928 on his own interpretation of the "social command" was ill-timed and of short duration. In the fol-

25 Zhurbina, "Mikhail Zoshchenko," p. 6.   26 *Ibid.*, p. 14.

lowing year the "social command" as understood by Leopold Averbakh, at the head of the powerful Party-backed RAPP (Russian Association of Proletarian Writers), became virtually law for Soviet writers, impressing them into the service of the First Five-Year Plan not merely as literary observers but as participants, sometimes actual factory workers, in the industrial development of the period.

By what inner struggle Zoshchenko came to an acceptance of an assigned role in the mobilization of all literary talent, there can be only conjecture. In any case, in October, 1930, he was sent to an industrial establishment to write *feuilletons* for the plant newspaper concerning the lack of discipline among the workers.[27] This task, hailed in the press as a great achievement not only for Zoshchenko, but for all the writers of Leningrad,[28] marked his debut as an *aktivist* in literary projects sponsored by the Party and government. Month after month throughout the thirties, the *Literary Gazette* chronicled Zoshchenko's comings and goings as a public figure. In 1931 he worked in various plants, with other members of the All-Russian Union of Soviet Writers, on an assignment of *Pravda* and *Izvestiia*, to portray the foremost workers of the Five-Year Plan.[29] In June, 1932, at the invitation of the regional committee of the Communist Party, Zoshchenko went to the Urals "to become acquainted with the largest construction projects and plants of the region." [30]

In the concerted effort to win over the "fellow travelers" during the First Plan, Zoshchenko was assiduously wooed by the Party critics and the dominant literary organizations. The participants in a discussion on satire in the *Literary Gazette* in 1929 had almost unanimously concluded that satire could be a powerful weapon in the fight against philistinism and other ugly survivals of the prerevolutionary regime, that despite the great need there were too few writing in this genre, and that satirists should be given encouragement.[31] At the meeting of the Federation of Organizations of

[27] Zoshchenko, "Na Baltiiskom zavode," *Lit. gaz.*, Oct. 29, 1930.

[28] M. Kazakov, "Chertëzh pisatel'skoi psikhiki izmenilsia," *Lit. gaz.*, Oct. 19, 1930.

[29] "Na boevoi proverke," *Lit. gaz.*, June 15, 1931.

[30] "Nad chem rabotaiut pisateli," *Lit. gaz.*, June 5, 1932.

[31] Lezhnëv, "Na puti k vozrozhdeniiu satiry," *Lit. gaz.*, April 22, 1929; G. Iakubovskii, "O satire nashikh dnei," *ibid.*, July 8, 1929; "O putiakh sovetskoi satiry,"

Soviet Writers on January 19, 1930, Zoshchenko was characterized as one of the fellow travelers who had come closest to the revolutionary writers, and his work was acclaimed as very important and valuable in the struggle against the remnants of the past in the minds of the people. At the same time he was cautioned against seeing philistinism in every aspect of Soviet life and development and against identifying the philistine with the present Soviet man. He was advised to generalize less and to concentrate on concrete, isolated examples of philistinism, as he did in his *feuilletons*.[32] As a portent of trouble ahead, Chumandrin indicated, as early as 1930, that popularity outside the USSR was not a salutary accomplishment for a Soviet writer, and that the great appeal of Zoshchenko's writings abroad might call into question his attitude toward the Soviet regime. The general tenor of Chumandrin's remarks, however, was one of encouragement and reassurance: he objected to the tendency of some critics to associate Zoshchenko himself with his philistine narrator and heroes.[33] Later, other critics followed suit, exonerating Zoshchenko in this respect.[34]

In 1931, Zoshchenko, described as "an outstanding satirist," attended a meeting of the Secretariat of RAPP for a discussion of the question of Soviet satire.[35] Soon afterwards he began to accept various administrative and educational responsibilities. In 1932,

ibid., July 15, 1929; M. Rogi, "Puti sovetskoi satiry," *ibid.*, July 22, 1929; "Nuzhna li nam satira?" *ibid.*, Jan. 13, 1930.

The only exception to the prevalent view was that of B. Blium ("Vozroditsia li satira?" *ibid.*, May 27, 1929), who believed that satire could be a weapon only in the struggle of classes, and that in a classless society it would be directed against the state, the form of government, the society itself. Therefore, stated Blium, there was not then and could not be any satire in the Soviet state. This is close to the point of view which actually triumphed in 1946.

[32] It is important to note the distinction made between "feuilleton" and "satire" in Soviet usage. A *feuilleton* is a short satiric story ridiculing one particular incident. It is based on an actual happening and follows the facts more or less closely, very often giving the names and sometimes even the addresses of the characters. It does not generalize, it does not imply that such incidents are frequent. It may even relate unique incidents. A "satire" is not necessarily based on actual happenings. A satirist may combine several incidents or invent the whole story. In so doing, he generalizes the occurrences described, and implies that the ridiculous, absurd, silly events depicted happen very often.

[33] Mikhail Chumandrin, "Chei pisatel'—Mikhail Zoshchenko?" *Zvezda*, No. 3 (1930), pp. 206–19.

[34] Zhurbina, "Mikhail Zoshchenko," pp. 1–19; Tsezar' Vol'pe, "Zametki o sovremennykh pisateliakh," *Zvezda*, No. 1 (1933), pp. 177–82.

[35] "Na Sekretariate RAPP," *Lit. gaz.*, Sept. 20, 1931.

he was elected to the new board of the All-Russian Union of Soviet Writers as well as of the Leningrad Writers' Publishing House, and was designated as one of the "qualified writers" who were to conduct seminars in the "workers' literary university" then in the process of creation.[36] When the humorous journal *Crocodile* was reorganized, Zoshchenko was appointed its representative in Leningrad.[37] As a sign of his standing among fellow writers, in 1933 Zoshchenko was a member of the presidium of the organizing committee of Leningrad writers, along with such authors as Alexei Tolstoy and Fedin.[38]

Meanwhile his short satirical stories maintained their former popularity with the public and gained in openly expressed esteem among the critics. *Literary Gazette* announced that he was one of those writers whose books sold so fast that there was always a shortage of them.[39] Critics, in an appeal for higher standards and greater recognition of the "small forms" of literature, so far scorned by writers, mentioned Zoshchenko as one of the very few who had been working successfully in this field.[40]

The first major fruit of the rapprochement between Zoshchenko and the powers-that-be was *Youth Restored*, in 1933. Zoshchenko himself, calling it a novel or novelette, describes it as a literary production, on the one hand, and, on the other, something quite different, in the way of a scientific treatise:

set forth, it is true, in simple, somewhat crazy, everyday language, understandable . . . to various strata of the population who have neither the scientific training nor the hardihood and desire to know what is going on beneath the surface of life.

This book will touch upon complex questions . . . for example, the search for one's lost youth, the recovery of health, freshness of feelings and such and the like and so forth. It will also touch on questions of the reconstruction of our entire life and of the possibilities of this reconstruction, on capitalism and socialism, and on the process of developing a philosophy of life.[41]

[36] B. Rest, "Konets apolitichnosti i neitral'nosti," *Lit. gaz.*, Feb. 29, 1932; B. R., "Pisateli—izdateli," *ibid.*, March 11, 1932; V. Saianov, *et al.*, "Vospitanie rabochikh kadrov," *ibid.*, Aug. 5, 1932.

[37] "Krokodil po-novomu," *Lit. gaz.*, Dec. 29, 1932.

[38] "Pis'mo iz Leningrada," *Lit. gaz.*, April 29, 1933.

[39] V. Sobolev, "Kniga derzhit ekzamen," *Lit. gaz.*, July 29, 1933.

[40] Brig, "Likvidirovat' zasilie khaltury i prisposoblenchestva," *Lit. gaz.*, May 20, 1931; L. Ovalov, "V zashchitu rasskaza i novelly," *ibid.*, Oct. 11, 1932.

[41] Zoshchenko, *Vozvrashchënnaia molodost'*, 3d ed. (Moscow, 1935), p. 9.

If there are those in scientific circles who look askance at his venture, as at the depredations of a pig rooting in their garden and munching their turnip, then, the author suggests, the book may be considered in the category of an educational film like some of those entitled "Abortion," "What Makes It Rain," "How Silk Stockings Are Made," or "The Difference between Man and the Beaver." First, he explains, there will be a scientific discussion with a number of footnotes, references, and commentaries, perhaps even with diagrams and documentary citations, which will definitively clarify the essence of the matter.

And only then the reader, a little tired and cockeyed from other people's thoughts, will get a section of entertaining reading matter, which will be a kind of graphic illustration to the foregoing thoughts and reflections.

Impatient readers . . . and those inflexible, rather coarse, and—why not say it?—low-brow minds who have no particular interest in the diverse phenomena of nature beyond the distribution of foodstuffs—such minds may, of course, skip the beginning and the commentaries and . . . proceed directly to the entertaining reading matter.[42]

In this vein, the long, rambling, saucy introduction, in which piquant wit and sardonic meditations on human nature are inextricably and deliciously interwoven, in which the author ranges with complete irrelevance from a zoo in the Caucasus to the cribside of an infant smiling out of the sheer joy of healthy being—at long last leads offhandedly into the story itself.

It is the story of a professor of astronomy who lived until middle age as most people live, without taking the slightest care of his physical and mental health, without realizing that his incorrect habits and way of life were aging him prematurely. He had no family happiness: his wife was stupid, and his daughter disapproved of him because, although he was not against socialism and even regarded it as a good thing, he nevertheless thought it would never be realized. No tendency toward the improvement of the species had been visible in the course of hundreds of years. At fifty-three, the professor suddenly realized that he was old. In order to restore his youth he resorted to the usual means. First, he took medical treatment, which made him feel neither younger nor healthier, but much worse. Then he attempted physical exercises, for which he was

42 *Ibid.*, p. 10.

too old and which almost brought him to heart failure. Finally, he began to study his condition and to read everything that could help him to understand it. With great difficulty, he changed his habits, and actually began to feel vigor returning. At last, he took the traditional step toward restoration of youth: a love affair with a young girl. Tulia was only nineteen, but her life had been long enough for five husbands and seven or eight abortions. Her dream was to have nothing to do, to eat sweets, and to recline languidly listening to all sorts of compliments, promises, proposals, entreaties, demands, and exclamations. From the professor she demanded an ermine wrap and a trip to Japan, or at least to Yalta on the Black Sea. On their honeymoon, she quickly found a younger lover. The affair ended with a stroke for the professor and a return to his family. Upon his recovery, he resumed his exercise—skating, volley ball, boating—and, on the whole, his health improved. He and his daughter were reconciled when he confided that he had enrolled in a shock brigade and now had no political deviations. But still he hankered after his Tulia.

At the end of the long, wickedly ingenuous commentaries which follow the narrative—on the life, health, neurasthenia, and death of great men of history and little men of Zoshchenko's observation—the author adds an autobiographical note purporting to explain his motive in writing the book:

The reader who is distressed by the change in my work may be reassured. Having published this book, I shall again continue the sort of thing I had begun. This book is merely a short breathing spell.

I have written this book for my own edification and that of others. . . .

In this way I simply wanted to be useful in the struggle for socialism which our country is carrying on. I have always been astonished at the extreme lack of knowledge and comprehension of the most elementary rules of taking care of one's body. It seemed to me that knowledge of all this is essential for people who work a great deal.

I wanted to tell in simple language what I have thought and learned. Perhaps here and there I have made mistakes—in which case I humbly beg pardon from science.

These medical opinions have not been copied out of books. I have been the dog on which I have performed all the experiments.[43]

43 *Ibid.*, pp. 233–34.

In the final lines, Zoshchenko describes the scene he is watching through the window: a summer scene of sun and clouds and a dog barking; a football flying through the air; a good-looking woman on her way to the river for a swim, rolling her eyes at a man who follows her as he flourishes a switch and whistles triumphantly; a little neighbor girl coming through the gate to play with the author's son. "The feel of well-being and serenity of these timeless pictures somehow rejoices and comforts me. I do not want to think any more. And on this I end my story." [44]

What *was* Zoshchenko up to? The current argument of the critics that writers should blend the literary with the scientific in works which, while remaining belles-lettres, would instruct, ennoble, and remold their readers for the better service of the Five-Year Plan will account for a little, but very little. Also Zoshchenko's own interest in preserving health was a natural one: he made no secret of his "heart ailment, bad nerves, and rather unruly psychological workings." [45] Given the precept and the author's personal concern with a subject to which it might well be applied, what actually was Zoshchenko's intention in *Youth Restored?* It is conceivable that he meant the narrative part of the book to illustrate the incorrect and sometimes harmful and ridiculous means to which people resort in order to restore their lost youth when it is already too late, and the commentaries to suggest means of preventing premature aging. It is conceivable. If so, on the face of it, he was congenitally unable to bend his talent to his will; as in the case of his beloved literary predecessor, Gogol, he intended one thing and produced another; he went into his work for edification and came out with mischief. He had admitted a few years before that the positive aspects of Soviet life, the description of achievements, had no place in his genre, that of the humorist. If here in this work, for the sake of compliance, of consent, he was attempting to accommodate the "positive" within his satire, the result is demonstration that the two were still fundamentally incompatible in his creative process. The satiric narrative and the straight-faced commentaries are physically separated in the book. He could juxtapose, he could not mingle, the two.

On the other hand, in *Youth Restored,* Zoshchenko may be

[44] *Ibid.,* p. 235.   [45] *Ibid.,* p. 234.

naughtily plucking away at the same string: there is no renascence for the professor, no metamorphosis of the incorrigible old Adam. The dream ends with a return to the old, the established, the inexorable. The professor seeks Tulia and his youth; the Communist Party, the regeneration of man. But life has its own laws, and defiance will not change them.

Youth Restored: science-fiction or an elaborate literary prank? Each reader must decide for himself.

Soviet critics approached the book with solemn gravity. Of all the works of Zoshchenko which were well received, this one was attended by more fanfare and more sober literary criticism than any other. Moreover, it was the subject of organized discussions in unexpected quarters such as the Scholars' Club, doctors' clubs, scientific institutes, and library circles. The colloquy in the Scholars' Club was attended by academicians, professors, and scientists outstanding in various fields, who dealt with the book as a scientific work rather than as a work of literature,[46] although the author had specifically stated that it was intended as an entertaining novel, not as a piece of scientific research. Even N. Semashko, People's Commissar of Health, pronounced on the book. In his opinion, Zoshchenko overemphasized biological factors and underestimated the role of social factors. Despite a number of questionable statements, Semashko praised Zoshchenko for his appeal to organize one's life, to strengthen and preserve one's mental and physical energies.[47]

The Leningrad organizational committee of writers arranged a discussion in May, 1934. "This was the first time that Zoshchenko was discussed not as a member of this or that bureau or committee, but as a writer." Zoshchenko, who was present, said that this was his "first meeting with 'high' literature in the fifteen years of his literary career." [48]

There was a deluge of newspaper and magazine articles. The author's search for a "positive hero" and his experiment in combining a satirical problem with a scientific one, in response to critical adjuration, were commended. Even friendly critics, how-

[46] B. R., "Pobeda ili porazhenie?" *Lit. gaz.,* March 26, 1934.
[47] Semashko, "Mozhno li vozvratit' molodost'?" *Lit. gaz.,* April 6, 1934.
[48] B. Rest, "Vozvrashchaiushchaiasia molodost'," *Lit. gaz.,* May 14, 1934.

ever, while calling the book a real aid in the fight for socialism, found his irony still excessive.[49] One critic labeled the book "ideologically narrow," and censured certain passages at variance with the orthodox Marxist point of view.[50] Another accused Zoshchenko of a "vulgar interpretation of materialism" in attributing all human emotions to the functioning of the kidneys, endocrine glands, and other organs; on the contrary, youth could be restored by social energy, by a new conception of work, by class solidarity, by willingness to sacrifice everything in the name of the Revolution. However, even this most severe critic saw a considerable advance for Zoshchenko in the fact that he brought into the gloomy realm of his heroes the idea of restored youth, of a new life, and of the necessity "to uproot the remnants of capitalism in the minds of the people." [51] In general, *Youth Restored* was viewed hopefully as the beginning of a new phase in Zoshchenko's literary career.[52] An editorial in the *Literary Gazette* deemed it a valuable contribution to Soviet literature.[53] The third edition of the book came out as early as May, 1935, in 15,000 copies.

Zoshchenko himself was dissatisfied with it, he acknowledged years later.[54] How the unanimously serious approach of the critics to the book affected him is not a matter of record.

In *Story of One Life* (1933) there is hardly a trace of the former Zoshchenko. The book in which this tale first appeared was the product of collective writing, the most highly approved method during the First Plan. As participant, Zoshchenko is collectivized into artistic obliteration.

In August, 1933, one hundred and twenty writers took an inspection trip through the White Sea–Baltic Canal, then under construction by prisoner labor under the direction of the OGPU. Immediately afterwards, thirty-six of the authors collaborated in a book devoted to the theme of the rehabilitation of criminals into

[49] G. Munblit, "Kak vazhno byt' ser'ëznym," *Lit. gaz.*, Feb. 20, 1934; B. Begak, "Povest' i kommentarii k nei," *ibid.*, March 18, 1934.
[50] N. Oruzheinikov, "Na poliakh zhurnalov," *Lit. gaz.*, Aug. 11, 1933.
[51] Anatolii Gorelov, "V poiskakh formuly molodosti," *Ispytanie vremenem* (Leningrad, 1935), pp. 89–98.
[52] Vol'pe, "O vozvrashchënnoi molodosti M. Zoshchenko," *Zvezda*, No. 8 (1934), pp. 161–71.
[53] "Privet pisateliam Leningrada," *Lit. gaz.*, Aug. 6, 1934.
[54] Rest, "Golubaia kniga," *Lit. gaz.*, March 15, 1936.

socially useful citizens through Soviet corrective labor, not punitive in intent but reeducative. Zoshchenko's contribution, in the form of a first-person narrative by a petty thief and swindler sentenced to work there, was later published separately under the title *Story of One Life*. According to Zoshchenko, the "autobiography" was written by the thief himself, and he only "polished it off."

The "reforging" of this wily and recalcitrant forty-year-old law-breaker, who had spent almost his entire life disdaining any kind of work as stupid degradation and enjoying a large and easy "income" from his various rackets, is accomplished by the camp authorities through heart-to-heart talks over tea and cookies and the issuance of good clothes and boots. Finally, moved by their considerate attitude and persuaded that in the new state, without capitalists, private-property owners, or poverty, his specialty of robbing will be an anachronism, Rottenberg, the hero, sees the wisdom of qualifying himself as a worker. Within a few days, he is a shock-brigader turning out 140 percent of his labor quota. From this time forward he is an exemplary prisoner, and is soon commissioned to reform a group of incorrigibles, to whom he applies the OGPU arguments he himself has embraced: "Gentlemen, the crash has come for our criminal world. . . . I do not speak for other countries, but with us this is so. And if it is not so at the moment, certainly it will be very soon." [55]

In his own comments at the end, Zoshchenko imagines the pride and joy of the man's homecoming:

R., thanks to proper correctional education, has transformed his psychology . . . and, at the same time, of course, has taken into account the changes in our life. And I have as much faith in this as in myself. Otherwise, I am a visionary, a naive man, and a nitwit. These are faults I have never had in my life.

For the new life of this man I would vouch, but I make this reservation: I would vouch for it only in our non-capitalist conditions. . . .

I want to live in a country where the doors will not be locked and where the grievous words robbery, thief, and murder will be forgotten.[56]

At the end of *Youth Restored*, Zoshchenko had promised that he would then resume his earlier manner. Instead, this is what he wrote. In almost calculable ratio, the more closely he adhered to

[55] Zoshchenko, "Istoriia odnoi zhizni," *Izbrannye povesti* (Leningrad, 1937), p. 292.
[56] *Ibid.*, p. 295.

officially prescribed formula, the fewer became the distinctive marks of Zoshchenko's hand on the printed page.

The critics who had earlier seriously analyzed his work and urged him into new directions of positive affirmation of Soviet life maintained silence upon this work. One or two others enthusiastically acclaimed this demonstration that, in the course of the brilliant victories of the First Plan, Zoshchenko had seen the changes occurring in the people and at last desired to portray a positive Soviet hero.[57]

In his persistent search for new genres acceptable both to his arbiters and to himself, Zoshchenko tried his hand in 1934–35 at a satirical history of human relations entitled *Blue Book*.[58] Gorky had indirectly suggested the idea of the book, and it is dedicated to him. Here Zoshchenko, at least in part, keeps the promise made in *Youth Restored* to revert to his former vein. He resurrects his familiar "philistine" narrator, and through him filters the life of mankind from the days of antiquity, not only Soviet life, discarding the sententiousness and sentimentality of *Story of One Life* for his old sharp, racy, derisive wit.

The book consists of five parts, dealing with "Money," "Love," "Perfidy," "Failures," and "Surprising Events," and their effect upon human relations throughout history. Under each heading, one section is devoted to the past, and another to the Soviet period. Again, Zoshchenko's motives can only be surmised. Given Marxist doctrine and the domination of the Communist Party as the known climate in which he functioned, no writer could expect to draw such a dividing line with impunity unless prepared to point up marked changes in favor of the new era. But again Zoshchenko is master of equivocation. Again his bitter laughter rings out over the whole gloomy picture of humanity. Whether or not deliberately to accentuate the constancy of his view, many of the stories dealing with the Soviet epoch were reprinted from earlier collections, some of them reworked. Possibly to gloss over this circumstance, the author mentions at the beginning of *Blue Book* that he wanted to

---

[57] A. Bolotnikov, "Kniga dostoinaia svoei temy," *Lit. gaz.*, Jan. 26, 1934; N. Simonov, "Istoriia odnoi zhizni," *ibid.*, Sept. 24, 1934.

[58] Zoshchenko, "Golubaia kniga," *Krasnaia nov'*, No. 3 (March, 1934), pp. 3–39; No. 10 (October, 1934), pp. 3–30; No. 6 (June, 1935), pp. 69–97; No. 7 (July, 1935), pp. 3–36; No. 12 (December, 1935), pp. 148–72.

unify many of his stories around one idea, but that it would have taken years to rewrite all of them.[59]

At this time of comparative relaxation and mutual accommodation between Zoshchenko and his Party watchdogs—after the completion of the First Plan, when socialism was considered to have already achieved considerable success and when Zoshchenko had given token of his acquiescence in *Story of One Life*—the critics were inclined to wink at a little backsliding. Zhurbina, a specialist on Zoshchenkiana, even announced that the *Blue Book* was conceived as a "balance of the man and culture of our time with the old world and the old culture," and saved the day by discerning that Zoshchenko showed perfidy to be "a feature of the man of capitalist 'training,'" whereas in the Soviet Union it was only a stray remnant. From this great step forward on Zoshchenko's part, she foresaw his use of his gift for ingenious innovation on the subject of the birth of new people and new human relations.[60] After the customary long disagreement among critics attacking and defending Zoshchenko,[61] the decisive last word was spoken in the Party paper *Pravda*. Gurshtein begins gently by referring to Zoshchenko as a writer who exposes philistinism and frequently does it very well: "His stories often hit the mark and show Zoshchenko's warm attitude toward the new life." Then the critic sternly admonishes the satirist for the future. As a result of using his old style (in which he demonstrates considerable mastery, but which is entirely inappropriate in the field of history) and his typical philistine narrator, Zoshchenko has filled his book with too much irony, both about history and about Soviet people and life. Too many Soviet writers, Gurshtein complains, do the same. In the chapter titles of the present book ("Money," "Love," and so forth), Zoshchenko has named subjects of works by Marx and Engels, Balzac, Shakespeare, and other famous writers, only to permit his narrator to treat these important ideas, as well as revolutionary events and people, in a trivial, "snickering" manner. In this, Zoshchenko demonstrates

[59] Rest, "Golubaia kniga."

[60] Zhurbina, "Golubaia kniga," *Lit. gaz.*, Sept. 20, 1935.

[61] For further comments, see "O formalizme i naturalizme v literature," *Lit. gaz.*, March 27, 1936; Rest, "Na sobranii leningradskikh pisatelei," *ibid.*, April 5, 1936; Anna Beskina, "Litso i maska Mikhaila Zoshchenko," *Literaturnyi kritik*, No. 1 (1935), pp. 107–31, and No. 2 (1935), pp. 59–91.

"his misreading of history, his ignorance." The *Blue Book* is "a collection of historical anecdotes to pander to the banality of the man in the street." [62]

Gurshtein was speaking in 1936 about a book which had been broadcast over the radio every other day in 1934.[63] The fault of the book was that its author had failed to anticipate the great ideological reversal of the mid-thirties, which followed soon after publication of *Blue Book*. Some Soviet social institutions against which satire had been officially invited earlier were now recanonized and shielded from the rude breath of derision.

Meanwhile, Zoshchenko, steadily active in literary organizations and projects, continued to rise in influence and esteem among his fellow writers and the publishing world. In June, 1934, he became a member of the new Union of Soviet Writers, and was elected as a delegate to represent the Leningrad group at the All-Union Conference of Writers in the autumn of that year.[64] In preparation for the Conference, it was announced that he had been selected as subject for one of the series of reports on individual writers to be given there.[65] At the Conference (August–September, 1934), he was made a member of the Board of the new Union.[66] Upon his return, he addressed a meeting of Leningrad writers on the proceedings of the Conference.[67] In the following year he served in the presidium of the organization of Soviet intelligentsia of Leningrad.[68] Literary journals and publishing houses boasted of the popularity of his works and plumed themselves with the distinction of purveying them to the public.[69] There was a flurry of critical works on his

[62] A. Gurshtein, "Po alleiam istorii," *Pravda*, May 9, 1936. This interpretation of the *Blue Book* was very soon dutifully echoed by the *Literary Gazette* (O. Tsekhnovitser, "Obzor pechati," *Lit. gaz.*, May 30, 1936), canceling its earlier praise ("Privet pisateliam Leningrada").

[63] "V Leningrade," *Lit. gaz.*, Sept. 8, 1934.

[64] *Lit. gaz.*, June 12, 1934; "Delegatsiia Leningrada," *ibid.*, Aug. 15, 1934.

[65] "Podgotovka k vsesoiuznomu s"ezdu pisatelei," *Lit. gaz.*, April 16, 1934.

[66] "Pravlenie Soiuza sovetskikh pisatelei," *Lit. gaz.*, Sept. 2, 1934.

[67] "Sobranie pisatelei Leningrada," *Lit. gaz* , Sept. 10, 1934.

[68] "Sobranie sovetskoi intelligentsii Leningrada," *Lit. gaz.*, Feb. 20, 1935.

[69] The Leningrad State Publishing House announced that 100,000 copies of his works would be released in 1935 ("Po Sovetskomu Soiuzu," *Lit. gaz.*, Nov. 26, 1934). In the spring of 1935, the periodical *Red Virgin Soil* countered criticism from the *Literary Gazette* by pointing out that a whole series of excellent works printed in its pages had been overlooked, including stories by Zoshchenko ("Literaturnyi dnevnik," *Krasnaia nov'*, No. 3 [March, 1935], pp. 254–56), and again in the next issue mentioned the *Blue Book* as one of the feathers in its cap. *The Literary Gazette*

career.[70] Fellow writers Fedin and Marietta Shaginian paid him un-stinting tribute.[71] Zoshchenko himself engaged in a number of col-lective literary projects under official auspices.[72] After Gurshtein's sobering onslaught on *Blue Book,* however, Zoshchenko drew in his literary horns and, if anything, redoubled his professional and civic activities.

From the beginning of 1937, his writing took a completely new tack. For the issue of the *Star* dedicated to Pushkin on the one-hundredth anniversary of his death, Zoshchenko wrote "Talisman; or, The Sixth Story of I. P. Belkin," an imitation of Pushkin's famous stories.[73] It was a politically innocuous piece, rather lightly received, but showing, according to one critic, the author's great respect for and appreciation of the classical heritage of Russian literature.[74]

Zoshchenko was feeling his way cautiously in a new direction with the historical sketch "The Black Prince," published in March, 1937. It describes with subtle irony the very costly and futile efforts made by several foreign countries, particularly Japan, to raise gold allegedly sunk aboard a British ship in the Black Sea during the Crimean War. Contrasted to this folly is the highly intelligent performance of "Epron," a branch of the Soviet Fleet assigned to the task, which after a few attempts abandoned the search for gold

itself gave credit to the *Star* for publishing some of the best works of Soviet literature, including Zoshchenko along with Gorky, Alexei Tolstoy, Fedin, and Iurii Tynianov ("Zvezda," *Lit. gaz.*, Oct. 4, 1935). It also pridefully quoted a favorable review of a collection of Zoshchenko's stories published in English, *Russia Laughs* ("Za rube-zhom," *Lit. gaz.*, Oct. 24, 1935).

[70] In 1934 the Leningrad Writers' Publishing House announced a series of mono-graphs on Leningrad authors, Zoshchenko among them ("Sorok knig kritikov i litera-turovedov," *Lit. gaz.*, Jan. 24, 1934). Zhurbina wrote extensively on Zoshchenko in 1935 (a work quoted in Zhurbina, "Variant sud'by 'intelligentnogo cheloveka,'" *Oktiabr'*, No. 2 [1936], pp. 246–57).

[71] K. Fedin, "Proza leningradskikh pisatelei," *Lit. gaz.*, Aug. 10, 1934; Shaginian, "Mysli k s"ezdu," *ibid.*, July 30, 1934.

[72] In 1935 he agreed to participate in a five-volume work suggested by Gorky in commemoration of the twentieth anniversary of the Revolution ("Dve piatiletki," *Lit. gaz.*, May 10, 1935). When work was begun on the history of "Epron" (Special Expedition for Submarine Operations), Zoshchenko was a member of the writers' "collective" for the book ("Knigi v grankakh," *Lit. gaz.*, Dec. 31, 1935).

[73] Zoshchenko, "Shestaia povest' Belkina, 'Talisman,'" *Zvezda*, No. 1 (1937), pp. 25–32.

[74] I. Sats, "Geroi Mikhaila Zoshchenko," *Lit. kritik*, No. 3 (1938), pp. 140–67.

and instead began very successful work in raising ships and scrap metal from the sea bottom.[75]

"Retribution" (1937) is a special-purpose piece (written for a volume planned, at the initiative of Gorky, to commemorate the twentieth anniversary of the Revolution but never realized because of the failure of other authors to produce their contributions).[76] It is the "autobiography" of a woman, a former cook, who became a Communist, participated in the Revolution, fought heroically in the civil war, and rose to an important position in the Soviet apparatus. The central idea is the revenge of the people on their former oppressors. The story is told in the woman's own colloquial language: as in *Story of One Life,* Zoshchenko ascribes the narration to the heroine herself, and states that he merely gave it literary form.[77] The critics expressed approval, almost without reservation. For the first time, they rejoiced, Zoshchenko had portrayed a character whom he himself regarded as a "positive hero," "one of the best people in our country," [78] a Soviet woman "transformed from a slave to a human being . . . aware of her dignity and ready to defend it," [79] "whose life teaches the reader the feelings of revolutionary heroism." [80] Throughout the ranks of the critics, an almost audible sigh of relief went up as Zoshchenko was proclaimed at last on the right track.

In "Inglorious End" (1938), the story of Kerensky, Zoshchenko continued to work these two veins of historical sketch and biography, where he escaped carping criticism. At the same time, the nature of the subject allowed free play for his restless irony and sarcasm.[81]

After his faltering climb up the ladder of compliance to the level of Communist approbation, Zoshchenko maintained himself there briefly by a series of works ostensibly didactic in intent. For several years he had been writing an occasional story for children. In 1939–40 he published four collections of his juvenile tales, one of

[75] Zoshchenko, "Chërnyi prints," *Literaturnyi sovremennik,* No. 3 (1937), pp. 30–68.
[76] V. Kremnev, "Pis'mo iz Leningrada," *Lit. gaz.,* Jan. 5, 1937.
[77] Zoshchenko, "Vozmezdie," *Novyi mir,* No. 10 (1937), pp. 81–116.
[78] Sats, "Geroi Mikhaila Zoshchenko."
[79] V. Vasilevskii, "Tri goda," *Lit. gaz.,* Oct. 15, 1938.
[80] I. Eventov, "Vospitanie chuvstv," *Zvezda,* No. 3 (1938), pp. 217–22.
[81] Zoshchenko, "Besslavnyi konets," *Lit. sovrem.,* No. 1 (1938), pp. 223–63.

them containing twelve stories about Lenin told in very simple language, which were praised by critics and fellow writers as of great value in Communist education, inspiring children with noble feelings and with the desire to be like Lenin.[82]

During this period Zoshchenko consistently displayed outward signs of yielding to the importunities of the critics. Objections had been made to his continued use of the jargon spoken by his "philistine" narrator.[83] In his short satirical stories and *feuilletons* at this time, his style underwent a certain change away from the bizarre, staccato, spicy, and mangled speech of the street toward the standard literary language. The moral and educational benefits of these stories, however, are seldom so apparent as the critics of the day found them. In "City Lights" (1937), a rough and pugnacious old peasant on a visit to his son in the city reforms immediately when two policemen speak politely and salute him. In "New Times" of the same year, a handsome young woman utterly devoid of moral principles and responsible for ruining the lives of several men, learns respect for a representative of the new Soviet man, who, resisting her feminine charms, treats her merely as a human being. The Soviet critic found in these stories the lesson that respect for human dignity and kind and considerate treatment reclaimed social offenders.[84] They might as easily be parodies on the current crop of Soviet fiction showing the "new morals" and the "new people" created through the precept and example of the Communist Party. When, perhaps under the influence of his more sedate literary language, Zoshchenko drifted off toward the fringes of active Soviet life, toward the wistful and superannuated misfits in the new regime, as in "Twenty Years Later" and "Quietude" (1937), critics jerked him back with reproaches that he too mercifully blunted his satire on the stupidity and pettiness of such philistines or that he wasted his talents on characters who were already "dead." [85]

[82] M. Slonimskii, "Rasskazy o Lenine," *Literaturnoe obozrenie*, No. 11 (June 5, 1940); M. Shkapskaia, "Rasskazy o Lenine," *Oktiabr'*, No. 1 (1941), pp. 185–93. The series as a whole was regarded as a significant contribution to literature for children ("Pisateli i redaktory," *Lit. gaz.*, Feb. 5, 1940; Vera Smirnova, "Chasy na bashne," *ibid.*, June 16, 1940).

[83] Gurshtein, "Po alleiam istorii"; S. Gekht, "Novye rasskazy Zoshchenko," *Lit. oboz.*, No. 6 (March, 1938), pp. 8–10.

[84] L. Levin, "Zametki o satiricheskoi proze," *Molodaia gvardiia*, No. 9 (1939), pp. 151–58.

[85] Eventov, "Vospitanie chuvstv"; Gekht, "Novye rasskazy Zoshchenko."

With the play *Dangerous Connections,* which he wrote in 1938–39, Zoshchenko came back to the politics-ridden scene, but he came back snarling. Every line of the play exaggerates to the point of absurdity the words and actions of the characters: the consummate hero, who makes noble speeches; the consummate villain, a Communist occupying an important position who turns out to be a former *agent provocateur;* the latter's secretary, a counterrevolutionary in disguise; and various "petty bourgeois" figures, all extremely repulsive. They are all merely bearers of the "positive" or "negative" principle, pushed to the last extremity of the Soviet definition. The play may well have been Zoshchenko's answer to the demand that writers expose the "wreckers" and conspirators in the Soviet Union, a goodly number of whom had recently figured in the sensational trials of the period.

The critics, either nonplussed or contemptuous, were unusually silent about this play. One complained anonymously and in general of "the low cultural and political level of some of our writers" who based their works on false ideas; in particular, called Zoshchenko's play a complete failure if it was meant to alert his audience against enemies like the villain or contrast them with the new Soviet people.[86]

If throughout these crucial years of conspiracy, trials, and purges, Zoshchenko's writings were sometimes ambiguous, his performance as literary mentor, consultant, and factotum, and his display of the proper political sentiments left little to be desired. In approved fashion, he drew up his authorial plans for the year 1937.[87] In that year he was reelected to the Board of the Leningrad branch of the Writers' Union, and next year became also a member of the Presidium.[88] His reliability and the soundness of his position would appear attested by his appointment to the committee for the reworking of the plan of the State Publishing House for 1939.[89] Together with another writer, he edited a collection of works selected in a competition of young Leningrad writers.[90] He served as chairman

[86] "Za ideinuiu bol'shevistskuiu printsipial'nost'," *Lit. kritik,* No. 9–10 (1940), pp. 9–19.
[87] Zoshchenko, "Moi plan," *Lit. gaz.,* Jan. 5, 1937.
[88] "Na obshchem sobranii leningradskikh pisatelei," *Lit. gaz.,* June 30, 1937; "Novyi prezidium pravleniia Leningradskogo Soiuza pisatelei," *ibid.,* Nov. 20, 1938.
[89] "Obsuzhdenie plana Goslitizdata na 1939 god," *Lit. gaz.,* Oct. 20, 1938.
[90] *Lit. gaz.,* July 15, 1937.

of a Writers' Union committee arranging the celebration of the
125th anniversary of the birth of Taras Shevchenko, on request
produced a group of biographical tales about Shevchenko, and
wrote the preface to a collection of his poems published for the
occasion.[91] He was a member of another committee organized to
mark the 50th anniversary of the death of Saltykov-Shchedrin.[92]

In the political sphere, he addressed a meeting of Leningrad
writers condemning the Trotskyites purged in 1937,[93] spoke at a
meeting dedicated to Gorky's memory,[94] worked on an election
committee in preparation for the general elections to the Supreme
Soviet in 1937,[95] urged Leningrad writers to take an active part in
the election preliminaries,[96] and appealed to them to follow the
example of the Moscow writing fraternity in delivering popular
lectures in railroad and industrial trade schools.[97]

Accolades honoring him as a Soviet artist were offered in all
quarters. In March, 1939, the Writers' Club of Leningrad organized
a meeting for discussion of Zoshchenko's work, and a Moscow State
University club paid its respects at a similar gathering.[98] The prominent actor Igor Il'inskii, expressing his admiration of Zoshchenko,
whose stories belonged to "the golden fund of Soviet literature,"
deplored the fact that the author had written no plays equaling
them in artistic and social value.[99] He was presented to the outside
world under seal of approval when several of his stories were published in English in *International Literature* of 1936 and 1938,
with a description of the author as "one of the most popular contemporary Soviet humorists." [100] In a *Literary Gazette* review of
Soviet literature produced in 1939, Zoshchenko's works were ac-
corded a place among the best.[101] As a culmination of his decade

91 "V Soiuze sovetskikh pisatelei," *Lit. gaz.*, Aug. 10, 1938; "Podgotovka k shevchen-
kovskim dniam v Leningrade," *ibid.*, Dec. 10, 1938; "Stikhotvoreniia Shevchenko,"
ibid., July 15, 1939.
92 "K 50-letiiu so dnia smerti M. E. Shchedrina," *Lit. gaz.*, April 10, 1939.
93 "Krov' Kirova stuchit v nashe serdtse," *Lit. gaz.*, Feb. 1, 1937.
94 "Na sobranii pamiati Gor'kogo," *Lit. gaz.*, June 30, 1936.
95 "Pisateli v izbiratel'nykh komissiiakh," *Lit. gaz.*, Oct. 26, 1937, and Dec. 5, 1937.
96 Zoshchenko, "Vpervye v istorii," *Lit. gaz.*, Oct. 20, 1937.
97 "Khoroshii pochin," *Lit. gaz.*, Dec. 31, 1940.
98 "Tvorcheskii vecher Mikhaila Zoshchenko," *Lit. gaz.*, March 30, 1939; "Vecher M.
Zoshchenko," *ibid.*, Dec. 5, 1939.
99 Igor' Il'inskii, "O samom glavnom," *Lit. gaz.*, Feb. 5, 1940.
100 *International Literature*, No. 1 (1938).
101 D. Moor, "Literaturnyi god," *Lit. gaz.*, Dec. 31, 1939.

of adaptation and triumph, he was awarded the Medal of the Red Labor Banner "for outstanding progress and achievement in the development of Soviet belles-lettres." [102]

On the face of it, by the end of the thirties, Zoshchenko and the Soviet powers, like the author's first hero and his bosom friend, appeared to sit "hugging each other all day." [103] The fictional character had been driven to refuge in his friend's home and embrace as "hired man": there was nowhere else to go. All doors were closed to him. He could not come to terms with life. Zoshchenko, too, had contrived a place for himself, one which he occupied with considerable uneasiness and ambivalence.

He had attempted to comply with the demands of the Communist Party by writing *Story of One Life*, "Retribution," "The Black Prince," "Inglorious End," the biographic sketches of Taras Shevchenko, and the "Stories about Lenin." With them he had won the plaudits of the Party-oriented critics as a serious writer of literature possessing moral and educational value for the new society. By any criteria other than those applied by Soviet critics at the moment, these stories belong to Zoshchenko's weakest works, and demonstrate his inability to go successfully beyond his own genre, the genre of a satirist, and to deny the dictates, conscious or subconscious, of his own esthetic imperatives. In response to demand, he had tried to do what one or two of the more forbearing critics had protested must not be asked of him: to interlard his satire with the "positive," in the manner of a layer cake.[104] The result was invariably flat and insipid. The vision of life as it should be, as it *must* be under Communist guidance, was not his forte. As ever, his eye lighted on human foibles and the shortcomings of Soviet life as they were, and, despite critical adjuration, they evoked in him no cheerful laughter nor cheerful certainty that there would soon be an end to all these "negative" things.[105] When, as in his conformist pieces, he forced an expression of certainty, there was no laughter; and when the laughter came, there was no certainty, even of his meaning, as in *Youth Restored* and *Blue Book*. In the first case the result was not the talented Zoshchenko; it might have

[102] *Lit. gaz.*, Feb. 5, 1939.
[103] Zoshchenko, "Chertovinka," *Rasskazy Nazara Il'icha*, p. 53.
[104] B. Malakhov, "Smekh," *Lit. gaz.*, April 15, 1939; Levin, "Zametki."
[105] Rest, "Na sobranii leningradskikh pisatelei."

been any hack. In the second instance, the Party critics looked askance.

The later thirties were not days when it was comfortable for a writer to feel the eyes of the critics looking askance at him. The brilliant writer Olesha, whom Zoshchenko referred to in *Youth Restored* as "my friend," [106] had invited distrustful attention by open and moving expression of his doubts and his artistic agonies in meeting the requirements of the literary arbiters; and after 1938 Olesha published no more for some years.[107] Zoshchenko never aired in public, as did Olesha, the conflict between his own creative compulsions and the "social command" laid upon writers. But the themes of the First and Second Five-Year Plans majestically sweeping socialism across the land were as foreign to him as to Olesha, who explained that he could not fulfill the assignments of living among workers at factories and construction plants, that understanding of the revolutionary hero-worker was hard for him, that he could not become one. Zoshchenko, like his old associates in the Serapion Brothers such as Tikhonov, Slonimskii, Fedin, and Kaverin, obeyed the "social command." He went to factories, and performed his writing assignments. He traveled along the White Sea Canal and collaborated on the book about it. He engaged in a veritable frenzy of civic activities from the early thirties. Polemics and beating of the breast in public were not for him. Shklovskii wrote about Zoshchenko in 1928: "Cautious bearing. He has a very quiet voice. The manner of a man who is trying very politely to put an end to a great uproar. . . . Zoshchenko breathes cautiously. . . . He is cautious about the moves he makes in life." [108]

If Zoshchenko the artist could not sincerely and wholeheartedly accept the Soviet regime, Zoshchenko the citizen, or at least the member of the Writers' Union, took a considerable interest in the life of his fellow countrymen, as demonstrated by his active participation in the work of various organizations and committees. Possibly the citizen was trying to make up for what the artist was

106 Zoshchenko, *Vozvrashchënnaia molodost'*, p. 235.

107 For Olesha's speech at the First Congress of Soviet Writers in 1934 and his later fate, see Gleb Struve, *Soviet Russian Literature 1917–50* (Norman, Okla., 1951), pp. 246–49, 267.

108 Viktor Shklovskii, "O Zoshchenko i bol'shoi literature," *Mikhail Zoshchenko*, p. 16.

unable to do. In the thirties, at any rate, what acceptance of the Soviet regime Zoshchenko manifested was as citizen rather than as artist.

IV

Of Zoshchenko's wartime work, little is available in this country except his autobiographical *Before Sunrise*. It is evident, however, that he continued to write, although perhaps with greatly diminished output.[109]

In the first year and a half of the War, while he was in Alma-Ata, Zoshchenko was associated with the Central United Film Studio, which was organized there jointly by the evacuated studios of Moscow and Leningrad and produced more than half of the entire film output of the country.[110] He wrote scenarios himself (work he had successfully tried earlier),[111] read all those which were received by the Studio, assisted in reworking them, and took part in the conference of scenario writers held there. He was officially thanked for "fast and good work." [112]

At a general meeting of the Writers' Union in November, 1942, in Moscow, the secretary of the Union, Fadeev, pointing out that most authors wrote about the front, praised Zoshchenko as one of the few devoting attention to the people behind the lines who worked very hard to produce the supplies needed for the War.[113]

Upon his return from the East in 1943, Zoshchenko again plunged into the thick of literary activities in Moscow, and on one or two occasions evidently expressed his opinion more freely than had been his custom in the past. At the Moscow Writers' Club in July, 1943, he may well have been venting pique accumulated over the years. In the course of discussing the subject "Satire and Humor during the War," he and others spoke of the critics who neglected

[109] In the early period he wrote at least one comedy on a wartime subject ("Novye p'esy sovetskikh dramaturgov," *Literatura i iskusstvo*, July 18, 1942; "Konkurs na odnoaktnuiu p'esu," *ibid.*, July 31, 1943) and a short story ("Chuchelo," *Velikaia otechestvennaia voina* [Moscow, 1942], pp. 574–75). For his later wartime work, see p. 238.

[110] Zoshchenko, "Pisatel' v kino," *Lit. i iskus.*, July 24, 1943; E. Andrikanis, "Na novykh mestakh," *ibid.*, April 4, 1942.

[111] "Khronika," *Lit. gaz.*, Dec. 10, 1938.

[112] Zoshchenko, "Pisatel' v kino"; "Za nedeliu," *Lit. i iskus.*, Sept. 26, 1942.

[113] "V soiuze pisatelei," *Lit. i iskus.*, Nov. 21, 1942.

works of this genre and of editors and workers in the Committee on Art Affairs who knew little about satire and humor and who "manifested intolerable disregard of writers working in this field." At the same meeting regret was expressed that Zoshchenko had abandoned the field of children's literature, in which very little was being written, and favorable mention of his juvenile stories was made by S. Marshak.[114] At another discussion of "Scenario Writing during the War," under the auspices of the Committee on Cinema Affairs, Zoshchenko spoke of the problems of subject matter and technique, as well as of some pointless and annoying disagreements between movie directors and authors of scenarios.[115]

In the summer of 1943, the journal *October* published the first two parts of Zoshchenko's autobiographical *Before Sunrise*.[116] In this cryptic work, curiously reminiscent of his *Youth Restored* and perhaps the continuation of the earlier book which he had planned ten years before,[117] Zoshchenko was undertaking to demonstrate the cure of a serious neurosis with the aid of Pavlov's theory of conditioned reflexes.

Before Sunrise is a series of episodes of the author's life from early childhood, from infancy indeed, to the age of thirty. In the second published installment, the author had worked back through bruising incidents of his life to its earliest days, and at the very end was groping for recall of a traumatic experience which, it is hinted, occurred at birth or even in a prenatal phase. In a society in which Freud is taboo and dianetics would certainly be banned without a hearing, Zoshchenko was skating on very thin ice, despite his explicit dependence on Pavlov and repudiation of Freud. The story is told in a completely serious tone and in standard literary language.

Objections on the grounds of taste might be made by some readers to certain of the frank autobiographical details, of a kind usually attributed only to a fictional character. Zoshchenko relied, unsuccessfully, on another device for making such incidents acceptable, which he mentions in the prologue: "I shall speak of things such as are not considered quite appropriate for discussion in novels. I find comfort in the fact that I shall be speaking of my youth. This is the

---

114 "Satira i iumor v dni Otechestvennoi voiny," *Lit. i iskus.*, July 10, 1943.

115 "Kinodramaturgiia v dni Otechestvennoi voiny," *Lit. i iskus.*, July 24, 1943.

116 Zoshchenko, "Pered voskhodom solntsa," *Oktiabr'*, No. 6–7 (1943), pp. 58–92; No. 8–9 (1943), pp. 103–32.

117 Zoshchenko, "Moi plan," *Lit. gaz.*, Jan. 5, 1937.

same as speaking of one deceased." By no stretch of imagination, however, can *Before Sunrise* be called, as it was by Zhdanov in 1946, an "outrageous" or "revolting" story, in which Zoshchenko, "with enjoyment, with relish, turns his mean and smutty soul inside out."

Publication of the work was suspended after the second installment, and the violent critical attack began three months later. This kind of intense and unblushing egocentrism, this confession-like probing into the dark recesses of the individual, neurosis-burdened past, was something Soviet literature had not seen in many a day. It was especially startling in wartime, when Soviet writers were focusing their attention almost exclusively on the War itself. Literary circles were stunned, but not speechless. Dmitriev led off in the chorus of revulsion, with an article in *Literature and Art* accusing Zoshchenko of distorting life, of intentionally selecting "the ugliest and most trivial facts of his biography," of evoking from memory the "filthy, repulsive, and disgusting," of ignoring social factors and the great events of his time, and of being preoccupied only by his own "philistine emotions, interests, and notions." [118]

Two days later the work was discussed at a meeting of the Presidium of the Writers' Union. Fadeev called it inimical to the interests of the people and of art, and stated that the serious discussion which should have taken place in advance would have prevented its publication. Others denounced it as pernicious, at a time of great war strain, in its proclamation of one's right to hypochondria. "The story is immoral; the most elementary standards of social behavior are violated in it; it preaches cynicism in regard to women." [119]

The next issue of *Bolshevik*, the theoretical and political journal of the Central Committee of the Communist Party, gave clear warning to Zoshchenko that he was skirting the danger zone. It carried an article in which four "rank and file Leningrad readers" voiced their indignation and disgust with *Before Sunrise* in terms anticipating those used in 1946 by Zhdanov and the Central Committee.[120] Soon Zoshchenko's new work was condemned at a plenary meeting of the Board of the Writers' Union,[121] and for some time

[118] L. Dmitriev, "O novoi povesti M. Zoshchenko," *Lit. i iskus.*, Dec. 4, 1943.
[119] "Na obsuzhdenii zhurnala 'Oktiabr','" *Lit. i iskus.*, Dec. 11, 1943.
[120] B. Gorshkov, *et al.*, "Ob odnoi vrednoi povesti," *Bol'shevik*, No. 2 (1944), pp. 56–58.
[121] "Sovetskaia literatura—boevoe oruzhie naroda," *Lit. i iskus.*, Feb. 12, 1944.

afterwards it was mentioned here and there as an illustration of the incorrect attitude of some writers toward events and requirements of the day.[122] At about the same time began a barrage of critical dissatisfaction with recent literary output in general, labeling it sketchy, didactic, and superficial. From February, 1944, until the summer of 1946, it was only a small, ominous wind blowing, not a blast, but enough to indicate to those writers who had availed themselves of the relaxation of Party controls during the War that it was time to mend their ways.[123]

For almost a year after the first attack by Dmitriev, Zoshchenko dropped out of the press. By the end of 1944, he was again active in literary circles in Leningrad. He read his new *Soldiers' Stories* in the Leningrad Writers' Club at the celebration of the twenty-seventh anniversary of the Revolution, and was again serving as a member of the presidium of the Leningrad branch of the Writers' Union.[124] On January 1, 1945, the *Literary Gazette* resumed publication of Zoshchenko's plan of work for the year. In it he mentioned two comedies then under way, a book about partisans in prospect, and daily *feuilletons,* for which he was trying to find a new form, the literary form of the prewar *feuilleton* having become too old and narrow for contemporary material.[125] In 1945 his satirical short stories began to appear in the journal *Leningrad*. The State Publishing House announced a collection of his stories for 1946, and he was appointed to the editorial board on books for children of preschool age to be published by the Leningrad branch of the Writers' Union.[126] Again he took to the speaker's stand at literary gatherings, served on committees, and went electioneering.[127]

---

122 "O chuvstve novogo," *Lit. i iskus.*, March 25, 1944.

123 N. Tikhonov, "Sovetskaia literatura v dni Otechestvennoi voiny," *Lit. i iskus.*, Feb. 12, 1944. "Zhanr korotkogo rasskaza," *Lit. gaz.*, March 31, 1945; Vera Maretskaia, "Obraz moei sovremennitsy," *ibid.;* Andrei Lobanov, "Litsa deistvuiushchie i mysliashchie," *ibid.*, April 22, 1945; Tikhonov, "Sovetskaia literatura v 1944–1945gg.," *ibid.*, May 17, 1945; A. Shvarev, "Ural—tema literatury," *ibid.*, July 14, 1945; "Dramaturgiia nashikh dnei," *ibid.*, Oct. 6, 1945; N. Moskvin, "Otnoshenie k geroiu," *ibid.*, April 20, 1946; "Zhanr korotkogo rasskaza," *ibid.*, Aug. 3, 1946; "Literatura i estrada," *ibid.*, Aug. 17, 1946.

124 "V Leningradskom Dome pisatelei," *Lit. gaz.*, Nov. 11, 1944; "Pod znakom vysokikh trebovanii," *ibid.*, Dec. 24, 1944.

125 Zoshchenko, "Novymi dorogami," *Lit. gaz.*, Jan. 1, 1945.

126 "Trëkhletnii plan Goslitizdata," *Lit. gaz.*, Oct. 13, 1945; "U pisatelei Leningrada," *ibid.*, Feb. 16, 1946.

127 In a series of weekly discussions on short-story writing organized by the editors

In April, 1946, Zoshchenko, among a number of fellow writers, received the medal "for valiant work during the Great Patriotic War of 1941–45." [128] In May he bought government bonds for 8,000 rubles, a quadrupling of his last reported token of patriotic loyalty and support.[129] In June, 1946, Zoshchenko was appointed to the new editorial board of the journal *Star*.[130] In its May–June issue his story "Adventures of a Monkey" was published. And in August of that year Zoshchenko was muzzled.

The action of the Central Committee of the Communist Party was endorsed by Soviet writers with the usual unanimous agreement on every word of the Resolution and of Zhdanov's report. In the *Star* and the *Literary Gazette,* the charges against Zoshchenko were repeated, and his stories and ideas crudely and maliciously misrepresented.[131] At the meeting of the Presidium of the Board of the Writers' Union in September, a number of writers made speeches "appropriate" to the occasion, and some of them (but not all) condemned Zoshchenko. The speeches did not show much conviction. Rather, they betrayed the desire of the speakers to say as little as possible and their embarrassment at having to declare themselves complete asses for the past twenty-five years.[132] More or less the same performance took place at meetings of writers in Leningrad and Moscow.[133]

---

of Leningrad, Zoshchenko's talk on "What Is a Short Story?" was reported as one of the most interesting events ("Sobraniia novellistov," *Lit. gaz.,* April 14, 1945). He participated in a discussion of the journal *Star* and criticized some of the works it had published ("Po sovetskoi strane," *ibid.,* Oct. 20, 1945). At a meeting in honor of Stalin prize winners, Zoshchenko congratulated the recipients in the name of all Leningrad writers ("Vecher pisatelei laureatov," *ibid.,* Feb. 16, 1946). He spoke at a Writers' Union discussion of the work of I. Brazhnin ("Razgovor s tovarishchami," *ibid.,* March 9, 1946). He was a member of the committee of the Leningrad Writers' Union to mark the tenth anniversary of the death of Gorky (*Lit. gaz.,* May 25, 1946). He was one of a delegation of writers cooperating with a Leningrad election committee in 1946, and at a writers' meeting spoke in favor of electing Tikhonov to the Supreme Soviet of the USSR ("Dzherzhinskii izbiratel'nyi okrug g. Leningrada," *ibid.,* Jan. 5 and 12, 1946).

[128] "Vruchenie medalei pisateliam," *Lit. gaz.,* April 27, 1946.

[129] "Pisateli s voodushevleniem podpisyvaiutsia na zaëm," *Lit. gaz.,* May 9, 1946; "Podpiska na novyi zaëm," *ibid.,* April 16, 1934.

[130] "Novaia redkollegiia 'Zvezdy,'" *Lit. gaz.,* June 13, 1946.

[131] L. Plotkin, "Propovednik bezydeinosti—M. Zoshchenko," *Zvezda,* No. 7–8 (1946), pp. 217–22; Anna Karavaeva, "Ob otvetstvennosti pisatelia," *Lit. gaz.,* Aug. 24, 1946.

[132] *Lit. gaz.,* Sept. 7, 1946.

[133] *Lit. gaz.,* Sept. 14 and 21, 1946.

V

This was the formal inauguration in literature of the postwar Party line. Under the new regulations, a license to practice could no longer be granted to a satirist of Zoshchenko's special and ineradicable stripe. In 1946 the Communist Party pronounced, by implication, that it had remade the people of the Soviet Union into a new image, into human beings morally superior to and culturally independent of the remainder of mankind, able to withstand all the machinations and depredations of the outside world, united, triumphant, and invincible. Henceforth Soviet literature was to be devoted to substantiation of this dogma. And this dogma Zoshchenko was congenitally unable to document. His entire past career demonstrated his incorrigible knack of seeing and arresting in his prose the ridiculous, the stupid, the mean and paltry, the tragic loneliness of human beings, the eternal irreconcilability between lofty programs of reform and the little man. Consummate master of his art, he had done his job of satire very well. He had soon become, and continued to be, one of the most popular Soviet writers. For about twenty years after the Revolution it was still possible to blame capitalist survivals for all the ills Zoshchenko depicted in Soviet life. As time went on and socialism was proclaimed *fait accompli,* it became awkward to explain away the widespread "philistinism" which he continued to see in the body politic.

Under pressure, Zoshchenko had attempted, particularly during the thirties, to "reforge" his work. But the effort was always a forced one and, what was worse, the result was dull. His biographies of the three "positive" heroes and his historical sketches are hardly more than bald records of events. His children's stories could have been no more than a sideline. To Party eyes, his avowedly didactic works, *Youth Restored* and *Before Sunrise,* must have appeared, at best, ambiguous and suspicious.

To his efforts as writer, he added his efforts as citizen. His indefatigable activities as committee member and public speaker, too, must have filled the notebooks of his mind with tantalizing material he dared not touch. He said once: "I am a fiction writer, and this capacity, unfortunately, never leaves me." [134] Everywhere,

---

[134] Zoshchenko, "Preduprezhdenie," *Mikhail Zoshchenko,* p. 7.

whether in associations within Party-sponsored projects or in company of the simple man-in-the-street, what Zoshchenko's sharp eye and keen ear picked out was the same. He could not confine himself to deriding rank-and-file Soviet citizens; sometimes he went so far as to portray members of the Party as entirely "negative" characters. Try as he would, he could not discipline his unruly genius to the extolling of socialism's great achievements and still write distinctive work. A little too far in one direction, and he risked his popularity with his readers and his own artistic self-esteem; a little too far in the other, and he could not remain in the favor of the Communist Party.

Early in his career, his self-knowledge forecast his future difficulties, when he admitted that he could not mix genres, could not accommodate Hamlet and the Inspector General in the same drama. Over the course of years, the Party arbiters learned slowly and graphically from the growing body of his work what he had known from the beginning: he could not blend the positive and the negative in the form of a layer cake without the cake falling flat. In the absence of stern regulation during the War, Zoshchenko seized the moment to write the self-preoccupied *Before Sunrise* and to revert, immediately after the War, to his earlier short-story approach in such pieces as "Adventures of a Monkey." This backsliding must have been proof enough to the official Party critics that what was thereafter desired from Soviet writers could never be delivered by Zoshchenko.

In 1946, the crystallization of the new Party line in foreign and domestic affairs authoritatively put an end to mention of those elements in Soviet life on which Zoshchenko's creative process fed. A people which had vanquished the greatest menace in history and was now advancing majestically toward the stage of full communism, the highest stage of development humanity had ever seen, could not logically go on its way trailing the sordid trappings of the unregenerate old Adam. Therefore, the bourgeois mentality, the mentality of the old world, no longer existed among Soviet people as a whole, the Party decreed. If Zoshchenko waywardly continued to see the old faults in Soviet life, he was falsifying. What is more, as is implicitly laid down in the new post-1946 Party line, many of the targets of Zoshchenko's satire in the past were also nonexistent.

The postwar ideology not only reappraises Soviet history, removing it completely from the influence of the West, but also recasts the past life of the Soviet people to bring it into conformity with the current image presented by the Communist Party. Book after book published in a new edition is revised, expunging the interpretation of the past which is discordant with what is proclaimed as present reality. Thus, Zoshchenko in 1946 became not only a distorter of the immediate scene, but of the past.

With the *raison d'être* of the satirist's existence thus eliminated, Zoshchenko, who had expected to find enough evidence of "philistinism" among his fellow citizens to last him the remainder of his life and who had never been able to function with distinction in any genre other than satire, became expendable. In the expenditure, the last drop of utility was wrung from him. To have quietly refused facilities for publishing in the future would have effectively silenced Zoshchenko. To condemn him as "the dregs of literature," however, killed a good many birds with the same stone. It enlightened other writers on the nature of the new line, while avoiding the necessity of direct intervention and dictation in their work. It guided publishers in their future practice. It provided the general public with a proper frame of opinion about literature. The Resolution of the Central Committee of the Communist Party dated August 14, 1946, was a most economical device. It was economical in all but the disbursement of literary talent and, conceivably, human life.

After the condemnation of Zoshchenko, the only role left for satirical works was to serve as anti-Western propaganda. For overcoming the deficiencies of Soviet life which, it was conceded, still existed as isolated survivals of the past, only one satirical form was permissible: the *feuilleton*, ridiculing one specific case without implication that such occurrences were typical or frequent. The result could only be that satire as a genre should vanish from Soviet literature.

That, by and large, satire has died out, even of the narrow type desired, is corroborated by numerous laments in later years over its disappearance.[135] There is still a wide field for this genre, Gor-

---

[135] "Za boevuiu sovetskuiu satiru!" *Lit. gaz.*, May 28, June 1, 1949; M. Matusovskii, "Na boi za mir!" *ibid.*, Oct. 5, 1949; N. Ignat'eva, "Za boevoi satiricheskii spektakl'!" *ibid.*, Oct. 8, 1949.

batov declared in 1949. Its main blow must be directed abroad, against the enemies of the USSR. Within the Soviet Union, where some survivals of capitalism still linger in the minds of the people, satire and humor must combat "plunderers of social property, grafters, bureaucrats, manifestations of conceit, obsequiousness, vulgarity." The attack is to be made in the form of the *feuilleton*.[136]

Even Zoshchenko has again appeared as author of a few contributions to the "new satire." After his four-year silence, unbroken except for several mediocre wartime stories of German barbarity and Russian heroism, which were published in the journal *New World* in 1947,[137] a trickle of *feuilletons* bearing Zoshchenko's name began, in 1950, in the pages of the humorous magazine *Crocodile*.[138] In them his "satire" is usually directed against "foreign enemies." These pieces are utterly devoid of the characteristic stamp of the former Zoshchenko. They might have been written by any hack. For whatever reasons, Zoshchenko's name, but not his talent, has been lent to these feeble lines.

Soviet literature has written off a heavy loss.

[136] Boris Gorbatov, "O sovetskoi satire i iumore," *Novyi mir*, No. 10 (1949), pp. 214–29.
[137] Zoshchenko, "Nikogda ne zabudem," *Novyi mir*, No. 9 (1947), pp. 148–72.
[138] *Krokodil*, June 20, 1950; Jan. 10 and 20, Sept. 10, Dec. 10 and 20, 1951.

Robert M. Hankin

Postwar Soviet Ideology and
Literary Scholarship

I

THE YEAR 1932 heralds the advent of a new era in Soviet literature. In that year a Communist Party Resolution "invited into a single Union of Soviet Writers all writers who support the platform of Soviet power and wish to participate in building socialism." [1] The reason for the establishment of this new organization is not absolutely clear. Perhaps it derived in part from a greater measure of support for the regime on the part of literary groups who had initially been indifferent. Perhaps the bitter antagonism aroused by the efforts of the Russian Association of Proletarian Writers to win hegemony over literature accounted for it. Or perhaps the Party decided that with the completion of the First Five-Year Plan the moment was at hand to advance its grand design for literature, which would call for increasing centralization of control. One or all of these factors might have prompted the change.

At the first All-Union Congress of Soviet Writers which assembled two years later, Zhdanov, speaking in the Party's name, surveyed the new demands which were to be made on literature. He asserted categorically that socialist realism would henceforth constitute the exclusive artistic method for Soviet literature; thus he definitively repudiated the Party's earlier abstention from a clear expression of preference in matters of literary policy. He elaborated upon the tasks which would confront writers in their ca-

[1] "O perestroike literaturno-khudozhestvennykh organizatsii, Postanovlenie TsK VKP(b) ot 23 aprelia 1932g.," *Sovremennaia literatura,* comp. A. Dubovikov and E. Severin (Moscow, 1946), pp. 14–18.

pacity as "engineers of the human soul." Drawing attention to the growth of international tensions, he sought to jostle the literary and ideological fronts into shouldering fresh responsibilities. Probably in response to ominous reverberations from the Reichswehr, Zhdanov sounded the initial call for a concerted offensive upon non-Soviet culture.[2] Italian aggression in Abyssinia and the Nazi invasion of the neutralized Rhine province soon were cogent reminders of the new threat.[3] No matter what the reasons for its establishment, the existence of a single Union of Soviet Writers now made it feasible for the Party to accelerate the ideological mobilization.

The years which remained before the outbreak of the Second World War witnessed a succession of campaigns designed to augment the striking power of the printed word and transform the corps of Soviet writers into a mobile task force. Accountability for ideological content in art grew greater, particularly as anti-Trotskyist pronouncements rose in frequency and concern with Axis intentions increased. As the War drew nearer, the Party elevated the political function of art to the paramount position, its intolerance of heterodoxy growing daily more emphatic.

The cultivation of mass patriotism became a major preoccupation of the day. Literary critics who ventured to deprecate works with sanctioned patriotic content were admonished to desist. It was symptomatic of the late hour that one critic should even have been upbraided for expressing his resolve to "discredit any work by an author who does not appear to have a sacred interest in creating a work of art." [4] Concomitant efforts were made to resuscitate interest in the nation's past. On one of those rare occasions which usually betoken turning points in Soviet ideological developments, Stalin, Kirov, and Zhdanov, in the middle thirties, made a number of recommendations for a proposed textbook on the history of the USSR—which furnished fresh impetus to the cultivation of mass patriotism.[5] This concentration on national traditions of fortitude

[2] "Russkaia literatura," *Bol'shaia sovetskaia entsiklopediia*, XLIX (1941), 667.

[3] "Bol'shevistskaia partiia i sovetskaia literatura," *Novyi mir*, No. 5 (1947), p. 119.

[4] "O nekotorykh literaturnykh khudozhestvennykh zhurnalakh," *Bol'shevik*, No. 17 (September, 1939), p. 54.

[5] P. Kerzhentsev, "Nekotorye voprosy iskusstva," *Bol'shevik*, No. 4 (Feb. 13, 1947), pp. 9–18.

and devotion to native soil in the face of external aggression
reached its apogee in the first two years of the War and challenged,
if it did not surpass, the dissemination of Communist ideology.

In 1939, the Eighteenth Party Congress introduced several fresh
currents into the ideological atmosphere. What was officially
dubbed "deference to the West" was singled out as a dangerous
trap for Soviet intellectuals; Stalin even went so far as to contend
that treason to the state could be traced to deference to foreigners.[6]
With the formal inception of what was termed the gradual transition to communism, the program of education and indoctrination was allocated a role of greater importance than ever before.
Party spokesmen gave notice, moreover, that the effectiveness of
the program would be determined not by domestic economic successes alone, but also by the outcome of the Soviet effort in the
"pending struggle with the forces of external aggression." [7]

During the War, literature climbed to new eminence in Soviet
society; daily newspapers featured entire plays and novels on timely
subjects, which undoubtedly played an effective role in sustaining
public morale.[8] The year 1944 saw the crucial hump of the national
peril surmounted and with it the Party's heightened concern with
ideological orthodoxy, and the reaffirmation of its unquestioned
leadership. As the year opened, Mikhail Zoshchenko was mercilessly belabored for his autobiographical *Before Sunrise,* and found
wanting in patriotism for writing what was called this "formal and
harmful" work.[9] Shortly thereafter, the list of delinquent writers
was lengthened to include others whose output in the period of national travail was termed substandard.[10] The process of ideological
stocktaking had begun in earnest. With incalculable implications
for all other categories of the Soviet "superstructure," the barb of
Party criticism was shortly applied to the philosophers. They were
called to task for their apologetic treatment of the idealist predeces-

[6] I. V. Stalin, *Voprosy Leninizma,* 11th ed. (Moscow, 1945), p. 590.

[7] V. M. Molotov, *XVIII s"ezd vsesoiuznoi kommunisticheskoi partii (b) (stenograficheskii otchët)* (Moscow, 1939), pp. 4–5.

[8] L. A. Plotkin, "Partiia i literatura," *Vestnik Leningradskogo universiteta,* No. 11
(November, 1947), p. 85.

[9] V. Gorshkov, *et al.,* "Ob odnoi vrednoi povesti," *Bol'shevik,* No. 2 (January, 1944),
p. 57.

[10] N. Tikhonov, "Otechestvennaia voina i sovetskaia literatura," *Bol'shevik,* No. 3–4
(February, 1944), pp. 36–37.

sors of Marx and Engels in German philosophy.[11] Thereby the achievement of Hegel and others was being reappraised so as to minimize their influence on Marx and Engels and indirectly on Russian Marxists. Concurrently, a campaign was launched glorifying the materialist tradition of Belinskii, Chernyshevskii, and Dobroliubov and portraying it as the crowning achievement of world pre-Marxist thinking. Anticipating the complaint that these men were virtually unknown in the West, elaborate attempts were made to ferret out every facet of their activities which might attest to their influence, however indirect, on the world.[12]

From 1941 to 1945 the Nazi invasion and the crisis of national survival had produced an impressive mobilization of all cultural and artistic media. The unprecedented intensity of the nation's anguish was succeeded by an understandable fatigue and a longing to relax. No respite was in store, however. After the briefest of interludes, the writers were summoned back into harness. Initially this ideological remobilization was oriented toward the needs of reconstruction, but when these early difficulties had been mastered, there was no demobilization. Despite revitalized economic optimism and resumption of the drive to achieve the next stage of social organization, dwindling hopes for international amity kept the propaganda mechanism functioning at top tension.

That reconstruction needs were enormous, the few foreign visitors to Russia after the War had occasion to observe in the gutted and wasted land, the plight of badly fed, scantily clad millions struggling to wrest bare sustenance from the neglected earth.[13] Official statistics accounted for seven million dead, but the true figure may have been far higher. Of prewar herds of livestock only a meager fraction remained in Soviet territory. Transportation, industry, and housing were in desperate straits.[14] On top of all this a fresh calamity descended in 1946 in the form of drought, which affected an unprecedentedly broad area and was aggravated by the

---

[11] "O nedostatkakh i oshibkakh v osveshchenii istorii filosofii kontsa XVIII i nachala XIX v.," *Bol'shevik*, No. 7–8 (April, 1944), pp. 14–19.

[12] M. Iovchuk, "Klassiki russkoi filosofii XIX veka," *Bol'shevik*, No. 12 (June, 1944), p. 25.

[13] Dwight D. Eisenhower, *Crusade in Europe*, excerpt from the New York *Herald Tribune*, Dec. 8, 1948.

[14] N. Voznesenskii, *Voennaia ekonomika SSSR v period otechestvennoi voiny* (Moscow, 1947), pp. 157–68.

wartime decline in sown area and the scarcity of agricultural equipment.[15] The derationing of foodstuffs had to be postponed as a result. Industry, too, failed to cope with the reconversion plan for 1946.[16] There were gaping spiritual wounds as well. The relaxation of Party controls during the War ushered in widespread corruption on the collective farms; officials and peasants alike were deemed culpable.[17] Lax economic morality was accompanied by alien ideological influences on Soviet soil. In pursuit of the retreating Nazis, millions of Red Army soldiers had seen Europe at first hand. Other millions lived for years under enemy occupation; some were admittedly deconditioned by the steady diet of anti-Bolshevik propaganda.[18] In newly acquired territories, the populations had been reared for a generation in a spirit of militant antipathy to Bolshevism.[19] To cap the climax, the prewar core of disciplined, finely indoctrinated Bolsheviks had suffered frightful casualties. Their replacements were youths whose chief qualification for membership had been front-line courage. They constituted an inflated army, itself in need of thorough theoretical and practical conditioning.[20]

By November, 1947, the domestic economic position was much improved, as evidenced by the abolition of rationing.[21] As the spirit of shoestring survival receded, throughout the press and periodical literature talk of the long-range view was revived. The prewar vision of communism in one country returned, and with it came a spate of speculation on ways and means of effecting the requisite

[15] A. Karavaev, "Narodnoe khoziaistvo," *Bol'shaia sovetskaia entsiklopediia*, supplement entitled "SSSR" (1947), col. 882.

[16] Molotov, "Tridtsatiletie velikoi oktiabr'skoi sotsialisticheskoi revoliutsii" (Doklad na torzhestvennom zasedanii Moskovskogo Soveta, 6 noiabria 1947g.), *Literaturnaia gazeta*, Nov. 7, 1947.

[17] "O merakh po likvidatsii narushenii ustava sel'skokhoziaistvennoi arteli v kolkhozakh, Postanovlenie Soveta Ministrov SSSR i Tsentral'nogo komiteta VKP(b), 19 sentiabria, 1946g.," *Vazhneishie resheniia po sel'skomu khoziaistvu za 1938–1946gg.* (Moscow, 1948), pp. 318–23.

[18] V. N. Zhukova, "Diskussiia po knige G. F. Aleksandrova, 'Istoriia zapadno-evropeiskoi filosofii,' 16–25 iiunia, 1947g." (stenograficheskii otchët), *Voprosy filosofii*, No. 1 (1947), p. 82.

[19] Iovchuk, "Diskussiia po knige Aleksandrova," p. 212.

[20] "Postanovlenie Tsentral'nogo Komiteta VKP(b), 'O roste partii i o merakh po usileniiu partiino-organizatsionnoi i partiino-politicheskoi raboty s novovstupivshimi v VKP(b),' Vospitanie molodykh kommunistov," *Pravda*, April 10, 1950.

[21] Molotov, "Tridtsatiletie."

economic and social transformations.[22] The obstacle to progress
was described as entrenched traditional "bourgeois" thinking and
habits, which would impede the adaptation of the masses to new
functions.[23] The solution recommended, apart from steady, rapid
economic progress, was an ideological campaign operative on two
levels: the widest possible propagandistic dissemination of the aims
and tenets of the regime, and the advancement of Soviet theory.
The ideologists thus received a dual assignment: to recover lost
ground and to pave the way for motion forward. As international
relations deteriorated, a third task was added: to temper the home
front for all eventualities. As though the brief interlude in which
the USSR and its Western Allies had joined forces to defeat a common foe had never been, mutual suspicions had reasserted themselves between the two camps.

Soviet intellectuals on all levels were instructed that their primary duty was to assist in the Party's program for the political and
cultural enlightenment of the population. To make the Party, now
numbering six million, an organization comparable in discipline
to its prewar membership, a mass study program was instituted.[24]
For Party officials an elaborate training program moved into high
gear. For the general public, series of lectures were organized on a
vast scale in May, 1947, with the establishment of the All-Union
Society for the Dissemination of Political and Scientific Knowledge.[25] The specific content of the enlightenment program was announced in the Central Committee's resolutions on literature, motion pictures, and the theater, and in Zhdanov's speech at the same
time. These documents were declared to have "established a fighting program . . . for many years." [26] The new line was laid down
with unprecedented stringency, taking many writers by surprise
despite their years of previous conditioning to Party hegemony.

[22] Ts. A. Stepanian, "O nekotorykh zakonomernostiakh perekhoda ot sotsializma k kommunizmu," *Voprosy filosofii*, No. 2 (1947), p. 28.
[23] Prof. V. A. Chagin, "Razvitie Leninym i Stalinym marksistskogo ucheniia o gosu-darstve," *Vestnik Leningradskogo universiteta*, No. 11 (1947), p. 19.
[24] "Teoreticheskaia podgotovka partiinykh i sovetskikh kadrov," *Pravda*, Nov. 1, 1946.
[25] "Obrashchenie ko vsem deiateliam sovetskoi nauki, literatury i iskusstva, k nau-chnym, obshchestvennym i drugim organizatsiiam i uchrezhdeniiam Sovetskogo Soiuza," *Lit. gaz.*, May 1, 1947.
[26] I. Ia. Shchipanov, "Diskussiia po knige Aleksandrova," p. 495.

Zhdanov conceded this was so, and endeavored to offer a justification for the policy:

Some people think it strange for the Central Committee to have passed such abrupt measures on the literary question. They are not accustomed to this. . . . They maintain that if industry produces defective goods and fails to meet the consumers' goods program, or if the lumbering plan is not fulfilled, it is natural that a reprimand be issued for this. But if human beings are damaged in their education, is this offense not worse than failure to meet the production program.[27]

In all postwar ideological pronouncements there is scarcely a passage which more accurately mirrors the militancy and rigidity of the day and the Party's anxiety over domestic weaknesses.

A survey of Soviet literary history since 1932 leaves no doubt that the Party's resolve to secure ultimate acceptance of its unqualified leadership and unshared control has been constant. But the tactics enlisted to achieve this end have varied. It would be misleading to describe the diversity of details in the postwar panorama as all merely the inevitable culmination of earlier lines of development. To suggest that specific details were painstakingly legislated long in advance is to ignore the distinctive demands of the contemporary situation. Numerous bald statements by Soviet leaders in 1946 reveal that their diagnosis of home-front infirmities and the potential menace of international developments spelled crisis in Soviet terms. A grave crop failure following hard on the heels of five years of near starvation on a nation-wide scale, industry's failure to meet its goals while goods were desperately short, rising tension with the West and its painfully tangible by-product—the failure of foreign reconstruction aid to materialize—all were factors judged to be acutely critical. Significantly, Party moves were initiated at the lowest ebb of Soviet postwar domestic fortunes, in the summer of 1946, when a protracted dry spell had already generated gloomy prognostications for the fall harvest.

Most observers recognize that the Soviet economy was subsequently successful in making good its war losses and raising the country out of its catastrophic decline of 1946. It is difficult to evaluate the contribution of the ideological campaign to this achievement. One assumption, however, appears warranted. The

---

[27] "Doklad tov. Zhdanova o zhurnalakh 'Zvezda' i 'Leningrad,'" *Sovetskaia kniga*, No. 8–9 (August–September, 1946), p. 16.

domestic ideological strategy which has been described was invoked because, generally speaking, similar tactics were considered to have been effective on earlier occasions in pulling the country out of critical situations.

II

Less than a week after the celebration of victory in Europe Soviet writers met for their first postwar conference. Liberal relaxation was the keynote of the proceedings. It was too early for the magnitude of the war devastation to have impressed itself on the jubilant *literati* just back from the front. The conviction prevailed, moreover, that the Soviets now occupied an established and respected place in the councils of nations. In this mood, several literary luminaries whose political loyalties were above suspicion cautioned against interference in the literary creative process and argued against the belief that in art a miracle could be "organized." [28]

In the next few months, steps were taken somewhere backstage to dampen these hopes, and finally in August and September, 1946, the Party resolutions and the Zhdanov report eliminated all doubts as to the Party's postwar demands on the arts.[29] An extensive range of charges was directed against literature described as "lacking in ideas and ideologically harmful." [30] As in 1944, Zoshchenko was again the chief target, this time for a story called "The Adventures of a Monkey." Zhdanov insisted that since 1922, when Zoshchenko had publicly confessed to being "politically immoral," nothing in his attitude had changed.[31] Another well-known writer, Anna Akhmatova, who on the eve of the War had emerged from almost twenty years of retirement, was spotlighted as an anomaly on the current scene. Zhdanov likened the reappearance of her poetry, "jelled in attitudes of bourgeois aristocratic estheticism," to the resurrection of a "museum piece." [32]

These two were old-timers, and this was not the first time they had taken the lash of the Party's tongue for reluctance to purge

[28] A. Tvardovskii, "Desiatyi plenum pravleniia Soiuza sovetskikh pisatelei SSSR," *Lit. gaz.*, May 22, 1945.
[29] *Lit. gaz.*, Aug. 24, 1946; *Pravda*, Sept. 21, 1946.
[30] "O zhurnalakh 'Zvezda' i 'Leningrad,' iz postanovleniia TsK VKP(b) ot 14 avgusta, 1946g.," *Sovetskaia kniga*, No. 8–9 (August–September, 1946), pp. 3–5.
[31] "Doklad tov. Zhdanova," p. 8.   [32] *Ibid.*, p. 10.

themselves of thought patterns inculcated in formative years under circumstances inimical to the present environment. But Soviet writers of considerably later vintage were also called to account. Akhmatova's melancholy and nostalgia for the past were matched by the sporadic appearance of "religious symbolism" (the employment of ecclesiastical terms, Biblical references, and evangelical imagery) in the work of young poets. This was judged as ill becoming an "engineer of souls" in Soviet society.[33] Shortly after the end of the War, what came to be known as "literature of consolation" was also brought under frequent attack. The agonies of the day notwithstanding, writers were adjured to handle reality fearlessly. The returning veteran, it was insisted, would have no truck with "sweet lyricism," "gastronomical promises," or a "lulling and caressing literature under the aegis of which to seek refuge from the storms of life." [34] Neither was this the time, in the Party's view, to use art purely for entertainment, since this might beget a mood of "false demobilization" and a yearning to "rest by the quiet stream." [35] The war years had been drenched in adoration of Russia's past glories, as part of a coordinated drive to resurrect national traditions of fortitude and devotion. From the moment the War ended, preoccupation with history evoked reprobation.[36]

Several other shortcomings completed the list of the Party's grievances. One complaint was that the quality of literary craftsmanship had fallen off. Another was that works had appeared manifesting "deference to the contemporary foreign culture of the West" and permeated with a "spirit of kow-towing to everything foreign." [37] This theme would soon swell to a major drive. Finally, there were aberrations such as the poet Sel'vinskii's "theory of socialist symbolism," which he proferred as a philosophy of art to replace socialist realism,[38] and the opinion of the Ukrainian writer, Petro Panch, that an author "had the right to make mistakes." [39] The two

[33] A. Surkov, "Poeziia naroda-pobeditelia," *Lit. gaz.*, Feb. 3, 1945.

[34] Iu. Iuzovskii, "Radost' bor'by," *ibid.*

[35] B. Platonov, "A. A. Zhdanov i problemy sovetskoi literatury," *Zvezda*, No. 8 (August, 1949), p. 174.

[36] Anna Karavaeva, "Desiatyi plenum pravleniia Soiuza sovetskikh pisatelei," *Lit. gaz.*, May 22, 1945.

[37] "O zhurnalakh 'Zvezda' i 'Leningrad,'" p. 4.

[38] N. Tikhonov, "Sovetskaia literatura v 1944–1945gg.," *Lit. gaz.*, May 17, 1945.

[39] "Rezoliutsiia Prezidiuma pravleniia Soiuza sovetskikh pisatelei SSSR ot 4 sentiabria 1946g.," *Lit. gaz.*, Sept. 7, 1946.

latter views reveal the extent to which the Party had relaxed its controls over literature during the War.

From the lowest to the highest echelons, every writer and Party functionary deemed responsible for the deplorable state of literature came in for his share of official opprobrium. This included the editors of two Leningrad literary magazines, the director of the Writers' Union, the Leningrad Municipal Party Committee and, on the highest level, the Central Committee's Propaganda Administration. Concrete action followed on the heels of the reprimands: Zoshchenko and Akhmatova were expelled from the Writers' Union; [40] the magazine *Leningrad* was summarily ordered to cease publication, and the *Star* (*Zvezda*) was brought under immediate Party supervision at the most responsible level by the appointment of the deputy chief of the Central Committee's Propaganda Administration as its editor; [41] the current chairman of the Presidium of the Writers' Union was removed and a secretariat elected to perform supervisory functions.[42]

Much of the Zhdanov address and of subsequent articles on the role of literature in the Soviet Union reformulated, with special stress on their postwar application, those canons of literature which have constituted literary orthodoxy since 1932: the cardinal function of literature is as an instrument of education in society; it must cater to the masses, employing literary forms meaningful to them (*narodnost'*); it should make use of the legacy of earlier cultures, critically reevaluating it and singling out as guiding models all its progressive elements; to fulfill its purpose in Soviet society it must subscribe to the world-view of the proletariat (*ideinost'*), and it must support the policies of the Party and State (*partiinost'*).[43]

The educational function of literature.—Zhdanov declared that it was the obligation of Soviet literature to assist in rearing the younger generation "to be bright and hearty, believing in its cause, fearing no obstacles, ready to master any difficulties." [44] He insisted that bitter experience had confirmed the efficacy of this course. To lend greater weight to his argument he even ventured to surmise that the War might have been lost had Soviet literature pursued

[40] *Ibid.*   [41] "O zhurnalakh 'Zvezda' i 'Leningrad,' " p. 5.
[42] "V Prezidiume pravleniia Soiuza sovetskikh pisatelei SSSR," *Lit. gaz.*, Sept. 7, 1946.   [43] Plotkin, "Partiia i literatura," p. 70.
[44] "O zhurnalakh 'Zvezda' i 'Leningrad,' " p. 4.

any other tack.[45] Zoshchenko and Akhmatova, he maintained, could only disorient and demoralize youth at a moment when, with the postwar transition to an economy of peace, the responsibilities devolving upon the ideological front and on literature primarily "do not diminish, but, on the contrary, grow." [46]

The narodnost' *of Soviet literature.*—To prove its devotion to the masses, said Zhdanov, Soviet literature must meet their demands, improve their tastes, and guide their development. To do this, it must not lag behind events. Historic themes need not be altogether excluded, but a healthier balance had to be established between past and present; history should be illuminated in such a way as to disclose its usefulness in solving the problems of the present. Writers should portray artistically the changes which had occurred in the people since the Revolution, laying special stress on new qualities developed during the recent war.

Attitude to the cultural heritage.—Pursuing the line introduced in 1944 by the *Bolshevik* articles on the contributions of the Russian Revolutionary Democrats, Zhdanov called attention to the debt owed by Soviet literature to the materialist current in native culture. Of the historical personages whom he showered with praise for contributing to the Soviet literary tradition, all were Russians.

The concepts of partiinost' *and* ideinost'.—Calling Lenin's article "Party Organization and Party Literature" the source of all the "foundations on which the development of our Soviet literature rests," Zhdanov adamantly insisted that writers were wrong to assume that politics was the Central Committee's business, whereas their approach to literature might be purely esthetic: "Our literature is not a private enterprise to titillate the various tastes of the literary market. We are not one whit obliged to accommodate . . . tastes and mores which have nothing to do with the morality and qualities of the Soviet people." [47] In the final analysis, it is this Leninist notion of *partiinost'* which most irrefutably disassociates the Soviet writer from his non-Marxist Western or prerevolutionary Russian counterpart. The modern Bolshevik will be the first to acknowledge the affinity of his ideas on *narodnost'*, art as education, and so forth, to those of prerevolutionary figures, primarily the materialists of the 1860s; similar opinions were entertained by

[45] "Doklad tov. Zhdanova," p. 11.   [46] *Ibid.*, p. 21.   [47] *Ibid.*, p. 11.

many other nineteenth-century giants as well. He will also concede the influence on Lenin of attitudes towards partisanship in literature contained in the writings of Chernyshevskii, Dobroliubov, and others. Yet by elevating *partiinost'* to a sacrosanct position, Lenin introduced a principle which was to become one of the most characteristic features of Soviet ideology. The Zhdanov speech in 1946 really constituted an exegesis on *partiinost'* in its postwar phase. It signified a major stride toward a thoroughly controlled literature.

Evidently the Party decided that the current situation allowed for less compromise in the execution of its purposes than had been necessary on earlier occasions. Hence its willingness to deal so summarily with writers as popular as Zoshchenko and Akhmatova. Hence its obduracy in demanding that writers sever all ties to earlier bourgeois thought, and its promptness to hold earlier deviations over the heads of recalcitrants. Hence its peremptory dismissal of the bare suggestion that a writer had the right to err. It accounts likewise for the stinging vituperation characteristic of this period, for the severity of the reorganizational measures and the resolve to secure absolute acceptance of *partiinost'* narrowly defined. And, finally, whereas for a generation Party spokesmen had championed the "critical absorption of past culture," criticism of the bourgeois legacy was now advocated far more vociferously than absorption.

Reference must be made to the polemic techniques of this period as a prerequisite for appraising any Soviet writings originating during the postwar Five-Year Plan. They were formulated in detail in 1947 when the philosophers of the USSR met in solemn conclave to overhaul the philosophical front in light of the new Party line. Again it was Zhdanov who worded the new requirement most bluntly. He qualified "annihilating criticism" as obligatory to the Party's polemic arsenal. To treat opposing views with a light hand would lead, he said, to professional "quasi-objectivism," "indifferent attention to good and evil," and would rob Marxism of its militancy and the aggressive spirit demanded by *partiinost'*.[48] In anticipation of a bitter world ideological contest, intellectuals were exhorted early in the postwar period to regard themselves as fighting publicists. The cry went out for total mobilization of the ideo-

[48] A. A. Zhdanov, "Diskussiia po knige Aleksandrova," p. 261.

logical front; waverers were warned that anyone preferring to by-
pass the challenge would be branded a "deserter." [49] In September,
1947, the reorganized *Literary Gazette* inaugurated an aggressive
program with an article entitled "Harry Truman," containing a
head-on assault upon the integrity of the American President.[50]
Here was unmistakable evidence of the intensity of the projected
drive.

The campaign which unfolded aimed at the universal annihilation of the tenets and contributions of "bourgeois culture in all its
guises." Zhdanov contributed a dogmatic restatement of the dependence of art upon society, and, in language glaringly reminiscent
of his characterization of bourgeois culture in 1934, drew the conclusion that in the contemporary crisis of capitalism the bourgeoisie
could no longer produce great art.[51] But in 1946 it was more than
present-day bourgeois culture which was attacked. The comparatively liberal prewar acceptance of earlier bourgeois cultural contributions as a treasured inheritance from which Soviet culture
should respectfully glean the best was supplanted by an attempt to
demonstrate how mankind had repeatedly been reduced to misfor-
tune by past bourgeois ideologies.[52] Literary movements on Russian soil which failed to satisfy the latest postulates or were at odds
with the materialist traditions of Russia were ferreted out one by
one and pilloried. The effectiveness of the denunciation was measured by the clarity with which a critic was able to trace the movement to Western, bourgeois origins.[53]

This inimical view of bourgeois culture was joined by insistence
upon Soviet cultural independence from the West. A Soviet biolo-
gist named Zhebrak submitted to an American magazine an article
in which he undertook to refute Lysenko's biological theories and
claimed that Soviet scientists were helping to build a "general
world-wide biology." [54] Using this incident as the provocation, the
Party advanced the "generally accepted thesis that under modern

[49] K. Simonov (from a speech at the Moscow Conference of Writers), *Lit. gaz.*,
Sept. 21, 1946.

[50] B. Gorbatov, "Garri Trumen," *Lit. gaz.*, Sept. 2, 1947.

[51] "Na peredovuiu liniiu ognia," *Lit. gaz.*, Sept. 28, 1946.

[52] V. Emdin, "Diskussiia po knige Aleksandrova," p. 10.

[53] D. Zaslavskii, "Mirovoe znachenie sovetskogo iskusstva," *Sovetskii teatr, k tridtsa-
tiletiiu sovetskogo gosudarstva* (Moscow, 1947), p. 27.

[54] A. Surkov, *et al.*, "K sudu obshchestvennosti," *Lit. gaz.*, Aug. 30, 1947.

conditions there is not and cannot be a single world science." [55]
This principle was deemed pertinent to all provinces of culture.
And in the contest of two world-views, the Soviets laid claim to the
role of the new teacher of mankind.[56]

Pursuing the principle enunciated in 1944 that notwithstanding
the affinities of Marxism with earlier philosophies it was the new
elements in Marxism which were far more significant than what
Marx had derived from his predecessors, Soviet thinkers everywhere claimed an original approach distinct from bourgeois culture. Russia, they said, had now assumed leadership among civilized
nations. They had, therefore, lived to see the fruition of Belinskii's
fond dream a century earlier that future generations would see
Russia "at the head of the educated world, giving laws in science
and art." [57] Soviet thinkers were told to make every effort to answer
the problems of intellectuals and masses in other countries who
were amenable to Soviet persuasion. Adequate Marxist solutions
should be offered for their problems.[58] From this, however, stemmed
an inevitable contradiction. Policies evolved under Soviet conditions would boomerang when offered as blanket solutions for the
problems of other cultures, damaging instead of enhancing Soviet
prestige. This issue arose late in 1947 during the gestation phase of
the Lysenko controversy. At that time the prevalent opinion seemed
to be that the validity of a particular viewpoint for Soviet conditions outweighed hesitancy concerning unfavorable foreign reaction. Indeed, one spokesman went so far as to anticipate that a
radical break with bourgeois tradition by Soviet thinkers, even in
the sciences, would in and of itself have telling effect in winning
the support of foreign intellectuals.[59]

But the effort to capture progressive sympathies in the West was
overshadowed by the domestic cultivation of Soviet patriotism and
national pride. Here the campaign candidly claimed Soviet superiority, both in the social organization and in the resultant human product. True, references were made to the services and con-

[55] Akad. V. Nemchinov, "Protiv nizkopoklonstva," *Lit. gaz.*, Oct. 4, 1947.
[56] "Bol'shevistskaia ideinost'—osnova sovetskoi literatury," *Lit. gaz.*, Sept. 21, 1946.
[57] "Natsional'naia gordost' russkikh revoliutsionerov-demokratov," *Lit. gaz.*, April 12, 1947.
[58] L. P. Trainin, "Diskussiia po knige Aleksandrova," p. 139.
[59] "Za darvinizm tvorcheskii, protiv mal'tusianstva," *Lit. gaz.*, Nov. 29, 1947.

tributions of other nations.[60] Nevertheless, that reinterpretation of
Russia's contribution to world culture which derived from the
premise that the intrinsic value of a cultural phenomenon must be
weighed by whether it is progressive or reactionary in Marxist
lights [61] gave Russia a clear advantage, it was felt, since historical
circumstances peculiar to Russia had generated so widespread a
native revolutionary tradition in the nineteenth century. It was
from this same premise that it was declared to be insufficient for a
Russian before the Revolution to have loved his country, to have
believed in its potential or in the great contribution which the
nation would some day make. The only patriots now fully acceptable were those who had consistently subscribed to the ideology of
revolutionary liberation.[62] Insistence on awarding full value only
to those cultural phenomena of the past which were associated with
the radical tradition meant repudiating some of the giants of Russian culture best appreciated outside of Russia.[63]

With this interpretation of patriotism as the touchstone, the
treatment of the past in historical novels was severely criticized. It
was charged that national solidarity had been illustrated to the
neglect of class antagonisms,[64] that novels in which Red Army men
were portrayed dreaming of past heroes failed to distinguish between the political consciousness of a Soviet citizen and that of a
Russian of an earlier day.[65] Two historical novels on the First
World War were said to have glossed over the social struggle of
the times. Other instances were cited. The critics rested on Lenin's
dictum that in any presocialist society two cultures coexist at any
given time. The two Russias of the past must be kept clearly separate, they said—the Russia of the tsars from the Russia of the
Decembrists, of Belinskii and the Revolutionary Democrats, and

60 "Patriotizm sovetskikh liudei," *Lit. gaz.*, April 12, 1946; Il'ia Erenburg, "Zametki
pisatelia," *Lit. gaz.*, Sept. 24, 1947; V. Kirpotin, "XI plenum pravleniia Soiuza sovetskikh pisatelei SSSR," *Lit. gaz.*, July 8, 1947.

61 "Obsuzhdenie postanovleniia TsK VKP(b) o zhurnalakh 'Zvezda' i 'Leningrad'
i doklad tovarishcha Zhdanova," *Izvestiia Akademii nauk SSSR*, V, No. 5 (1946), 515.

62 Kirpotin, "Odinnadtsatyi plenum pravleniia Soiuza sovetskikh pisatelei," *Lit.
gaz.*, June 29, 1947.

63 A. Fadeev, "Sovetskaia literatura posle postanovleniia TsK VKP(b) ot 14 avgusta
1946g. o zhurnalakh 'Zvezda' i 'Leningrad,' " *Lit. gaz.*, June 29, 1947.

64 S. Dolubov, "X plenum pravleniia Soiuza sovetskikh pisatelei SSSR," *Lit. gaz.*,
May 26, 1945.

65 L. Subotskii, "Zametki o teme i teorii," *Lit. gaz.*, April 22, 1945.

the Marxists. Oversight on this score, it was charged, had resulted in the idealization of tsarist culture.[66] Literary scholarship was felt to be vulnerable on this account. One work was said to "smell of Slavophilism." Another was repudiated for its efforts to discover a continuum of patriotism from the soldiers of 1812 to those of the Patriotic War.[67] Still a third had treated the Russian literary process as a single stream.[68] Analogous instances were multiplied at length. A terse summation of the official disapproval of these excesses and deviations, which were ascribed to wartime exigencies, was: "We cannot disguise ideologies sharply hostile to our entire outlook, our whole system, our entire structure!" [69]

Zhdanov complained that Soviet periodicals had published Western "trash" and works which "groveled" before the bourgeois West.[70] In time elaborate explanations were produced for the origin of this malady, which was characterized as "ideological waverings by individual representatives of our intelligentsia . . . and rotten servility to bourgeois culture." [71] It was referred to an old inferiority complex generated by Russia's prerevolutionary backwardness. As far as official statements went, the phenomenon was confined to the intellectuals. However, an article by a popular Soviet poet, Antokol'skii, entitled "On the Party, the Education of Youth, and Culture," disclosed that youths who had spent time abroad were enthusiastic over the amenities of Western life and disappointed by the contrast upon their return home.[72] From this it must be assumed that the vice of "deference," which the Party in public pronouncements restricted to the remnants of the prerevolutionary intelligentsia or to their influence, also applied in some measure to the younger generation of intellectuals born and reared in Soviet surroundings. Moreover, postwar novels and plays attest that it was true likewise of returning workers and peasants.

[66] Fadeev, "Zadachi literaturnoi teorii i kritiki," *Problemy sotsialisticheskogo realizma*, sbornik statei (Leningrad, 1948), p. 29.

[67] "Obshchee sobranie nauchnykh sotrudnikov INLI im. Gor'kogo Akademii nauk SSSR," *Izvestiia Akademii nauk SSSR*, V, No. 6 (1946), 523.

[68] *Ibid.*, p. 522.

[69] Kirpotin, "Ob otnoshenii russkoi literatury i russkoi kritiki k kapitalisticheskomu zapadu," *Oktiabr'*, No. 9 (September, 1946), pp. 174–75.

[70] "Doklad tov. Zhdanova," p. 12.

[71] Akad. N. Mitin, "O kritike i samokritike," *Lit. gaz.*, Oct. 4, 1947.

[72] P. Antokol'skii, "O poezii, o vospitanii molodykh, o kul'ture," *Znamia*, No. 1 (1947), p. 137.

In imaginative writing it was only a lapse here and there—five or six minor cases—which was adduced as proof that Soviet literature was actually guilty of groveling.[73] Literary scholarship, on the other hand, was declared to be permeated with a deferential spirit. The trend selected as most opprobrious was the disposition to consider Russian literature primarily in the light of foreign influences. From the standpoint of methodology, this was called an interpretation of literature as a hermetically enclosed process divorced from the realities of social life. One critic described it as a deleterious concept which belittled the achievements of Russian culture by portraying the great writers of the nineteenth century as imitators.[74]

The approach advocated for future scholarly research was the following: without repudiating the importance of international cultural influences, it had primarily and repeatedly to be stressed that the Russians had developed an *original* culture. The literature of the nineteenth century should be regarded mainly as a reflection of the Russian historical process—the rise of the revolutionary movement and the struggle with tsarism—which had, it was maintained, placed its stamp on all Russian writers and which alone could explain their fearlessness, liberational pathos, and zeal for social justice. These qualities, it was further contended, had in the latter half of the nineteenth century elevated Russian writers to the role of mentors of their Western confreres. Innumerable quotations were gleaned from the writings of Western authors attesting the inspiration they had derived from Russian literature.[75] This interpretation of the rise of Russian culture was accompanied by a series of broad recommendations. The drive to disseminate these views should be sustained until the "legend of the complete dependence of Russian thought on foreign sources is uncrowned." The contributions of the Russian classical materialists should be

[73] Tikhonov, "Iz vystupleniia na zasedanii Prezidiuma pravleniia SSP SSSR," *Lit. gaz.*, Sept. 7, 1946; "Rezoliutsiia Prezidiuma pravleniia Soiuza sovetskikh pisatelei SSSR ot 4 sentiabria 1946g."; A. Egolin, "Za vysokuiu ideinost' sovetskoi literatury," *Protiv bezydeinosti v literature* (Leningrad, 1947), p. 28; "Za vysokuiu ideinost' sovetskoi literatury," *Lit. gaz.*, June 21, 1947.

[74] Plotkin, "Sovremennye zadachi literaturovedeniia," *Izv. Akad. nauk*, V, No. 6 (1946), 459.

[75] T. Motylëva, "Russkaia literatura—peredovaia literatura mira," *Lit. gaz.*, April 12, 1947.

widely and loudly publicized,[76] so as to focus attention on the materialist traditions from which the present socialist society had sprung.

This obsessive and blatantly one-sided concentration on national individuality and the uniqueness of the Russian cultural contribution understandably gave rise to speculation, some of it bitter, among Soviet critics regarding the validity of the new approach. How reconcile the new line with the more traditional Marxist stress upon the primacy of class factors?

The champions of the new line declared that Marxism admitted nationality to be a major historical force. They sought to support this contention with traditional materialist reasoning.[77] That is, ran their argument, since the development of ideas is dependent upon the development of things, the immediate national environment deserves precedence over international ideological influences in tracing cultural phenomena to their source. While it is true that similar cultural phenomena appear in different countries as they pass through similar social formations, they bear obvious national features. To illustrate, they maintained that while bourgeois revolutions brought with them in all countries the phenomenon of Enlightenment, in each country the Enlightenment acquired peculiar traits.[78] In approaching any school of philosophy, art, or literature, this side of the debate insisted, the requirements of the internal development of a country and people should be considered the dominant source of inspiration, without denying the importance of international influences.[79] It was charged that Marxist studies of the causation of similar cultural phenomena in different environments were scarce.

Until the philosophers' discussion in 1947 there was a vociferous Marxist opposition to this approach. The philosopher Kedrov argued that it was a gross simplification of Marxism to dig for the roots of a philosophy always within a country, thus elevating the concept of "national spirit" to a decisive position. He reminded his colleagues that Marxists must look beyond the immediate national framework and regard ideologies in terms of separate epochs,

[76] Iovchuk, "Diskussia po knige Aleksandrova," p. 217.
[77] Fadeev, "Sovetskaia literatura."
[78] S. Meilakh, "Diskussiia po knige Aleksandrova," pp. 398–99.
[79] Ts. Chertkov, *ibid.*, p. 79.

national peculiarities being subordinate to the general class character of the theories prevalent in a given age. The philosophy of one country would then emerge as the best expression of one of several ideologies competing across national boundaries in that epoch. To take a specific instance, Kedrov maintained that Hegelianism would be seen as a bourgeois-aristocratic response to the French Revolution taking place across the German border.[80] What Kedrov cautioned against was exclusive interest in the national self-generation of ideas; he insisted on reemphasizing the play of ideas across national frontiers as reflections of conflicting class ideologies.

Another philosopher of the opposition, Smirnova, may have come nearer an understanding of the spirit of the day when she questioned whether it was theory which was the issue at all but rather a possible inferiority complex. For, she contended, it was simply absurd to deny international influences, nor would any Russian think to deny them where other nationals were concerned. But just as soon as it was a Russian whose theory came under scrutiny, merely to recognize that he had been influenced by foreign thinkers was taken as a challenge to his originality: "People apprehensive for the independence of the Russians upon contact with Western culture fail to see in the simplicity of their minds and hearts that, by fearing constantly for Russian nationality, they thereby insult it cruelly." [81]

Clearly, therefore, the question of abstract theoretical cogency is not the crucial one. Light must be sought from other sources. The origin of the national solidarity upon which the psychological entity of modern Russia rests has been explained in large measure by the upsurge of patriotism provoked by the Napoleonic invasion of 1812 and the defensive war which ensued. To overlook similar feelings induced in the Russians by the Nazi attack is to sidestep a basic clue to the postwar attitudes which have been described. Freshly roused national pride and sensitized patriotic feelings must be considered in any attempt to comprehend the Central Committee's resolutions and the Zhdanov report. These were the feelings on which Zhdanov was playing when he complained that Zoshchenko had caricatured the Soviet people as fools and idlers, of

[80] B. Kedrov, *ibid.*, p. 43.   [81] Z. V. Smirnova, *ibid.*, p. 112.

primitive culture and philistine tastes. It is likely that the Party would have been more circumscribed in its broadsides upon Western culture and upon the slightest suspicion of kow-towing to things foreign had it not relied confidently on the prevalent pride in the recent national achievement. The desire to reinforce, as well as capitalize on, this pride in the war effort surely played its part, also, in the Party's insistence that attention be shifted from the distant past to the mass heroism displayed in the Second World War.

Several other factors should be mentioned briefly as helping to explain the new national emphasis: first, the wish to spread confidence in Russia as the source of ideas and inspiration for the infant regimes in Eastern Europe and, somewhat later, China; and, second, the need, described above, to counteract the inevitable doubts and perhaps feeling of hopelessness generated in hundreds of thousands of Red Army men by their contact with superior Western technology and living standards.

But one factor probably far outweighs the others. In consequence of the all but absolute break which exists in social intercourse with the Western powers, the Soviets are divorced from what was formerly a rich and invaluable source of information to them. The decision, whether prompted by choice or dictated by necessity, to place reliance on their own resources, physical and spiritual, very likely influenced this gigantic effort to convince every citizen that native talent and genius were inexhaustible. Is this not essentially what Zhdanov was revealing when he declared that never before had it been so vital to inculcate a universal spirit of optimism? Since great progress had been made by Russian science and thought not only in the Soviet period, but before the Revolution as well, even in the face of tsarist oppression, Russia could, the propaganda implied, look forward confidently to that day in the near future when it would "outstrip the level of scientific achievement in the leading capitalist countries." In other words, the propaganda sought to eradicate the slightest doubt as to Russia's capacity for unlimited progress on her own.

The new line may perhaps best be viewed as a fusion, a mutual reinforcement, so to speak, of (*a*) the ideological currents inherited from the prewar period, (*b*) the ramifications which appeared during the War, and (*c*) the postwar conceptions delineated above.

Clearly discernible in the composite picture are trends which can largely be separated from peculiar current pressures and will appear to represent much longer-range developments. Thus, the unification of men of letters in one tightly centralized, highly concentrated organization, their obligatory adherence to a uniform literary program in which art is esteemed principally as an educational implement, its political orthodoxy being regarded as of paramount importance—these conditions have existed since 1932. The concerted portrayal of an anathematized foreign foe, in conjunction with dire threats to any Soviet national suspected of a "deferential" attitude toward the external enemy—this, too, was typical of the prewar scene. The intensive implantation of a flaming brand of patriotism, the expanding scope of a program of education and indoctrination to ready the masses for contemplated economic changes at home as well as for a possible military contest abroad— these, likewise, were common before the War. In 1944, months before Soviet relations with the Western powers began to assume the shape by which they are now recognizable, the cardinal political significance of art came to be reemphasized; the process of glorifying Russian culture was magnified and accelerated with the studious revision of earlier attitudes toward the Russian Revolutionary Democrats and the adulation now awarded them over the philosophical antecedents of Marx and Engels in Germany.

What, then, is essentially new in the postwar picture? From the organizational, implementational standpoint, the vital innovation is the abrupt tightening of the Party control mechanism aimed finally at total, exemption-free concentration of intellectual cadres on specific goals strictly defined by Party authorities; secondly, the vast expansion in the scale of mass indoctrinational activities. What should be said of the new line itself? An attempt has already been made to trace the broad trends which followed from the Zhdanov speech and the Party decrees in 1946. Patently, the main fact underlying these tendencies, absent from the prewar conjuncture, is the contemporary position of the USSR as a contender with the West for world ideological leadership amidst tensions which threaten fateful risks. The Soviet adaptation to this situation lay in the unprecedented intensity of the stress on Russian originality, the denigration of bourgeois culture, and the pervasive efforts to eradicate from the Soviet scene the slightest proclivity for ideas current in the West.

In the months that followed the Party moves in 1946, no province of intellectual concentration was exempted from the application of the new directives. Significantly, transcending the technicalities at issue in each field, there would emerge generalized pronunciamentos at once hailed as pertinent to all other ideological areas. Roughly by the time the five years of the Plan period had run out, all the arts, biology and the other physical sciences, philosophy, scholarship in the humanities, in short, the complete intellectual edifice, had stage by stage been scrutinized and jolted into adjustment with the new requirements. Like relay runners, Party spokesmen in each of these fields, as its turn came, seized the baton from its bearer over the previous lap. Slightly short of the halfway mark of the five-year period, the runners covered that stretch of ideological terrain which interests us most, literary scholarship. The Party spokesmen warmed to their assignment in a comparatively relaxed spirit. They seemed willing to listen to argument and to welcome discussion as a device for arriving at truth. Toward the end, however, their tone altered sharply. A new militancy was introduced which was then carried on to new fields by the spokesmen of the offensive at its next stage and made to apply to all that had gone before as well.

III

For almost a year following Zhdanov's address, criticism of deference to the West in literary scholarship remained sporadic and desultory. When at last the big guns opened fire, the target in the foreground proved to be Professor Nusinov, who had been the butt of Party criticism before the War, too. Curiously enough, the work which attracted the critics' ire was written in 1941, but the reason for its selection is suggested by the title, *Pushkin and World Literature*.[82] The attack on Nusinov's work presaged an onslaught on the entire comparativist approach in literary scholarship. It was to Nusinov that the term "passportless wanderer in humanity" was first applied in the postwar period. His study was declared to have derogated from Russian national individuality by constantly comparing Pushkin's creations with abstract, cosmopolitan stereo-

[82] "Za vysokuiu ideinost' sovetskoi literatury," *Lit. gaz.*, June 21, 1947.

types.[83] His critics complained that Nusinov had divided Pushkin's works into those dealing with Russia and written for Russians, and those which treated "world" themes, solved "world" esthetic problems.[84] The end result, they said, had been to portray Pushkin as "nationless," [85] whereas the poet's stature derived from the *new* themes and images which he contributed to world literature and which reflected his Russian background. Pushkin's works on Western themes, moreover, held interest not for what they had in common with Shakespeare, Goethe, and Byron, but because of what was distinctive in them.[86] Nusinov's methodology was regarded as servile. Artificially separating Russian from world culture, his critics alleged, he had implied that "light comes from the West and Russia is an 'Oriental nation,' " hence Nusinov's theory that Pushkin was more of a European than either Dostoyevsky or Tolstoy, both of whom repudiated the West and preferred their own "Oriental ideals," the ideals of Russia.

An uproar ensued among Soviet scholars when Nusinov's views were traced to the celebrated prerevolutionary scholar, Alexander Veselovskii. He was singled out as the "chief grandparent of a number of Russian literary scholars, past and present, deferential to the West." [87] This accusation was contested. The debate raged throughout the Soviet Union and attracted the interest of intellectuals in all walks of life. Initially, the altercation centered about Veselovskii's methodology. With the passing weeks, however, no aspect of the scholar's life and thought was left unexamined; his theory of art, philosophical views, political orientation, all came in for an airing.

The poetics of plots, upon which rests Veselovskii's historical comparativism, aspires to identify in any literary work the formulae which constitute its skeletal framework. According to this theory, "motifs," defined as the simplest primitive elements of folk creation, combine to form plots. The same motif can arise in diverse ethnic formations if their psychological processes are parallel. The more complex the plot, however, and the greater the number of motifs involved, the less likelihood of polygenesis and the more

---

[83] "Protiv burzhuaznogo liberalizma v literaturovedenii," *Kul'tura i zhizn'*, March 11, 1948.

[84] A. Tarasenkov, "Kosmopolity ot literaturovedeniia," *Novyi mir*, No. 2 (February, 1948), pp. 124–37.   [85] Fadeev, "Sovetskaia literatura."

[86] Tarasenkov, "Kosmopolity," p. 128.   [87] Fadeev, "Sovetskaia literatura."

legitimate is it to assume that plots developed by one people were borrowed by another.[88] The modern novel would appear some-what to transcend this hypothesis and to be a departure from the laws of literary development. Here, too, however, the migration of plots makes itself felt:

Contemporary narrative literature with its complex plot structure and photographic reproduction of reality would appear to obviate this very possibility. When future generations see it, however, from the same distant perspective in which we view ancient times, from prehistoric to medieval, when the synthesis of time, the great simplifier, running over the complexity of the phenomena, shall have reduced them to the size of dots retreating into the distance, their lines will merge with those which are now revealing themselves to us as we glance back over the distant literary past. Schematicism and repetition will emerge over the whole.[89]

What, then, is the task of historic poetics? It is "to determine the role and limits of tradition in the process of individual creation." [90]

This theory, say Soviet critics, halts at the threshold of literature, embraces the "first timid steps of literature," but stops short of literature itself.[91] Through its concern with immutable formulae, in their opinion, it reduces the importance of art as a reflection of society. If literature is viewed as the product of interminable bor-rowing, the role of world literary tradition comes to be preponder-ant and art appears as nationless.[92] They termed Veselovskii's ideas incompatible with Marxism, first, because his comparativism was of a highly formal nature, and, second, because the sociological facets of his work, while clearly evident, appeared to be tangential, inconsistent, and superficial, prompted only by the need to per-ceive the state of society in order to determine the genesis of litera-ture.[93]

---

[88] Veselovskii, *Istoricheskaia poetika,* ed. V. M. Zhirmunskii (Leningrad, 1940), p. 498.
[89] *Ibid.,* p. 494.　　　　[90] *Ibid.,* p. 51.
[91] Kirpotin, "Ob otnoshenii," p. 173.　　[92] *Ibid.,* p. 171.
[93] Veselovskii's defenders averred, and his Party critics acknowledged, that Veselov-skii believed that literature *did* bear the imprint of the society in which it arose; that his theory of the polygenesis of motifs in similar environments stemmed from this conviction; and that his work revealed a conscious effort to link the growth of art to the development of society. The sociological grounding of Veselovskii's approach emerges most clearly in his definition of the task of historic poetics. Veselov-skii's Party critics protested, however, that his economic materialism could be re-duced to highly amorphous concepts (*ibid.,* p. 172). They conceded that his method-

In Veselovskii's conception did art influence society or did it not? Kirpotin, the critic whose voice dominated the attack, charged that Veselovskii had not even thought to pose this question, since he regarded art as at best passive reflection. The allegations of Veselovskii's defenders notwithstanding, said Kirpotin, Veselovskii had written only on the origin of art and not on its social function. Indeed, he had denied utterly that a work of art could or should be utilized in social and political struggle. Therefore, continued Kirpotin, his views were inferior to those of Chernyshevskii and the Revolutionary Democrats, who championed the candid intervention of art into life. For Veselovskii there could be no thought of coopting esthetics in the transformation of the world. Under present circumstances, Veselovskii's ideas clashed in a practical sense with the clearly designed function of Soviet literature and literary science, which was "to lead the way to an advanced art and literature and to help them to influence the consciousness of the masses . . . accelerating the coming of the bright day of communism." [94] Thus, Veselovskii's critics concluded, his views on the role of art in society were unacceptable. [95]

Veselovskii's defenders and attackers alike concurred that his failure to accomplish his purpose was attributable to his philosophical premises. He was a positivist and characteristically sought analogies for cultural phenomena in the natural sciences:

He would have liked to examine motifs and their association in plots as a sort of Mendeleevan system of elements in which all the complexities

---

ology was superior to that of the "myth" school, but insisted that in tracing the genesis of plots his primary concern with borrowing led him to ignore the originality of Russian folklore and literature (Kirpotin, "O nizkopoklonstve pered kapitalisticheskim zapadom, ob Aleksandre Veselovskom, o ego posledovateliakh, i o samom glavnom," *Oktiabr'*, No. 1 [January, 1948], p. 4).

[94] Kirpotin, "Ob otnoshenii," pp. 172–73.

[95] Kirpotin called Veselovskii's career a tragedy since, despite his enormous erudition, he had failed to effect the genuine reform in the presentation of literary history to which he had aspired. He buttressed this contention with a quotation from Zhirmunskii, a strong champion of Veselovskii: "Veselovskii failed to show the laws in the process of literary development at all its stages and to finish construction of the edifice of the history of world literature as a science" (*ibid.*, p. 172). To this Veselovskii's defender, Shishmarëv, retorted that, if Veselovskii's failure was a tragedy, then this same tragic fate had befallen all but a very few of those who attempted to erect the structure of an entire science which would embrace the literature of all times and peoples (Akad. V. P. Shishmarëv, "Aleksandr Veselovskii i ego kritiki," *Oktiabr'*, No. 12 [December, 1947], pp. 158–64).

of plot and analysis might receive exhaustive scientific explanation as a mechanical combination of a group of the simplest elements, poetic formulae.[96]

As a positivist, moreover, his Party critics continued, he lacked genuine historicism and failed to explain historical development scientifically. In Veselovskii's view, progress could be equated with the repetition of old phenomena, a philosophy which was reflected in his approach to literature. While countenancing change in literature, he interpreted it mainly as the variation of things seen before, a simple quantitative increase or a new combination of old components.[97] This, of course, contrasted with the Marxist view of progress as a shift from the gradual accumulation of quantitative changes to radical qualitative changes, a skip from one stage to another, development from a lower to a higher state.[98] Any efforts to make of Veselovskii a dialectician interested in new qualitative factors were simply misguided.[99]

It was further charged that Veselovskii's commitment to the

[96] Kirpotin, "Ob otnoshenii," p. 171.

[97] I. Dmitrakov, I. Kuznetsov, "Aleksandr Veselovskii i ego posledovateli," *Oktiabr'*, No. 12 (December, 1947), pp. 165–74.

[98] Stalin, *Voprosy Leninizma*, p. 537.

[99] Shishmarëv demurred at this presentation. Veselovskii had, he acceded, been a positivist, but as early as 1860 he had affirmed his belief that "history is not physiology. If it develops exclusively on physiological principles, it is no longer history." He had, moreover, believed that history moved forward by jumps. Without benefit of Marxist theory, his historical perspicacity had enabled him to trace literature as it developed from a syncretic state in preclass society to "group divisions" later on (Shishmarëv, p. 163). To refute Shishmarëv, Kirpotin adduced Veselovskii's insistence that the modern novel, which, because of its predilection for lifelike images, appeared momentarily to defy classification according to motifs and plots, would generations hence be seen as an extension of earlier lines of development. This was further proof, he declared, that in all things Veselovskii's emphasis was on finding the old in the new.

Shishmarëv was not alone, the attack continued, in his efforts to make Veselovskii's views acceptable to Marxists. Zhirmunskii had also described Veselovskii's thinking as "close to a historical materialist understanding of family and social relationships" and "close to a genuinely scientific, materialist understanding of the decisive role of the masses in the socio-historic process." A. N. Sokolov held that Veselovskii had drawn upon the Hegelian dialectic for his theory of history and that his method was not only permeated with a materialist spirit, but was close to materialism in its very premises. Veselovskii's critics repudiated these contentions. Marxism held no interest for Veselovskii, they said, though he lived at a time when the *narodnik* movement had already suffered ideological defeat and Marxism was rapidly winning adherents. Nowhere in his writings had he even used the word "class"; the closest he came to a similar concept was "social group" (N. Glagolev, "K voprosu o kontseptsii A. N. Veselovskogo," *Oktiabr'*, No. 12 [December, 1947], p. 182).

philosophy of positivism had led to "bourgeois objectivism," which Kirpotin characterized as passive factology evincing an erroneous metaphysical position. A Marxist approach demanded that both past and present be described with the new progressive elements in the life of the society in the foreground. Moreover, Veselovskii's philosophy of history as continual repetition negated the value of criticism.[100] Veselovskii was also censured for subscribing to the cult of "pure science," which was reprehended as a phenomenon which appeared "when human thought is condemned to inactivity," leading to the loss of civic consciousness among scholars who fell under its influence. As the embodiment of this type of scholar, the epitome of "armchair learning," of academic objectivism, Veselovskii was declared unacceptable as a model for Soviet youth.[101]

According to the new line, what were the criteria by which any one active in the 1860s should be judged? His attitude to materialism, to the revolution and to Utopian socialism. Veselovskii would be astonished, said Kirpotin, to see the attempts now being made to build a bridge between himself and the Revolutionary Democrats. His first journalistic activities had been in liberal periodicals engaged in combating the "men of the sixties": "Veselovskii's biography in no way resembles the biographies of the so-called men of the sixties. The biography of Veselovskii is typical of a liberal of the sixties and not of a man who sympathized with the Revolutionary Democrats." [102]

---

[100] Kirpotin, "Ob otnoshenii," p. 170.   [101] Kirpotin, "O nizkopoklonstve," p. 22.

Shishmarëv deplored any attempt to make Veselovskii appear reactionary. Admittedly, he said, he had not been a revolutionary, socialist, or consistent materialist, but could it be said that he had broken completely with the Revolutionary Democratic tradition? This would mean underestimating the pervasive influence which the publicist writings of the day had exerted on public opinion (Shishmarëv, pp. 160–61). Veselovskii's critics agreed that he had not been a reactionary, citing a passage in which Veselovskii had written that the growth of democratic views assured the flowering of literature, whereas literary aristocratization meant the constriction of thematic material and the impoverishment of content (Glagolev, "K voprosu," p. 183). But, they maintained, Veselovskii was at most a timid, liberal critic of tsarism. Nowhere in his writings did he say that his views had been formed under the influence of the progressive ideologists of the sixties (Kirpotin, "O nizkopoklonstve," p. 9).

[102] *Ibid.*, p. 11.

At the end of the discussion an article in *Culture and Life* asserted that Kirpotin had been too indecisive in his views on Veselovskii's politics. "Veselovskii was one of the enemies of revolutionary-socialist thought in the nineteenth century. Obviously, Kirpotin forgot this truth." The authors of the article agreed with Kirpotin's view that no significance whatsoever should be attached to Veselovskii's clandestine

Since it was the problem of overcoming deference to the West which had initially prompted concern with Veselovskii's followers, this issue received most attention. The discussion fell into two categories: (1) was Veselovskii himself deferential to the West? and (2) to what extent had his work generated deference among his pupils? The hard-and-fast criterion of the role played by the Revolutionary Democrats again obtruded itself. To show that Veselovskii was himself deferential, he was quoted as having stated in 1868 that in Russia a scientific treatment of the history of literature was impossible ("Among us science is still at the stage of primitive economy") and that in a Russian university the function of a department of world literature was to "transmit the results of Western learning." This, it was asserted, was obsequiousness, because it was expressed notwithstanding the writings of Belinskii, Chernyshevskii, and Dobroliubov.[103] Veselovskii's scholarship was combed for evidence that he had belittled Russian culture. Guided in his studies by the theory of borrowing, his critics found, he had as a rule concluded that Russian and Slav works were reworkings of other peoples' images.[104]

---

reading of Feuerbach and Herzen in his university days. "One needs a powerful imagination to build on this a theory of Veselovskii's dependence" on progressive Russian philosophy ("Protiv burzhuaznogo liberalizma").

[103] Kirpotin, "Ob otnoshenii," p. 171.

[104] Kirpotin, "O nizkopoklonstve," p. 7. To this Shishmarëv retorted that it was not true that deference was intrinsic in Veselovskii's methodology or in his training. Mere study abroad, he insisted, was in and of itself irrelevant: "Quite a few of our scholars and artists went abroad to study. From this neither Sechenov, Mendeleev nor Butlerov, who worked in European laboratories, nor Glinka, who studied with Dehn, shed their Russian personalities or became kow-towers" (Shishmarëv, p. 150). There was the statement of the prerevolutionary literary scholar Kotliarevskii that Veselovskii was simply compelled to go abroad because in Russia there was no one with whom to study world literature. Though significantly influenced by Western schools of literary investigation, Veselovskii had throughout his life remained an independent thinker. In his later years he had grown increasingly dissatisfied with Western science, detecting in it "shrinking thought, narrowing scope and the splintering specialization which deflected scholars from large problems" (*ibid.*, p. 160). In time Veselovskii's former Western teachers had become his pupils, the scholar taking great pride in the turn of events which had produced more favorable conditions in Russia than in Western Europe for the development of science. As for the theory of borrowing, Shishmarëv insisted that it contained nothing essentially deferential. There were, strictly speaking, no "chance" plots but only "deeply rooted" ones: "In any literature one can point to elements of influence or absorption from without, but the literature does not for that reason lose its individual personality (*ibid.*, p. 162). Veselovskii, Shishmarëv continued, was interested less in "ours or someone else's" than in how "someone else's" became "ours."

Party spokesmen repeatedly affirmed that, whatever his intention, the end result of Veselovskii's comparativism was to portray Russian culture as borrowed and imitative. Because of his enormous influence in his day in founding an entire school of scholarship, declared to be still vigorous and flourishing, he was dubbed the "grandparent of deference to the West" [105] in literary investigation and adjudged the major source and "theoretical justification" of comparativism in Soviet literary scholarship. The comparative method, the charge continued, had distorted the true picture of Russian literature, dissecting it and handing over its components piecemeal to the West. One book after another alleged that the task of scholarship was accomplished when evidence could be adduced that Gogol derived from Hoffmann, Griboedov from Molière, *Boris Godunov* from Shakespeare, Dostoyevsky from Balzac, and so on.[106] As evidence of this approach before the Revolution, Kirpotin cited a work by Alexander Veselovskii's brother, Alexei, *Western Influence on Modern Russian Literature*.[107]

Party critics charged that within the past decade there had been a strong revival of Veselovskii's views, initiated before the War with a collection of articles on the centennial of his birth. At that time Shishmarëv's declaration had contained the prevalent opinion: "We trace our scientific genealogy in large measure from Veselovskii, but even where our theses have been erected on other principles, we are dealing with the general tendency formulated under the influence of Veselovskii." [108] The followers of Veselov-

---

In his rebuttal, Kirpotin expressed surprise that Shishmarëv should have felt it necessary to justify Veselovskii's foreign study: "Where in print or in oral statement has Shishmarëv encountered the opinion that anyone who went abroad to study was called a kow-tower solely on that account? This is a bad and simply a foolish figment. Or does Shishmarëv really think that this is what the Soviet public means by deference to things foreign?" On the other hand, the justification offered for Veselovskii's trip, namely the poverty of Russian scholarship, "breathes deference," since Russia did have outstanding scholars at that time: "If Shishmarëv seriously considered Belinskii a scholar and thinker and not merely a 'critic,' he would not have repeated this categorical statement of Kotliarevskii's. Veselovskii's concern to discover how "someone else's" became "ours," Kirpotin went on, in no way altered the fact that "ours" is "someone else's," that to understand "ours" it must be compared with "someone else's." The total impression, he concluded, was to exaggerate the importance of "someone else's" and underestimate the importance of "ours" (Kirpotin, "O nizkopoklonstve," p. 24).

105 Fadeev, "Sovetskaia literatura."   106 Kirpotin, "Ob otnoshenii," p. 173.
107 *Ibid.*, pp. 161–62.   108 "Protiv burzhuaznogo liberalizma."

skii were regarded as numerically significant and of considerable influence in the universities.[109]

It was persistently maintained that not Veselovskii so much as his followers were the target. It was Veselovskii and not Buslaev, Afanas'ev, Tikhonravov, Pypin, or other bourgeois literary scholars of the past who had been singled out, said the Party critics, because his ideas were still very much alive among Soviet scholars.

If those who wrote books and taught in the universities did not create an atmosphere of deference in literary scholarship, did not rely on Veselovskii, did not take cover behind him, did not portray him as comrade-in-arms and successor to the Revolutionary Democrats and as a spontaneous Marxist, the critical examination of Veselovskii's theory would not have acquired such social significance.[110]

What, then, was specifically wanted? It was demanded that Veselovskii be used only within the framework of Marxism, materialistically, "the way V. I. Lenin taught us to read Hegel." [111] Soviet literary science must not try to erect Marxist theories on Veselovskii's foundations but should uncompromisingly attack his errata.[112]

[109] Kirpotin, "O nizkopoklonstve," p. 4.

[110] *Ibid.,* p. 24. The Party critics declared that there would be no attempt to disparage those aspects of Veselovskii's work regarded as still fruitful for scholarship. Before criticizing him, Professor Plotkin characterized Veselovskii as follows: "Alexander Veselovskii was an outstanding Russian scholar. A man with enormous research talent, a brilliant creative mind, and knowledge striking for its scope, he remains to this day one of the remarkable figures in the history of Russian and world literary science" (Plotkin, "A. Veselovskii"). Others went still further, maintaining that Veselovskii stood head and shoulders above his contemporaries among Western European bourgeois scholars and laying claim to Veselovskii's work as the legitimate legacy of Soviet scholarship (Dmitrakov and Kuznetsov, p. 167). Fadeev on several occasions paid tribute to Veselovskii's enormous accumulation of precious factual data (Fadeev, "Zakliuchitel'noe slovo," *Lit. gaz.,* July 8, 1947). Kirpotin asserted that no one was asking scholars to cease reading Veselovskii or using the extensive material which he had collected. Nor, said Kirpotin, did the attack on Veselovskii signify repudiation of international literary ties (Kirpotin, "O nizkopoklonstve," p. 3).

[111] Dmitrakov and Kuznetsov, p. 170.

[112] Kirpotin, "O nizkopoklonstve," p. 3.

Shishmarëv presumed there would be some scholars abroad who would be overjoyed to see these attacks on Veselovskii, particularly since the Russians themselves were attacking him. The campaign, he declared, was a scientific blunder and a political mistake from start to finish (Shishmarëv, p. 160). To this Kirpotin retorted that neither Revolutionary Democrats nor Communists had ever spared a Russian from criticism on the grounds solely that he was a Russian, or had concealed his deficiencies from the world on that account. To tolerate Veselovskii's views for purposes of foreign prestige would mean permitting deference to the capitalist West at home in the field of literary scholarship. Moreover, said Kirpotin, criticism of the views of Veselovskii was absolutely indispensable if Marxist scholarship was to progress (Kirpotin, "O nizkopoklonstve," pp. 24–25).

Literary scholars must remain alert to their responsibility to youth
studying with them; to idealize Veselovskii, gloss over his weaknesses, seek to accommodate his views to Marxism would impede
the training of new literary scholars and critics in the consistent and

---

The debate on Veselovskii was launched broadside and gained in intensity and
acrimony with each successive stage. Fadeev's initial remarks on the subject appeared to be directed as much against Shishmarëv as against Veselovskii. He accused
him of venerating foreign names, of enumerating "pseudo-scientists" among whom
Veselovskii had made his contribution. His speech was replete with irony and sar-
castic references to Shishmarëv's description of Veselovskii's activities abroad. In
conclusion he thundered: "Should not the Presidium of the Academy of Sciences and
the Ministry of Higher Education take an interest in the fact that in the Gorky
Institute of World Literature in Moscow and in Moscow and Leningrad Universities
all the literary education of youth is in the hands of Veselovskii's parrots, his avid
apologists" (Fadeev, "Zakliuchitel'noe slovo").

Shishmarëv was afforded a chance to answer Fadeev's speech and Kirpotin's lengthy
article which followed it. Remarking upon the characteristic "forcefulness" with
which Fadeev had delivered his attack, Shishmarëv claimed that the new appraisal
of Veselovskii had provoked "enormous perplexity in the widest circles of our Union
among representatives of different generations and various nationality cultures." He
brushed aside some of Fadeev's strictures on Veselovskii with the remark that both
in form and substance these were among the least successful pages he had ever written. Peeved by Kirpotin's characterization of Veselovskii as a tragic figure, he retorted that a critic who preferred a vague and superficial analysis of a scholar to a
detailed and profound one seemed to him far more tragic. He accused Kirpotin of
unfair tactics in trying to fix an ideological kinship between Veselovskii and the
reactionary scholar Leont'ev on the mere ground that Veselovskii had studied under
Leont'ev. As for the influence of Western scholarship upon Veselovskii, his comment here was that Engels would hardly concur that Grimm, Humboldt, and Ben-
fey were "pseudo-scientists." Veselovskii, he said, had once written that Russians had
a rare gift of historical objectivity, which they could put to use by developing "critical
tact." Veselovskii had possessed this "tact," that is, genuine historical objectivity, in
the highest degree, but "Kirpotin does not suffer from it." Rejecting the charge that
his teacher had been indifferent to the influence of literature on life, he remarked,
again with apparent irony: "It goes without saying that he did not raise the fighting
themes which agitate us now, [themes] which socialist realism has posed not only
for our literature but for literary science." He was embittered by Kirpotin's reference to the "pile" of facts which Veselovskii had assembled but failed to integrate.
Culminating his defense, he lavished encomium upon Veselovskii and closed with
the remark, "Respect for names bathed in glory is the first sign of an enlightened
mind, said Pushkin" (Shishmarëv, p. 164).

Kirpotin, in rebuttal, asserted that the heat of the dispute over Veselovskii's legacy
showed how tenacious were survivals of the deference inculcated in the past century. He insisted that in defending their positions, Veselovskii's followers had even
reversed opinions which they had expressed about Veselovskii's methodology ten
years earlier, and modified their earlier representation of him as a comparativist. Kirpotin sought repeatedly to bring his opponents' attention back to the immediate
framework of the Veselovskii dispute: "It must not be forgotten that the quarrel over
Veselovskii arose and grew out of the problem of clarifying the significance of the
Russian, and in general the Soviet, contribution to world culture, out of the urgent
need to overcome kow-towing to the capitalist West." And again, "The quarrel over
Veselovskii has raged not outside time and space, but over the problem of over-

creative use of Marxism. Scholars should examine the appraisal of Western classics contained in Belinskii, Chernyshevskii, and Dobroliubov and recognize that, besides the "progressive influence of the West" on Russian literature, there was also the vast influence of Russian literature on the literature of the rest of the world:

Have our literary scholars said anything resounding and convincing on this? Have they grasped the great world-wide significance and power of Russian and Soviet art? Have they explained it from a class, Leninist point of view? There are individual articles on this theme, but so far not a single serious piece of research.[113]

In the issue of *New World* of February, 1948, the critic Tarasenkov hinted that the debate had not much longer to run and revealed that the Party intended to emerge from the dispute with nothing less than total victory. Evidence that this was the Party's resolve was provided when Tarasenkov resurrected dread names:

Contempt for Russia, its culture, its great ideas typified the Jesuit Bukharin and the bandit-cosmopolitan Trotsky. These are fearful memories. They show us with what the spirit of deference to bourgeois culture and civilization is related under present-day political conditions and whom it serves.[114]

Tarasenkov addressed Nusinov in this spirit, observing threateningly that the sooner he reexamined his principles the better for him and for Soviet literary scholarship.[115] The time had come, he said, to have done "once and for all" with the survivals of the comparative-historical school: "It is time to see that it is the living

coming kow-towing to the capitalist West" (Kirpotin, "O nizkopoklonstve," p. 22). Ignoring the history of deference in Russia, Shklovskii and others, he lamented, had been "unwilling to make a contribution to overcoming deference to the bourgeois West."

The acid tone which the debate assumed as it proceeded forced Kirpotin to take special note of it, for he entitled an entire section of his article of refutation "On the Polemic Techniques of Veselovskii's Apologists." To the opposition's charge that "ulterior motives" lay behind the attack on Veselovskii, Kirpotin retorted that the discussion was open to public scrutiny and could be explained only by the demands of society and theory (*ibid.*, p. 24) and not by a desire to institute a new RAPP (Russian Association of Proletarian Writers), to prohibit citations from Veselovskii or to banish him, as rumor had it. He concluded by charging that the refusal of Veselovskii's supporters to join in the campaign to eradicate deference to the West, a policy prompted by the Soviets' new role as "teacher and leader of contemporary mankind," was motivated by vested interest, "poorly concealed alarm for the tranquillity of the backwaters of 'pure truth' and 'pure science'" (*ibid.*, p. 27).

113 Tarasenkov, "Kosmopolity," p. 134.
114 *Ibid.*, p. 127.   115 *Ibid.*, p. 131.

historical practice of the class struggle which has determined and determines the history of literature, and not notorious literary 'influences.' " [116]

The discussion terminated when an article in *Culture and Life* of March, 1948, condemned it as entirely wrong and unnecessary. Not one critic, the article maintained, had correctly diagnosed the political import of the resurrection of Veselovskii's followers. Veselovskii's name was being used to champion independence from Party ideology, to revive bourgeois literary scholarship. Reactionary German literary scholarship, continued the article, had now been replaced by liberal-positivist science, its locus in the United States of America, well-financed and influencing the cultural life of other peoples. The Party implied that the revival of the Veselovskii school signified the establishment on Soviet home territory of a locus of enemy ideology. "The exposure of Professor Nusinov clearly shows that Veselovskii is a symbol of prerevolutionary tradition in science, a bridge to an ideologically hostile shore." Besides failing to place the Veselovskii dispute properly in relation to the world struggle, the article went on, Veselovskii's critics had been wrong to squander their efforts on matters which were beyond dispute, namely, was Veselovskii a Revolutionary Democrat, did he come close to Marx? The correct approach would have been not to discuss his ideas but to unmask their bourgeois-liberal nature, to prove the ideological harm in liberal apologies for Veselovskii.[117]

Clearly by late 1947, the climate of opinion demanded that a high irreducible minimum of ideological orthodoxy be attested in order to qualify for mere participation in the debate over Veselovskii. Shishmarëv, Shklovskii, and others were hesitant forthrightly to defend the scholar for what he *was,* and for what he *did* accomplish. Instead, they squandered their energies on confronting complaints as to what Veselovskii was not, and did not accomplish. They endeavored to accommodate his views to Marxism, to represent Veselovskii as all but a confrere of the Revolutionary Democrats. Veselovskii's traducers, on the other hand, though contending that they were primarily exercised about the uncritical disciples, were nevertheless all too eager to evaluate the scholar's contributions not on

[116] *Ibid.,* p. 137.   [117] "Protiv burzhuaznogo liberalizma."

their own merits but as they reflected his character, faulty philosophy, and political shortcomings.

The specific demands of the new line, however, had not yet thoroughly penetrated all the pores of society, and momentarily the Party's imputation of antipatriotism to recalcitrant scholars was hotly rejected. When on one occasion, in the interests of rigid fidelity to the new line, Fadeev high-handedly slandered some of the great names in nineteenth-century Western European scholarship, thereby flouting even the opinions of Marx and Engels concerning these men, Shishmarëv was given a good reason to challenge the very premises of the attack. His deepest ethical instincts appeared aroused. This seemed to him to be a demand that he join in reviling the achievements of Western scholars out of motives which seemed suspect and which at best had little apparent connection with scholarly theoretical issues.

The Marxist arguments against comparativism were not new, nor was this the first time that Veselovskii was being challenged from the Marxist standpoint. Soviet reference works published in the early thirties attacked Veselovskii's premises with many of the same arguments reviewed in 1947. It is the postwar context of the attack, the atmosphere of national adulation, which is new. The contrast of Veselovskii's views with the new line may have been aggravated by a possible reanimation of Veselovskii's followers. The excellent introduction to Academician Iurii M. Sokolov's *Russian Folklore,* the first edition of which appeared in the USSR in 1938, showered high praise upon Veselovskii's great contributions to literary studies and, while specifying that Veselovskii's was far from the one correct interpretation of the history of society given by scientific Marxism, concluded the survey of his works by advocating attentive study of his heritage as "one of the essential conditions for future progress." [118] In 1938, on the occasion of the centennial of the scholar's birth, the Academy of Sciences of the USSR organized a celebration at which some of the most distinguished Soviet literary scholars read papers in which "the scientific activity of A. N. Veselovskii received new treatment." [119] The alacrity with

[118] Sokolov, *Russkii fol'klor* (Moscow, 1941), p. 86.
[119] *Ibid.*

which the tributes led to more tangible action may lend credence to the contention that Veselovskii's ideas were in process of revivification. Within the brief space of two years, on the eve of the War, two weighty tomes were published, Veselovskii's *Historical Poetics* [120] and a volume of *Selected Works*. [121] Again in 1946, shortly after the War, Academician Shishmarëv wrote a new article on Veselovskii which evidently provided the Party with one of the pretexts for its attack.

But surely the explanation for the broad scope of the Party's attack on Veselovskii does not lie in the question of whether or not Veselovskii's admirers had increased their activity. That Veselovskii's heritage was attractive to many Soviet scholars there can be little doubt. The Party's onslaught makes sense only in so far as it illustrates the manner in which the new line stressing national individuality to the exclusion of all competing views on culture was instituted in this particular field. The crux of the debate, its wellspring, its key motive, lacking which the dispute would have seemed a tempest in a teapot, lies in the editorial allegation of *Culture and Life* that Veselovskii was a "bridge to an ideologically hostile shore." In the analysis of some of the factors underlying Soviet postwar ideology, it was surmised that one reason probably transcends all others as the explanation for the national glorification. This was the belief, whether adopted with deliberate calculation or whether compelled by circumstances, that the Soviets were isolated from the non-Soviet world, and that therefore theirs would be a lone course. If one recalls the total nature of postwar ideological controls, it is easy to see where Veselovskii fits in the picture. There seems little doubt that Veselovskii was a comparativist. His concern with Russian culture was primarily as it related to the culture of the rest of the world. Intrinsically this approach was a link, a "bridge" to an outer world viewed as hostile. It was, moreover, the sort of link which would at every turn provoke doubts regarding the unadulterated "originality" of Russian cultural phenomena. Furthermore, since Veselovskii was not in sympathy with Russian materialism, his comparativism would lack the peculiar slant

[120] Veselovskii, *Istoricheskaia poetika*, ed. V. M. Zhirmunskii (Leningrad, 1940).
[121] Veselovskii, *Izbrannye stat'i*, ed. M. P. Alekseev, V. A. Desnitskii, V. M. Zhirmunskii, and A. A. Smirnov (Leningrad, 1939).

—so significant since 1944—which gave Russian culture advantages over the West in the eyes of Party spokesmen, namely its powerful materialist tradition. On these two cardinal counts, Veselovskii's views clashed headlong with the expressed resolve—deriving from factors ultimately related to the generation of a new national morale—to stress at all costs, all other issues being secondary, the originality, the uniqueness, the independence of Russian culture, the quality, in short, which would enable Russia to "go it alone."

IV

The attack on Veselovskii's followers had provoked genuine discussion; at least some of the opposition spokesmen courageously defended their positions notwithstanding the charged atmosphere. In the finale, however, the principle of debate surrendered in the face of slashing censure. Heeding their own admonition, the Party critics administered the next phase of the literary offensive, their attack on the "cosmopolitan" critics, with uncompromising tactics. The tension mounted steadily until February–March, 1950, when finally an overzealous critic, A. Belik, who spoke, he thought, in the name of superorthodoxy, overstepped the mark. From higher up, the Party interceded at this point, and subsequently hints were released portending developments which might greatly transcend the significance of this isolated case. The Party's stand on literature had frequently in the past reflected policy toward all Soviet ideology.[122]

The timing of this development is crucial. Almost a year earlier, in April, 1949, Belik had collaborated with another critic, N. Parsadanov, on an article in the literary magazine *October* entitled "On Errors and Distortions in Esthetics and Literary Scholarship." At the time this attracted scant notice, although the opinions expressed were akin to those which elicited a torrent of abuse a year later. This was the period when the "cosmopolitan, anti-patriotic" critics were under fire, accused, *inter alia*, of championing universal human ideals and the unity of world science, and of the error

---

122 "Obsuzhdenie redaktsionnykh statei v gazetakh 'Pravda' i 'Kul'tura i zhizn',' v Akademii obshchestvennykh nauk pri TsK VKP(b)," *Voprosy filosofii*, No. 1 (1950), pp. 393–97.

of "objectivism." The two critics blusteringly descended upon one Soviet professor who ventured to suggest that the principles of Marxist esthetics were actually as yet poorly developed, and upon a second who advanced the catholic belief that progress toward a Marxist esthetic might be accelerated by examination of pre-Marxist systems. The interpretation which Belik and Parsadanov had given to the philosophy discussion of 1947 was that it barred sedulous scrutiny and exposition of the philosophical systems of the past. Shifting their attention to the "cosmopolitan" critics, they berated one who held that an artist could produce great realistic works of art, even if his world-view was defective, and another who contended that Soviet literature had to be more than the bearer of progressive ideas since the "development of our literature cannot be appraised unless juxtaposed with world literature." These views, they alleged, violated Leninism. Both the literary process as a whole, declared Belik and Parsadanov, and its specific aspects were subject to interpretation solely as a reflection of objective reality, that is the life of society, the class struggle. Since the Soviet system was something entirely new, its reflection in literature was equally unique and hence was not measurable with standard yardsticks. They took issue with a prominent scholar who characterized socialist realism as a combination of the "best traditions of the artistic legacy of the past and the principles of socialist *ideinost'*." This, they argued, ignored the dialectically new character of socialist realism, its qualitative distinction from all the artistic methods of presocialist history.[123] Manifestly, what these two critics were after was to divorce all things Soviet from the prerevolutionary Russian past and the experience of the rest of mankind.

To repeat, this article aroused little comment. It was Belik's article in the February issue of *October,* 1950, "Some Errors in Literary Studies," [124] which promptly evoked a response from *Pravda,* entitled "Against Banality in Literary Criticism," [125] and

[123] Belik and Parsadanov, "Ob oshibkakh i izvrashcheniiakh v estetike i litera-turovedenii," *Oktiabr',* No. 4 (1949), pp. 166–74.
[124] Belik, "O nekotorykh oshibkakh v literaturovedenii," *Oktiabr',* No. 2 (1950), pp. 150–65.
[125] "Protiv oposhleniia literaturnoi kritiki," *Pravda,* March 30, 1950.

innumerable hints that some basic change was in the air. Enumeration of the views expressed by Belik this time reveals where the Zhdanov line had led by 1950 on these cardinal issues: (1) the connection between Marxism, Soviet ideology, and past thought; (2) the relationship of Russian to Western European culture; and (3) the meaning of *partiinost'*. Belik alleged that the lag in Soviet criticism stemmed from an inadequate grasp of dialectical materialism and the failure to heed the decisions of the philosophy discussion which condemned "neutrality" and a pseudo-academic approach and opposed the divorcement of any given philosophy from its historic milieu. Belik upbraided Professor A. Egolin, one of the leading Party spokesmen in literary studies, for years in command of that entire sector of ideological work and himself one of the Party's most vigorous exponents of the new Zhdanov line, for a postwar work entitled *Liberational and Patriotic Ideas in Russian Nineteenth-Century Literature*. Egolin's opinion that Gorky's work embraced the classical traditions of Russian literature while simultaneously marking a new phase in the development of Russian literature was held to repudiate the revolutionary essence of socialist literature and to misinterpret the dialectical development of art. Socialist realism, fulminated Belik, was certainly neither a *step* nor a *level* but nothing less than a *revolutionary upheaval* in world literature. To settle for less would be to gainsay its total newness! On the issue of Russia *vis-à-vis* the West, Belik complained that Egolin exaggerated the influence of Western thinkers on Russians. Egolin's temperate judgment that it was pointless to deny the patent benefits derived by Russians from progressive Western thinkers was interpreted as a sly ruse to resurrect "Veselovskii-ism," "condemned by the Party." But Belik's most heinous offense in interpreting current demands was to call the principle of *partiinost'* the "basic law" of socialist realism. Significantly he selected from Lenin's article "Party Organization and Party Literature" a rarely invoked passage which stated "writers must without fail join Party organizations."

This was the extreme to which the Zhdanov line had led by early 1950, three and a half years after its inception. Belik's convictions were entertained by a minority, it is true, but a significant one; there is reason to believe that this group comprised almost the entire editorial staff of the magazine *October*.[126] Belik was now charged with having outraged common sense, fair play, and Marxist ideology. The *Pravda* editorial and ancillary comment denounced him for vulgarizing Marxism, attempting to revive the odious RAPP ideology by enjoining all writers to become Party members, turning criticism into sensation-pandering, and employing unscrupulous tactics to gain his point by distorting facts and quotations. They accused him of a shouting, arrogant tone "having nothing to do with the nature of Bolshevik criticism," of nihilism in his attitude to the Russian classics as seen in his disparagement of past culture, and of a multitude of other shortcomings. Crucial was the unequivocal statement that Lenin's article was meaningful only in the context of 1905 polemics, that any attempt to decry writers not in the Party could do immeasurable harm under contemporary circumstances, and that (quoting Stalin in 1929) intra-Party concepts could not profitably be applied to literature, where it was more appropriate to judge a writer by such general criteria as whether he was pro-revolution or anti-revolution.[127] A symptom of change in the air was implicit in the reinvocation of this liberalizing view on the handling of writers voiced by Stalin on an earlier occasion.

The turning point arrived three months later when Stalin personally delivered a major pronouncement on Soviet ideology for the first time since 1934. The immediate pretext for Stalin's intervention was the deplorable condition of the science of linguistics. A Westerner may wonder at the rationale behind the choice of this of all domains for a disquisition of such transcendent import, since in most countries linguistics is a highly esoteric discipline. Not so, however, in the USSR. The compelling tasks of language development in a land embracing so many nationalities rid the subject of its customary exclusiveness. Moreover, linguistic problems necessarily concern *all* the Soviet nationalities without exception; hence any major ideological promulgation in this province would be certain to attract general attention. Furthermore, notwithstanding its

[126] "Obsuzhdenie redaktsionnykh statei." (The following statement occurs on p. 393: "A. Belik's new RAPPist attacks on Soviet literature [are] supported by the editors of the magazine *October*.")   [127] "Protiv oposhleniia."

importance, linguistics lacks direct involvement in economic plans. The new line, introduced so abruptly in this relatively innocuous field, could subsequently be debated, analyzed, and applied more cautiously in more sensitive areas. In short, linguistics was significant without being crucial. But doubtless there was a more important reason: the increasing spread of monopoly direction since the War, illustrated by the sketch on the Veselovskii controversy above, attained perhaps its most constraining and stultifying limits in language studies and terminated in unrelieved stagnation. There was a crying need for emergency remedies.

The substance of the linguistics controversy which unfolded in the summer of 1950 need not detain us here. Broadly speaking, what happened was this. A theory of linguistic development which claimed to be the one authentically Marxist approach, developed by a Soviet scholar, N. Marr, and therefore appropriately unique and ostensibly a pathfinder, a theory which proceeded from a Marxist generalization and then carefully selected the facts in such a way as to validate this generalization while the preponderance of evidence substantiated the reverse, a theory the fallacies of which were sufficiently apparent so that by the eve of the Second World War it had in large measure been discredited, rejected, universally challenged—such a theory was rehabilitated in the key year of 1946. In a few years it succeeded in establishing a monopoly in the field.[128]

The timetable in linguistics parallels the pattern in literary scholarship and roughly reflects the periodization of the Party's ideological moves over this entire time span. In the first few months after the War, the monopolists-to-be, the followers of Academician Marr, held their fire. Between the middle of 1945 and the middle of 1946 they revived gradually, proceeding warily, however. With the Zhdanov report and the ideological decrees of the Central Committee, the tempo of their movements was accelerated. A linguistics discussion in October, 1946, marked the first major drive for the

128 We are indebted to the periodical *Soviet Studies,* published under the auspices of the University of Glasgow and edited by J. Miller and R. A. J. Schlesinger for an article "The Crisis in Soviet Linguistics," in No. 3 (January, 1951), pp. 209–64, the best survey of the discussion which has as yet appeared. A verbatim transcript of the entire debate is now available in English: J. V. Murra, *et al.,* trans., *The Soviet Linguistic Controversy,* (New York, 1951).

Marrist monopoly. The tenor of this discussion resembled unmistakably that of the Veselovskii controversy. A Marrist advocate called linguistics a part of the struggle between socialism and capitalism. He forewarned that any departure from Marr's teaching would be impermissible. The impetus for the next stage was probably furnished by the meeting which discussed Alexandrov's *History of Western European Philosophy* and by the Veselovskii controversy. In June, 1948, another linguistics conference heralded the second Marrist offensive; complete triumph followed the Lysenko controversy in biology that same summer. Dictatorial measures increased throughout 1949 amid the acrimonious assault on "cosmopolitanism." Any suggestions of possible kinship between Marrism and "bourgeois" linguistics were run into the ground. Meanwhile, under pressure to produce results with their lame theory, the Marrist defenders became more uncritically dogmatic. They excoriated their opponents, endeavored to expel them from linguistics. In the spring of 1950 another conference convened and produced such a dismal impression that genuine alarm was voiced. Finally, on May 9, 1950, *Pravda* opened its pages to a thorough airing of complaints in an effort to terminate stagnation by initiating discussion. The climax of the debate came on June 20, with the publication of Stalin's contribution.[129]

Stalin insisted that although he was not a linguist, he could speak authoritatively on Marxism and on its appropriate application, whatever the specific subject involved. A detailed elucidation of his opinions on linguistics need not concern us here. What is relevant is his reference to the calamitous decline of the entire science over the previous five years, and his remedial recommendations. Stalin seconded *Pravda*'s decision to initiate an airing of the controversy, "since no science can develop and flourish without a conflict of opinions, without freedom of criticism," and this, he declared, had lamentably been absent from linguistics. Indeed, the slightest criticism of Marrism had been cruelly suppressed under an "Arakcheev-like regime." [130] Stalin's first major contribution, therefore, was to order a halt to the trend toward the elimination of

---

[129] "The Crisis in Soviet Linguistics," pp. 221–34.

[130] Stalin, "On Marxism in Linguistics," *The Soviet Linguistic Controversy*, trans. Murra, *et al.*, pp. 75–76.

controversial give-and-take in the sciences. The importance of this attitude can be judged without superfluous comment by simply contrasting it with the editorial opinion in *Culture and Life* in 1948 (see p. 276), which challenged the very principle of discussion. There may be room to question whether Stalin's statement was anything more than repetition of the oft-heard demand for criticism and self-criticism which figured abundantly in the Soviet press in the previous five-year period even at moments when friction of ideas was most conspicuous by its absence. But the invocation of such an abhorrent name as Arakcheev to label Soviet scholars should probably be construed as a sharp warning and advocacy of at least some mitigation of stringency. Numerous statements by academicians and professors could be cited as evidence that this was precisely how they interpreted Stalin's words.[131]

Stalin's second contribution lay in his insistence on less contemptuous examination of prerevolutionary "bourgeois" science. Marrism represented the acme of inflexibility with its blanket exclusion of any knowledge stigmatized as "bourgeois." Demanding what he termed a genuinely Marxist approach to replace Marr's vulgar oversimplifications, Stalin called for creative development of the contributions of earlier linguists.[132]

Stalin's article broached anew the sensitive subject of the reliability of scientific data derived in a bourgeois or feudal environment and gave rise to abundant speculation which seemed to point to a somewhat less imperious repudiation of the contributions of non-Marxists in all sciences, natural and social. From 1944 on, stress had been laid on the qualitative newness of Marxism, which, it was claimed, had elevated Soviet thinking generally to a loftier sphere, strangely isolated from all that had gone before. Stalin contrasted Marr's disdain for all antecedent linguistics with the appreciative awareness of Marx and Engels that "their dialectical materialism was the product of the development of the sciences, philosophy included, over preceding periods."

It has been noted above that, over the entire period of the postwar Five-Year Plan, polemic devices of the most scathing and uncom-

[131] I. I. Tolstoi, Shishmarëv, Egolin, *et al.*, "Otdelenie literatury i iazyka," *Izv. Akad. nauk,* IX, No. 1 (1950), 61–80.
[132] Stalin, "On Marxism in Linguistics," p. 76.

promising variety prevailed, intended to "annihilate" opponents. In this, too, Stalin's remarks appeared to sound a note of moderation. He rebuked Marr for introducing into science an immodest, arrogant tone, which Stalin contended was alien to Marxism. In a transparent effort to apply his own admonition against indiscriminate, vitriolic denunciation in place of circumspect analysis, Stalin recommended that Marr's scholarship be drawn upon when it was distinguished and scrupulous, for whatever factual data might be useful.

New perspectives were unfolded by Stalin's comments on the relationship of superstructure to base. Prior to Stalin's article it was avowedly customary for Soviet philosophers to assume that all social phenomena should be assigned either to the superstructure or to the base, that is, were either part of the totality of economic relationships or of their reflection in a given society's laws, religion, morals, and art, and their corresponding institutions. Stalin, however, argued that language was neither in the base nor in the superstructure. It was a means of communication, he averred, and its life span extended far beyond that of any single social formation. Since language served all members of society impartially and was, generally speaking, comprehensible to all classes it could not be regarded as a class phenomenon. This common-sense notion contained sweeping implications for Marxist theory on other phenomena hitherto regarded as exclusively part of the superstructure.

How, specifically, could this reasoning affect the sphere of literary studies? First, a note of caution is in order. Stalin took pains to distinguish language from culture. As we have seen, he excluded language from the superstructure; culture, however—and hence literature—was the superstructure and hence did bear class tags. With this dichotomy clearly comprehended, it seems valid to assume that no such wholesale reversal is in the offing in literary scholarship as occurred in linguistics. On the other hand, the appeal for more discussion and the warning against monopolies were interpreted as the green light in literary studies for: (*a*) a more sympathetic, less nihilistic attitude to the Russian scientific heritage; (*b*) the eradication of the Arakcheev-like regime which "regrettably obtains also on the editorial boards of some of our magazines"; (*c*) a struggle against name-calling and offensive labeling of "persons utterly devoted to science"; and (*d*) more frequent discussion on a variety of subjects.[133]

Within a comparatively short time, several interesting hints appeared as to how Stalin's article might temper reigning Soviet attitudes toward art. The most provocative was from the pen of the philosopher P. S. Trofimov, who resolutely confronted the problem of the relationship of art to superstructure. In his view, a Marxist would insist that art was incontrovertibly part of the superstructure, serving the economic base as a weapon in the hands of one class against another, and containing in imagery the political, religious, and philosophical ideas of a given epoch. However, he continued, it was equally true that much of the great art of past ages was still great art today. Its capacity for continuing to convey pleasure, he insisted, could be explained by the "objective historical content" of works of the past, and their "lofty esthetic value." Art contained elements which were not superstructural, which did not atrophy with the passing of the economic base upon which it had arisen. The "objective esthetic values" of art were the product of a number of social stages and survived any one stage. As a materialist, Trofimov repudiated any suggestion that these esthetic values existed in and of themselves and were everlasting and unchanging. His contention was, however, that inasmuch as they were the cumulative product of many social formations, they metamorphosed far more slowly than did the superstructural features of art, that is, than the complex of ideas and images reflected.[134]

This new tone of argument is in contrast to the earlier tenor. Only months earlier Belik had been denying with all the vehemence at his command that the merits of Soviet art should be judged ultimately by comparative juxtaposition with the art of other epochs. Now one Soviet scholar confessed that in literary studies as well as in linguistics, Marxism had been oversimplified and vulgarized over the past few years. Another maintained that problems of theory had been dealt with in primitive fashion before Stalin's article appeared. A third concluded that the way now lay open for an attempt to arrive at the universal, world-wide principles underlying the

133 "V Institute mirovoi literatury," *Izv. Akad. nauk* (Otdelenie literatury i iazyka), IX, No. 2 (1950), 149–51.
134 "Izuchenie novykh trudov I. V. Stalina v Institute filosofii Akademii nauk SSSR," *Voprosy filosofii*, No. 2 (1950), pp. 361–62.

development of literature.[135] There was even an intimation that some of the excesses tolerated in the preceding space of years might be rectified. A distinguished scholar, Professor Blagoi, was challenged by a colleague for distorting the truth by alleging that in the 1820s Pushkin was wholly free of Byronic influence. His critic wrote that this was the period in which Pushkin himself had testified that he was "mad" about Byron and in which his work had shown unmistakable Byronic influence.[136]

These developments may be the harbinger of a meliorative approach in Soviet literary studies. Students of literature may be permitted somewhat to flex their talents after the confinement of postwar insularism and to arrive at a more persuasive version of Russia's contribution to world culture. The most recent periodicals to arrive in the United States from the Soviet Union, dated over a year after Stalin's speech, contain signs of a greater willingness to countenance new suggestions, at times of a nature startling by contrast with the previous period. As an example, one such proposal even advocated repudiating the very concept *"partiinost'* of literature" on the ground that it would be more apt, at the present time under what it referred to as the "state of moral-political unity," to speak of "communist ideology" or of "Soviet patriotism." [137] Stalin's remarks on the superstructure are being applied in literary studies by more and more of the guiding lights in the field in the direction here indicated. Increasingly, the lasting values of literature are cited as deserving of scholarly attention. At the same time the pace of change is slow. After a year, the new theories themselves appear very little advanced.

It would be illogical to anticipate anything more momentous at this juncture. Statements which followed shortly after the Zhdanov report in 1946 made it clear beyond a doubt that the new Party line was destined to hold sway for a very long time to come (see p. 249). Thus far there is no evidence that anything in the hard core of this line has been radically altered. The Soviet ideological

[135] "V Institute mirovoi literatury," p. 151.

[136] A. I. Beletskii, "Znachenie trudov I. V. Stalina po iazykoznaniiu dlia sovetskogo literaturovedeniia," *Izv. Akad. nauk* (Otdelenie literatury i iazyka), X, No. 1 (1950), 15–16.

[137] "Voprosy literaturovedeniia v svete trudov I. V. Stalina po iazykoznaniiu," *Izv. Akad. nauk* (Otdelenie literatury i iazyka), X, No. 3 (1951), 311.

front appears to be entering a period which one might hazard naming the phase of refinement of the Zhdanov line. It is the rough edges which are likely to absorb the attentions of Party ideologists in the near future. The overwhelming factor in the tempo of change in Soviet ideology from now on will be the role played by relations with the West. Presumably, the invocation of a certain relaxation in Stalin's speech was prompted by the domestic economic successes of the USSR, the accomplishment in broad terms of the ideological shifts desired by Party planners, and the excesses in the execution of the Zhdanov line which had reduced the effectiveness of many distinguished intellectuals. As for the external sphere, it is hard to see what cause there might have been for optimism. Whereas the domestic crisis appeared markedly reduced, the crisis in foreign relations was acutely aggravated. As of this writing, the relaxation of tension in this vital sector, which alone might enable the Stalin pronouncement of 1950 to bear fruit rapidly, has not occurred.

The pattern by which the Party has in the past imposed tight controls in direct ratio to its interpretation of the acuteness of crisis may be expected to obtain indefinitely. Any prognostication of trends in Soviet ideology must give this due consideration. This factor is constant, however. The truly profitable subject for investigation as the dynamic reflector of current conditions, therefore, lies in the variables, that is, in month-by-month policy mutations. These are diagnosable from close attention to recent acquisitions from the USSR. This paper has endeavored to highlight some of the changes which occurred over the period of the postwar Five-Year Plan, emphasizing that for all their seeming abruptness of innovation, they contained indissoluble and clearly visible links with developments in the decade before the War. Changes from now on, too, are bound to reveal the same lucid evidence of close kinship with the period we have just been considering.

Index

Index